H. A. Gleason, Jr.
Hartford Seminary Foundation

An Introduction to

DESCRIPTIVE LINGUISTICS

Revised Edition

D1336155

HOLT, RINEHART AND WINSTON
LONDON · NEW YORK · SYDNEY · TORONTO

A HOLT INTERNATIONAL EDITION

First printed in Great Britain May 1969
Copyright © 1955, 1961 by Holt, Rinehart and Winston, Inc.
All Rights Reserved
Library of Congress Catalog Card Number : 61–8588

SBN 03 910023 5

Printed by offset by William Clowes and Sons, Limited
London and Beccles

1   2   3   4   5   6   7   8   9

Preface

Language is one of the most important and characteristic forms of human behavior. It has, accordingly, always had a place in the academic world. In recent years, however, its position has changed greatly: at one time the study of language was almost entirely restricted to specific languages, primarily those of Western Europe and classical antiquity; over the last few generations, a much broader consideration of language has taken a place at the side of the study of individual languages.

As each of the social sciences has developed, it has encountered language problems within its domain. Psychology, sociology, and anthropology have each investigated language both as a type of human activity and as a system interacting with personality, society, or culture. Language has intruded even upon technological problems, and engineers have found themselves driven to basic research on human speech. Today, as a result, we have well-established techniques for the study of language from a number of different points of view. Each of these techniques supplements all the others in contributing to theoretical knowledge and the practical problems of the day.

One approach has, however, received little attention until very recently: descriptive linguistics, the discipline which studies languages in terms of their internal structures. It differs from the other approaches in that it focuses its attention on different facets of human speech. The common general subject matter and its special competence to handle certain types of problems bring it into important relationships with many other disciplines.

Concurrent with the broadening of interest in language, there has been a fundamental change in the teaching of specific languages. Tongues which a past generation would have thought unworthy of serious attention are now taught in regularly scheduled classes. The variety of linguistic structures which must be dealt with has increased markedly, and the need has arisen for a broader perspective. Descriptive linguistics has thus become an essential concomitant to the newer language program.

iii

This trend is evidenced by the addition of courses in descriptive linguistics in many American colleges and universities. Moreover, the courses are having a wider influence than before. Anthropologists have traditionally had some introduction to linguistic field methods in their training. Language majors have often had courses in Romance Philology or the like. These courses have been very different in content and outlook. But today the needs and interests of both groups seem to be converging, so that in many institutions they can meet in common courses in descriptive linguistics. Students in other social sciences are beginning to feel a need for a similar background. Linguistics courses are ceasing to be appendages to single specialized curricula, and are attracting an ever more diverse enrollment.

This textbook was written with this development in mind. It is not directed to prospective linguists alone; rather, widely various academic backgrounds and interests are assumed. Many of the students who use it will be particularly interested in understanding the place of descriptive linguistics among related disciplines, but will not be able to take specialized courses in these related fields. It has therefore been thought best to interpret the field rather broadly. Brief treatments of historical linguistics, dialect studies, communication theory, and acoustic phonetics have been included primarily to show their very close relationship to descriptive linguistics. In courses of more narrowly defined purpose or more restricted dimensions, these chapters can be omitted.

The first edition of this book was developed out of several years of teaching introductory linguistics at the Hartford Seminary Foundation. In a preliminary draft it was tested at a number of other institutions in a variety of courses. It appeared just at the beginning of a new upsurge of interest in linguistics, and has had its small part in producing and sustaining the impetus. In six years it has had much more extensive use than I dared dream of. On the whole, it seems to me, it has stood the test and found favor with a growing number of teachers. The basic plan of the work, therefore, remains unchanged, though a number of small changes have been made.

New theoretical developments have come with increasing frequency. Questions which formerly were considered quite esoteric have come to be familiar subjects of discussion and debate. There

is an increasing wealth of material which is available for inclusion
in introductory courses, and teachers have differed greatly in what
they have selected. It would not be possible to treat all the possibilities within one reasonably sized volume. Yet it has been
necessary to provide a somewhat wider selection of topics than in
the first edition, and four chapters have been added. There are a
considerable number of other matters that I regretfully had to
omit, or give only the most incidental mention. The book remains
an *Introduction*; only material judged to be suitable for first courses
has been included. I have tried to present widely held viewpoints
and tested procedures. There are, however, a few places where
this would not be possible without leaving damaging lacunae.
The treatment of all subjects is, of course, only introductory; suggestions for further reading can be found in the bibliography.
It is perhaps indicative of the growth of linguistics that the bibliography is now eighty percent longer, though if anything even more
rigorously selected. Most of the increase comes from the rapid
expansion of the literature of the field.

This textbook may be used in an upper-class or graduate single-
semester course by omitting the more marginal chapters. With
some supplemental reading assignments, it is adaptable for a full-
year course in general linguistics. It should be used with the *Workbook in Descriptive Linguistics*, which was prepared to accompany
this text and which gives carefully graded problems for analysis
selected to illustrate the techniques in this textbook. It is also
desirable to have some oral instruction and practice in phonetics.
At the Hartford Seminary Foundation this is given in drill sessions
meeting in small groups for three hours each week. These drill
sessions are devoted at first to drill on the English phonemic system and its transcription. Then attention is gradually shifted to
sub-phonemic detail, and thence into more general phonetics. In
the meantime, the lectures and assigned workbook problems are
devoted to morphology. Halfway through the course, Chapter 15
provides a summary and systematization of the phonetics which
has been drilled. This provides a basis for discussion of the phoneme
principle in subsequent chapters. If the students have had previous
work in phonetics, or if this separation of phonetic drill from the
class discussion is not possible, a different arrangement might be
desirable. Chapters 15 to 21 are written in such a way as to be

largely independent of the morphology chapters. They can accordingly be assigned before Chapter 6. Chapter 5 might in such a case be best treated as a part of the introduction.

Almost all the material of the original edition remains. The contributions of all those who helped in one way or another to make it what it was can still be felt, and my indebtedness remains as great as ever. Special mention should be made of my colleague, Professor J. Maurice Hohlfeld, who has shared with me for many years in the teaching of introductory linguistics and who contributed in so many other ways; of Professor W. Freeman Twaddell, who generously gave both criticism and encouragement; and of Professors Winfred P. Lehmann, Raven I. McDavid, and Mark Hanna Watkins, who used the experimental edition in their classes. I am indebted to Dr. Franklin S. Cooper and the Haskins Laboratory who permitted me to use their equipment for the preparation of the spectrograms on page 366. Professor Ku Tun-Jou and Mr. 'Tariho Fukuda assisted with illustrations in Chapter 25. Frances Gleason typed and retyped the manuscript and assisted in unrecountable ways, not the least of which has been constant encouragement.

For the revision I have had the benefit of an ever widening number of people who gave me comments or suggestions or relayed to me the difficulties of their students. I cannot acknowledge all of them personally, but my debt is nonetheless heavy. A number of colleagues and friends have helped by reading and meticulously criticizing preliminary drafts of one or more chapters of the new material. As they read the chapters here they will see many places where their suggestions have made very material improvements. I would like to acknowledge such extensive help from Gilbert Ansre, Donald Böthel, Noam Chomsky, T. Gerald Dyar, Morris Halle, Eric P. Hamp, Charles Hein, J. Maurice Hohlfeld, Dell H. Hymes, Ashok Kelkar, Leonard Newmark, and W. Freeman Twaddell. Many others responded to my pleas for suggestions and comments on the bibliography, so many that space prohibits any listing. I am grateful to all of them.

Finally, major acknowledgment must go to my students at the Hartford Seminary Foundation, Trinity College, the Linguistic Institutes, and the Summer Schools of the Indian Linguistic Society. They suffered through my mistakes and taught me, in many cases, perhaps more than they themselves learned. Special appreciation goes to the few who, with courage rare among students, told me what they thought was wrong with my teaching, with the course, and with the subject in general, and to those who encouraged me by testimonies as to the value of their preparation as they became immersed in their language learning or their research.

A twelve-inch LP record, "Phonemic Field Work," with transcript, accompanies Chapter 18 of this text and can be ordered from the publisher.

H. A. G.

Hartford, Connecticut
March 16, 1961

Contents

Language

1.1 As you listen to an unfamiliar language you get the impression of a torrent of disorganized noises carrying no sense whatever. To the native speaker it is quite otherwise. He pays little attention to the sounds, but concerns himself instead with some situation which lies behind the act of speech and is, for him, somehow reflected in it. Both you and he have failed to grasp the nature of the phenomenon. Neither the casual observer nor the usual native speaker can give any real information about a language. To be sure, some people, Americans perhaps more than most others, have decided notions about language. But the ideas held and discussed come far short of giving a complete picture of the language and sometimes have very little relationship to the facts. Even people with considerable education are often wholly unable to answer certain quite simple questions about their language. For most people language is primarily a tool to be used, rather than a subject for close and critical attention.

It is probably well that it is so. Yet there are important human problems into which language enters intimately and on which it exerts such a profound influence that an understanding of its mechanism would contribute materially to their solutions. Moreover, every phase of human activity is worthy of study. Thus, for practical reasons, as well as to satisfy man's innate curiosity, language deserves careful and intelligent study.

1.2   Language has so many interrelationships with various aspects of human life that it can be studied from numerous points of view. All are valid and useful, as well as interesting in themselves. Linguistics is the science which attempts to understand language from the point of view of its internal structure. It is not, of course, isolated and wholly autonomous, but it does have a clearly and sharply delimited field of inquiry, and has developed its own highly effective and quite characteristic method. It must draw upon such sciences as physical acoustics, communications theory, human physiology, psychology, and anthropology for certain basic concepts and necessary data. In return, linguistics makes its own essential contributions to these disciplines. But however closely it may be related to other sciences, it is clearly separate by reason of its own primary concern with the structure of language.

1.3   What then is this structure? Language operates with two kinds of material. One of these is sound. Almost any sort of noise that the human vocal apparatus can produce is used in some way in some language. The other is ideas, social situations, meanings — English lacks any really acceptable term to cover the whole range — the facts or fantasies about man's existence, the things man reacts to and tries to convey to his fellows. These two, insofar as they concern linguists, may conveniently be labeled *expression* and *content*.

The foreigner who hears merely a jumble of sounds has not really heard the language, not even the part of it which we have called *expression*. All that he has heard is sounds, the material which language uses to carry its message. This is not the domain of the linguist, but that of the physicist. The latter can analyze the stream of speech as sound and learn many things about it. His findings have both theoretical and practical importance; the designs of telephones, radios, and much other electronic equipment depends in an essential way upon such findings. They also contribute basic data to linguistics, and to numerous other sciences, including psychology and physiology, as well as to physics itself.

The linguist is concerned with sound as the medium by which information is conveyed. To serve in this way, speech must be something quite different from the jumble of sound apparent to the foreigner. It is, in fact, an organized system or structure, and it is this structure that lies within the subject field of linguistics.

The linguist analyzes speech as an orderly sequence of specific kinds of sounds and of sequences of sounds. It is orderly in terms of a very complex set of patterns which repeatedly recur and which are at least partially predictable. These patterns form the structure of **expression,** one major component of language in the sense that the linguist uses the term.

The native speaker has his attention focused on something else, the subject of the discourse. This may be a situation which is being described, some ideas which are being presented, or some social formula which is being repeated. None of these things are language, any more than are the sounds which convey speech. The subject of the discourse stands on the opposite side and in much the same relationship to speech as do the sounds. The speaker comprehends what he is talking about in terms of an organizing structure. This structure causes him to select certain features for description and determines the ways in which he will interrelate them. It also cuts the situation up into portions in a characteristic way. These selected features, like the sounds mentioned above, also form patterns which recur, and which are at least partially predictable. These recurrent patterns are the structure of **content,** a second major component of language as the linguist treats it.

Finally, these two structures are intimately related and interacting. Parts of the structure of expression are associated in definite ways with parts of the structure of content. The relations between these two complex structures are themselves quite complex. In every language they are different from what is found in every other language. The differences may be profound and extensive, or they may be relatively slight. But in every instance, the two structures are intricate and their relationships quite characteristic.

1.4 The native speaker uses this complex apparatus easily and without conscious thought of the process. It seems to him simple and natural. But to a speaker of another of the world's three thousand languages it may present quite a different picture. It may give an impression of being cumbersome, illogical, or even ridiculous. Actually, of course, the strange language is merely different. A true picture of language can only be had by seeing languages more objectively. Such a view will emphasize the immense complexity, the arbitrariness, and the high degree of adequacy for their purposes — features which are shared by all languages in spite of their divergencies.

1.5   The dual structure of language can best be made clear by an example. The more technical description which will follow later in this book will afford more refined examples, but the following will indicate something of the possibilities without involving complicated terminology or technical concepts.

Consider a rainbow or a spectrum from a prism. There is a continuous gradation of color from one end to the other. That is, at any point there is only a small difference in the colors immediately adjacent at either side. Yet an American describing it will list the hues as *red, orange, yellow, green, blue, purple,* or something of the kind. The continuous gradation of color which exists in nature is represented in language by a series of discrete categories. This is an instance of structuring of content. There is nothing inherent either in the spectrum or the human perception of it which would compel its division in this way. The specific method of division is part of the structure of English.

By contrast, speakers of other languages classify colors in much different ways. In the accompanying diagram, a rough indication is given of the way in which the spectral colors are divided by speakers of English, Shona (a language of Rhodesia), and Bassa (a language of Liberia).

English:

purple	blue	green	yel-low	orange	red

Shona:

cips^{w}uka	citema	cicena	cips^{w}uka

Bassa:

hui	ziza

The Shona speaker divides the spectrum into three major portions. *Cips^{w}uka* occurs twice, but only because the red and purple ends, which he classifies as similar, are separated in the diagram.

Interestingly enough, *citema* also includes black, and *cicena* white. In addition to these three terms, there are, of course, a large number of terms for more specific colors. These terms are comparable to English *crimson, scarlet, vermilion,* which are all varieties of *red.* The convention of dividing the spectrum into three parts instead of into six does not indicate any difference in visual ability to perceive colors, but only a difference in the way they are classified or structured by the language.

The Bassa speaker divides the spectrum in a radically different way: into only two major categories. In Bassa there are numerous terms for specific colors, but only these two for general classes of colors. It is easy for an American to conclude that the English division into six major colors is superior. For some purposes it probably is. But for others it may present real difficulties. Botanists have discovered that it does not allow sufficient generalization for discussion of flower colors. Yellows, oranges, and many reds are found to constitute one series. Blues, purples, and purplish reds constitute another. These two exhibit fundamental differences that must be treated as basic to any botanical description. In order to state the facts succinctly it has been necessary to coin two new and more general color terms, *xanthic* and *cyanic,* for these two groups. A Bassa-speaking botanist would be under no such necessity. He would find *zĩza* and *hui* quite adequate for the purpose, since they happen to divide the spectrum in approximately the way necessary for this purpose.

1.6 Now for a simple statement of structure in the expression part of language: The sounds used by English are grouped into consonants and vowels (and some other categories). These are organized into syllables in a quite definite and systematic way. Each syllable must have one and only one vowel sound. It may have one or more consonants before the vowel, and one or more after the vowel. There are quite intricate restrictions on the sequences that may occur. Of all the mathematically possible combinations of English sounds, only a small portion are admitted as complying with the patterns of English structure. Not all of these are actually used, though the unused ones stand ready in case they should ever be needed. Perhaps some day a word like *ving* may appear in response to a new need. *Shmoo* was drawn out of this stock of unused possibilities only a few years ago. But *ngvi* would be most unlikely: it simply is not available as a potential English word, though it contains only English sounds.

Six of these permissible sequences of sounds are somehow associated with the six portions into which English language-habits structure the spectrum. These are the familiar *red, orange, yellow, green, blue, purple*. This association of expression and content is merely conventional. There is no reason why six others could not be used, or why these six could not be associated with different parts of the spectrum. No reason, that is, except that this is the English-language way of doing it, and these are conventions to which we must adhere reasonably closely if we are to be understood. Sometime in the past history of the language, these conventions became established and have persisted with only gradual changes since. In their ultimate origins, all such conventions are the results of more or less accidental choices. It is largely fortuitous that the spectrum came to be so divided, that the specific words were attached to the colors so distinguished, or, indeed, that the sounds from which they were formed were so organized that these words were possible. These irrational facts, with many others like them, constitute the English language. Each language is a similarly arbitrary system.

1.7   The three major components of language, as far as language lies within the scope of linguistics, are the structure of expression, the structure of content, and vocabulary. The latter comprises all the specific relations between expression and content — in the familiar terminology, words and their meanings.

Vocabulary comes and goes. It is the least stable and even the least characteristic of the three components of language. That portion of the vocabulary which changes most freely is sometimes referred to as "slang." But even staid and dignified words are constantly being created and continually passing out of active use, to be preserved only in literature which is dated by their very presence. While certain types of words are more transient than others, none are absolutely immortal. Even the most familiar and commonly used words, which might be expected to be most stable, have a mortality rate of about twenty percent in a thousand years.

Moreover, in the life history of an individual speaker the birth and death of words is very much more frequent than in the language community as a whole. Every normal person probably learns at least three words every day, over a thousand a year, and forgets old ones at an appreciable but lower rate. This figure must be a minimum, because most people have total vocabularies which could only be reached through even more rapid acquisition of vocabulary during at least part of their life.

We have no comparable method by which the rate of change of content structure can be estimated. The learning of new vocabulary, particularly technical terms associated with the learning of new concepts, does of course imply certain minor changes. But it is quite evident that change rarely touches the most basic features in any given language. With regard to the structure of expression the facts are clearer. Few, unless they learn a second language, will add, subtract, or change any of their basic sound patterns after they reach adolescence. Grammatical constructions may increase, but at a rate much slower than the increase of vocabulary. Vocabulary is indeed the transient feature of language.

1.8   In learning a second language, you will find that vocabulary is comparatively easy, in spite of the fact that it is vocabulary that students fear most. The harder part is mastering new structures in both content and expression. You may have to free yourself from the bondage of thinking of everything as either singular or plural. Perhaps the new language will organize content into singular, dual, and plural (here meaning 'three or more'). Or perhaps the new language will not give routine consideration to the matter. English speakers can never make a statement without saying something about the number of every object mentioned. This is compulsory, whether it is relevant or not. In Chinese, objects are noted as singular or plural only when the speaker judges the information to be relevant. The Chinese experience suggests that it actually seldom is, for that language operates with only occasional references to number.

You will have to make similar changes in habits of thought and of description of situations in many other instances. You may, for example, have to learn to think of every action as either completed or incomplete, and to disregard the time of the action unless it has special relevance. The reorganization of thinking and perception may extend much deeper than such changes. In some languages, situations are not analyzed, as they are in English, in terms of an actor and an action. Instead the fundamental cleavage runs in a different direction and cannot be easily stated in English. Some of these divergencies between languages have been described by Benjamin L. Whorf. His formulation has been widely debated and perhaps is not at present susceptible to rigorous testing. Yet the papers are very suggestive and can be read with profit by every student of linguistics or languages.

You will also have to reorganize your habits of making and hearing sounds. You will have to discriminate between sounds that you have learned to consider the same. You will find that others, in clear contrast in English, function as one, and you will have to learn to respond to them as to one sound. Patterns which seem impossible will have to become facile, and you will have to learn to avoid some English patterns that seem to be second nature.

The most difficult thing of all, however, is that these profound changes will have to become completely automatic. You will have to learn to use them without effort or conscious attention. In this learning process constant disciplined practice is essential. Special ability may be helpful, but probably much less so than is popularly supposed. An understanding of the basic principles of language structure — that is, the results of modern linguistic research — while not indispensable, can contribute in many ways.

1.9   As we listen to a person speaking our native language we hear not only what is said, but also certain things about the speaker. If he is an acquaintance, we recognize him. If not, we identify him as male or female and perhaps obtain some idea of his age, his education, and his social background. A person's voice serves at least two functions in communication. One is linguistic, in that it serves as the vehicle of the expression system of language. The other is non-linguistic, in that it carries information of a quite different sort about the speaker.

This distinction is made, at least roughly, even by the unsophisticated. If we are told to REPEAT exactly what another says, we will duplicate (provided our memory serves us adequately) every feature which is included in the language expression system. We can do that, if it is our own language, even without understanding the content. In repeating we will make no effort to reproduce anything beyond the linguistically pertinent features. If, however, we are asked to MIMIC another, we attempt to reproduce not only the linguistic features, but every discernible characteristic.

Few can mimic with any degree of success, whereas every normal native speaker can, perhaps with a little practice, repeat exactly up to the limit imposed by his memory span.

1.10 The most basic elements in the expression system are the **phonemes.** These are the sound features which are common to all speakers of a given speech form and which are exactly reproduced in repetition. In any language, there is a definite and usually small number of phonemes. In English there are forty-six. These will be identified and described in the next three chapters. Out of this limited inventory of units, the whole expression system is built up. In many respects the phonemes are analogous to the elements of chemistry, ninety-odd in number, out of which all substances are constructed.

The phoneme is one of those basic concepts, such as may be found in all sciences, which defy exact definition. Yet some sort of working characterization is necessary before we go on. The following is hardly adequate beyond a first introduction to the subject, but will make it possible to proceed with the analysis and enumeration of the phonemes of English. It will be expanded and modified several times. Indeed, the very process of application in the next three chapters will constitute such emendation.

With this in mind, we may define a **phoneme** as a minimum feature of the expression system of a spoken language by which one thing that may be said is distinguished from any other thing which might have been said. Thus, if two utterances are different in such a way that they suggest to the hearer different contents, it must be because there are differences in the expressions. The difference may be small or extensive. The smallest difference which can differentiate utterances with different contents is a difference of a single phoneme. This description is best illustrated by a full-scale application in the presentation of the phonemic system of a language. Since this cannot be done in brief compass, no illustration will be given until the English phonemes are presented in Chapters 2, 3, and 4.

1.11 There are two things about phonemes that must be explicitly pointed out in anticipation of any such presentation:

Phonemes are part of the system of one specific language. The phonemes of different languages are different, frequently incommensurable. It is for this reason that a foreigner hears only a jumble which he cannot repeat. The sounds of the unfamiliar language do not fit into his phonemic system, and so he can comprehend no order in a simple utterance. If anything which is said about the phonemes of one language happens to apply to those of another, we must regard it as fortuitous.

Phonemes are features of the spoken language. Written language has its own basic unit, the grapheme. Something will be said about this later. If, of necessity, written words are cited as illustrations, it must be constantly borne in mind that the written form is not, and cannot be, an illustration of a phoneme. Instead, it is the spoken form which the written form is expected to elicit which illustrates the phoneme under discussion. This inevitably introduces a major difficulty into the presentation. The illustrative words have been selected with the intention that they should be as generally as possible pronounced by all Americans in the same way. Undoubtedly this principle of selection fails in some instances because of dialect and individual peculiarities of the writer and the reader. Such instances will not vitiate the argument. For some Americans other examples might be needed, but examples can be found which will lead to the same results.

1.12   The thinking that most Americans do about language is almost exclusively concerned with written English. A written language is, of course, a valid and important object of linguistic investigation. It can, however, easily mislead the unwary. Most of the misunderstandings which Americans have about language arise from a failure to keep clearly in mind the nature and limitations of a written language.

A written language is typically a reflection, independent in only limited ways, of spoken language. As a picture of actual speech, it is inevitably imperfect and incomplete. To understand the structure of a written language one must constantly resort either to comparison with the spoken language or to conjecture. Unfortunately, recourse has been too largely to the latter. Moreover, conjecture has been based not so much upon an intimate knowledge of the ways of languages in general (the results of descriptive linguistics) as to a priori considerations of supposed logic, to metaphysics, and to simple prejudice. While logic and metaphysics are important disciplines and can make significant contributions to an understanding of language, the customary manner of applying them has redounded neither to their credit nor to the elucidation of language structure. Linguistics must start with thorough investigation of spoken language before it proceeds to study written language. This is true of languages with long histories of written literature, such as English, no less than those of isolated tribes which have never known of the possibility of writing.

1.13   The second basic unit in the expression system is the **morpheme.** This again cannot be exactly defined, and several chapters will be given to discussing it. For the present, however, let us characterize a **morpheme** as follows: It is the unit on the expression side of language which enters into relationship with the content side. A morpheme is typically composed of one to several phonemes. The morpheme differs fundamentally from the phoneme, which has no such relationship with content. That is, phonemes have no meanings; morphemes have meanings.

The simpler words of English are morphemes. Other words consist of two or more morphemes. Like the phonemes, the morphemes enter into combinations in accordance with definite and intricate patterns. The expression structure is merely the sum of the patterns of arrangement of these two basic units.

1.14   Using the phoneme and the morpheme as their basic units, linguists have been able to build a comprehensive theory of the expression side of language, and to make detailed and comprehensive statements about the expression systems of specific languages. This is what is ordinarily called **descriptive linguistics.** It is the basic branch of linguistic science. Others are **historical linguistics,** dealing with the changes of languages in time, and **comparative linguistics,** dealing with the relationships between languages of common origin. Descriptive linguistics is conventionally divided into two parts. **Phonology** deals with the phonemes and sequences of phonemes. **Grammar** deals with the morphemes and their combinations.

In some respects linguistics has developed more precise and rigorous methods and attained more definitive results than any other science dealing with human behavior. Linguists have been favored with the most obviously structured material with which to work, so this attainment is by no means due to any scientific superiority of linguists over other social scientists. It is also the direct result of the discovery of the phoneme, a discovery which allows the data to be described in terms of a small set of discrete units. Within a given language, a given sound is either a certain phoneme or it is not; there can be no intergradation. This fact eliminates from linguistics a large measure of the vagueness and lack of precision characteristic of most studies of human behavior. It would be presumptuous to claim that this advantage has been thoroughly exploited by linguists, but it is certainly fair to say that in some places, linguistics has achieved an appreciable measure of scientific rigor and has the foundations for further development in this regard.

The chief evidence for the high order of development of linguistics as a science lies in the reproducibility of its results. If two linguists work independently on the same language, they will come out with very similar statements. There may be differences. Some of these differences will be predictable. Very seldom will any of the differences be deep-seated. Usually it will be quite possible to harmonize the two statements and show that by simple restatements one result can be converted into the other. That is, the two results will have differed largely in inconsequential ways, often only in external form.

1.15   The content side of linguistics has developed much less rapidly and to a very much less impressive extent than the study of expression. Indeed, it cannot as yet justifiably be called a science. Undoubtedly this has been a source of frustration in linguistics as a whole. One of the greatest shortcomings of descriptive work with the expression aspect of language has been a lack of understanding of the relationships between expression and content, and the inability to use the analysis of content in attacking related problems in expression. Here is the great frontier in linguistic knowledge on which we may look for progress in the next decades.

There have been three reasons for this neglect of the content side. First, linguists have been late in comprehending the real significance of the two-sided nature of language. Their attention has been diverted from this basic problem by the great advances being made within the analysis of expression.

Second, there has been no way to gain access to the content structure except through the expression structure. This requires an inferential method which has not appealed to linguists busy with building a highly rigorous method for the handling of more directly observed data. Content has therefore had an inferior status in the eyes of linguists.

Third, the content, apart from its structure, has not been amenable to any unified study. The substance of content is, of course, the whole of human experience. Thousands of scientists have labored, each in some one of numerous disciplines, in elucidating this mass of material. But there is no one approach which can comprehend the whole and so serve as a starting point for comparison of the different structures which can be imposed upon it. Only isolated portions of the content system can as yet be studied as structure imposed on a measurable continuum of experience. The examples of structuring of color concepts discussed above suggest the possibilities and make the lack of further opportunities for comparison the more tantalizing.

1.16 In contrast, the expression plane starts with much simpler materials. The sounds producible by the human voice can be studied comprehensively by several approaches. Two of these have reached the degree of precision which makes them useful to linguistics: **articulatory phonetics,** a branch of human physiology, and **acoustic phonetics,** a branch of physics. These are discussed in Chapters 15 and 22. It is hard to imagine the scientific study of the expression aspect of speech attaining anywhere near the present degree of development without the aid of phonetics. The structure can be systematically described only because the underlying sounds can be accurately described and measured.

The study of content structure must proceed, at present, without equivalent source of order in the totality of its primary data. Because of this it is relatively poorly developed. It is equally as important as the expression plane, yet it will be necessary to give it much less attention in this book. What little can be said is often semi-scientific at best. We do not even have a clear idea of the basic unit or units, and hence no basis for the high degree of precision which characterizes the study of language expression.

English Consonants

2.1 The first step in studying any spoken language is to determine the phonemes. For a linguist studying his own native speech, this is relatively easy. He is accustomed to using the phonemic system, so his feeling about the sounds will often assist materially. For a person of a different background, the problem is much different. Some points which will seem obvious to a native speaker will require proof to the non-native. It is profitable in any case to seek rigorous demonstration, as there are occasional features which contradict popular prejudices. Not infrequently the difficulties arise from confusion of spelling and pronunciation.

At this stage something less than full rigor will be demanded. The demonstration which follows is designed primarily for educated Americans. A person of a different mother tongue might consider some points in it rather unconvincing. All the results which are arrived at here can be demonstrated more objectively by techniques which minimize the effects of the investigator's language background. The basic principles of these methods will be presented later in Chapters 16 to 18. They will be much more meaningful if the student has first acquainted himself with the phonemic system of one language and worked with it as a tool in language study.

2.2 In this chapter attention will be restricted to the consonants. The familiar meaning of the term will be adequate for the present. That is, we are considering the sounds that are not ordinarily thought of as vowels. For convenience of presentation, we will restrict our attention in this chapter and the next to words of one syllable. It will also be necessary to base the discussion on some one form of spoken English. This will be the author's ordinary pronunciation of words in his active vocabulary. Another person's speech will yield identical or nearly identical results, though some of the particular examples used may be pronounced quite differently.

2.3   To find the phonemes we must compare samples of spoken English that are distinct both in expression and content. We must be careful to ensure that both types of differences are present. *Bill* (a man's name) and *bill* (a request for payment) are obviously different in content. But they are not recognizably different in expression. If one of the two is said without context, no other person can distinguish which one of the two has been said. The difference in content is not matched by a difference in expression. Such a pair is of no use in determining the phonemes of English.

If two different persons say *bill*, the two utterances may be recognizably different. But the difference is not in the linguistic expression. One pronunciation will be considered, by a native speaker, as a repetition of the other. The difference between the two utterances conveys information about the speakers, not about the message. Linguistically the two are identical, and hence do not afford a contrast useful for our purpose.

Occasionally it will be necessary to ascertain by experiment that two words are actually different. Two similarly pronounced words may occur in such different contexts that a native speaker may never have compared their pronunciation closely. To be certain, you can prepare a list of random repetitions of the two words in question. If they are different in expression, a second speaker of the same dialect should be able to identify them when read. If the two words are not distinguishable, mere chance will produce about one half correct identifications.

2.4   If the two samples are *bill* and *pill*, there is both a difference of content and a difference of expression. The latter enables the hearer to recognize the word and associate it with the proper content. Irrespective of the context or lack of it, an American can distinguish these two words as they are said by any native speaker.

The two must therefore differ in at least one significant feature in the expression system, that is, in at least one phoneme. This follows from the definition given in the last chapter. The **phoneme** is the minimum feature of the expression system of a spoken language by which one thing that may be said is distinguished from any other thing which might have been said. We will find that *bill* and *pill* differ in only one phoneme. They are therefore a **minimal pair.**

2.5   In calling *bill* and *pill* a minimal pair we assume that they differ by only one phoneme. Can we justify this? If these two words differed by two phonemes it might be possible to find a word that differs from both *bill* and *pill* but which differs from each of these in a smaller degree than these two differ from each other. This would be a word which shares with *bill* one of the phonemes by which *bill* differs from *pill* and with *pill* one of those by which *pill* differs from *bill*. Diligent search through the vocabulary of English will fail to reveal any such word. This, of course, proves nothing, for we know that only a small portion of the possible words are actually used. The word which we are seeking could easily be one of the unused possible forms. But if we could find no such word to compare with *bill* and *pill*, we might expect that one could be found to compare with some other pair which differs in a similar way.

We can conduct a similar search for a word differing from *bat* and *pat* in some smaller feature than the difference between these two. And so likewise for numerous other pairs: *tab* and *tap, but* and *putt*, etc. No matter how many such pairs we examine, no evidence can be found that any smaller difference than that between *bill* and *pill* exists in English. This will establish that *bill* : *pill* is a minimal pair.

2.6   To make a complete inventory of the consonant phonemes of English we will need to find a large number of such minimal pairs. Since we may expect that the number of phonemes will be considerable, this may be quite laborious. Time and effort can be conserved by finding sets of words which seem to be minimally different rather than mere pairs. One such set is the following:

pill	*bill*	*till*	*dill*	*chill*	*Jill*
kill	*gill*	*fill*	*ville*	*sill*	*hill*
mill	*nil*	*rill*	*Lil*	*will*	

We are not concerned that many of these words show similar spellings, nor that some do not. Our interest is in spoken English, hence we are looking for sets of words which are alike in pronunciation. In some cases, the words of such a set will rime.

2.7 The set of seventeen words just cited proves that the initial consonant in each is phonemically distinct from each of the other sixteen. There is no evidence that this is the total list of English consonants. We may proceed by adducing additional sets of the same sort. These should be matched with the sets already found, as follows:

pill	*pet*	*kill*		*mill*	*met*
bill	*bet*	*gill*	*get*	*nil*	*net*
till		*fill*		*rill*	
dill	*debt*	*ville*	*vet*	*Lil*	*let*
chill	*Chet*	*sill*	*set*	*will*	*wet*
Jill	*jet*	*hill*	*het*		*yet*

Fourteen pairs of words match in the two sets. Each set includes some word or words without counterparts in the other. We must find some evidence that the initial of *yet* is phonemically distinct from those of *till, kill, fill,* and *rill.* Perhaps the next set of words we find will provide this, but if not, pairs can be sought for each contrast. *Ten : yen, tot : yacht,* or *two : you,* etc., will prove one of these pairs to be phonemically distinct. *Kelp : yelp, coo : you, call : yawl,* etc.; *fell : yell, fail : Yale, fen : yen,* etc.; and *rung : young, rue : you, roar : your,* etc., will establish the others.

Proceeding in this way we will gradually build up a list of phonemes. Before long the discovery of new additions to the list will become less frequent and finally cease. There are exactly twenty-four in most dialects of English. Search for more than this will prove fruitless.

2.8 It is desirable to have some less awkward means of referring to these phonemes than by saying "the initial of *bill.*" We may provide a convenient notation by selecting twenty-four symbols, each of which will, by definition, refer to one and only one of the consonant phonemes. The most satisfactory will be the ordinary letters of the alphabet, eked out by a few additional signs of the same type. But if this system is used, symbols for phonemes may be confused with letters in various other uses. It will be necessary to mark them as representations of phonemes. This we will do, following well established convention, by enclosing phoneme symbols in / /. Thus /p/ means the phoneme found, among other places, at the beginning of the word *pill* as usually pronounced. Phonemes always refer to sounds, never to spellings. To indicate the letter we will write *p*.

2.9 The twenty-four symbols selected are the following. There is reasonable agreement among linguists on all of these, and unanimity on most. Throughout the remainder of our discussion of English structure a knowledge of these symbols and the values given will be assumed.

/b/	*bill*	*tab*	/t/	*till*	*tat*
/d/	*dill*	*Tadd*	/v/	*ville*	*have*
/f/	*fill*	*taff*	/w/	*will*	
/g/	*gill*	*tag*	/y/	*yet*	
/h/	*hill*		/z/	*zeal*	*has*
/k/	*kill*	*tack*	/θ/	*thigh*	*cloth*
/l/	*Lil*	*till*	/ð/	*thy*	*clothe*
/m/	*mill*	*tam*	/š/	*shall*	*hash*
/n/	*nil*	*tan*	/ž/		*rouge*
/p/	*pill*	*tap*	/č/	*chill*	*hatch*
/r/	*rill*	*rear*	/ǰ/	*Jill*	*edge*
/s/	*sill*	*Tass*	/ŋ/		*tang*

Two of these, /ŋ/ and /ž/, never occur initially. As we have defined it, /h/ never occurs finally; and /w/ and /y/ do not occur finally in the material under consideration here. These facts account for the blank spaces in the table.

2.10 It may be calculated that twenty-four phonemes will form 276 pairs. To prove each of the twenty-four phonemes to be distinct by the method discussed above, it will be necessary to find at least one minimal pair of words for each of the 276 pairs of phonemes. In most cases this is easy. For some, hundreds of pairs can be found readily. But for other pairs of consonants, suitable pairs of words are few, and many involve comparatively rare words. It may therefore take considerable searching to find them. For example, only five minimal pairs are known to me for the contrast /θ/ : /ð/. These are *thigh : thy, ether : either, mouth* (noun) : *mouth* (verb), *wreath : wreathe*, and *thistle : this'll* (the last is a contrast between a word and a phrase). For /š/ : /ž/, minimal pairs are even rarer, and only the following are known in my speech: *dilution : delusion, glacier : glazier,* and *Aleutian : allusion.* Some speakers pronounce *azure* to form a minimal pair with *Asher.* There may of course be other pairs which I have not yet found, but there certainly are not many of them. Diligent and systematic search has been made for both these pairs of consonants.

At the moment of writing, there are twelve pairs of consonants for which I know no minimal pairs in the material we are considering. These are:

$$/ž/ : /v \text{ š č } ɉ \text{ ŋ y w h}/$$
$$/ŋ/ : /ž \text{ ð y w h}/$$

That these should not be found is understandable enough, though that does not help to prove the phonemic distinctness of the pairs concerned. In English, /ž/ is a rare phoneme, and particularly so in monosyllables. The author knows only three such words, *loge, beige,* and *rouge.* The odds are against finding contrasts with only three words with which to work. /ð/ also occurs in comparatively few words. Both /ž/ and /ŋ/ occur in monosyllables only after vowels. In the material under consideration, /y w h/ occur only initially. This, of course, renders minimal pairs impossible. We will, however, later find that the distribution of /y/ and /w/ is much wider and that minimal pairs can be found. These are rather numerous for /y/ : /ŋ/ but somewhat rarer for /w/ : /ŋ/.

As mentioned above, some pairs are known for /š/ : /ž/. These involve three-syllable words. Presumably by diligent search through the total vocabulary, minimal pairs might be found for all English consonant phonemes. But there is no guarantee that all will be found, and in any case, it is hardly a feasible procedure. Reliance on minimal pairs would be particularly difficult for a foreigner whose English vocabulary might be small. Other techniques are available which are more efficient and leave less to chance.

2.11 The expression system of a language is a structure imposed by the language on the sounds which are used in speech. The phonemes are the units in this system. They cannot be considered as pure abstractions remote from the physiological and acoustic realities of the sounds concerned. Any further examination of English consonants must be based on an understanding of the phonetic nature of the sounds themselves.

There are two points of view from which sounds can be profitably studied and described. The oldest and best established of these is known as **articulatory phonetics.** It is based on the assumption that the characteristics of speech sounds are the results of their modes of formation. They may accordingly be described and classified by stating the position and action of the various speech organs. This physiological approach has been one of the basic tools of linguistics for many years and has proved very productive.

Only recently has it been possible to study the linguistically significant features of speech sounds from an acoustic point of view. The method is so new that the full impact on linguistics has not yet been felt. Acoustic phonetics, however, promises to be of great significance as linguists gain access to the expensive equipment necessary and familiarize themselves with the techniques and with the interpretation of the results. To date, the chief effect has been to validate and reinterpret slightly some of the older ideas derived from articulatory phonetics. The following discussion is necessarily based on the older methods.

2.12   The sounds used in English are produced by a few basic mechanisms combined in various ways. One of the more important of these is **voice,** a regular periodic vibration generated through the action of the vocal cords. The latter are two bands of elastic tissue in the larynx. They may be opened to permit free breathing, or brought together to produce various types of sounds, the most important of which is voice. In this instance, they are closed, but somewhat lightly. The air behind is moderately compressed by contraction of the thoracic cavity. This air pressure forces the cords apart. A small amount of the air passes through, and they again snap closed because of their elastic nature. In this way an alternating opening and closing of the cords is produced. This generates the sound waves which we call voice. Voice has a definite pitch or frequency, which depends on the number of openings of the cords per second. This frequency is controlled, among other ways, by tension on the cords. In singing, the control is careful and obvious, and with a good singer highly precise.

2.13   The shapes of the passages between the vocal cords and the outside air modify the quality of the voice in various ways. Sounds that involve no other mechanism than these two are called **resonants**. All English vowels and /m n ŋ l r y w/ are resonants. They may be divided into three groups.

In /m n ŋ/ the passage through the mouth is completely closed at some point, but the passage through the nose is open. They are called **nasal resonants** or merely **nasals**. The three differ only in the point at which the mouth passage is closed.

In /l/ the mouth is closed at the mid-line by the contact of the tip of the tongue against the gums. There is an opening at one or both sides. It is called a **lateral resonant**, or merely a **lateral**.

In /r y w/ the passage through the mouth is open at the mid-line. They are therefore called **median resonants**. This term includes also all English vowels. Because of the close similarity of /r y w/ to the vowels, they are sometimes called **semivowels**. A more detailed description will be given in connection with that of the vowels in the next chapter.

2.14 If the vocal cords are brought together sufficiently to obstruct the passage of air, but not to produce voice, a different sort of sound results. This is **glottal friction**. Friction differs from voice in that there is no clearly marked fundamental pitch. The effect is therefore not musical. It may be modified by the shapes of the passages above in the same way as voice, so that different whispered sounds are distinguishable, though not as clearly as when spoken.

The phoneme /h/ in normal speech consists largely of glottal friction. Since the mouth normally is moving toward the position for the following vowel, /h/ is frequently similar to a whispering of that vowel. This means that /h/ varies widely in quality with its environment. It may even be a whispered nasal, as in /mhm/ 'yes.'

2.15 Friction can be produced at various other points in the air passage by any very narrow opening. The sounds /f θ s š/ are largely such friction produced at a narrow constriction in the mouth. They are therefore called **fricatives**. The sounds /v ð z ž/ are similar except that there is simultaneous voice. They are therefore called **voiced fricatives**, and in distinction /f θ s š/ are called **voiceless fricatives**.

Fricatives differ also in the shape of the narrow opening in which they are produced. In /f v θ ð/ it is relatively wide from side to side but very narrow from top to bottom. Because of the slit-like shape of the opening, these sounds are called **slit fricatives.** In contrast in /s z š ž/ the opening is much narrower from side to side and deeper from top to bottom. These sounds are called **grooved fricatives.**

2.16 The sounds /p t k b d g/ are formed by the complete closure of the air passages. There may be either closure and opening, or only closure, or only opening. These differences are not significant in English. The sounds /b d g/ are further characterized by voice at the moment of closing or opening; they are called **voiced stops.** /p t k/ have no voice at the moment of opening or closing. They are therefore called **voiceless stops.** English voiceless stops usually have a rather strong release of breath between the opening and the beginning of voicing for the following vowel. This is **aspiration,** and the stops are said to be **aspirate.** The amount of aspiration in /p t k/ is rather variable in most English dialects, but the variation is never significant. Aspiration may be nearly or entirely lacking in certain environments. The commonest of these is after /s/ in such words as *spill*, which should be contrasted with *pill* and *bill*. Aspiration may most easily be detected by holding a thin strip of paper before the lips. It should be so adjusted that it will jump for *pill* but not for *bill*. A similar failure to jump on the pronunciation of *spill* will indicate that the /p/ here is unaspirate.

2.17 If it is desired to symbolize some feature of sound which is not phonemic, the transcription is enclosed in brackets [ ]. Thus we may write *pill* as /pil/ or as [pʰil] and *spill* as /spil/ or as [sp⁼il]. The symbol [pʰ] represents an aspirated stop, whereas [p⁼] represents an unaspirated stop. Such a method of indicating pronunciation is called a **phonetic transcription.** One in which the phonemes are indicated is a **phonemic transcription.** The significance of the distinction will be made much clearer by the more comprehensive definition of the phoneme in Chapter 16.

2.18 **Affricates** are stops in which the opening is relatively slow. They therefore are composed of a stop plus a movement through a fricative position: /č/ starts with a sound similar to /t/ and moves through one rather similar to /š/; /ǰ/ starts with a sound similar to /d/ and moves through a sound rather similar to /ž/. In some languages such sequences of sounds function as single phonemes, in others as sequences of phonemes. In English the treatment as single phonemes seems most closely to accord with the evidence, though some linguists have advocated treating them as /tš/ and /dž/. In any case the movement is relatively rapid and the fricative element is not very long.

2.19 All the consonants are characterized by a closure or a decided narrowing at some point in the mouth. They may be classified by this **point of articulation.** In each case there are two parts, known as **articulators,** which are brought together. These two serve to define the various articulations. The following are used in English:

	LOWER ARTICULATOR	UPPER ARTICULATOR
Bilabial	(lower) lip	upper lip
Labiodental	(lower) lip	(upper) teeth
Dental	tip of tongue	(upper) teeth
Alveolar	tip of tongue	upper gums
Alveopalatal	front of tongue	far front of palate
Velar	back of tongue	velum (soft palate)
Glottal	the two vocal cords	

Bilabial stop
/p/ or /b/

Labiodental fricative
/f/ or /v/

Dental fricative
/θ/ or /ð/

Alveolar nasal
/n/

Alveopalatal fricative
/š/ or /ž/

Velar stop
/k/ or /g/

ENGLISH ARTICULATIONS

The lower lip is much more important as an articulator than the upper. The term "lip" without specification may be assumed to refer to the lower lip. Similarly, "teeth" may be assumed to refer to the upper front teeth unless some others are specified.

2.20 The consonants of English can be classified according to the accompanying chart on the basis of the types of sounds and the points of articulation:

		Bilabial	Labiodental	Dental	Alveolar	Alveopalatal	Velar	Glottal
Stops	voiceless	p			t		k	
	voiced	b			d		g	
Affricates	voiceless					č		
	voiced					ǰ		
Fricatives								
slit	voiceless		f	θ				h
	voiced		v	ð				
groove	voiceless				s	š		
	voiced				z	ž		
Lateral	voiced				l			
Nasals	voiced	m			n		ŋ	
Semivowels	voiced	w			r	y		

2.21 An examination of the phonemes of English as sounds rather than as units in a linguistic system reveals that some of them are actually quite variable in their pronunciation. A **phoneme** is a class of sounds so used in a given language that no two members of the class can ever contrast. This is the first modification of our original definition of a phoneme given in 1.10. Its full implications will not be discussed until a later chapter. However, one closely connected observation must be made here. All the sounds in any such class must be, in some measure, phonetically similar. This is the case, for example, with [p⁼] and [pʰ]. Both are voiceless bilabial stops. It is also the case with the numerous varieties of /h/ which were mentioned. These are all voiceless and characterized by glottal friction. There is similar phonetic similarity in each of the classes of sounds that constitute English phonemes.

2.22 If some measure of phonetic similarity is made a necessary condition for two sounds to be one phoneme, we can dismiss from further consideration some of the pairs for which minimal pairs were lacking. For example [ŋ] and [ð] have nothing in common beyond the fact that both are voiced. The likelihood of their constituting a single phoneme is rather remote. However, [θ] and [ð] are much more similar, so that it is worthwhile to seek conclusive proof that they are distinct. It is for this reason that diligent search has been made for minimal pairs bearing on the contrast of [θ] and [ð], whereas no such effort has been expended on some of the other pairs mentioned in 2.10. Equal effort might be expected to prove equally successful.

2.23 However, it is still conceivable that extensive search might fail to uncover any minimal pairs for two closely similar sounds. In some languages, minimal pairs are much more difficult to find than is the case in English, so much so that the analyst cannot afford to depend upon them. They are by no means necessary, but merely the most definitive evidence when they can be found. Other methods can, however, provide a quite reliable analysis.

We may demonstrate one of these methods by assuming that no minimal pairs for [š] : [ž] are known. A non-English investigator might not find *dilution* : *delusion, glacier* : *glazier, Aleutian* : *allusion*, even if these should occur in the speech of his informant. Or perhaps the speaker might not use some of these words at all, and so not actually have any minimal pair. This is not all hypothetical. I taught linguistics for two years before I became aware that these pairs existed in my own speech. Since [ž] is rare in English monosyllables, it will be necessary, for this demonstration, to relax our restriction and use words of two syllables.

Numerous pairs can be found that differ in only one phoneme in addition to the sounds under discussion. One such is *treasure* [trežər] : *pressure* [prešər]. Here there are two contrasts, /t/ : /p/, and [ž] : [š]. The first is known to be phonemic from the existence of many minimal pairs, and hence is written /t/ : /p/. The second is under discussion; phonetic transcription is used to indicate that the phonemic status is unknown.

The use of [ž] and [š] in these words is not haphazard. If an informant is asked to repeat these words several times, *treasure* will always have [ž] and *pressure* always [š]. There must be something about these words which determines which of the two occurs. There are only two possibilities. They are used consistently either because they are two different phonemes, or because of the presence of /t/ or /p/. We may assume as a hypothesis to test, that if a word has /t/, it will have [ž] rather than [š], and if it has /p/, it will have [š] rather than [ž]. This will explain the two words *treasure* and *pressure*, but will not work elsewhere: *pleasure* has /p/ and [ž]; and *trashy* has /t/ and [š]. Either we must abandon the hypothesis or introduce additional complications. As we examine additional data, we will be forced to conclude that to predict [ž] : [š] on the basis of other sounds in the words is either unworkable or unbelievably complex. They must be considered as separate phonemes.

What we have just done is to conclude that /š/ and /ž/ are separate phonemes because they occur in similar environments. Minimal pairs afford more direct proof because they show the two sounds occurring in identical environments. The more nearly similar the words on which we base our argument, the more direct and conclusive it is.

2.24   That /š/ and /ž/ are two separate phonemes is no surprise to an American. He knows this without the marshalling of evidence. But it might be quite otherwise with a non-native. The way people hear sounds is determined by their language background. Americans are used to hearing /ž/ and /š/ in similar environments, and so have learned to distinguish them. They are not accustomed to hearing [p⁼] and [pʰ] in similar environments, and have never needed to distinguish them. A native speaker learns to rely for the recognition of utterances on the phonemes of the language, and to disregard everything else as not pertinent. That is, he learns the phonemic system of the language. The task of an American student of linguistics is not one of learning a set of phonemes — he already knows them well — but of learning to make conscious formulations about the system, to attach symbols to the individual phonemes, and to lay a basis for understanding the relations between the English system and the phonemic systems of other languages.

The English Vowel System

3.1 The analysis of the vowels of English presents certain difficulties which are not encountered in the case of the consonants.
These necessitate a presentation somewhat different from that
which was used in the last chapter. Two of these peculiarities must
be pointed out at the beginning. No discussion can be fruitful
unless they are kept clearly in mind throughout.

3.2 Most American and at least some British dialects have
exactly the same total inventory of vowel phonemes. However,
few words have the same vowels in all dialects. For example, east
of the Allegheny Mountains, *marry, merry,* and *Mary* are generally
all pronounced differently. West of the Alleghenies *merry* and *Mary*
are usually alike, and in some areas all three may be alike. Numerous other comparable differences can be cited, not only between
the speech of East and West, but also between smaller subdivisions
in each. The total list of available phonemes is the same, but the
distribution of the phonemes varies widely from dialect to dialect.

Because of this it is impossible to select words that will illustrate
the vowel phonemes to speakers of all dialects. An example that
is excellent for one area of the country may be quite misleading
for another. The phonemes must not be identified solely from the
words which are stated to contain them. Preferably there should
be oral presentation by an instructor who is thoroughly acquainted
with the vowel system of English and this analysis of it. Lacking

this, dependence must be placed more on the phonetic description than on key words. Throughout this chapter, unless otherwise stated, my own pronunciation is the subject of analysis. This will prove quite different from that of most speakers from the Atlantic coast or the Southeast.

3.3 What Americans usually think of as vowels are often not single phonemes but sequences of phonemes. In these instances, however, the two phonemes are very intimately related, much more so than a vowel and an accompanying consonant. This closely knit sequence of phonemes must sometimes be studied as a single unit. We will call it a **syllable nucleus,** since it serves as the center of a syllable. A syllable nucleus will be defined as a vowel, or a vowel and a following semivowel.

3.4 Because of the intimate relationship between the parts of a syllable nucleus, it will be easier first to identify whole nuclei as single entities, and then to divide them into their segments.

We may obtain a partial list of syllable nuclei by the same method we used with the consonants. In this case we will obtain a set of one-syllable words in which the consonants are identical, and which are all distinguishable by a native speaker. It then follows that each word will contain a distinct syllable nucleus. The longest list known to me in my own speech is the following:

bait	*bet*	*boat*	*bought*
bat	*bit*	*boot*	*bout*
beat	*bite*	*bot*	*but*

A number of other possibilities must be eliminated. *Beet* is not distinguishable from *beat,* nor *bight* from *bite.* Another person might distinguish between some of these words, or fail to distinguish between some others which I have listed as distinct; or he might have a different vocabulary. For example, relatively few Americans can consider *bot* 'a parasite of horses' as an item in their vocabulary.

Other lists can be adduced and compared as we did with the consonants. In this way our inventory of nuclei can gradually be increased. The maximum number that can be found will vary with the dialect under investigation from about fifteen to over thirty. Some will prove quite rare in the speech of a given person. I have at least two which occur with a frequency of considerably less than once in a thousand syllables. There is no need of a laborious searching to determine the full list. For our present purpose the sample of the twelve established by our first set of similar words will be adequate for the next step in the analysis.

3.5 If we compare the nuclei in *bout* and *boat* we may observe certain features in common. In both cases, during the pronunciation of the nucleus the lips may be seen or felt to round noticeably. The speaker himself may feel that his tongue moves upward and backward at the same time. These similar movements of the vocal apparatus produce an audible similarity in the last portion of these nuclei.

A similar comparison of the nuclei of *bite* and *bait* yields comparable results. In both, the tongue may be felt to rise and move somewhat forward. There is no rounding of the lips. There is an audible similarity in the last portion of the nuclei.

Comparison of *bout* and *bite* demonstrate that the final portions of these nuclei constitute two phonemes. These words are in fact a minimal pair. The two consonants and the first element in the nuclei are the same. They differ only in the glides with which the nuclei end. We will transcribe the glide of *bout* and *boat* as /w/, and that of *bite* and *bait* as /y/. The justification for using these symbols will be discussed later.

3.6 We have just demonstrated by means of minimal pairs that four of our nuclei can be divided, since each half enters into a separate set of contrasts. With this in mind we may now examine the remaining nuclei of our sample, comparing each of them with these four. We will find one more with /y/, *beat;* the movement of the tongue is less prominent in this word than the others, but it is clearly discernible. We also find one more with /w/, *boot;* here, likewise, the tongue movement is slight but observable, but the presence of the glide is most clearly seen in the lip rounding. This leaves six nuclei with neither /y/ nor /w/ glides. One of these, *bought*, presents some special problems; we will postpone the discussion of it until later. The remaining five have simple vowels without glides. We will assign symbols for the phonemes as follows: *bit* /bit/, *bet* /bet/, *bat* /bæt/, *but* /bət/, and *bot* /bat/. The first four of these are pronounced the same in most dialects.

3.7 The next problem is that of identifying these simple vowels with the first elements in the compound nuclei. We have already found that the first elements in *bite* and *bout* are the same. We may start with this vowel for our first identification. There are two ways in which to proceed. A very drawn-out pronunciation of *bite* will so prolong the vowel that we may more easily hear the quality. It may also, of course, introduce some small distortion, but probably not enough to change the phoneme. We may also try deliberately pronouncing /y/ after each of the short vowels we have found. Both procedures will suggest that *bite* should be transcribed /bayt/ — that is, that the vowel is the same as that of *bot*. (Compare *kite* and *cot* if you do not have *bot* in your vocabulary.)

Actually, most Americans pronounce /a/ slightly differently in /bayt/ and /bawt/ from the way they pronounce it in words like /bat/. We cannot expect exact identity of any phoneme in different contexts or even in different repetitions of a word. But here the difference is more regular than a chance variation. As we will show later, both /y/ and /w/ exert a considerable and regular influence on any preceding vowel. When the simple vowels have all been identified, it will be found that the vowel of *bite* is nearer that of *bot* than to any other, and that it will have the same sort of relationship to this vowel that we find in the case of each of the other vowel phonemes.

3.8 Making allowances for similar differences in other cases, we may arrange the nuclei of our sample as follows:

/i/	*bit*	/bit/	*beat*	/biyt/		
/e/	*bet*	/bet/	*bait*	/beyt/		
/a/	*bot*	/bat/	*bite*	/bayt/	*bout*	/bawt/
/o/					*boat*	/bowt/
/u/					*boot*	/buwt/
/æ/	*bat*	/bæt/				
/ə/	*but*	/bət/				

We find no simple nucleus to match the vowel of *boat* or *boot*, nor any complex nuclei containing the vowels of *bat* and *but*. Of course, our sample has been a restricted one. As additional nuclei are found, some of them may be expected to fit into the vacant spaces in this tabulation. The search for nuclei should be conducted with this chart in mind. We must also search for additional simple vowels and additional types of diphthongs.

3.9 Some of the missing nuclei will be found very readily by examining further sets of monosyllabic words. Consider the following:

lack	/læk/	*lick*	/lik/	*look*	
lake	/leyk/	*like*	/layk/	*luck*	/lək/
leak	/liyk/	*lock*	/lak/	*Luke*	/luwk/

Most of these can be readily matched by a native speaker with the members of the set we have been examining. The matching is indicated by the transcriptions. Only *look* seems new. It contains neither /y/ nor /w/ and seems to be a simple vowel. The vowel of *look* stands in the same sort of relationship to that of *Luke* as we have seen before in the case of, say, *bot* and *bout*. We may transcribe *look* as /luk/, and so fill one of the vacant places in the table in 3.8.

3.10   It will be somewhat harder to find /o/. Most Americans, including myself, have this in very few words. The colloquial pronunciation of *going to* /gonə/ is the commonest and most widespread. New Englanders often have this simple nucleus in such words as *home* /hom/ or *whole* /hol/. Elsewhere these words would usually be pronounced /howm/ and /howl/.

3.11   Careful search will also uncover some of the missing compound nuclei. Most of the remaining ones, however, are missing from certain dialects, or are of sporadic occurrence only. For example, I sometimes use /əw/ in words where most speakers of similar dialects would say /ow/. Thus *road* is pronounced either /rowd/ or /rəwd/. This is the result of dialect mixture; in some dialects /əw/ is the usual pronunciation in these words and /ow/ is rare or sporadic. Such pronunciations are more widespread than is often realized. Somewhat less frequent is the use of the /ew/ in all or some of these words.

The diphthong /æw/ is a similar case. *House* is /haws/ in most areas; in a few areas, however, it is regularly pronounced /hæws/. In such dialects /aw/ may be rare. In still less frequent types of English, *house* may be /hews/ or /həws/.

In New York City, *bird* is said to be pronounced "boyd." This description is erroneous. The pronunciation that is actually heard is /bəyd/, something clearly different from what the spelling would convey to most readers. The legend is the result of the inadequacy of our traditional alphabet to indicate pronunciation, coupled with the unfamiliarity of the pronunciation to the uncritical observer from another dialect area.

Every possible sequence of vowel and semivowel can be found in some American dialect. Some are quite widespread, occurring in all or most English speech; others are comparatively infrequent.

3.12 Our tabulation in 3.8 shows only seven vowel phonemes. Actually, there are nine in English. The two not included there are difficult to identify in print. They are highly susceptible to dialect variation and even to individual differences within major dialects. Both occur, either as simple vowels or in compound nuclei, in most dialects, and one or both are usually quite frequent.

Some dialects make a distinction between *just* as in *a just judge* and *just* as in *He just came*. If this is done, the first is usually /jəst/ and the second is /jɨst/. Both of these pronunciations contrast with *gist* /jist/ and *jest* /jest/. Other Americans use the same pronunciation, usually /jəst/, for both words. Their doing so does not prove that they do not have the phoneme /ɨ/. Indeed, it may be quite common in other words. The pronunciation /jɨst/ has long been singled out as an earmark of "poor English." In response, many Americans have by considerable effort eradicated /jɨst/ from their speech, usually replacing it by the more acceptable /jəst/. Some people who consider /jɨst/ inelegant nevertheless use it freely in unguarded moments. The pronunciation is certainly commoner than many people suppose.

The word *pretty* as in *pretty good* commonly is said with /ɨ/. It is quite variable in pronunciation: both /pritiy/ and /pɨrtiy/ are frequent; /pərtiy/ is not rare. In this context it is almost never /pritiy/, though in such a use as *a pretty girl* /pritiy/ is probably the commonest form. Both *pretty* and *just* will almost always be said with some other vowel in isolation. For a pronunciation which will illustrate /ɨ/ they must be said in natural context.

Children has two common pronunciations. The first syllable may by /čild/ or /čɨld/. In the South *sister* is commonly /sister/. For some speakers the name *Willie* /wiliy/ contrasts with *will he* /wɨliy/ and *wooly* /wuliy/. All these illustrative words must be used with caution, however, since many speakers who use /ɨ/ in any of these words will substitute /i/ when speaking carefully.

The examples just cited do not illustrate the most characteristic uses of /ɨ/, which are in unstressed syllables in longer words and in certain words which do not normally receive stress in a sentence. Thus the second syllable of *children* may either be /rɨn/ or /rən/. *Can* is pronounced /kæn/ when said in isolation, but in sentences it is more frequently /kɨn/. In these positions /ɨ/ can be easily overlooked or confused with /i/ or /ə/. A little practice is required to recognize and discriminate between these vowels in unstressed syllables. In most dialects it will be found that /ɨ/ is one of the commonest vowels. It is particularly common in a very colloquial pronunciation, or in utterances containing many longer words.

3.13 Simple /ɔ/ is relatively common in the speech of eastern New England in such words as *cot* /kɔt/. Elsewhere in America these words are usually pronounced like /kat/. It is also the most usual pronunciation for "short o" in Southern British, but not in some other British dialects. In the dialects which say /kat/, /ɔ/ is one of the rarest of syllable nuclei. It usually occurs in only a very few words and under somewhat unusual conditions. By the same token, /a/ is a very rare nucleus in some of the dialects which say /kɔt/.

The vowel /ɔ/ is somewhat more common in compound nuclei. Many Americans use this vowel in words like *boy*, saying /bɔy/. Others pronounce such words like /boy/. /ɔ/ is also used as the vowel in nuclei like that of *bought*, though here too, /o/ occurs in other dialects.

3.14 For some speakers *cot* and *caught* form a minimal pair for another type of glide. We write it as /ʜ/. *Caught* is pronounced either as /koʜt/ or /kɔʜt/, the latter contrasting in some dialects with /kɔt/. Unfortunately, over much of the continent no minimal pairs can be found for simple nuclei as against diphthongs. The following are some of the most likely examples.

A good pair is *bomb* and *balm*. Both words vary considerably in pronunciation from place to place. In the West they are most frequently pronounced alike. Some Eastern dialects say /bam/ and /baʜm/. Others say /bɔm/ and /baʜm/. Some Southerners say /bəm/ and /baʜm/. Some speakers pronounce *balm* with an /l/.

In many Eastern dialects both /æ/ and /æʜ/ occur. The contrast can frequently be heard in the pair *can* meaning 'be able' /kæn/ and *can* meaning 'tin can' /kæʜn/. Some speakers make an even greater difference and say /kæn/ and /keʜn/. These are the pronunciations of these words said in isolation. In context, 'be able' is usually /kɪn/. Another frequent minimal pair is *have* /hæv/ : *halve* /hæнv/.

Some Americans make a contrast in pronunciation between *reel* /riyl/ and *real* /riнl/. For some who do this the further comparison of *rill* /ril/ can also be made.

The semivowel /н/ occurs with each of the nine vowel phonemes; but, for most of the combinations, dependable key words are even harder to find than for those already cited. There is great variation in the use of these diphthongs from dialect to dialect. In most, nuclei with /н/ are commoner before /r/ and /l/ than elsewhere.

Some dialects are popularly considered as "r-less." These either do not pronounce /r/ after vowels, or else use a kind of /r/ which is so different from that of other speakers that it is often not recognized as an /r/. In these dialects /н/ quite regularly appears in words that would have /r/ in other dialects. Thus *here* may be pronounced /hir/, /hiнr/, or /hiн/ in different areas.

3.15   In summary, there are a total of nine simple vowels. Each of them can occur alone, with /y/, with /w/, or with /н/. This makes a total of thirty-six possible nuclei. Probably no single dialect has all of them, though some approach it closely. Every one of the thirty-six occurs, however, in some American dialect.

The thirty-six nuclei can conveniently be exhibited in a chart. No key words have been inserted because of the variations which exist between dialects. The student is advised to fill in key words for all those which occur in his own speech. The result will be much more useful than any ready-made tabulation.

The names of the vowel letters are quite confusing, and the addition of four more symbols makes matters worse. These are sometimes called: "digraph" for /æ/, "barred I" for /ɨ/, "open O" for /ɔ/ and /šəwaн/ for /ə/. For certain purposes, a number system has been found to be a more convenient method for oral identification of the nuclei. In this system the tens digits represent the vowels and the unit digits the semivowels. The numbers under this system are given with the transcriptions:

10 /i/ ___	11 /iy/ ___	12 /iw/ ___	13 /iн/ ___
20 /e/ ___	21 /ey/ ___	22 /ew/ ___	23 /eн/ ___
30 /æ/ ___	31 /æy/ ___	32 /æw/ ___	33 /æн/ ___

40 /i/ ___	41 /iy/ ___	42 /iw/ ___	43 /iн/ ___
50 /ə/ ___	51 /əy/ ___	52 /əw/ ___	53 /əн/ ___
60 /a/ ___	61 /ay/ ___	62 /aw/ ___	63 /aн/ ___
70 /u/ ___	71 /uy/ ___	72 /uw/ ___	73 /uн/ ___
80 /o/ ___	81 /oy/ ___	82 /ow/ ___	83 /oн/ ___
90 /ɔ/ ___	91 /ɔy/ ___	92 /ɔw/ ___	93 /ɔн/ ___

3.16 In view of the variations in pronunciation from dialect to dialect, it is particularly necessary to understand the mode of formation for the various vowel sounds. This will provide an essential check on the accuracy with which they have been identified from the examples.

An articulatory phonetic description would not be adequate by itself. Each of the nine vowel phonemes varies somewhat in pronunciation. Dialect differences include not only differences in the vowels or nuclei used in certain words, but also minor variations in the quality of the vowels themselves. Nevertheless, this variation always occurs within certain limits, so that close attention to both phonetic quality and distribution will generally provide accurate identification of the vowel phonemes and compound nuclei.

3.17 Three variables in the positions of the vocal organs are particularly significant in the phonetic description of English vowels. The most important is the position of the highest part of the tongue. This varies in two dimensions. It may be relatively high, mid, or low. It may also be relatively front, central, or back. Note the difference in meaning between central (intermediate between front and back) and mid (intermediate between high and low). These two variables provide a symmetrical charting of the English vowel phonemes:

	FRONT	CENTRAL	BACK
HIGH	i	i	u
MID	e	ə	o
LOW	æ	a	ɔ

The third variable which is of importance in English vowels is the rounding of the lips. In /u/ there is always moderate rounding. In /o/ there is usually somewhat less, but always enough to be noticeable. In /ɔ/ the rounding is still weaker. In some pronunciations it may be so slight as to be hardly noticeable, or even lacking. The front and central vowels are never rounded.

3.18   /i/ is neither extremely high nor extremely front. The high front vowels of many other languages are both higher and nearer the front. For this reason /i/ is often difficult for foreigners. They often tend to use a higher vowel, one which impresses most Americans as more nearly /iy/. Frequently, however, this foreign vowel is a simple vowel, not a diphthong like /iy/.

/u/ is likewise not as high nor as back as comparable vowels in many other languages. For this reason it also gives many foreigners difficulty. Some degree of lip rounding is always present.

/ɨ/ has the same height as /i/ and /u/ or may be higher than either. It may be produced by starting from /i/ and drawing the tongue backward toward the /u/ position. There is no lip rounding. The tongue position is distinctly higher than for /ə/. Most students have their greatest difficulty in learning to distinguish /ɨ/ and /i/. This may require considerable practice with such pairs as *gist* /ǰist/ : *just* /ǰɨst/ and *pretty* /pritiy/ : /prɨtiy/, or with the contrast between different pronunciations of such words as *children* /čildrin/ : /čɨldrən/ and *sister* /sistər/ : /sɨstər/.

/a/ is somewhat variable in pronunciation, not only between speakers, but also between various contexts in the speech of a single person. The more fronted varieties are generally quite a bit lower than /æ/, and seldom quite as far front. The more backed varieties may approach rather closely to /ɔ/. In general, speakers who have a rather back /a/ have appreciable rounding in /ɔ/. Those that lack rounding in /ɔ/ have no variety of /a/ far enough back to be confused. The greatest difficulty in attempting to transcribe another dialect of English is, in the majority of instances, with the identification of the low vowels. Apparently most dialects have three phonemes in this territory, but the discrimination of the three varies from dialect to dialect. To be certain, it is always necessary not only to observe the phonetic details but also to watch for the contrasts between the several phonemes.

/ɔ/ is sometimes confused with /a/ and also sometimes with /o/. In most dialects it is hard to find minimal pairs for the /ɔ/ with either of these. Some dialects have /o ow ɔy ɔH/ but not /ɔ ɔw oy oH/. To make matters worse, some dialects use /ɔy ɔH/ in the same words in which others use /oy oH/. As a result many Americans are more or less accustomed to equating /ɔy/ with /oy/ and /ɔн/ with /oн/. If the nucleus of *boy* starts from a noticeably lower tongue position than does that of *beau*, the transcriptions /bɔy/ and /bow/ are probably correct. If these two seem to start from about the same place, then /boy/ and /bow/ are probable. Many people say *boy* with no trace of lip rounding such as can be observed in *beau*, or even in *going to* /gonə/. In this case *boy* is probably /bɔy/, and /o/ and /ɔ/ differ not only in tongue position but also in lip rounding.

3.19   The glide or semivowel /w/ was defined in 3.5 as a movement of the tongue upward and backward with an accompanying increase in lip rounding. In /uw/ the lips start with moderate rounding, and this is noticeably increased. In /aw/ the lips are unrounded at the start, but then rounded somewhat. /uw/ ends with considerably more lip rounding than does /aw/. Indeed, the beginning of /uw/ may be more strongly rounded than the end of /aw/. The characteristic feature is not any given degree, but a marked increase in lip rounding during the course of the pronunciation of /w/.

Both /y/ and /w/ involve a raising of the tongue. In /y/ the movement is up and forward, in /w/ it is up and backward. Neither semivowel represents movement to one definite position; rather, each is characterized by movement in a particular direction. In /ay/ the tongue does not usually rise as high as the starting point of /iy/; similarly, in /aw/ the tongue does not rise as high as the starting point of /uw/. Moreover, /y/ represents a longer rise in /ay/ than in /ey/, and still less of a rise in /iy/. The rise in /aw/ is greater than that in /ow/, and in /uw/ it is even slighter.

3.20   The symbols /y/ and /w/ were proposed in 2.9 for the initial consonants in *yes* and *would*. The description of the pronunciation of /y/ and /w/ just given will obviously not fit in these cases. Our definition of phonemic transcription requires that every phoneme have an unambiguous symbol, and that every symbol represent one phoneme. Writing /y/ in *yes* /yes/ and *say* /sey/, or /w/ in *would* /wud/ and *do* /duw/ implies that we have identified sounds as members of a single phoneme.

Before vowels, /y/ and /w/ also represent glides. They are in fact precisely opposite movements to those just described. In /yes/ the tongue starts a little higher and nearer the front than the tongue position of /e/ and glides rapidly to the latter. In /sey/ the tongue starts at the position of /e/ and glides rapidly to a higher and fronter position. If a tape recording of /yes/ is played backwards, the result is very similar to /sey/. Moreover, the /y/ before /i/ in *ye* /yiy/ starts much higher than that before /a/ in *yacht* /yat/. Before /i/ the glide is relatively short. Before /a/ it is much longer. In these respects the behavior of /y/ before vowels parallels the observed behavior of /y/ after vowels. The same things are true also of /w/.

The differences between initial and final /y/, or initial and final /w/, must be taken as the consequences of their position rather than as any significant differences in their function in the language. Treating each pair as a single phoneme is thus quite justifiable. This is another instance of the kind of variation within phonemes which can be observed in all languages and within most phonemes.

3.21   The glide /н/ sometimes represents a movement of the tongue toward a more relaxed position. The highest point of the tongue may move toward a mid-central position, the position of rest, or there may be only a general relaxation of the tongue. The extent of either movement varies widely from speaker to speaker and from nucleus to nucleus. For many, particularly in /aн/, movement is hardly perceptible; but /aн/ is always distinctly different from /a/. When a movement of tongue position is not discernible, the difference is largely one of duration. That is, /н/ represents either glide or prolongation, or both. No contrast can be found between nuclei which end in a central glide and those which are merely prolonged.

3.22   The fact that the /y/ and /w/ glides after vowels have counterparts before vowels naturally suggests that /н/ should also. The only possible candidate is /h/, as it is the only consonant which does not occur after vowels. There are certain tenuous similarities, but these are by no means as great as those found in /y/ and /w/. Since there is no clear evidence that /н/ has or has not a counterpart in /h/, linguists differ as to the direction in which the evidence points. I consider that keeping the two separate is the better solution, and hence use two symbols, /h/ and /н/. Many other linguists feel that the weight of the evidence is on the other side, and so use /h/ for both. On this basis the last column in the chart of 3.15 will read: 13 /ih/, 23 /eh/, 33 /æh/, etc. In any case, the two systems are closely equivalent, and either can be readily converted into the other.

3.23   In many American pronunciations /r/ is a glide comparable in a number of ways to /y/ and /w/. Most often the top of the tongue is turned upward, though other speakers obtain very similar sounds by different types of motions. Probably no single phoneme varies so widely from dialect to dialect as does /r/; in some pronunciations it is a trill or a flap, or one of a variety of other types of sounds. Certain American dialects pronounce /r/ after vowels so weakly that hearers accustomed to other dialects do not hear it at all. A few do not ordinarily pronounce /r/ in this position.

The phoneme /r/ differs from /y/ and /w/ in that it is not as closely knit with a preceding vowel. That is, in most instances /r/ is not part of the syllable nucleus. Nevertheless, the relationship between /r/ and a preceding vowel is often closer than is the case with other consonants.

In the pronunciation of many Americans, /ər/ is phonetically a single /r/-like vowel. That is to say, the turning up (retroflexion) of the tongue tip which characterizes /r/ occurs throughout the /ə/. This seems to be quite generally the case in the Western dialects. In Eastern dialects /ər/ may be clearly divided into two parts. The first is a non-retroflexed vowel /ə/ and the second a retroflexed glide /r/. These two pronunciations give quite different impressions, but seem to be phonemically equivalent.

4

English Stress and Intonation

4.1 In our discussion of the last two chapters we restricted our attention largely to the comparison of one-syllable words spoken in isolation. From this body of material we were able to obtain evidence for the consonant and vowel phonemes of English. The restricted nature of the data used rendered it impossible to discover some of the English phonemes. In this chapter the inventory will be completed through examination of a more varied body of evidence.

4.2 If two-syllable words are examined, it will be found that they are of two kinds. One group is stressed ("accented" is a familiar alternate term) on the first syllable and includes such words as *going, spoken, phoneme*. The others are stressed on the second syllable, among them *obtain, because, above*. Having observed such a difference, we should inquire as to whether it is phonemic. A search for minimal pairs is one method of investigation. A very large number of pairs can be found in which there are relatively minor differences in addition to the contrast in stress. Many of these are pairs of nouns and verbs, and most are spelled alike in the traditional orthography. For example *present* is [prézint] as a noun but [prizént] as a verb. In such instances, most English-speaking people will feel that the difference in stress is more important than the **difference** in the vowels. This impression does not constitute proof, but it does encourage further search for true minimal pairs. A few pairs can be found in which there is no difference in the vowels (for some speakers at least). One of these is *permit;* as a verb it is pronounced /pərmít/, but as a noun /pə́rmit/. However, since there are other pronunciations in use (e.g., /pə́rmit/), these do not constitute a minimal pair for all speakers. Another is *pervert,* /pə́rvərt/ and /pərvə́rt/.

These prove that stress is phonemic in English; thus two additional phonemes have been established. We will call /′/ **primary stress,** and /˘/ we will call **weak stress.** We will follow a convention that /˘/ will not be written in a transcription of words or longer portions unless it is desired to call special attention to it. In an example where stresses are shown, any vowel with no stress marked will be understood to have weak stress.

4.3 Having determined that stress is phonemic, we must now turn back to the one-syllable words we considered in Chapters 2 and 3 and determine whether they have stress. One way of doing this is to read a list of words, alternating monosyllables and disyllables, for example, *bill, permit, pill, present, beat,* etc. These must be read with a slight pause between them so that they will be, in effect, isolated. If this is done, it will be evident that the stress on the monosyllables will match closely that on the more heavily stressed syllable in the longer words. We accordingly conclude that all monosyllables, when said in isolation, have primary stress. This means that a transcription of *bill* as /bil/ is not complete. It should be /bíl/.

The stress was not discovered in our first comparisons because all words said in isolation have one /′/; hence no stress contrast — minimal or otherwise — is possible in monosyllables. The full phonemic system of English cannot be considered as established until we have examined the full range of types of utterances which are amenable to linguistic study.

4.4 The next type of data that should be examined is words of more than two syllables. These will easily enable us to discover a third degree of stress. In this case it will prove more difficult to discover suitable minimal pairs, but many very suggestive cases can be found. A technique comparable to that used in 2.23 to establish the phonemic status of /š/ and /ž/ will prove that this third degree of stress is phonemic. We will mark it /ˆ/ and call it **tertiary stress**. It may be heard in such words as *dictionary* /díkšənèriy/ or *animation* /æ̀niméyšin/.

Having discovered the contrast between tertiary and weak stress, it is necessary to go back and re-examine the two-syllable words. It will be found that the more weakly stressed syllable most often has /˘/, but not infrequently has /ˆ/. For example *contents* is usually pronounced /kántènts/, very rarely /kántĭnts/.

4.5   These two cases show how essential it is to restudy all data in the light of each new discovery. In each of them, phonemic distinctions which could not easily have been discovered through work with limited data have proved to be easily identifiable when other data has suggested their existence and nature. This is a frequent experience in linguistics. For example, to suggest that stress is phonemic only in polysyllabic words will produce many unnecessary complications. Experience has shown that the most satisfactory policy is to consider that, if stress is phonemic at all, it is phonemic throughout English. Conversely, no feature which is not established as phonemic can be considered as linguistically significant even in a highly specialized context. The discovery of any new phonemic contrast imposes the obligation to examine the data to determine the full range of its occurrence.

4.6   A contrast of another sort may be discovered through comparing such sequences as *night rate* with *nitrate*. The average American will hear the difference as a break between *night* and *rate*, contrasting with no break in *nitrate*. Since this break serves to distinguish utterances, it is a phoneme. It may be called **open transition** and transcribed /+/.

Having found /+/, the principle just mentioned compels us to examine the language closely to find how widely it is distributed. It is reasonable to expect that it will be found in many more places than the few minimal pairs would indicate. It will prove convenient and helpful to search next for pairs which, while not minimal, show the contrast in similar environments. One such case is, for many speakers, *minus* /máynis/ : *slyness* /sláy+nis/. Such pairs will help us to discover the characteristics by which we recognize /+/ in different contexts. We will then find it easier to identify it as we begin to examine an increasing range of data.

By this procedure we will find that /+/ is, in fact, a frequently occurring feature of English pronunciation.

The phonetic nature of /+/ is complex, and many of the details cannot be mentioned at this time. When /+/ follows immediately after a syllable nucleus, as in *slyness*, it is expressed, in part, by a prolongation of the syllable nucleus. This is certainly the most noticeable difference in such a pair as *minus* : *slyness*. After certain consonants, notably /m n ŋ/, it is also expressed by prolongation of the preceding consonant. After some other consonants it takes the form of a weakening of the voicing. After voiceless stops it is shown by contrasts in the degree of aspiration. /+/ also has certain noticeable effects on the following vowel or consonant. In short, in a pair like *night rate* and *nitrate*, though a native speaker interprets the facts as a break or even a very short pause between *night* and *rate*, the differences are actually in the details of pronunciation of both the /t/ and the /r/.

4.7 Most of the traditionally defined words of an utterance are separated from their neighbors by a /+/, a fact which has misled some to consider it as more or less identical with the traditional word division. Nothing could be more confusing than to do so. Word divisions are part of our system of spelling conventions. Why, for example, is *cannot* one word, when *must not* is two? As a spelling convention, word division follows its own, largely arbitrary, rules. These are uniform, except for minor departures, for all educated Americans. Arbitrariness is the price of uniformity.

The /+/ is of an entirely different nature. It is a feature of pronunciation. As such it varies from speaker to speaker, and indeed one speaker may be quite inconsistent in his usage at certain points. /+/ is a phonemic feature. As such it may be written in a transcription only because it is heard in the pronunciation of the speaker being observed.

Actually, /+/ will be found in many places where word divisions customarily occur. The correlation is far from exact, however. Certain commonly written word divisions are almost never paralleled by /+/ in natural speech. Certain words are commonly pronounced with /+/ within them. One case is *unknown*, usually /ən+nówn/. Some others vary: *Plato* is pronounced by some as /pléytòw/, by others as /pléy+tòw/. As we shall see later, the occurrence of /+/ is associated in definite ways with the stresses.

4.8   When the discussion turns from words to whole sentences a new difficulty arises. The necessary data cannot be presented in writing. A cited sentence may be read in a variety of ways. In actual speech a native speaker would not be in the least capricious in his selection of a certain intonation for a given sentence. Nor will the average American fail to react differently to sentences which are alike in the words composing them but different in intonation. The latter differences are correlated with differences of content, and hence are clearly within the domain of linguistics. The difficulty of presentation is merely that we have no feasible means of informing the reader which pronunciation is intended. What we call a "sentence" in written English may stand as a written symbolization of several different spoken utterances. The distinction between them cannot be indicated in such a way that the reader will know what spoken sentence is cited as an example.

The result can easily be that the wrong reading is selected. The example then fails to prove the point at issue, or may even seem to contradict the description flatly, so that the reader remains unconvinced. Even experienced professional linguists have been grievously misled in this way and have failed utterly to understand presentations of facts about English intonation which are perfectly clear when the author presents his data orally.

It will, therefore, be necessary to use a different approach for the remainder of this chapter. Instead of adducing evidence from which the phonemes can be demonstrated, it will be better to state the conclusions first and then present the supporting or illustrative data. Your instructor will, of course, demonstrate these features in detail, perhaps in a manner more nearly in accord with the presentation up to this point than the printed text can be.

4.9   The nature of this difficulty is shown by the very existence of a special art, the oral interpretation of literature, which promotes the ability to select the oral rendition which will be accepted by the native speaker as most suitable for the context. That it is an art, rather than a science, demonstrates that there is no reliable method currently in use by which an author can inform his readers how he wants his work to be pronounced. If there were, expressive reading could be largely mechanical. As it is, mechanical reading is far from expressive. Moreover, if the public did not react differently to different pronunciations, there would be no need to even attempt to make a selection. That is, the art would be unnecessary if it did not involve the manipulation of some features of pronunciation (phonemes) which are significant in the structure of the language.

4.10   We have established the existence of three phonemic degrees of stress. There is one more which we will write /ˆ/ and call **secondary**. It may be heard in an ordinary pronunciation of such a sentence as *I'm going home.* Normally there will be only one /ʹ/ in such a sentence. Most frequently it will be on *home*, but it may be on *going*. Two possible pronunciations are (marking the stresses on only these two words) *I'm gôing hóme.* and *I'm góing hôme.* These have different meanings and hence constitute a minimal pair establishing that /ˆ/ is distinct from /ʹ/.

The contrast of /ˆ/ with /ˋ/ may be seen in such a pair as *bláck bîrd* : *bláckbìrd.* The first implies a bird that is described as being black; the second a particular kind of bird which, incidentally, may or may not be black. *That white bird is an albino bláckbìrd.* makes sense if the stresses are as indicated, but nonsense if we substitute *bláck bîrd.*

4.11   The four stresses /ʹ ˆ ˋ ˇ/ and /+/ are closely related and form a special system within the phonemic structure of the language. There is always at least one /+/, or some higher-ranking break, between every successive pair of /ˆ/ and /ʹ/. *Bláck bîrd* must have a /+/ between the /ʹ/ and the /ˆ/. Any American other than a phonetic virtuoso will inevitably either pronounce a /+/ or change one of the stresses. /blǽk+bə̂rd/ or /blǽkbə̀rd/ are both possible, but /*blǽkbə̂rd/ is not. (Forms which are impossible or unknown are marked with *.) It does not, however, follow that there must be a /ʹ/ or /ˆ/ between every two /+/. Both /blǽk+bə̀rd/ and /blǽk+bə̂rd/ are possible. Few words cited in isolation have both /ʹ/ and /ˆ/. This is because few words contain a /+/, and only such words could have both. Moreover, the few words that do have /+/ within them do not necessarily have /ʹ/ and /ˆ/; they may have /ʹ/ and /ˋ/ or various other combinations.

4.12   Some of the breaks in a long utterance will be markedly different from /+/. There will be exactly one of these between every pair of /ʹ/, and it will always be found at a place where a /+/ might otherwise occur. These breaks divide the utterance into portions which are characterized by two prominent features: the break at the end, and the presence of a /'/. Such a unit may be called a **clause**. The term is here used to refer to a unit in the spoken language which is evident from the pronunciation only. It may frequently prove to be equivalent to a clause in the conventional grammatical sense, but it will often be different. The breaks marking the ends of clauses are **clause terminals**. They may easily be shown to be phonemic because there are three different terminals, and these contrast.

Clause terminals are popularly referred to as "pauses." There may be an actual pause, but this is not necessary. If there is a pause, it is always preceded by one of the characteristic English clause terminals. The clause terminal is, properly speaking, a means of ending a clause, not of separating two clauses, and for this reason one such terminal will be found at the end of the last clause in an utterance.

Clause terminals are of three kinds:

/↘/   **fading:** a rapid trailing away of the voice into silence. Both the pitch and volume decrease rapidly.

/↗/   **rising:** a sudden, rapid, but short rise in the pitch. The volume does not trail off so noticeably, but seems to be comparatively sharply cut off.

/→/   **sustained:** a sustention of the pitch accompanied by prolongation of the last syllable of the clause and some diminishing of volume.

4.13   The clause terminals are heard at the very end of the last syllable in a clause. Over the remainder of the clause, the pitch varies in such a way that four contrasting phonemic levels can be recognized. The normal pitch of the voice of the speaker is /2/, called **mid.** It varies, of course, from speaker to speaker. Moreover, most people raise the pitch somewhat when they are speaking more loudly, and at various other times. Pitch /2/ is relatively common and serves as a standard of comparison for the others. Pitch /1/, called **low,** is somewhat lower, perhaps two or three notes below /2/, but the interval will vary from speaker to speaker and from time to time. Pitch /3/, called **high,** is about as much higher than /2/ as /2/ is above /1/. Pitch /4/, called **extra high,** is higher than /3/ by about the same amount, or may even be somewhat higher. /4/ is much less frequent than the other three. In any utterance of any length /1 2 3/ will all be heard. The native speaker will identify them with little difficulty by comparing the three commonly occurring pitches in the utterance.

Some variation of pitch within these four levels will be noticed by some observers. Others (i.e., native speakers) may have great difficulty in convincing themselves that this variation exists. It is not a significant variation, as can be demonstrated by techniques of the sort presented in Chapter 17. In any case, no minimal contrasts can be found for any other pitches, whereas they can be found between all of the pitches here considered as phonemic.

4.14 Unfortunately, two systems of numbering the pitch phonemes have arisen. A minority of American linguists use /1/ for extra high, /2/ for high, /3/ for mid, and /4/ for low.

An alternative graphic system avoids the confusion of these competing notations and has certain pedagogic advantages as well. On the other hand, it has various limitations, not the least of which is that it is wasteful of space. It is as follows:

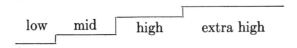

Clause terminals can be indicated by arrow heads continuing the line. In some of the examples below, both systems will be used: /1 2 3 4 ↘ ↗ →/ with phonemic transcriptions, and graphic marking with the orthography.

4.15 The pitch is frequently the same over long sequences of syllables (phonemically the same, that is: there will usually be sub-phonemic variation from syllable to syllable). It seems best to consider most such instances as containing only a single occurrence of the pitch phoneme concerned. In transcribing spoken English, we need therefore only note the pitch at certain critical points. One of these is at the beginning of the syllable which has /'/. This syllable will commonly have a different pitch from that of the preceding syllables, usually a higher pitch. In the instances where it is the same, it should be noted anyway. It will be indicated in a phonemic transcription by a raised numeral immediately before the syllable.

If the clause contains any syllables before the /'/, these will usually have a single continuing pitch; most often, but by no means always, this will be a /2/. An indication of this pitch should be written at the very beginning of the clause.

Another critical point is at the end of the clause immediately before the clause terminal. The pitch here will be indicated by a raised numeral immediately before the symbol for the terminal.

Normally, these three are all the points at which contrasts can be found. It is therefore necessary to symbolize pitch at these places, and only these. If the /'/ is on the first syllable, there must always be two pitches indicated. (They may be the same, of course.) If the /'/ is not on the first syllable, three must be indicated. A few speakers have occasional patterns in which a rise in pitch occurs at a syllable with /^/; in these cases, four pitches must be marked.

4.16 Frequently the /'/ is on the last syllable of the clause. In this case, the pitch frequently glides from one level to another on this one syllable. In most instances the pitch will fall. If the /'/ is farther from the end, the fall may be spread over all the intervening syllables, or may occur anywhere between the /'/ and the end. No contrasts can be found in the time, rate, or manner of this fall, so no details need be recorded in a phonemic transcription.

4.17 The four pitches and three clause terminals constitute another sub-system within the total phonemic system of English. Every clause is marked and held together by an **intonation contour** consisting of two, three, or four pitch phonemes and one clause terminal. Intonation contours are not, of course, phonemes, but morphemes. Their mention in a chapter on English phonemes is logically out of place, but it will be somewhat easier to cite intelligible illustrations if this concept is introduced now. Of course, examples of morphemes are examples of the phonemes of which they are composed, but the two must be kept clearly distinct.

4.18 The commonest intonation contour in English is /(2)31↘/. The parentheses indicate that the /2/ will occur if there are syllables before the /'/, but not otherwise. That is, /231↘/ and /31↘/ are considered as variants of the same morpheme conditioned by the context. This contour may be used in different ways with what is, apart from stress and intonation, the same utterance. Each of the following examples has a slightly different meaning, as will be evident to any native speaker.

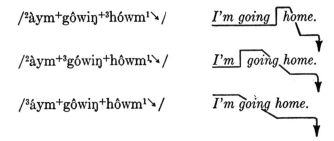

/²àym⁺gôwiŋ⁺³hówm¹↘/   *I'm going home.*

/²àym⁺³gówiŋ⁺hôwm¹↘/   *I'm going home.*

/³áym⁺gôwiŋ⁺hôwm¹↘/   *I'm going home.*

The /(2)31↘/ intonation contour does not necessarily indicate a statement. It is quite commonly used with questions.

/²hwèn⁺əryə⁺³gówiŋ⁺hôwm¹↘/   *When are you going home?*

Another common contour is /(2)32→/. This usually indicates some close connection between the clause so marked and the clause closely following.

/²ày⁺wəz⁺³gówiŋ⁺hôwm²⁻²bət⁺it⁺³réynd¹↘/

I was going home, but it rained.

The contrast between /↘/ and /↗/ can be seen in a question such as that below. The first of these pronunciations is somewhat less polite or deferential than the second, and the third commonly means something like 'Did you say, "What are we having for dinner?"'?'

/²hwət⁺ər⁺wìy⁺hǽviŋ⁺fər⁺³dínər¹↘/
/²hwət⁺ər⁺wìy⁺hǽviŋ⁺fər⁺³dínər¹↗/
/²hwət⁺ər⁺wìy⁺hǽviŋ⁺fər⁺³dínər³↗/

Both /22↗/ and /11↘/ are used to mark the person addressed. They differ primarily in politeness. /23↗/, as in the third example below, asks a yes-or-no question repeating the question in the preceding clause.

/²hwət⁺ər⁺wìy⁺hǽviŋ⁺fər⁺³dínər²↗²mə́ðər²↗/
/²hwət⁺ər⁺wìy⁺hǽviŋ⁺fər⁺³dínər²⁻¹mə́ðər¹↘/
/²hwət⁺ər⁺wìy⁺hǽviŋ⁺fər⁺³dínər²↗²mə́tin³↗/

How clear the contrast between these contours may be is seen by switching them in the following way:

/²hwǝt⁺ǝr⁺wìy⁺hǽviŋ⁺fǝr⁺³dínǝr² ↗²mǝ́ðǝr³ ↗/
/²hwǝt⁺ǝr⁺wìy⁺hǽviŋ⁺fǝr⁺³dínǝr² ↗²mǝ́tin²↘/

Pitch /4/ is much rarer than the others. It occurs most commonly in utterances characterized by at least mild emphasis or expressing surprise. Contrast *I'm going home.* said as a matter-of-fact statement with the same words said impatiently by a person who has started home but is being nagged to move a bit faster. He might say:

/²àym⁺⁴gówiŋ⁺hôwm¹↘/   *I'm going home.*

4.19 We may now list the complete inventory of English phonemes as follows:

24 consonants /p b t d k g č ǰ f v θ ð s z š ž m n ŋ l r w y h/
9 vowels /i e æ ɨ ǝ a u o ɔ/
3 semivowels /y w н/ (/y w/ were listed also with the consonants.)
1 open transition /⁺/
4 stresses /ʹ ˆ ˋ ˇ/
4 pitches /1 2 3 4/
3 clause terminals /↘ ↗ →/
46 total (eliminating duplications in the listing)

5

The Morpheme

5.1 In the last three chapters the basic elements of English pronunciation were shown to be forty-six phonemes. By describing these in detail (an undertaking not attempted here), and stating the characteristic distribution of each (which was merely hinted at), a great deal can be said about the English language. By recording the phonemes occurring in it, any possible English utterance can be so identified as to be exactly repeatable from the written record alone.

These are valuable results, and an essential part of any full description of the language; but they fall far short of a complete analysis. No matter how far this line of investigation is pursued, nothing is revealed about the meanings of utterances in the language. Yet the social function of any language is to carry information from speaker to hearer. Without this, speech would be socially useless and presumably would not exist. A phonologic study of language, no matter how detailed, can tell us nothing about meaning, because the phonemes themselves have no direct connection with content. They are merely the units by which the speaker and hearer identify the morphemes. For any further study of language, the morphemes and combinations of morphemes must be examined. When this is done, the analysis of language structure proceeds on a fundamentally different plane.

5.2 Morphemes are generally short sequences of phonemes.

These sequences are recurrent — but not all recurrent sequences are morphemes. For example, the sequence /in/ occurs thirteen times in a reading of the preceding paragraph; /əv/ occurs ten times. Such sequences as /in/ and /əv/ can profitably be studied as phenomena of English phonology, and some important generalizations can be made about these and similar sequences. Such a study of /in/ about exhausts everything worth serious attention regarding this sequence. Not so in the case of /əv/; for /əv/, in addition to being a sequence of phonemes, is in each of these ten occurrences a morpheme, and so participates in a higher level of organization. On this plane /in/ is not relevant. The fact that /in/ is commoner than /əv/ does not affect the situation.

5.3   The difference between /əv/ and /in/ rests on the fact that /əv/ in each of its ten occurrences above has a meaning — that is, some connection with some element in the structure of the content aspect of the language — while /in/ does not have meaning, except as it forms a fragment of certain sequences, such as /kin/ *can.*

As a morpheme, /əv/ also has demonstrable relationships with other morphemes in the language. These are of two kinds: In the phrase *study of language,* there are certain significant relationships between /əv/ and the morphemes which precede and follow it in this particular fragment of an utterance. These are features of this sample of English as such. There are also certain more general relationships of the morpheme *of* which are not limited in this way, and so constitute a part of the system of the language as a whole. These are generalizations arrived at by comparing *study of language* with many other similar sequences. For example, *of* can be followed by a noun, but not usually by a verb. In some constructions, *of* can be replaced by *on.* Compare *the hat of the man* with *the hat on the man.* In another way, *of* can be replaced by *'s.* Compare *the hat of the man* with *the man's hat.* These broader relationships are the subject of study in the division of linguistics known as **grammar.**

5.4   The **morpheme** was mentioned in 1.13 as the second of the two basic units in linguistics. No definition was given, and it was stated that an exact definition is not feasible. Perhaps the best that can be done is to define the morpheme as the smallest unit which is grammatically pertinent. But it would then be necessary to define grammar as the study of morphemes and their combinations. This is obviously circular and hence is no definition. Nevertheless, it does serve to point out something significant. As a basic concept, a morpheme cannot be defined beyond some such circular statement. In place of a definition, therefore, we must merely describe certain features of morphemes and give some general rules for their recognition. This we will do here and in succeeding chapters.

5.5 Some morphemes can be usefully described as the smallest meaningful units in the structure of the language. A more precise statement would, of course, be in terms of relationship between expression and content, but for the present purpose a less exact statement is convenient. By "smallest meaningful unit" we mean a unit which cannot be divided without destroying or drastically altering the meaning. For example, /streynǰ/ as in *strange* is a morpheme; as a whole it has meaning. If it is divided, we obtain fragments such as /str/ or /eynǰ/, which have no meaning, or /strey/ as in *stray* or /streyn/ as in *strain*, which have meanings which are not significantly related to that of /streynǰ/. Any division of /streynǰ/ destroys or drastically alters the meaning. Therefore, /streynǰ/ qualifies under our description of a morpheme as the smallest meaningful unit in the structure of the language.

However, /streynǰnis/ as in *strangeness* is not a single morpheme, though it does have meaning. It may be divided into /streynǰ/ and /nis/. Each of these pieces does have meaning, and the meaning of the combination is related to the meanings of the two pieces. Therefore /streynǰnis/ is two morphemes.

5.6 A morpheme is not identical with a syllable. The morpheme /streynǰ/ happens to be a syllable, and so are many English morphemes. But /kənetɨkɨt/ as in *Connecticut* is a single morpheme, though it contains four syllables. Both /gow/ and /z/ in *goes* are morphemes, though together they are but a single syllable. Morphemes may consist of one or several whole syllables, parts of syllables, or, in fact, any combination of phonemes without regard to their status as syllables.

5.7 A morpheme may consist of only a single phoneme. The /z/ in *goes* just cited is a case. But the phoneme /z/ and this morpheme are by no means identical. The phoneme occurs many times where it has nothing to do with this morpheme. Instances are *zoo* /zúw/ and *rose* /rówz/, both of which contain /z/ but have no meaning in common with the /z/ in *goes*. Most English morphemes are intermediate in size between /z/ and /streynǰ/, and consist of two to six phonemes.

5.8 Frequently two morphemic elements are alike in expression but different in content. Such pairs are said to be **homophonous,** literally "sounding alike." Thus /z/ is a morpheme both in *goes* /gówz/ and in *goers* /gówərz/, but not the same morpheme. /z/ meaning 'third person singular actor' and /z/ meaning 'plural' are homophonous. Sequences of morphemes can also be homophonous, either with other sequences or with single morphemes. Compare /rowz/ in *He rows the boat. They stood in rows.* and *That flower is a rose.*

5.9 If the morpheme is to be described as the smallest meaningful unit in the structure of a language, care must be taken not to misconstrue the words "meaningful" or "meaning." "Meaning" is intended to represent the relationship which exists between morphemes as part of the expression system of a language and comparable units in the content system of the same language. A morpheme is the smallest unit in the expression system which can be correlated directly with any part of the content system.

Using the term *meaning* in its ordinary familiar sense without careful control will in some cases be quite misleading. In many instances, however, it will serve as a workable approximation, if used with caution. For example, *cat* may be said to have a meaning since it refers, among other things, to a specific kind of animal. But it is also used of humans with certain personality characteristics. In a like sense, *go* may be said to have a similar kind of meaning, since it refers (among other things) to a motion of an object. But it is difficult, even fruitless, to attempt to specify exactly what motions are indicated. Compare *He goes home. John goes with Mary.* and *The watch goes.* Indeed, it may be used of a quite immobile subject as in *This road goes to Weston.* These variations of reference to the outside world can in part be accounted for by the assumption that a speaker of English has learned to structure content in such a way as to bring these diverse elements of experience together into a single category. The meaning of *go* rests in the interrelationship between the morpheme /gow/ and the point within the content system where these things are brought together.

5.10 The content system of a language is not directly observable, so that we can only with great difficulty check any such statement as that just made. It does, however, serve this useful function: It should be a distinct warning against relying on translations to get access to meanings. If the structure of content imposes a filter between the expression system and human experience, translation must impose two such. Translation can only be accurate where the content structures of the two languages coincide. Such places are too infrequent to be depended upon. Where translation must be used (and there are many such instances in practical language work) the user must be constantly alert against its pitfalls.

5.11 With some morphemes, meaning in the sense of reference to human experience outside language is wholly or largely lacking. Consider *to* in *I want to go*. The elements *I*, *want*, and *go* are referable, through the intermediary of English content structure, to aspects of human experience. But it is impossible to find a specific factor in the situation which can be considered as the "meaning" of *to*. Nevertheless, *to* does have a function, since without it **I want go.* means nothing. (The symbol * is used to indicate that a form cited is either unattested or known to be impossible.) *To* merely fulfills a requirement of English structure, in that *want* cannot be followed by *go* without *to*. Such a function cannot be included within the traditional meaning of "meaning," but in the sense in which we are using it (the interrelationship between expression and content), "meaning" — with a little stretching, perhaps — can comprehend it.

5.12 The meaning of *cat* might be explained (partially, to be sure) to a non-English speaking person by pointing out the animal to which it refers. It would not be possible to explain *to* in this way. Instead, it would be necessary to cite a number of cases of its use, and thereby point out the contexts in which it occurs regularly, those in which it may occur, and those in which it cannot occur (e.g., **I can to go.*). That is to say, *to* has a characteristic distribution. For the foreigner, this distribution is the most easily observable feature of such a morpheme, and hence the chief clue to its meaning.

Morphemes like *to* are not alone in having a characteristic distribution. Every morpheme has. *Cat* may occur in *I saw the ——.* but not in *I will —— home. Go* can occur in the second, but not in the first. The **distribution** of the morpheme is the sum of all the contexts in which it can occur in contrast to all those in which it cannot occur. A full understanding of any morpheme involves understanding its distribution as well as its meaning in the familiar sense. It is partly for this reason that a good dictionary always cites instances illustrative of usage. One that does not is of very restricted usefulness, or even very misleading.

5.13 Morphemes can be identified only by comparing various samples of a language. If two or more samples can be found in which there is some feature of expression which all share and some feature of content which all hold in common, then one requirement is met, and these samples may be tentatively identified as a morpheme and its meaning. Thus *boys* /bɔ́yz/, *girls* /gɔ́rlz/, *roads* /rówdz/, etc., are all alike in containing *s* /z/ and meaning 'two or more.' We therefore identify *s* /z/ as a morpheme meaning 'plural.' This is not actually sufficient. In addition there must be some contrast between samples with similar meaning and content, some of which have the tentative morpheme and some of which do not. Comparison of *boy* /bɔ́y/ will serve to confirm the example we have just discussed. That such a condition is necessary is shown by the following words: *bug* /bɔ́g/, *bee* /bíy/, *beetle* /bíytɨl/, *butterfly* /bɔ́tərflày/. It seems ridiculous to suggest that since these all include /b/ and all mean some kind of insect, /b/ must be a morpheme. But this is only because, as native speakers, we know that /əg/, /iy/, /iytɨl/, and /ətərflay/ do not exist as morphemes that can be associated with these words. Finally, it is necessary to ascertain that what we have isolated are actually single morphemes rather than combinations. (See 5.5.) The procedures for carrying out such an analysis will be sketched in the next two chapters.

5.14 When a person is dealing with his own native language, much of this seems superfluous. This is simply because such comparisons have been made repeatedly and subconsciously, if not consciously, in the past. We can identify English morphemes without detailed comparison because we have already identified most of them. That this is true, even of young children, can be seen from a common type of mistake. The child hears and learns to associate *show* /šów/ with *showed* /šówd/, *tow* /tów/ with *towed* /tówd/, etc. Then he assumes *go* /gów/ must be associated in the same way with /gówd/. He is, of course, wrong in detail, but right in principle, and has obviously made a morphemic analysis. He must merely learn the limits within which the pattern he has discovered is valid.

5.15 Certain constructions composed of morphemes have a rigidly fixed order. For example *re–con–vene* (the hyphens merely separate the morphemes) is a familiar English word. But **con– re–vene* or **re–vene–con* are not. They are not only unfamiliar in sound and appearance, but also are actually meaningless to a native speaker. The meaning of a word depends not only upon the morphemes that are present but also on the order of their occurrence.

Other constructions allow some, but only partial, freedom of order. *Then I went.* and *I went then.* are both possible and have at most only slight difference of meaning. But **Went then I.* is unintelligible because it departs from established English structure. In general, the more intimate constructions, like words, have the most rigidly fixed order, and the less closely knit constructions, like sentences, allow more freedom. But even longer sequences have some definite restrictions on order, sometimes of a subtle sort. For example, *John came. He went away.* might imply that John did both. But *He came. John went away.* certainly could not have that meaning. A specific reference to a person must precede a pronoun reference to the same person, unless some special device is used. This is a peculiarity of English structure, not of logic, nor of the general nature of speech, since some other languages have quite different rules.

5.16 The fixed order of morphemes in certain constructions, and the definable degree of freedom, are basic to language. They are expressions of the systematic structure which is the real essence of speech. It is the business of linguistic science to describe these principles of arrangement in the most comprehensive and concise way possible. Such a description is the **grammar** of the language. The term is in poor repute with some, largely because of lack of precision in its use, and because it has frequently served as a label for legislation as to how a language should be used, rather than as a description of how it actually is used. These implications are not, of course, inherent in the term, but it is necessary to take care to avoid them. As used in this book, **grammar** will comprehend two convenient, but not precisely delimitable, subdivisions:

morphology, the description of the more intimate combinations of morphemes, roughly what are familiarly called "words"; and **syntax,** the description of larger combinations involving as basic units the combinations described under the morphology of the language. Some linguists use the term morphology to cover both subdivisions, in which case it is equivalent to **grammar** as used here.

5.17   The grammar of a given language cannot conveniently be stated in terms of the arrangement of specific morphemes, because the total number of morphemes in any language is far too large to permit this. However, it is always found that the morphemes can be grouped into certain classes, each with a characteristic distribution. The structure of utterances in the language can then be stated in terms of these classes of morphemes. In this way the material which must be described is reduced to manageable proportions.

For example, *walk, talk, follow, call,* etc., form an extensive class of morphemes. So likewise *s* (marking the third person singular), *ed* and *ing* form a smaller class. The latter can occur only immediately following one of the former (or some equivalent construction). The members of the first group can be found immediately preceding one of the second group, or they may be found alone. That is, *walks, walked, walking,* and *walk* all occur. But in **swalk* or **ingwalk* the order is wrong and the forms are accordingly impossible. **Walkeding* is unintelligible because *ing* cannot follow *ed*. **Shelfed* is not found because *shelf* belongs to another class which never precedes *ed*. All such facts, and many more like them, can be comprehended in a relatively few simple statements about the classes of morphemes. The complete listing of all possible and impossible sequences, on the other hand, even within a closely restricted sample of English, would be cumbersome and rapidly becomes utterly impossible as the number of morphemes treated increases.

5.18   The broadest and most comprehensive classes of morphemes in English, and the most nearly universal in the languages of the world, are **roots** and **affixes.** *Walk, talk, follow,* etc., is one class of roots. *Shelf, rug, road,* etc., is another. The vast majority of English morphemes are roots, and the number runs into many thousands. Such morphemes as *–s, –ed, –ing,* etc. are affixes. Hereafter affixes will ordinarily be cited with hyphens to indicate the manner in which they are affixed.

A definition of these two classes which would be universally applicable would be immensely complex and is probably unnecessary here. A definition which will fit the needs of one specific language is commonly feasible. In general, affixes are subsidiary to roots, while roots are the centers of such constructions as words. Roots are frequently longer than affixes, and generally much more numerous in the vocabulary.

5.19 Two different types of affixes can be defined here. Both are found in English and in many other languages. **Prefixes** are affixes which precede the root with which they are most closely associated. Examples are: /priy–/ in *prefix*, /riy–/ in *refill*, and /iŋ–/ in *incomplete*. Prefixes are also common in many other languages. Hebrew examples are /bə–/ 'in' in /bəbáyit/ 'in a house' and /hab–/ 'the' in /habbáyit/ 'the house'; compare /báyit/ 'house.' **Suffixes** are affixes which follow the root with which they are most closely associated. Some English examples are: /–ɨz/ in *suffixes*, /–iŋ/ in *going*, and /–iš/ in *boyish*. Suffixes are also common in many other languages. Some Swedish examples are *–en* 'the' in *dagen* 'the day' and *–ar* 'plural' in *dagar* 'days'; compare *dag* 'day.'

Note that in English many speakers have both a prefix /iŋ–/ and a suffix /–iŋ/. Both may occur with the same morphemes. *Incomplete* /ìŋkəmplíyt/ and *completing* /kəmplíytiŋ/ are however clearly different. The position of these affixes in the word distinguishes between them unquestionably.

5.20 Affixes may be added directly to roots, or to constructions consisting of a root plus one or more other morphemes. All these may be called stems. A **stem** is any morpheme or combination of morphemes to which an affix can be added. The English word *friends* /fréndz/ contains a stem /frend/ which is also a root, and an affix /–z/. *Friendships* /fréndšips/ contains an affix /–s/ and a stem /fréndšip/, which, however, is not a root since it consists of two morphemes. Some stems or words contain two or more roots, and are said to be **compound**. *Blackbird* /blǽkbərd/ is a compound word, containing two roots, /blæk/ and /bərd/. *Blackbirds* contains a compound stem and an affix.

5.21 In some languages, certain affixes function primarily to form stems, and as such have little meaning other than this linguistic function. Such morphemes may be called **stem-formatives.** The Greek word /thermos/ 'warm' consists of a root /therm–/, a stem-formative /–o–/, and a final affix /–s/. The latter, which indicates among other things that the word can be the subject of a sentence, cannot be attached directly to the root. That is, /*therms/ is impossible. Stem-formatives of this kind are very common in Greek.

Greek compound words are usually formed by compounding stems rather than roots. English words derived from Greek, or formed on the Greek pattern, commonly lose or distort suffixes at the end of the word, but the stem-formative of the first stem is usually quite evident. *Thermometer* is composed of the stems *thermo-* and *meter*. The first of these is formed from the root *therm–* by adding the stem-formative *–o–*. This accounts for the very common occurrence of *–o–* in words of this type. Compare *morph–o–logy, ge–o–graphy, phil–o–sophy,* etc.

At this point a word of warning is in order: *–o–* is a morpheme in English, not because it is one in Greek, but because certain facts of English structure require it to be so interpreted. We cannot be satisfied with dividing *thermometer* as either *thermo-meter* or as *therm-ometer*. Comparison of *isotherm* indicates that *therm–* is a morpheme. *Meter* can stand alone as a word. Therefore neither *thermo–* nor *–ometer* is a single morpheme. The Greek origin of the morpheme *–o–* may contribute to an understanding of the history of this English feature, but is not otherwise relevant to English structure.

5.22 Some morphemes have a single form in all contexts. English /–iŋ/ in *coming, walking,* etc., is an example. (The fact that some speakers pronounce this /–in/ or /–iyn/ does not alter the matter. Typically, a person pronounces *–ing* the same in all linguistic contexts regardless of which pronunciation he uses.) In other instances there may be considerable variation. The plural *–s* is pronounced in three different common ways: in *boys* /bóyz/ it is /–z/; in *cats* /kǽts/ it is /–s/; and in *roses* /rówziz/ it is /–iz/. In spite of this difference in form, every native speaker would be quite certain that these are in some sense the same thing. The impression of the native speaker is corroborated by an examination of the way in which these three are used. Inspection of large volumes of material will reveal that /–iz/ occurs only after /s z š ž č ǰ/ and that neither of the others ever occurs in this place. /–s/ occurs only after /p t k f θ/ and neither of the others ever occurs here. /–z/ occurs after all other consonants and all vowels. The selection of the correct one of these is purely automatic with the native speaker, and he very rarely makes any mistake; indeed, it requires conscious effort to contravene these patterns. It does not matter whether the native speaker has ever heard the word before. Given a phrase like *two taxemes*, most people will read it /tûw⁺tǽksiymz/. But though not all agree in their guess as to how to pronounce the stem *taxeme*, all will agree in pronouncing –*s* in this case as /–z/.

To provide for description of such cases (and they are frequent), linguists distinguish between allomorphs and morphemes. An **allomorph** is a variant of a morpheme which occurs in certain definable environments. A **morpheme** is a group of one or more allomorphs which conform to certain, usually rather clearly definable, criteria of distribution and meaning. Thus /–z/, /–s/, and /–iz/, above, are three allomorphs of a single morpheme. They are such because they show the definite definable distribution which was mentioned, and because they have the same meanings.

5.23   The concept of allomorphs and morphemes, and of other "allos" and "emes," is one of the most basic in descriptive linguistics. Its importance both as a tool and as an insight into the operation of language can hardly be overestimated. It stands behind the two basic units of linguistic description, the phoneme and the morpheme, as well as behind other lesser concepts such as the grapheme. The principle involved is largely responsible for the high development of linguistic theory and techniques. The inapplicability (so far as we now know) of the concept in certain related disciplines is the chief differentiating factor between the science of linguistics and other treatments of human behavior.

5.24   Any phenomenon is said to be **conditioned** if it occurs whenever certain definable conditions occur. This is not identical with saying that it is caused by these conditions. All that is implied is that they occur together in some way, so that one can be predicted from the other. *Where there's smoke there's fire.* and *Where there's fire there's smoke.* are both statements of conditioning. Only one of them can possibly be a statement of cause, and there is no need to assume that either necessarily is. The three allomorphs of the plural morpheme, /-z/, /-s/, and /-ɨz/, are conditioned, since each occurs when certain clearly defined conditions occur. In this case the conditioning factor is the phonetic nature of the preceding phonemes. /-z/ occurs only after voiced sounds; /-s/ only after voiceless sounds; and /-ɨz/ only after groove fricatives and affricates. We may therefore say that they are **phonologically conditioned.** This means that, if we understand the facts of distribution, we can accurately predict which of the three will occur in any place where any one of them could occur. As native speakers of English we make this selection automatically and subconsciously. As linguists we may formulate a descriptive statement of our own habits and on the basis of this statement make the proper selection deliberately. The formal statement is valid only insofar as it produces the same result as the subconscious habit of the native speaker.

This automatic selection is part of the structure of English and has to be learned. It is not "just natural," even though it may seem so to us. To a foreigner it may seem very unnatural. Indeed, it is not a universal feature of English. In the Blue Ridge Mountains of Virginia /-ɨz/ is used not only after /s z š ž č ǰ/ but also after /sp st sk/. Thus *wasps*, *posts*, and *tasks* are pronounced /wáspɨz/, /pówstɨz/, and /tǽskɨz/, not /wásps/, /pówsts/, and /tǽsks/ as in most dialects. In both dialects the form is phonologically conditioned; in both the selection is completely automatic and quite regular. They are merely different, and each seems entirely natural to the speakers.

5.25   The selection of allomorphs may also be **morphologically conditioned.** In this case the selection is determined by the specific morpheme or morphemes forming the contexts, rather than by any phonologic feature. The plural of *ox* is *oxen* /áksin/. /-in/ is an allomorph of the plural morpheme which is used only with this one root /aks/. For the native speaker familiar with the word (a dwindling minority but for its use as a grammatical example!), /-in/ is automatically selected after /aks/ and /*áksiz/ is rejected as incorrect. There is nothing phonologic about this selection. *Boxes*, *foxes*, *axes* are phonologically similar, but use /-ɨz/. The peculiarity rests in the morpheme /aks/ as a morpheme; the selection is morphologically conditioned.

5.26   The concept of allomorph and morpheme necessitates some additional notation to avoid long circumlocutions. Variation, as that between allomorphs, will be indicated by the sign $\sim$, to be read as "varies with" or "alternates with" or simply "or." We may thus write $/\text{-z} \sim \text{-s} \sim \text{-iz}/$ to indicate that these three are to be taken as allomorphs of one morpheme. The same symbolization can be used to identify the morpheme.

If the morpheme has numerous allomorphs, as many do, it is awkward to have to list all of them every time the morpheme is mentioned. Instead, it is desirable to have a single symbol to indicate a morpheme as such, comprehending all the variant forms in which it can appear. For this purpose we use braces { }. Within the braces we may place any convenient designation of the morpheme at hand. Of course, once such a symbol has been defined, we are no longer at liberty to choose arbitrarily. For example, we could choose {-s} or {-z} or various other designations for the English plural morpheme. However, to conform to one established notation we will select the symbol $\{-Z_1\}$. Having defined this symbol as equivalent to $/\text{-z} \sim \text{-s} \sim \text{-iz} \sim \text{-in} \sim \ldots/$, we will not again need to specify the allomorphs included. $\{-Z_1\}$ will be read as "the morpheme Z one."

5.27   It will be convenient at this place to recapitulate the various types of notation which we will use:

[ ]   indicate a phonetic transcription, in which the pronunciation is transcribed as heard, not necessarily representing the significant features.

/ /   indicate a phonemic transcription in which the pronunciation is transcribed so as to represent all significant features and nothing else.

{ }   indicate a morphemic representation in which one arbitrarily selected symbol is used to represent each morpheme and comprehend all its allomorphs. It does not directly give any information about pronunciation.

Italics indicate orthography, the traditional spelling which may approach being phonemic or may give almost no direct information about pronunciation. The relationship between spelling and pronunciation varies from language to language.

' ' indicate glosses, translations, or other indications of the meaning of items.

* indicates that a form is impossible or unknown.

The uses of [ ] and / / are well established and used by the vast majority of American linguists. { } is used by a considerable group, but other notations are also in vogue. There are no universally established conventions for citing orthography or glosses, but those used here are not uncommon.

The Identification of Morphemes

6.1 The investigation of the grammar of any language proceeds from the examination of a **corpus,** a sample of utterances which have been gathered for the purpose of analysis. It will seldom be possible to recognize the morphemes within this corpus by any simple inspection. The task of the investigator is, therefore, to select out of the corpus those pairs or sets of utterances which can most profitably be compared, to draw the most reasonable deductions from them, and to build these together into an integrated and consistent system that will account for the data in the corpus. This analysis is then checked against additional utterances. On the basis of this increased corpus it may be corrected and extended until it seems probable that the results will apply usefully to any sample of the language.

The first objectives are: to **segment** the corpus — that is, to divide it into portions, each of which represents a single morpheme; and to **class** these segments together into morphemes. Unfortunately, there is no procedure which will lead automatically to a correct segmentation or classing unless, like some of the elementary problems in the workbook accompanying this text, the corpus is highly artificial in selection or arrangement. False starts are almost inevitable. Some of the most promising comparisons may lead to nothing useful. The most significant contrasts may be difficult to see at first. Very frequently the several aspects of the problem are so interrelated that many tentative decisions must be made before any of them can be subjected to a real test. It is, therefore, essential that the analyst should bear in mind the tentative nature of all his results until many lines of evidence can be made to converge in support of each, and until they can be fitted together into a system.

6.2   There are several levels of structure in a language. For the most useful description, each must be clearly distinguished from all the others. They are not, however, wholly independent. Each higher level of structure is best stated in terms of the units of the preceding level. Thus, the statement of the morphemes is best made in terms of the phonemes. But, on the other hand, the phonology should be stated without any reference to the grammar. So likewise, the syntax must be stated in terms of the morpheme sequences described in the morphology, but the description of the morphology must not be dependent upon that of the syntax.

It is not ordinarily feasible to analyze each level separately. Instead, the work must be carried on more or less simultaneously on all levels. All that is required is that it be done in such a way that the results can be stated in terms of an orderly hierarchy of levels, each dependent on those below and describable without dependence on any above.

The processes of linguistic analysis, though carried on more or less together, must be described separately. In this textbook it has seemed best to present grammar before phonology. We must, therefore, assume that at least a preliminary analysis of the phonology has been made. The examples in the text and the problems in the workbook are all either in a phonemic transcription, or in some notation which is nearly phonemic.

6.3   The identification of morphemes is done almost wholly by variations and refinements of one basic technique. This is the comparison of pairs or sets of utterances which show partial contrast in both expression and content. Unless the contrast is partial (that is, unless there is some apparent identity somewhere in the utterances), and unless it exists in both expression and content, the comparison is fruitless. In many important respects this is the same general procedure as was used in Chapters 2, 3, and 4 to identify English phonemes. For the identification of phonemes we wanted the smallest possible difference in expression with ANY DIFFERENCE in content whatever. For the identification of morphemes we seek the smallest differences of expression which exist with A PARTIAL DIFFERENCE of content. This difference of procedure rests in the fundamental difference between phoneme and morpheme. The phoneme is the smallest significant unit in the expression which can be correlated with ANY difference in the content structure. The morpheme is the smallest significant unit in the expression which can be correlated with any ONE PARTICULAR difference in the content structure.

Because we cannot tell what are, properly speaking, morphemes until we have nearly completed the task of analysis, it will be permissible to use the term *morpheme* somewhat loosely. We must gradually become more precise in our use of it, however, as we attain to a more precise knowledge of the structure. Above all, we must be aware of the tentative nature of all our preliminary findings and never allow ourselves to be misled by appearances of precision.

6.4 The process of analysis is best shown by detailed discussion of an actual example. For this purpose we will use a series of Hebrew verb forms. The data will be introduced a few words at a time. This is an artificial feature of the presentation. The preceding step is merely implied: namely that we have selected from the corpus those pairs or sets of items that can be profitably compared. The order of presentation is not necessarily that which is most efficient for the analysis of the data, but that which most effectively illustrates the methods used.

1. /zəkartíihuu/   'I remembered him'
2. /zəkartíihaa/   'I remembered her'
3. /zəkartíikaa/   'I remembered thee'

Comparison of items 1 and 2 reveals one contrast in expression, /–uu/ : /–aa/, and one in meaning, as shown by translation, and hence presumably in content 'him' : 'her.' This may (tentatively!) be considered as a pair of morphemes. However, comparison of 1, 2, and 3 suggests that the first identification was wrong. The contrast now seems to be /–huu/ 'him' : /–haa/ 'her' : /–kaa/

'thee.' We can be reasonably sure that the morpheme meaning 'him' includes the sounds /–uu/ or /–huu/, but until we can identify the remaining parts of the word we cannot be sure how much else is included.

6.5 4. /zəkarnúuhuu/ 'we remembered him'
5. /zəkarnúuhaa/ 'we remembered her'
6. /zəkarnúukaa/ 'we remembered thee'

Comparison of 4, 5, and 6 with 1, 2, and 3 reveals a contrast in expression and meaning between /–tíi–/ 'I' and /–núu–/ 'we.' However, as before, we cannot be sure how much is to be included until the remainders of the words are identified. It is conceivable that the morphemes might be /–rtíi–/ 'I' and /–rnúu–/ 'we.' Incidentally, comparison of 4, 5, and 6 with one another confirms our conclusion in paragraph 6.4.

6.6 7. /qətaltíihuu/ 'I killed him'
8. /qətalnúuhuu/ 'we killed him'

Comparison of 7 and 8 with the foregoing gives us a basis for identifying /zəkar–/ 'remembered' and /qətal–/ 'killed.' By so doing we have tentatively assigned every portion of each word to a tentative morpheme. We have, however, no reason to be certain that each portion so isolated is only a single morpheme. We have only reasonable assurance that by dividing any of these words in a manner similar to /zəkar–tíi–huu/ we have divided between morphemes, so that each piece consists of one or more essentially complete morphemes; that is, each piece is probably either a morpheme or a morpheme sequence.

6.7 The problem is somewhat simpler if one sample is identical with another except for an additional item of meaning and of expression:

/koohéen/ 'a priest'
/ləkoohéen/ 'to a priest'

There can be little doubt as to the most likely place to divide, and we can be rather confident in identifying two tentative morphemes /lə–/ 'to' and /koohéen/ 'priest.' Nevertheless, there are significant possibilities of error, so that this sort of division must also be considered tentative. Consider the following English example:

/hím/   'a song used in church'
/hímnəl/   'a book containing /hímz/'

The obvious division is into two morphemes /hím/ and /–nəl/. Reference to the spelling (which is, of course, never conclusive evidence for any thing in spoken language!), *hymn* : *hymnal* suggests that this is not very certain. Actually the two morphemes are /him ~ himn–/ and /–əl/, as may be shown by comparing additional data: *confession* : *confessional*, *hymnology* : *geology*, *hymnody* : *psalmody*.

6.8   9. /zəkaarúuhuu/   'they remembered him'
        10. /zəkaaráthuu/   'she remembe ed him'

If we compare 9 and 10 with the foregoing we find /–huu/ 'him,' /–úu–/ 'they,' and /–át–/ 'she.' But where 1–6 have /zəkar–/, 9 and 10 have /zəkaar–/. There is an obvious similarity of form between /zəkar–/ and /zəkaar–/ and the meaning seems to be identical. We may guess that they are two different allomorphs of one morpheme, and proceed to check whether this hypothesis is adequate. The method of doing so will be discussed in Chapter 7. We must leave the question until that time, but must anticipate the result. /zəkar–/ and /zəkaar–/ will be shown to be variants of one tentative morpheme.

But though we will proceed on the basis that the hypothesis can be sustained, we must recognize that there are certain other possibilities. 1) /zəkar–/ and /zəkaar–/ may be different morphemes. This seems unlikely because of the similarity of meaning, but we must always remember that English translation may be misleading. 2) A somewhat less remote possibility is that /zəkar–/ and /zəkaar–/ are each sequences of morphemes and contain two contrasting morphemes. We can do nothing with this possibility from the data at hand, because there is no evidence of a contrast in meaning, but this may well be the kind of difference that does not show up clearly in translation. 3) We may have divided wrongly. Perhaps 'I' is not /–tíi–/ but /–a–tíi–/ and 'they' is similarly /–aa–úu–/. This would mean that the morpheme for 'remembered' would have to be /zək–r–/. Our only present reason for rejecting this possibility is the comparative rarity of discontinuous morphemes. We would ordinarily assume that morphemes are continuous sequences of phonemes unless there is cogent reason to believe the contrary.

6.9   11. /zəkartúunii/   'you remembered me'

We have as yet no item which forms a wholly satisfactory comparison with 11. We may, however, tentatively divide it into /zəkar-/ + /-túu-/ 'you' + /-nii/ 'me.' We do this because we have come to expect words similar to this to be divisible into three pieces, stem + actor + person acted upon, in that order. A division on such a basis is legitimate if done with caution, though obviously such an identification is not as certain as it would be if based on contrasts for each morpheme separately.

6.10   12. /šəmartúuhaa/   'you guarded him'
             13. /ləqaaxúunii/   'they took me'

Even without providing minimal pairs, 12 and 13 pretty well corroborate the conclusion which was drawn from 11 in paragraph 6.9. They thus confirm the two morphemes /-túu-/ 'you' and /-nii/ 'me.' Words 11, 12, and 13 would be rather unsatisfactory words from which to start an analysis. However, as the analysis proceeds, the requirements for satisfactory samples relax in some respects. This is because we are now able to make our comparisons within the framework of an emerging pattern. This pattern involves certain classes of elements, stems, actor affixes, and affixes stating the person acted upon. It involves certain regular types of arrangement of these elements. In short, the pattern we are uncovering is a portion of the structure of the language at a level a bit deeper than mere details of individual words.

6.11   14. /zəkaaróo/   'he remembered him'

This word cannot be analyzed by comparison with the foregoing only. We can easily identify the stem as /zəkaar-/, identical in form with that of 9 and 10. But the remainder /-óo/ neither seems to consist of the expected two parts (actor and person acted upon), nor to contain the morpheme /-huu/ 'him' which meaning would lead us to expect. Since the pattern does not assist us here in the way it did with 11, we must seek some more direct type of evidence.

6.12 15. /zaakártii/   'I remembered'
16. /zaakárnuu/   'we remembered'
17. /zaakár/   'he remembered'

These three forms differ from all those examined before in that they do not express a person acted upon. If we compare these words with each other, and if we compare 15 and 16 with 1 and 4, we can easily identify the affixes expressing the actor. These are /–tii/ 'I' and /–nuu/ 'we,' identical with those we found before except for a difference in the stress. In 17, however, there is no affix expressing actor. We will tentatively list Ø (zero) 'he' with the other actor affixes. This is intended merely as a convenient notation for our conclusion that the actor 'he' is expressed by the absence of any affix indicating some other actor. These three forms also show another variant of the stem: /zaakár/; we shall proceed on the hypothesis that like /zǝkar–/ and /zǝkaar–/, it is merely another conditioned variant. This proposal should be carefully checked by methods to be discussed later.

6.13 The analysis attained in the last paragraph suggests that item 14 can be considered as divisible as follows: /zǝkaar–Ø–óo/. The zero is, of course, a fiction, but it does serve to indicate that the form does show a rather closer parallelism with the others than we could see at first. That is, it contains a stem and a suffix expressing the person acted upon, and these are in the same order that we have found before. Whereas the pattern we had found did not seem to fit this word, closer examination shows that it does fit in with only slight modification. The pattern is therefore valid.

One problem posed by item 14 is taken care of in this way, but the other remains. We have identified two forms meaning 'him,' /–huu/ and /–óo/. These are not so obviously similar in form as /zǝkar–/ and /zǝkaar–/, so the hypothesis that they are allomorphs of one morpheme is not so attractive. Nevertheless, the similarity in meaning, and certain peculiarities in distribution which would be evident in a larger body of data, should induce us to check such a hypothesis. It will be sustained; /–huu ∼ –óo/ is one morpheme.

6.14 In the course of the discussion we have found four stems: /zǝkar–/ 'remembered,' /qǝṭal–/ 'killed,' /šǝmar–/ 'guarded,' and /ləqaax–/ 'took.' Comparison of these forms reveals that they all have the same vowels and differ only in consonants. /ləqaax–/ is not an exception, since it compares directly with /zəkaar–/. More data would yield a much longer list of such forms. This similarity in vowels could be a coincidence, but that possibility is slight. Another hypothesis is that these forms consist of two morphemes each. This is very attractive, but there is no means of checking it without a contrast. The following will provide such:

18.	/šooméer/	'watchman'
19.	/zookéer/	'one who remembers'
20.	/qooṭéel/	'killer'

By comparing these with some of the earlier samples we may identify the following morphemes: /z–k–r/ 'remember,' /q–ṭ–l/ 'kill,' /š–m–r/ 'guard,' /l–q–x/ 'take,' /–oo–ée–/ 'one who,' and /–ə–a– ~ –ə–aa– ~ –aa–á–/ ' –ed.' The first four of these are roots; the last two are some sort of affixes.

6.15 Note that we were wrong in considering /zəkar–/, /zəkaar–/, and /zaakár/ as allomorphs of a single morpheme. No damage was done, however, since these three forms, each composed of two morphemes, are distributed in exactly the same way as are allomorphs. What we assumed to condition the selection of one of these three (/zəkar–/ etc.) can just as well be considered as conditioning the selection of one of the allomorphs of the affix contained in these stems. Treating larger items as morphemes is, of course, wrong, but not seriously so at preliminary stages, provided the larger units consist of associated morphemes. Ultimate simplification is, however, attained by full analysis in any case like that just discussed.

6.16 That the analysis in paragraph 6.14 should yield morphemes such as /z–k–r/ and /–oo–ée–/ seems at first sight somewhat disconcerting. We expect morphemes to be sequences of phonemes. These, however, are discontinuous and interdigitated. Of course there is no reason why such morphemes cannot occur, as in fact our sample has indicated they do. They are much less common than compact sequences of phonemes, but they occur in a wide variety of languages and are quite common in some. Any combination of phonemes which regularly occur together and which as a group are associated with some point in the content structure is a morpheme. We need give no regard to any peculiarity of their arrangement relative to each other and to other phonemes. Rarely do morphemes consist of separate portions widely separated by intervening material. A linguist must always be prepared for such a phenomenon, however, rare as it may be.

Hebrew and related languages are unusual in the large number of discontinuous morphemes they contain. In fact the majority of the roots are similar to {zkr}, consisting of three consonants. Various allomorphs occur: /z–k–r/ in /zaakár/ 'he remembered,' /–zk–r/ in /yizkóor/ 'he was remembering,' and /z–kr–/ in /zikríi/ 'my remembrance.' The three consonants never occur contiguously in any utterance; such roots are discontinuous in all their occurrences.

6.17   In other languages, discontinuous allomorphs of otherwise quite usual morphemes occur. These commonly arise as a by-product of a special type of affix not mentioned before, an infix. An **infix** is a morpheme which is inserted into the stem with which it is associated. In comparison with suffixes and prefixes, infixes are comparatively rare but of sufficiently frequent occurrence to warrant notice. An example is the common Greek stem formative /–m–/ in /lambanɔ·/ 'I take' from the root /lab–/. Another is Quileute (Oregon) /–¢–/ 'plural' in /ho¢kʷat'/ 'white men' from /hokʷat'/ 'white person.' Such infixes produce discontinuous allomorphs /la–b–/ and /ho–kʷat'/ of the root morphemes with which they occur.

6.18   An affix should not be considered as an infix unless there is cogent reason to do so. Of course, any affix which actually interrupts another morpheme is an infix. In Tagalog *ginulay* 'greenish blue' is formed from the root *gulay* 'green vegetables.' The *–in–* is clearly an infix. But it is not justifiable to consider English *–as–* in *reassign* as in infix. This word is made by two prefixes. First *as–* and *sign* form the stem *assign*. Then *re–* is added. The alternative would be to consider *re–* and *sign* as forming a stem *resign* to which an infix *–as–* is added. The latter would be immediately rejected by any native speaker of English, since he would sense that *reassign* has a much closer connection with *assign* than with *resign*. It is always better, unless there is good reason to the contrary, to consider words as being constructed of successive layers of affixes outward from the root.

6.19   Most English verbs have a form that is made by the addition of the suffix *–ed* /–d ∼ –t ∼ –id/. This is usually known as the past. The verbs which lack this formation do, however, have some form which is used in all the same syntactic environments where we might expect such a form, and in comparable social and linguistic contexts. For example, in most of the places where *discover* /diskə́vər/ can be used, *find* /fáynd/ can also. Similarly, where *discovered* /diskə́vərd/ can be used, *found* /fáwnd/ generally can also. *Found* must therefore be considered as the past of *find* in the same sense that *discovered* is the past of *discover*.

Most of the past tenses which lack the *–ed* suffix are clearly differentiated from the base form by a difference of syllable nucleus. We may express the facts by the following equations:

discovered = *discover* + suffix *–ed*
found   = *find*   + difference of syllable nucleus

When it is so stated, it becomes evident that the difference of syllable nucleus functions in some ways like the suffix. We may consider such a difference in phonemes (they are not restricted to nuclei; consider *send* : *sent*) as a special type of morphemic element called a **replacive.**

We will use the following notation for a replacive: /aw ← (ay)/. This should be read as "/aw/ replaces /ay/." The equation above can be stated in the following form:

found   = *find* + *ou* ← (*i*)
/fáwnd/ = /fáynd/ + /aw ← (ay)/

If this is done, then we must consider /aw ← (ay)/ as another allomorph of the morpheme whose most familiar form is *–ed* and which we can conveniently symbolize $\{-D_1\}$. This morpheme has a number of replacive allomorphs, some of which will be listed in 8.10. All of them are morphologically conditioned. $\{-Z_1\}$, the English noun plural affix, also has replacives among its allomorphs.

6.20   It is, of course, possible to describe a language like English without recourse to replacives. Thus, *geese* /gíys/ can be described as containing a root /g–s/ and an infix allomorph of the plural morpheme $\{-Z_1\}$ of the form /–iy–/. Then the singular would have to be described as containing an infix /–uw–/, an allomorph of a singular morpheme *$\{X\}$. Except for the cases under consideration, there are no infixes, nor discontinuous morphemes in the language. To consider plurals like *geese* as formed by an infix turns out to involve many more complications than the alternative of describing replacives. As is often the case, the simpler explanation accords more closely with the native speaker's feeling about his language.

6.21   With replacives it is not easy to divide a word into its constituent morphemes. Obviously /giys/ is two morphemes, but the four phonemes cannot be neatly apportioned between them. A morpheme does not necessarily CONSIST of phonemes, but all morphemes are stateable in terms of phonemes. A replacive must be described in terms of two sets of phonemes: those that appear when it is present (/iy/ in *geese*) and those that appear when the replacive is absent (/uw/ in *goose*). A morpheme can consist of any recurring feature or features of the expression which can be described in terms of phonemes, without restriction of any sort.

6.22   A further, and in some respects more extreme, type of morphemic element can be seen in the past of some other English verbs. Words like *cut* and *hit* parallel such forms as *walked* in meaning and usage. There is, however, no phoneme difference of any kind between the past and the non-past form. Nevertheless, it is in the interests of simplicity to consider all English past verb forms as consisting of a stem plus an affix. Moreover, the description must in some ways note the lack of any overt marker of the past. An expedient by which both can be done is to consider *cut* 'past' as containing a root /kət/ plus a zero affix. (Zero is customarily symbolized Ø to avoid confusion with the letter O.) Ø is therefore another of the numerous allomorphs of {-D₁}.

The plural affix {-Z₁} also has a zero allomorph in *sheep*. The reason that it is necessary to describe these forms in this way rests ultimately in English content structure. Native speakers feel that the dichotomy between singular and plural is a basic characteristic of nouns. Every individual occurrence of any noun must be either singular or plural. *Sheep* is ambiguous, but not indifferent to the distinction. That is, in any given utterance the word is thought of by speaker and hearer as either singular or plural. Sometimes they may disagree, plural being intended and singular being perceived, or vice versa. It requires conscious effort for a person accustomed only to English patterns to conceive of noun referents without consideration of number. To attempt to do so impresses many people as being "too abstract." Yet they feel under no such compulsion to distinguish the exact number if it is more than two.

In other words, there is a covert difference between *sheep* 'singular' and *sheep* 'plural,' and this is linguistically significant, as may be seen from the fact that it controls the forms of certain other words in *This sheep is* . . . . : *These sheep are* . . . . The recognition of a $\emptyset$ allomorph of $\{-Z_1\}$ is merely a convenient device for entering all this into our description.

6.23   The other possible use of the zero concept in morphology would be to set up a $\emptyset$ morpheme, that is, one in which there is no overt allomorph whatever. To do so is quite unnecessary, and will generally lead to increased complexity of statement, the precise opposite of our desired goal. Moreover, it is logically indefensible. If we are to make such free use of zero, there is no definable place to stop. We could freely add zeros of all kinds to our descriptions, and each would be as justifiable as the last. The situation is decidedly different in cases in which zero is an allomorph of some morpheme which more commonly has an overt form. We can never add zeros beyond the limits of the gaps clearly visible in the structure being described.

Sometimes it is convenient to use the symbol $\emptyset$ as a temporary expedient in analysis. That was done in 6.12. Here it merely served as a short notation to indicate that no morpheme for the third person masculine singular was found. This fact demanded record during the course of the investigation. At a later stage some other less artificial method can be found to state the facts. If zero is used in this way as a temporary device, no harm will come; but the temptation to take such a zero too seriously must always be resisted. Unless it later proves to be an allomorph of some morpheme having some observable forms, then it will have to be eliminated in a final statement.

6.24   In 6.5 the principle was laid down that all parts of a sample must be identified before it is possible to consider a division into morphemes as established. However, some morphemes occur only in a very limited distribution, so that this is not always possible. In *cranberry* /krænbèriy/ the division would seem to be between /kræn/ and /beriy/. The latter can be confirmed by numerous words including *berry, blueberry, blackberry*, but the first element does not seem to occur in any other context. We are justified in considering this as a morpheme only after a thorough analysis of a large segment of English morphology. This will reveal certain widespread patterns of word formation which will confirm a division between /kræn/ and /beriy/ in the lack of any more direct evidence. Nevertheless, /kræn/ cannot be considered as securely established as a morpheme as, say /beriy/, where both morphologic patterns and direct contrasts converge.

6.25 Morphemic analysis is hardly practical without close attention to the meanings of forms. This must ordinarily be manipulated in the form of translations. Translation can obscure some features of meaning and falsify others. A contrast in meaning is not relevant unless there is also a contrast in form. Consider the following additional data for the problem which was discussed above.

21. /zəkartíihuu/   'I remember him'
22. /zəkartíihuu/   'I will remember him'

The contrast in meaning between these two items and item 1 must be disregarded because there is no contrast in form. Actually, this contrast is introduced in translation. It involves a category (time of action) which is not expressed in the inflection of the Hebrew verb. It is, however, impossible to cite an English verbal phrase without specifying time. The category must be added in the gloss, even though there is no justification in the Hebrew.

6.26 The following word may also be added to the data of the same problem:

23. /ʔezkəréehuu/   'I remember him'

There is a profound contrast in expression between 21 and 23, but none in meaning as shown by the translations. This form cannot be fully analyzed until the difference in meaning is established. The contrast in form is, however, much more significant than the apparent identity in meaning, since the latter may be purely a matter of translation. Finding these or similar words in actual contexts may supply the contrast in meaning which is lacking in the translation. Translation is a very inadequate means of expressing meanings and must always be used with great caution.

Classing Allomorphs into Morphemes

7.1 The analytic procedures described in Chapter 6 yield a list of tentative morphemic elements. Even before the procedures are completed, it is necessary to begin organizing the resulting elements in such a way as to make clear the existing structural relationships. One step in organization is to determine which of the elements are to be classed together as allomorphs of a single morpheme.

In the example discussed in Chapter 6, two very similar elements, /zəkar–/ and /zəkaar–/, were isolated. These were observed to have similar, but not identical, phonemic form, and to be apparently the same in meaning. The hypothesis was suggested that these two are allomorphs of one morpheme, and the work was carried forward on this assumption. Of course, such a hypothesis should have received at least preliminary checking before further analysis was based on it. In a practical situation it would have. But, for clarity of presentation, the discussion of the methods used in such a check had to be deferred to this chapter. This is another instance of the fact that various stages in the analysis cannot be neatly separated, though logically they should follow one after another. To go back and forth between various steps in analytic procedure and to perform many of them more or less simultaneously is essential for efficient work. It is, however, never necessary, and often dangerous, to confuse them. After an analysis has been achieved, it should always be possible to go back to the original data and demonstrate all the conclusions systematically in the logically prescribed order. If this is not possible, that is, if the various levels of structure are inextricably mixed, the whole result must be considered suspect.

7.2   A morpheme is the smallest element in the expression which has a direct relationship with any point in the content system. For any two items to qualify as allomorphs of a single morpheme it is essential merely that both have the same relationships to the same structure points in the content. Unfortunately, this is not directly observable. The process of grouping elements into morphemes therefore depends on finding, through various subsidiary or even incidental criteria, classes of items which may be assumed with reasonable probability to have such relationships. Two observable features may be expected to show some correlation with the expression-content relationship which would certainly class elements into morphemes: these two are meaning (in the vague and somewhat unscientific sense) and distribution. Of these the most objectively observable is distribution. Nevertheless, we must take care to select the most pertinent features of distribution. When samples are small, we must be particularly cautious to discriminate between significant and chance occurrences. Meaning is subject to a different kind of difficulty. It will ordinarily have to be judged from translations or from the non-linguistic context. The latter is the continuum upon which the content structure is arbitrarily imposed. We have no direct way of judging the extent or nature of the arbitrariness, but we can be sure that it exists. Translation meanings, on the other hand, include such arbitrary structuring, but they include not only that of the language under consideration but that of the language of the glosses as well. Meaning is, therefore, a variable which is not subject to any precise control. It will never be safe to use it alone, but only in combination with some facts of distribution. But it will not be possible to use distribution alone (except perhaps in special cases), since meaning will be needed to assess the pertinence of the distributional features. It follows that in each case we must use a double criterion, both parts of which must be satisfied.

Various types of distributional criteria must be used in different ways. We will therefore state and discuss separately two different sets of criteria for the classing of allomorphs into morphemes.

7.3   Two elements can be considered as the same morpheme if (1) they have some common range of meaning, and (2) they are in complementary distribution conditioned by some phonologic feature. (Morphologic conditioning will be discussed below.)

Two elements are said to be in **complementary distribution** if each occurs in certain environments in which the other never occurs — that is, if there are no environments in which both occur. For the present this means environments definable in terms of certain phonemes, types of phonemes, or combinations of phonemes. Complementary distribution is one of the basic concepts of linguistic theory and method, and will recur repeatedly in various contexts in this book and all linguistic literature. It is frequently abbreviated CD.

7.4   Note that the criterion of 7.3 does not include any reference to phonemic similarity. There is no need that allomorphs be similar in form. Occasionally the difference may be as great as that in the root of *go* /gów/ and *went* /wént/. Most often, however, allomorphs are phonemically similar. Commonly they differ by the smallest degree possible within the phonemic system of the language. For this reason, phonemic similarity is important in the analysis, but not as a criterion for uniting elements. Instead it serves primarily to indicate pairs of elements that should be tested. This was the case in the last chapter with /zəkar-/ and /zəkaar-/.

7.5   To determine whether two elements are in complementary distribution, it is necessary to tabulate a considerable number of occurrences of each. The next step is to examine each list, looking for some feature in the environment in one group which is never present in the other. Continuing the example of 6.8 but disregarding all later conclusions, we may tabulate the relevant forms as follows (the hyphens are inserted merely to separate the elements under discussion from their environments):

With short vowel		With long vowel
1. /zəkar–tíihuu/	5. /zəkar–núuhaa/	9. /zəkaar–úuhuu/
2. /zəkar–tíihaa/	6. /zəkar–núukaa/	10. /zəkaar–áthuu/
3. /zəkar–tíikaa	11. /zəkar–túunii/	14. /zəkaar–óo/
4. /zəkar–núuhuu/		

If we examine these lists, we find that /zəkar-/ occurs before a consonant, whereas /zəkaar-/ occurs before a vowel. Unfortunately the evidence is rather scant, so that any conclusion must be very tentative. Nevertheless, this will be sufficient to permit us to continue with the analysis as we did in 6.8.

7.6 Cases frequently arise, such as that just discussed, in which the available evidence is too restricted to afford any high degree of certainty. In this case, even if all the occurrences of /zəkar-/ and /zəkaar-/ in a much larger corpus were to be examined, it would still leave much room for doubt. However, similar patterns in other morphemes will emerge as the work progresses. Each of these strengthens the case for all the others. Finally, it will be possible (for Hebrew) to establish a pattern of changes in vowel length which are repeated over and over through the language. This general pattern will provide the confirmation for our analysis which could never be obtained from the examination of one such case alone. The pattern includes the following generalizations which apply to our example: (1) Any vowel followed by two consonants is short unless stressed, when it may be either long or short, /zəkartíihuu/. (2) Ordinarily any vowel followed by one consonant is long if the next vowel is stressed, /zəkaarúuhuu/.

Conclusions concerning individual morphemes can often be confirmed by very general patterns in the language, and not infrequently can be firmly established in no other way. A language is not an assemblage of unconnected patterns, but a system which is integrated to a high degree. The individual patterns will not emerge until a number of lesser patterns have been discovered. It is, therefore, necessary to make tentative conclusions based on relatively slender support, in order to establish a base from which they can be confirmed. We must never let the apparent reasonableness of such conclusions beguile us into treating them as fully established before all relevant data has been examined.

7.7 As has just been suggested, there are often widespread patterns determining the selection of allomorphs of a large number of morphemes. It is of course possible to state the facts independently for each such morpheme. This may, however, be very inefficient, because it requires endless repetition of the same statements. Moreover, it is theoretically unsatisfactory in that it obscures a general pattern. Such general patterns are important parts of the structure of the language. The objective of a person who is analyzing a language is to make such patterns of structure as clear as possible. The objective of a person who is learning a language is to comprehend these basic patterns in the most thorough way possible, and in the shortest time, so that he can manipulate them naturally. Both objectives are served by the same type of analysis. It is desirable to find simple and general methods of describing the distribution of allomorphs.

One way to make simple statements of variations within a series of morphemes is to select one allomorph of each morpheme as a **base form.** Then the other allomorphs can be considered as resulting from describable changes from this base form under certain statable conditions. Thus, parallel changes in a number of morphemes can be described once. Sometimes it is necessary to append a list of the morphemes to which the description of changes applies.

Changes of this sort are called **morphophonemic changes.** In some languages they are extensive and complicated, in others relatively few or relatively simple. They are usually referred to as "changes," but this is merely a convenient fiction; they are the changes that must be made if you start from the assumed base form. They do not represent changes that have occurred in the history of the language, unless the base form selected fortuitously happens to coincide with an older form.

7.8   It is sometimes of little importance which allomorph is selected as the base form. The English noun plural morpheme $\{-Z_1\}$ has three common allomorphs $/-z \sim -s \sim -\text{i}z/$ which are phonologically conditioned. Any one of these can be selected as the base form. If we assume $/-s/$ to be basic, we may say that after a voiced sound it becomes voiced, $/-z/$; after $/s\ z\ š\ ž\ č\ ǰ/$ a vowel $/\text{i}/$ is inserted and, as the vowel is voiced, the morpheme becomes $/-\text{i}z/$. Or we could select $/-z/$ as basic, in which case we would say that after a voiceless phoneme (other than $/s\ š\ č/$) it becomes voiceless $/-s/$. Or we could start with $/-\text{i}z/$ and describe under what conditions the vowel is dropped. One is about as convenient as the other.

It might be suggested that, since all are equally convenient, we should choose that one which is historically correct. If we do this, our statements of morphophonemic changes would be also statements of development. Unfortunately, this cannot be done in any way that is useful. The reason is that the phonemic system of

English has changed; [s] and [z] were at one time not phonemically distinct. Any attempt to state the present situation in terms of phonemes of Old English, or vice versa, will inevitably falsify the facts. Moreover, the historical development of the language, interesting as it may be, is not our present concern. Our purpose is to state the existing structure of the language. If we are to turn later to historical linguistics, our work then must be based on good descriptive statements of the structure of the language at various periods. The opposite procedure, basing descriptive work on a historical foundation, is of necessity much less satisfactory and has generally worked out to obscure various important details of structure.

7.9   One of the commonest types of morphophonemic change is **assimilation**. This is a label for the situation where some phoneme is more nearly like its environment than is the phoneme sound in the base form. "Similarity" is defined in terms of the phonetic description of sounds, as was sketched in 2.12ff and 3.17ff, or in terms of a classification of the phonemes directly suited to the language concerned. The details of application of such a definition will rest on some principles of phonology which will be discussed later. The definition can be illustrated by an English word like *imperfect* /impə́rfɨkt/, which contains a root /pərfɨkt/ and a prefix whose base form may be given as {in-}. The change of /n/, an alveolar nasal, to /m/, a bilabial nasal, makes it more similar to /p/, a bilabial stop. The assimilation of /n/ is said to be conditioned by /p/.

Various relationships exist between assimilated sounds and those by which the assimilation is conditioned. As might be expected, the two are usually very close together. Most commonly they are immediately adjacent in the stream of speech. For example, {in-} in *intemperate* /intémpərɨt/ : *incalcitrant* /iŋkǽlsitrɔ̀nt/ : *impossible* /impásɨbil/ shows assimilation conditioned by the immediately following phoneme. The two commonest allomorphs of {-D₁} are an instance of assimilation conditioned by the immediately preceding phoneme, being voiced after voiced sounds as in *buzzed* /bə́zd/, and voiceless after voiceless sounds as in *wished* /wíšt/. The two types are sometimes distinguished as **progressive,** in which the assimilated sound follows the conditioning sound, as in Turkish *gitti* 'he went' from base form *git* plus *-di*; and

regressive, in which the assimilated sound precedes the conditioning sound, as in Hebrew /mibbáyit/ 'from a house' from the base forms /min/ 'from' and /báyit/ 'house.'

Assimilation conditioned by an immediately adjacent sound, as in Greek /pʰleps/ 'vein' from /pʰleb–/ plus /–s/, is sometimes called **contiguous** in contrast to **noncontiguous,** in which one or more phonemes intervenes between the sounds concerned. The latter is much less frequent. A good example is Sanskrit /puṣpa·ṇi/ 'flowers' where without the assimilation we would expect /*puṣpa·ni/. Under certain circumstances /n/ becomes retroflex /ṇ/ conditioned by the occurrence of retroflex /ṣ/ earlier in the word. Probably the commonest type of noncontiguous assimilation is **vowel harmony,** in which vowels of successive syllables must be similar in some way. This occurs in a limited way in many languages and in some is very extensive and quite systematic. In Hungarian most suffixes have allomorphs exhibiting vowel harmony. For example 'toward'/–hoz ∼ –hez ∼ –höz/ takes the form /–hoz/ after all back vowels, /a parthoz/ 'toward the shore'; /–hez/ after unrounded front vowels, /a kerthez/ 'toward the garden'; and /–höz/ after rounded front vowels, /a fölthöz/ 'toward the earth.'

Assimilations also differ in the degree and kind of similarity to the conditioning sound. In Arabic the prefix /ʔal–/, often translated 'the,' assimilates completely to certain following sounds. Thus 'the peace' is /ʔassala·m/. When the two sounds involved differ in more than one feature, assimilation is commonly only partial. Any feature or any combination of features may be concerned. English {–Z₁} shows assimilation in voice; {in–} shows assimilation in point of articulation. The possibilities are best shown by an arbitrary example: English /n/ and /p/ differ in three respects, alveolar : bilabial, voiced : voiceless, and nasal : stop. These may be shown in the form of a three dimensional diagram:

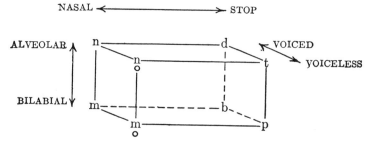

/n/ could assimilate to /p/ by becoming:

m	i.e., by becoming bilabial
d	stop
ŋ	voiceless
m̥	voiceless and bilabial
b	stop and bilabial
t	stop and voiceless
p	voiceless, bilabial and stop.

Of these, the first occurs in English, as we have seen. Two of the others are impossible in English because there are no voiceless nasal phonemes such as */ŋ/ and */m̥/ in the language. The remaining possibilities just do not occur. This is because they are not included in the morphophonemic patterns of English, an ultimately arbitrary matter, not because they are inherently less easy or less natural. Other languages may select other types of assimilations.

One type of assimilation which is very widespread and occasionally particularly troublesome is **palatalization.** This is the assimilation of velar or dental consonants to high front vowels or semivowels, which are similar in articulation to palatal consonants — for example, Italian /mónači/ 'monks' from /*mónaki/, /léjje/ 'he reads' from /*légge/, and /kuéʎʎi/ 'that' from /*kuélli/. (/ʎ/ is a palatal lateral.)

7.10 By no means all of the common morphophonemic changes are assimilations. Some are of types so infrequent in occurrence as not to warrant special terms; almost any conceivable type of change can and does occur. In addition to assimilations, a few other kinds are of simple character and can conveniently be given generally applicable labels.

One of these is **dissimilation,** in which the affected phoneme becomes less like the conditioning sound than it might otherwise be. For example, in Greek the root for 'hair' is /tʰrikʰ–/. In the nominative (the form used as a subject) the suffix /–s/ is added and, by a regular morphophonemic change of /*kʰs/ to /ks/, this becomes /tʰriks/. In the genitive the suffix is /–os/. This does not condition any change in the /kʰ/. However, no Greek word ever has two aspirate phonemes in successive syllables. The /tʰ/ therefore changes to /t/, giving the form /trikʰos/ 'of a hair.' The change of /tʰ/ to /t/ is dissimilation.

Another relatively rare morphophonemic change is **metathesis,** a change in the order of phonemes. For example, there is a prefix /hit–/ in the Hebrew system of verbal stem formatives. With roots beginning with groove fricatives (/s z š ṣ/), the /t/ of the prefix and the fricative change places. This may be seen in /hištamméer/ where we would otherwise expect /*hitšamméer/.

Much more common than either of these are changes involving the addition or loss of phonemes. These are common in many languages including English. The /–ɨz/ allomorph of {–Z₁} in *dishes* /dišɨz/ may be described as a case of the addition of a phoneme. Similar additions are common in Hebrew in such words as /šébet/ 'sitting' from /*šébt/. Consonants are commonly dropped in English from what would otherwise be long and awkward (from an English point of view!) sequences. For example, *landgrant* is commonly pronounced /lǽngrænt/ rather than /*lǽndgrænt/ as both spelling and etymology would suggest. /grǽnməðər/ for *grandmother* is a similar case. In Hebrew certain consonants (/ʔ ʕ h x r/) are not pronounced double even where doubling is morphologically significant. Thus, /haaʔíiš/ 'the man' has only one /ʔ/ when we might expect two /*haʔʔíiš/ after the same pattern as seen in /hammélek/ 'the king,' /haššéem/ 'the name,' etc. The fact that in such cases the preceding vowel is long is sometimes labeled "compensatory lengthening." The term should not be so interpreted as to suggest some sort of causal over-simplification, but merely (as is true of all other morphophonemic changes) as a label for certain observed phenomena. Phonemes are not dropped only from clusters. In Greek, for example, only a very few consonants ever occur at the ends of words. Many which might be expected are regularly dropped. Thus the word /stoma/ 'mouth' is from the root /stomat–/, the formation involving the dropping of the final /t/.

The voicing of consonants between vowels and the unvoicing of final consonants are both common. In German the latter is regular with all stops. Thus /tak/ 'day' is from the root /tag–/. Voicing of consonants is often conditioned by the position of the stress, as is shown by the two competing pronunciations of English *exema* /ɛ́ksɨmə/ and /ɨgzíymə/.

7.11 In many instances it is desirable to select base forms of morphemes with care. Often one choice will permit of a relatively simple and convenient description of morphology and morphophonemics, whereas another will necessitate a much more complex and awkward statement. This may be illustrated by the following data from Latin:

/re·ks/	'king'	/re·gis/	'of a king'	stem /re·k– $\sim$ re·g–/
/greks/	'flock'	/gregis/	'of a flock'	/grek– $\sim$ greg–/
/noks/	'night'	/noktis/	'of a night'	/nok– $\sim$ nokt–/
/duks/	'leader'	/dukis/	'of a leader'	/duk–/

The suffixes are /–s/ in the forms in the first column, and /–is/ in the forms in the second. The stems, except /duk–/ each show two allomorphs. These are listed in the third column. The problem under consideration is the selection of base forms in such a way as to permit the simplest description. The allomorphs show two kinds of differences, /k/ : /g/ and single consonant : cluster.

It would be possible to select the base form independently for each stem; but to do so would introduce another complexity. It is preferable to select for each stem either the form occurring in the first column or that occurring in the second. This will enable us to make parallel statements about each. If that in the first column is selected, it will prove necessary to state individually for each stem what, if any, of these changes apply. On the other hand, if the forms in the second column are selected, then the other allomorph can in every instance be predicted by a general rule as follows: all stem-final consonants become voiceless, if not already voiceless; all final clusters are reduced to a single consonant by dropping the second.

Given only four sets of forms, as in the data above, the rule may seem more complex than a simple listing of the allomorphs. However, each of these is representative of a number of others. Given the whole list of similar words in the language, the rules are far simpler.

7.12 As a general rule of thumb, an analysis should be based on that series of forms which shows the greatest diversity. In the case just described, that is the second column. These words exhibit the following endings of the stems: /g k kt/, whereas all forms in the first column have stems ending in /k/. It will ordinarily be easier to state how such differences are suppressed than to describe the ways in which diversity replaces uniformity.

The same rule of thumb is also useful in language learning. In learning vocabulary comparable to that in the example above, learn that set of forms which shows the greatest diversity. It will usually be easier to associate the other forms of each word with this base form than with any other. That is, /re·gis/ carries all the structural information which /re·ks/ does, plus an indication of the morphophonemic changes in the stem which are not clearly shown in /re·ks/. If /re·ks/ is learned, you must learn in addition what changes must be applied to produce /re·gis/.

In some instances there is no single set of allomorphs from which all the others can be predicted in this way. This is true for some other Latin nouns not included in the data above. When this occurs it is necessary to learn either more than one form for each stem, or one form plus some indication of the changes to be expected. Common practice in many languages is the former. This is the reason for learning **principal parts** of verbs in German, Latin, or Greek — that is, a selection of those forms of each verb which indicate the necessary morphologic and morphophonemic facts about each.

7.13   In the last several paragraphs something was said about "rules." The term is open to misinterpretation to such an extent that many linguists studiously avoid using it at all. The trouble arises from the fact that many people have expected "grammar" to tell them how a language "ought" to be spoken. Of course, this is no proper function of descriptive linguistics. If it can be clearly understood that a "rule" is merely a statement of what DOES occur, without any connotation of what SHOULD occur, the term is harmless. A legislative type of grammar is of very questionable value to a person who speaks the language, and absolutely worthless to a learner.

7.14   In 7.3 and the sections following it a criterion for classing allomorphs into morphemes was presented; however, its application was specifically restricted to those instances in which the conditioning factor is phonologic. When the conditioning is morphologic, different criteria must be applied. Two elements can be considered as allomorphs of the same morpheme if: (1) they have a common meaning, (2) they are in complementary distribution, AND (3) they occur in parallel formations. Note that there are three requirements. All three must be met. The third requirement in particular is inadequately stated, but a better statement would involve a number of complexities. Some of these, and some of the other possibilities in morphologic conditioning, are beyond the scope of an introductory treatment.

7.15   The meaning of this criterion is best shown by some examples. The three allomorphs of the English plural /–z ∼ –s ∼ –ɨz/ can be established as members of the same morpheme by the criterion presented in 7.3, since they are phonologically conditioned. /–ɨn/ is another allomorph which can be grouped with them for the following reasons: (1) The meanings are alike, 'plural.' (2) They are in complementary distribution — /–ɨn/ occurs only with *ox;* none of the others do. (3) The constructions in which they occur are parallel; /–ɨn/ occurs only in the construction *oxen* /áksɨn/, while *cows* /káwz/ is representative of the constructions in which /–z ∼ –s ∼ –ɨz/ occurs. These can be said to be parallel because /áks/ and /káw/ occur in some identical and many similar environments, and so likewise do /áksɨn/ and /káwz/. This suggests that /–ɨn/ and /–z/ have the same functional place in the grammatical structure of the language.

7.16   As a second example we may take the problem raised in 6.13. Two affixes, /–huu/ and /–óo/, both meaning 'him' were found. They were there assumed to be allomorphs of the same morpheme. The justification for this assumption depends on the criterion just presented. (1) Their meanings seem to be alike. (2) They are in complementary distribution: /–óo/ occurs after Ø 'he' and /–t–/ 'thou' (in /zəkartóo/ 'thou remembered him'), whereas /–huu/ occurs after all other suffixes expressing the actor. Because this distribution is morphologically conditioned, it is necessary to consider the third requirement. (3) They occur in parallel constructions. This may be seen most clearly if the morphemes are separated thus:

$$/\text{z–k–r}/ + /\text{–ə–aa–}/ + \frac{/\text{–úu}/ + /\text{–huu}/ \quad /\text{zəkaarúuhuu}/}{\text{Ø} \quad + /\text{–óo}/ \quad /\text{zəkaaróo}/}$$

  'they remembered him'
  'he remembered him'

$$/\text{z–k–r}/ + /\text{–ə–a–}/ + \frac{/\text{–tíi}/ + /\text{–huu}/ \quad /\text{zəkartíihuu}/}{/\text{–t–}/ + /\text{–óo}/ \quad /\text{zəkartóo}/}$$

  'I remembered him'
  'thou remembered him'

These four forms show a parallelism in internal construction. In addition they occur in very similar environments so that they also show the type of parallelism which was found in the case of /áksin/ and /káwz/.

7.17 A third example will also be drawn from Hebrew:

/zaakártii/	'I remembered'	/lii/	'I have'
/zaakártaa/	'thou remembered'	/ləkaa/	'thou hast'

From these (preferably of course by comparison with additional data) we can isolate two elements meaning 'I,' /–tii/ and /–ii/, and two meaning 'thou,' /–taa/ and /–əkaa/. In addition to the similarity of meaning they seem to be in complementary distribution, though of course it is exceedingly rash to base any such conclusion on such slender evidence. They are not, however, in parallel formations — /l–/ + /–ii/ is not parallel with /z–k–r/ + /–aa–á–/ + /–tii/. There is nothing to support considering /–tii/ and /–ii/ as members of the same morpheme, nor /–taa/ and /–əkaa/. Note that the conclusion is stated negatively. It may be that further investigation will show that, while these particular constructions are not parallel, they do actually occur in comparable structures. This does not happen to be the case, but the data at hand does not prove that it is not.

7.18 Some morphemes are highly various, while others have only a single allomorph in all environments. Moreover, allomorphs may be quite similar or wholly unlike. Both conditions can be illustrated in English. The prefix in *intolerant, impossible, incoherent, illegal,* etc., has the forms /in– $\sim$ im– $\sim$ iŋ– $\sim$ i–/. By contrast the morpheme {–Z₁} 'plural' includes such diverse allomorphs as those in *cows, oxen, stomata, mice,* and *deer,* /–z $\sim$ –in $\sim$ –tə $\sim$ ay $\leftarrow$ (aw) $\sim$ Ø/.

7.19 A special case of affixes of highly variable form, **reduplications** in which the affix is identical with some part of its environment, can be seen in the Tagalog words in the following list:

/isá/	'one'	/iisá/	'only one'	prefix	/i–/
/dalawá/	'two'	/dadalawá/	'only two'		/da–/
/tatló/	'three'	/tatatló/	'only three'		/ta–/
/píso/	'peso'	/pipíso/	'only one peso'		/pi–/ etc.

Reduplications can be prefixes, infixes, or suffixes. An example of the latter can be seen in the following Mam words. In all the words cited there is a suffix /–ŋ/ added after the reduplication.

/šp'iliŋ/ 'it is smooth'	/šp'ililiŋ/ 'it is slippery'	suffix /–li–/
/toloŋ/ 'roll (a log)'	/tololoŋ/ 'water is rolling'	/–lo–/
/tunuŋ/ 'hang'	/tununuŋ/ 'it went out hang-ing'	/–nu–/

In the examples of reduplications, several different words were cited. If this is not done, affixes may sometimes appear to be reduplications by accident. For example the English word *singing* /síŋiŋ/ from /síŋ/ could, if nothing more were known, be interpreted as a reduplication. But if other words are compared — perhaps *riding* /ráydiŋ/, *going* /gówiŋ/ — this interpretation is easily seen to be untenable. The significant thing about a reduplication is the allomorphic variation which occurs; reduplications can only be identified when sufficient data is available to indicate the extent and nature of such variation.

Outline of English Morphology

8.1 English grammar is traditionally described in terms of eight **parts of speech**: nouns, pronouns, adjectives, verbs, adverbs, prepositions, conjunctions, and interjections. These eight classes are of quite diverse character and validity. The familiar definitions overlap and conflict, or are so vague as to be nearly inapplicable. Some parts of speech gather together a number of not very obviously related types of words. In other cases, the line of demarcation between parts of speech is rather arbitrary. Before any thoroughgoing description of English morphology can be attempted, it is necessary to refine these definitions, recognize the differences in status between the classes, and make various other alterations.

8.2 One of the sources of difficulty with the English parts of speech is the tradition of defining them on the basis of meaning. Thus, nouns are defined as words that "name persons, places, or things." There are numerous nouns that have no such reference: *goodness, home run, fatherhood,* etc. To cover these, the definition is commonly expanded by the addition of some such list as "... qualities, action, relationships, etc." The "etc.," of course, immediately disqualifies this description as a definition, but this criticism is trivial. The serious problem is that adjectives are defined as words that "indicate a quality," and verbs as words that "specify actions, states, feelings, etc." Since "quality" and "action" each occur in two of these definitions, each fails as a basis of discrimination between parts of speech. Presumably a word referring to a "quality" cannot be a verb, unless the "etc." will cover such a case. But whether a word is a noun or an adjective cannot be determined from the reference to a "quality." If such differences are ruled out as nondistinctive, recourse must be had to an apparent distinction between "name," "indicate," and "specify." These are the only distinctive elements in the three definitions. Yet there is no evidence that these words are used with sufficient precision to warrant resting any significance on the difference, if any such is in fact discernible.

In short, the traditional definitions of parts of speech are largely unworkable. In practice, these overlappings and confusions have little effect. Ultimate recourse is always had to other criteria. The assignment of *tallness* to a certain part of speech does not rest on whether it "names" or "indicates" a "quality," but upon its linguistic behavior. In short, *tallness* is USED as a noun. Every American knows this, and hence assumes that it must "name" rather than "indicate" (or whatever distinction is made in the particular set of definitions which he is attempting to apply). Conversely, *tall* is considered to "indicate" rather than "name" because it is used as an adjective. The controlling criterion is always usage, not meaning, a fact which is being increasingly widely recognized among scholars of the English language.

8.3 The second difficulty with such definitions is more serious. Our one reason for desiring to classify words into parts of speech is to simplify our description of the structure of the language. To achieve this simplification we must class together words which play essentially identical rôles in the structure of the language. If this is done, statements can be made about the structural relationships of a class as a whole which will apply rather precisely to all members individually. But if they do not have structural function in common, then the classes become useless for our purpose. In fact, the usefulness of a classification depends directly on the uniformity of structural relationships of the words included. Words of similar meaning do not necessarily have common function. Consider *tall* and *tallness*. These certainly both refer in some vague and indefinable way to a quality. Suppose we were to set up a class of "quality words" including these and many others. There would be nothing useful we could do with such a class, at least not in morphologic analysis. Some (e.g., *tall*) would occur in such an environment as *The —— man came.*; others (e.g., *tallness*) in *—— is to be desired.* Only very few environments could be suggested in which all could occur, and even fewer, perhaps none, in which "quality words" could occur but not members of other classes. In other words, *tall* and *tallness* have very little in common grammatically which is distinctive of any class including them.

8.4   The only classes that will necessarily be grammatically useful are those which are grammatically defined. Others may, by more or less fortuitous coincidence, not be obviously bad. This is unfortunate because it can be so misleading. Most nouns (grammatically defined) do in fact refer to "persons, places, or things." This is a useful fact to know, and it is not wholly accidental. Nevertheless, nouns are not nouns because of this, but because of something else which is only rather distantly connected, namely the grammatical structure of English. The meaning-based class and the grammar-based class are different in just enough cases to cause endless confusion if the two are not clearly distinguished in any discussion of the language.

8.5   At this point a quite legitimate objection can well be raised: is not our chief interest in language its use as a means of conveying meanings? Certainly, one very easily justifiable reason for language study is to understand it in this capacity. Why then do we set meaning aside so brusquely?

We must answer these questions by saying that we rule meaning out of our analysis precisely because it is meaning in which we are ultimately interested. We hope that the study of the structure of English, or of any other language, will lead ultimately to an understanding of the meanings it conveys, as far as they may be accessible to us. We also hope that it will make them more accessible to us than they were before such study was undertaken. But, if our understanding of structure is based on meaning, and our understanding of meaning on structure, we are in a most vicious circle. All kinds of meanings can be read out, if in the course of analysis they are first put in. In order to make the study of meaning as effective as possible, we must first have an objective understanding of structure. Only a person wholly uninterested in any ultimate understanding of meaning can afford to base his structural analysis on meaning to any greater extent than may be unavoidable.

8.6 Returning to English parts of speech, we find that an attempt to find definitions based on grammar necessarily resorts to two types of criteria. Some words (we will continue for the present to use *word* in the rather loose familiar sense without close definition) are found in a small set of related forms. These sets fall into four patterns, each of which is a **paradigm**. They may be typified by the following examples:

man	/mǽn/	*I*	/áy/	*ride*	/ráyd/	*fine*	/fáyn/
men	/mén/	*me*	/míy/	*rides*	/ráydz/	*finer*	/fáynər/
		my	/máy/	*rode*	/rówd/	*finest*	/fáynɪst/
		mine	/máyn/	*ridden*	/rídɪn/		
				riding	/ráydɪŋ/		

The first of these is representative of a large class of words, in each of which occur two forms corresponding to the two forms of *man*. That they correspond is shown by certain parallelisms of usage: *one man: one ox, two men: two oxen, man is: ox is, men are: oxen are*, etc. Examples are:

ox	/aks/	*child*	/čáyld/	*boy*	/bóy/	*table*	/téybil/
oxen	/áksɪn/	*children*	/číldrin/	*boys*	/bóyz/	*tables*	/téybilz/

Any of the thousands of words which occur in this paradigm may be defined as a **noun**. Similarly, there are a few others like *I*, and these may be defined as **personal pronouns**. A very large number occur in a paradigm like that of *ride* and may be labeled **verbs**. A moderate number are like *fine* and are called **adjectives**. Note that by this definition *beautiful* is not an adjective, because it does not occur in the paradigm *beautiful, *beautifuler, *beautifulest*. At least, these forms are not heard in the speech of most Americans. For the few who use them, of course, *beautiful* is an adjective.

These four paradigms define four **paradigmatic classes**. The remaining parts of speech, so far as they have any validity, are of a different sort. They are classes of words which occur in the same or comparable environments in English utterances. They are **syntactic classes**. Syntactic classes sometimes comprehend paradigmatic classes. For example, we have just pointed out that *beautiful* is not in most dialects an adjective. It does, however, occur in the type of environments in which adjectives are found. It therefore belongs to a large syntactic class which also includes the adjectives. This class we will call **adjectivals.** Some features of syntactic classes will be mentioned in Chapter 10.

8.7   We may abstract from each paradigm a set of morphemes by which it is formed. Leaving the pronouns with their complications aside for a moment, the paradigms may be summarized as follows:

noun stem	verb stem	adj. stem
noun stem $\{-Z_1\}$	verb stem $\{-Z_3\}$	adj. stem $\{-\text{ər}\}$
	verb stem $\{-D_1\}$	adj. stem $\{-\text{ist}\}$
	verb stem $\{-D_2\}$	
	verb stem $\{-\text{iŋ}\}$	

These affixes are **inflectional suffixes.** They may be contrasted with **derivational affixes,** a term which covers all other suffixes and all prefixes in English. They serve to form stems that can function in these paradigms, or to form words of other classes. For example /–ayz/ is a verb-stem-forming derivational suffix. Every word containing /–ayz/ is a verb and can be found in the five forms of the verb paradigm, unless some further derivational suffix has been added. For example, *phonemicize* is a verb; *phonemicization* with an additional suffix, the noun-stem-forming /–eyšin/, is a noun.

English inflectional suffixes typically do not form stems. That is, once such a suffix is added, another suffix or a prefix is not ordinarily added to the word. Thus *rereads* is a member of a paradigm *reread, rereads, reread, reread, rereading* based on the verb stem /riyriyd/, not a formation from *reads* by the addition of the prefix /riy–/. Inflectional suffixes are an outer layer in word formation.

8.8   This suggests three convenient divisions of English grammar. The first will be the analysis of the paradigms of the four parts of speech: noun, pronoun, verb, and adjective. It will involve largely the discussion of the inflectional suffixes and their allomorphs. The second will be the analysis of the formation of stems and of words which are not inflected. In this short outline very little can be said about this division. These two together comprise **morphology.** The third will be the description of the longer sequences into which the words enter. This is called **syntax** and will form the subject of Chapters 10 and 11.

Of course, these three are not wholly distinct nor always clearly separable. But in general they constitute the most useful divisions of the subject matter of English grammar. In other languages similar divisions may be found, or one or the other of these may be missing, or there may be other divisions. The utility of such an organization of the subject depends on the structure of the language. Such a division is practically dictated by English structure, but may be worse than useless in another form of speech.

8.9 As described here English nouns have only one inflectional suffix $\{-Z_1\}$. There is another morpheme which is commonly listed as participating in noun inflection. This is symbolized by $\{-Z_2\}$. On this basis nouns would have a paradigm of four members:

man	/mǽn/	*boy*	/bɔ́y/	noun stem
men	/mén/	*boys*	/bɔ́yz/	noun stem $\{-Z_1\}$
man's	/mǽnz/	*boy's*	/bɔ́yz/	noun stem $\{-Z_2\}$
men's	/ménz/	*boys'*	/bɔ́yz/	noun stem $\{-Z_1\}$ $\{-Z_2\}$

To treat these two within the same framework presents some serious difficulties. With many nouns $\{-Z_2\}$ is extremely rare. Occasionally it is found with a word not clearly a noun, or what seems to be the wrong noun: *that man over there's, a friend of mine's, the mayor of Hartford's.* Such usages are avoided in good formal speech and writing, and can easily be considered as outside the bounds of Standard English. Yet their frequency is so great that there must be something about $\{-Z_2\}$ which favors them. In 10.18 it will be shown that $\{-Z_2\}$ is much better handled in the syntax than in the inflection. When so treated an explanation is indeed forthcoming for examples like those just cited. Therefore only a two-member paradigm is given for nouns here.

8.10 The plural affix of the noun, $\{-Z_1\}$, has a very large number of allomorphs. Instead of a detailed listing they will be described in general groups.

1. /-z ∼ -s ∼ -iz/ These three are by far the commonest, occurring with the overwhelming majority of noun stems, including most of the new words which are produced each year. Though many of the stems using other allomorphs are among the com-

monest nouns in the language, the large majority of plurals in any body of English will be formed with members of this group of allomorphs. Within the group they are phonologically conditioned:

/–z/ occurs after stems ending /b d g v ð m n ŋ r l ə y w ʜ/
/kə́b kə́bz/ *cub cubs* /bíy bíyz/ *bee bees*
/–s/ occurs after stems ending /p t k f θ/
/kə́p kə́ps/ *cup cups* /klέf klέfs/ *clef clefs*
/–ɨz/ occurs after stems ending /s z š ž č ǰ/
/glǽs glǽsɨz/ *glass glasses* /wíč wíčɨz/ *witch witches*

2. /–z ∼ –ɨz/ plus a change of the final consonant of the stems.

/z ← (s)/ in one word only
/háws háwzɨz/ *house houses*
/v ← (f)/ in about a dozen words
/náyf náyvz/ *knife knives*
/ð ← (θ)/ in about eight words
/pǽθ pǽðz/ *path paths*

3. /–ɨn/ with or without additional changes in three words.

/áks áksɨn/ *ox oxen*
/čáyld číldrɨn/ *child children*
/brə́ðər bréðrɨn/ *brother brethren* (Only in specialized senses; as a common kinship term the plural /brə́ðərz/ *brothers* is used.)

4. Various replacives in a few very common nouns.

/e ← (æ)/   /mǽn mén/ *man men*
/i ← (u)/   /wúmɨn wímɨn/ *woman women*
/iy ← (u)/   /fút fíyt/ *foot feet*
/iy ← (uw)/   /gúws gíys/ *goose geese*
/ay ← (aw)/   /máws máys/ *mouse mice*

5. Zero in a few nouns, mostly referring to animals. Some of these are pluralized in this way by some speakers and with /–z ∼ –s ∼ –ɨz/ by others; and some speakers use both forms in different contexts.

/šíyp šíyp/ *sheep sheep*

6. Certain loan words from other languages, mostly Latin, have retained the plural formation used in the original language, at least in the spelling. There is a strong tendency to make these conform to the English pattern by changing the form of {–Z₁} to /–z ~ –s ~ –ɨz/.

From Latin:	/ələ́mnə ələ́mniy/	*alumna alumnae*
	/kǽktəs kǽktày/	*cactus cacti*
	/kráysɨs kráysìyz/	*crisis crises*
	/índèks índisìyz/	*index indices*
	/díktəm díktə/	*dictum dicta*
From Greek:	/stówmə stówmətə/	*stoma stomata*
	/kritíriyən kritíriyə/	*criterion criteria*
From Hebrew:	/čérəb čérəbim/	*cherub cherubim*

8.11   The listing of the noun plural formations just given does not include a full list of the allomorphs of the inflectional morpheme {–Z₁}. It does, however, suggest some of the items that would have to be included in it. The significant thing is the nature of the variation that is shown. The first group is by all odds the commonest. It defines a subclass of nouns into which most new words find their way. In addition, this type of plural formation occurs as an alternative to any of the others, whenever there is any variation in usage. Such a subclass, defined by an allomorph or a phonologically conditioned set of allomorphs, may be called a **productive subclass.**

Groups 2 to 5 in the tabulation represent vestiges of older English patterns which were once much more widespread than they now are. In the course of several centuries, large numbers of nouns which were formerly pluralized in ways comparable to those listed in groups 2 to 5 have altered their paradigms and come to use the /–z ~ –s ~ –ɨz/ type of plural. For example, the Old English form which became modern *cow* had a plural which, if it had continued to modern times, would be expected to be pronounced /*káy/. That is, *cow* would follow the same paradigm as *mouse*. Instead, at some point in the history of the language, this plural was replaced by that which developed into /káwz/ *cows*. Such a process of alteration is likely to affect the less common words first. As a result, a few, but mostly very common, words continue to use the less common allomorphs. This is quite typical of the situation to be found in many languages. The "irregular" forms (those belonging to smaller paradigmatic subclasses) are usually the commoner words of the language.

Group 6 is a somewhat different case. These are recent loan words from classical languages. They are mostly technical or learned words, used only by people with classical education or in contact with classical traditions. Because of this, they succeed partially in retaining unassimilated paradigms in spite of their comparative rarity. The few which have become part of the common vocabulary of the American public have almost all received new plurals. Sometimes the Latin singular has become the stem, sometimes the Latin plural. Many people use *criteria* as a singular from which a plural /kràytíriyəz/ is formed (the pronunciation varies widely!). *Data* is very commonly used as a singular, from which the plural /dǽtəz/ can be formed. Indeed, many people use *data* and *datum* side by side in different meanings without recognizing the relationship between them. Only the eternal vigilance of classics-minded teachers, editors, and scholars has preserved these irregular (for English) plurals, and even that has been powerless in a large and increasing number of cases.

The process involved is illustrated in the case of the word *shmoo*. Al Capp, in coining and publicizing this word through his comic strip, stated clearly and repeatedly that the plural was to be *shmoon*, presumably /šmúwn/. The effort was entirely unsuccessful. *Shmoo* was readily accepted, *shmoon* not at all. The American readers immediately formed the plural /šmúwz/, thus assigning it, as they felt new words should be, to the productive subclass. Formation of new words is a ceaseless activity in English. Anyone has both a right to indulge in it and a reasonable prospect of success. Tampering with the morphologic patterns of the language is probably equally within an American's constitutional rights, but the chances of successful promulgation are infinitesimal. Morphology is much more basic to language than is vocabulary.

8.12 The morpheme $\{-Z_2\}$, while standing outside the inflectional system, shows interesting relationships to $\{-Z_1\}$ in form. It has four allomorphs /$-z \sim -s \sim -iz \sim \emptyset$/. The first three are phonologically conditioned and follow the same distribution as the similar allomorphs of $\{-Z_1\}$ and $\{-Z_3\}$: *Rosa's* /rówzəz/, *Jack's* /jǽks/. *Rose's* /rówzɨz/. $\emptyset$ is used after $\{-Z_1\}$ when the latter ends in /z/ or /s/, but not after other allomorphs: *boy's* /bóyz/, *cat's* /kǽts/, *men's* /ménz/. In addition, the Ø allomorph is occasionally used after proper names ending in /z/ or /s/: *James'* /jéymz/ or /jéymzɨz/. With the majority of noun stems, forms containing {-Z_1}, {-Z_2}, or both are exactly alike in pronunciation, though spelled differently. The non-distinctive form of {-Z_2} is perhaps a factor in its rather erratic use.

8.13   The verb paradigm presents some similar problems, as well as some that are rather different. Of the four inflectional affixes, {-iŋ} is unique in having only one allomorph in most forms of English, but varying widely from one dialect to another. {-Z_3} has only three /-z ∼ -s ∼ -ɨz/. These are phonologically conditioned throughout, and hence require little discussion. In three verbs, however, there are minor irregularities, *do does* /dúw dʌ́z/, *have has* /hǽv hǽz/, and *say says* /séy séz/. We may consider these cases as formed by three special allomorphs of {-Z_3}, /z/ plus /ə ← (uw)/, /z/ plus /Ø ← (v)/, and /z/ plus /e ← (ey)/; or we may consider the changes as part of the stem, in which case each stem has two allomorphs /duw ∼ də-/, /hæv ∼ hæ-/, and /sey ∼ se-/. The latter has much to commend it, since the same stem forms occur before {-D_2} in *done* /dʌ́n/, *had* /hǽd/, and *said* /séd/. Either analysis is acceptable. In the next section, however, all changes will be considered as assignable to the affix.

8.14   Both {-D_1} and {-D_2} have numerous allomorphs of various types. In the majority of instances the two forms are exactly alike, but in a few verbs they are different, and so must be considered as two morphemes. Both are like {-Z_1} in having a set of phonologically conditioned allomorphs /-d ∼ -t ∼ -id/ which taken together define the productive subclass of verbs. The remaining allomorphs are all morphologically conditioned, and all have rather restricted distributions. In the tabulation below, some statistics on occurrence will be given. These are based on the author's personal usage. The figures are, of course, not necessarily the same as might be found in another person's speech. There are three reasons for possible differences: (1) Some verbs commonly listed as "irregular" have been omitted because I do not regularly use them. Another person might have a different active vocabulary. (2) Some verbs have two paradigms, both acceptable, and commonly others which are considered as substandard. Another person might select differently among the alternatives. (3) Since the analysis is based on phonemic transcription, dialectal differences in pronunciation will affect it in many, though usually minor, ways.

The verbs of English may be classified into the following subclasses based on differences in paradigms. These are **paradigmatic subclasses.** They are arranged in order of descending size.

1. {–D₁} and {–D₂} = /–d ∼ –t ∼ –ɨd/ with the following distribution:

   /–d/ after /b g ǰ v ð z ž m n ŋ l r ə y w ʜ/
   /rə́b rə́bd rə́bd/ *rub rubbed rubbed*
   /–t/ after /p k č f θ s š/
   /stép stépt stépt/ *step stepped stepped*
   /–ɨd/ after /t d/
   /síyt síytɨd síytɨd/ *seat seated seated*

2. {–D₁} and {–D₂} = ∅ in nineteen verbs:

   bet burst cast cost cut hit hurt let put quit rid set shed shut spit split spread thrust wet
   /kə́t kə́t kə́t/ *cut cut cut*

3. {–D₁} and {–D₂} = /ə ← (i)/ in fourteen verbs:

   cling dig fling shrink sink (transitive) *sling slink spin sting stink string swing win wring*
   /spín spə́n spə́n/ *spin spun spun*

4. {–D₁} and {–D₂} = /–t/ plus /e ← (iy)/ in nine verbs:

   creep deal feel keep leap mean sleep sweep weep
   /míyn mént mént/ *mean meant meant*

5. {–D₁} and {–D₂} = /e ← (iy)/ in eight verbs:

   bleed breed feed lead meet plead read speed
   /líyd léd léd/ *lead led led*

6. {–D₁} = /æ ← (i)/ and {–D₂} = /ə ← (i)/ in seven verbs:

   begin drink ring sing sink (intransitive) *spring swim*
   /dríŋk drǽŋk drə́ŋk/ *drink drank drunk*

7. {–D₁} = /ow ← (ay)/ and {–D₂} /–in/ plus /i ← (ay)/ in seven verbs:

   drive ride rise smite strive thrive write
   /ráyd rówd rídɨn/ *ride rode ridden*

8. $\{-D_1\}$ and $\{-D_2\}$ = /t ← (d)/ in six verbs:

   bend build lend rend send spend
   /sénd sént sént/ *send sent sent*

9. $\{-D_1\}$ = /ow ← (iy)/ and $\{-D_2\}$ = /–in/ plus /ow ← (iy)/ in four verbs:

   freeze speak steal weave
   /spíyk spówk spówkin/ *speak spoke spoken*

10. $\{-D_1\}$ and $\{-D_2\}$ = /aw ← (ay)/ in four verbs:

    bind find grind wind
    /báynd báwnd báwnd/ *bind bound bound*

11. $\{-D_1\}$ = /uw ← (ow)/ and $\{-D_2\}$ = /–n/ in four verbs:

    blow grow know throw
    /nów núw nówn/ *know knew known*

12. $\{-D_1\}$ = /ɔн ← (e)/ and $\{D_2\}$ = /–n/ plus /ɔн ← (e)/ in four verbs:

    bear swear tear wear
    /tér tɔ́нr tɔ́нrn/ *tear tore torn*

13. $\{-D_1\}$ = /u ← (ey)/ and $\{-D_2\}$ = /–in/ in three verbs:

    forsake shake take
    /téyk túk téykin/ *take took taken*

14–19. Six subclasses, each containing two verbs.

20–53. Thirty-four subclasses, each containing only a single verb.

8.15 One of the latter single-membered subclasses comprises the verb *be*. This is exceedingly irregular, and in addition has certain additional forms which are not distinguished in other verbs. The forms may be listed as follows, using *ride* as a comparison:

		ride	/bíy ár ǽm/	*be are am*
——	$\{-Z_3\}$	*rides*	/íz/	*is*
——	$\{-D_1\}$	*rode*	/wɔ́z wɔ́r/	*was were*
——	$\{-D_2\}$	*ridden*	/bín/	*been*
——	$\{-iŋ\}$	*riding*	/bíyiŋ/	*being*

The verb *be* is exceedingly common and highly specialized in its usages. These two facts combine to make possible continued resistance against conformity of *be* with the prevailing patterns. Such additional complications are quite characteristic of such highly specialized and common words in all languages.

8.16   There is a small group of words, *can could will would shall should may might must*, which are traditionally included with the verbs. By the definition used here, it is impossible to classify them as verbs since they show none of the verbal inflection, with the possible exception of {$-D_1$}. That is, some people consider *could* as *can* plus {$-D_1$}, and similarly, *would should might* as the past forms of *will shall may*. There is doubtful value in this analysis, but in any case the class is quite distinct from verbs in many other respects and quite uniform within itself in usage, and so must be recognized as a clearly marked class in English structure. Whether it is treated as a highly specialized subclass of verbs (auxiliary verbs) or as a separate class closely associated with verbs (verbal auxiliaries) does not matter greatly. We will here elect the latter alternative. The definition of a **verbal auxiliary** must be based largely on syntax rather than on the somewhat debatable inflection, and is therefore a syntactic rather than a paradigmatic class.

8.17   The inflection of adjectives is relatively simple and regular, {$-ər$} and {$-ist$} being constant in form in the vast majority of adjectives. Only with a few are there any irregularities. In these cases there is variation not only in the form of the suffix, but also in the form of the stem. Only one requires attention here:

/gúd bétər bést/   *good better best*

Probably the best way to analyze this is to assume three allomorphs of the stem /gud $\sim$ bet- $\sim$ be-/. The suffix {$-ər$} is then of the usual form, while {$-ist$} occurs in the allomorph /$-st$/. The sort of complete change in form seen in the stem has been called **suppletion**. The term, as such, is not particularly important, but the phenomenon does deserve some attention. It can be a source of unnecessary confusion to students. There is, after all, no reason whatever why a stem cannot have widely divergent allomorphs. Considering the languages of the world, we find the phenomenon very widespread, though seldom very common in any particular language. The English verb *go went gone* /gów wént góʜn/ is another familiar example. The verb *fero tuli latus* 'carry' is one of the plagues of Latin students, as is /pʰerɔ· oisa hæ·neka/ 'carry' for Greek students.

8.18 The **personal pronouns** are eight in number. Each of them occurs in a paradigm of four forms. While it is, of course, possible to analyze these into stems and affixes, the small number of items and the high degree of complexity makes such a procedure somewhat questionable as a practical device. The paradigms are as follows:

/áy	míy	máy	máyn	*I*	*me*	*my*	*mine*
wíy	ə́s	ár	árz	*we*	*us*	*our*	*ours*
yúw	yúw	yɔ́ʜr	yɔ́ʜrz	*you*	*you*	*your*	*yours*
híy	hím	híz	híz	*he*	*him*	*his*	*his*
šíy	hə́r	hə́r	hə́rz	*she*	*her*	*her*	*hers*
ít	ít	íts	íts	*it*	*it*	*its*	*its*
ðéy	ðém	ðér	ðérz	*they*	*them*	*their*	*theirs*
húw	húw	húwz	húwz/	*who*	*whom*	*whose*	*whose*

These are subject to considerable variation from speaker to speaker. Such forms as /yɔʜrn hízin hə́rn/ sometimes replace /yɔ́ʜrz híz hə́rz/ as the fourth form, but since they are considered quite inelegant, they are usually avoided. While the older distinction between *who* and *whom* is frequently preserved in writing, the distinction /húw/ : /húwm/ is very seldom maintained in speech. Some people use /húwm/ after prepositions but not in other places where /míy/ or /hím/ would be used. Moreover, /húwm/ frequently carries some taint of pedantry or snobbishness, so that some people deliberately avoid it.

8.19 In addition, most of the personal pronouns vary quite widely in the pronunciation of any given speaker, different forms being used in different contexts. The pronunciations indicated in the tabulation are those which I use when the pronouns are cited in isolation. In connected speech the stress is most commonly /ˊ/ or /ˇ/, and the vowels and consonants often differ from those in the base forms listed. Few Americans are aware of the extent of the variation. This is partly because the spelling seldom reflects the differences. *'Em* is occasionally written for *them*, but not nearly as frequently as the pronoun is pronounced /əm/. This spelling gives some suggestion of substandard speech, and any others, for example *'im* for *him*, have a strong implication of this sort. Actually /im/ is with most people the commonest pronunciation of *him*. There is no difference between educated and uneducated in this; all alike very rarely use pronunciations with /h/. Each item in the table must, therefore, be understood to represent a small group of pronunciations varying in accordance with complex morphophonemic patterns.

8.20   There are a few vestigial remains of other inflections or of other inflected words. As typical may be cited the old personal pronoun *thou thee thy thine* /ðáw ðíy ðáy ðáyn/ now practically restricted to use in oral reading of older literature or in prayer. With it is associated an additional inflectional suffix used with verb stems. This takes the form /–ist/ or /–est/. The pronunciation varies somewhat, partly at least because of the unfamiliarity of most speakers with the forms.

More conservative members of the Society of Friends have preserved this pronoun, but generally in a special "plain speech" paradigm /ðíy ðíy ðáy ðáyn/. The accompanying verb is used in the {–Z₃} form. This usage is probably best interpreted as a partial assimilation to prevailing patterns, perhaps influenced by the similar spread of the old second form of the paradigm /yíy yúw yóʜr yóʜrz/ to replace the old first form. Quaker "plain speech" arose from a deliberate attempt to resist the developing patterns of the language. Ironically, the paradigm was formed on the analogy of the usage they were resisting.

8.21   The remaining parts of speech must be defined on the basis of syntax. This is in many ways a much less sure basis. The possible syntactic uses of words are so many, and often so varied, that it is quite difficult to determine which are the significant ones on which the classification should be based. There is accordingly less possibility of reaching a classification on which all will agree, though the broad outlines are generally clear. For example, the group of words traditionally called *prepositions* are a reasonably definite class with characteristic syntactic uses. They are used before nouns and at the ends of clauses with certain characteristic stress patterns. This is, of course, nothing more than a hint at a definition. A better one would have to be based on certain concepts which will be developed in Chapters 10 and 11.

The paradigmatic classes, nouns, verbs, adjectives, and pronouns, also have their characteristic usages. For example, no noun, adjective, or pronoun can occur in the place a verb usually occupies in the predicate of a sentence. Conversely, a verb or a pronoun never occurs after *the*, though either a noun or an adjective may. Such facts as these make it possible to recognize a noun, adjective, or verb in the base form, or indeed in any of the others when the full paradigm is not known.

This is important because a very large proportion of English stems can be used in two or more parts of speech. For example, many, such as *run, walk, nap, breakfast* can be used as either nouns or verbs. That is, both the verb paradigm *run runs ran run running* and the noun paradigm *run runs* occur. It is not possible to assign *run* in isolation to either class. But in contexts, such as *I run a store.* or *There's a run on the bank.*, there is no difficulty. Not all noun stems can also be used as verb stems, nor all verb stems as noun stems. If this were the case, the two parts of speech could not be distinguished. Nevertheless, the increasing use of words in other classes than those to which they originally belonged gives promise of drastic changes in English structure if present trends continue.

8.22   There are two basic processes of stem formation in English: (1) the addition of derivational affixes to roots or to stems of two or more morphemes, and (2) the combination of two or more stems to form compounds. A full description of these processes in all their ramifications would be lengthy. We can only give a few illustrative examples of the problems involved:

Stem formation of the first type is customarily described on the basis of the affixes used. Thus, for each affix is noted: (1) the class or classes of stems (including roots) with which it is used, and any pertinent restrictions within the class or classes; (2) the class of stems produced; and (3) any morphophonemic changes in either the affix itself or the stem. For example, /-θ/ is a suffix used with verb and adjective roots to form nouns: /grówθ/ *growth* is from the verb root /grow/, and /dépθ/ *depth* from the adjective root /diyp/. /-iy/ is a suffix which forms adjectives from noun stems: /glúwmiy/ *gloomy* from /gluwm/. It is used with some stems formed with /-θ/; /fílθiy/ *filthy* from /filθ/ from /fawl/; /hélθiy/ *healthy* from /helθ/ from /hiyl/.

None of the derivational affixes can be used freely with any stem, even with any stem in the proper class. Some approach this rather closely. /-ər/ 'one who does' forms nouns from a very large number of verb stems: /dúwər/ *doer*, /ráytər/ *writer*, etc. It is a productive formation. That is, it is quite freely extended to new verb stems as the occasion arises. However, it is not used with all verb roots; **meaner* 'one who means' or **seemer* 'one who seems' do not occur and are rejected by many Americans as strange or impossible. At the other extreme, /-θ/ is restricted to less than twenty stems. New formations are not currently being made through the use of this suffix. In fact, the historic connection between some of the words containing /-θ/ and the roots from which they were formed has been almost completely lost sight of. Not everyone would recognize the morphologic connection between /déθ/ *death* and /dáy/ *die*, and still fewer that between /fílθ/ *filth* and /fáwl/ *foul*.

8.23 A first analysis will yield a large number of tentative morphemes with more or less similar meanings and functions. For example, /-nis/ *-ness*, /-itiy/ *-ity*, and /-θ/ *-th* all have much the same meaning and are used in similar ways to form nouns from adjective stems. The question arises as to whether these can be considered as allomorphs of one morpheme. As between /-nis/ and /-θ/, the question is settled by a contrasting minimal pair, /wɔ́Hrmθ/ *warmth* : /wɔ́Hrmnis/ *warmness*. They are clearly to be kept separate. But what about /-nis/ and /-itiy/, or /-itiy/ and /-θ/?

Actually, this question is of more theoretical than practical importance. A person learning English will have to learn what stems can take /-nis/ and which /-itiy/, whether they are allomorphs of one morpheme or distinct morphemes. The problem here is very different from that with inflectional affixes. There is practical value in knowing that /-in/ in *oxen* is an allomorph of {-Z₁}, for this tells us that *oxen* functions in the language in a similar way to *boys, tables,* etc. — that is, that we must say *The oxen are* . . . and not **The oxen is* . . .

8.24 If we take English words apart into their constituent morphemes, we find that the stresses present a problem. An isolated word typically has one and only one primary stress. Where in the word it occurs has no particular connection with the roots or affixes concerned, but seems to be a feature of the word as a whole.

To leave the stresses on the vowels on which they are found in the word is not a satisfactory division.

An alternative method is to divide a word in the following manner: *reading* /ríydĭŋ/ = /′ ˇ/ + /riyd/ + /–iŋ/. /riyd/ is, of course, a root, and /–iŋ/ is an inflectional suffix. This leaves only /′ ˇ/ to be accounted for. This combination of stresses is structurally significant for three reasons: (1) *Reading* is never said (at least in normal speech) with any other pattern of stresses, such as /*rĭydíŋ/ or /*rĭydĭŋ/. (2) The same pattern occurs in numerous other words, among them /ríydə̆r/ *reader*, /gówĭŋ/ *going*. (3) Other patterns occur with the same constancy on other words, for example, /ˇ ′/ in /ə̆bə́v/ *above*, /bĭfə́ʜr/ *before*, etc. Indeed, minimal pairs can be found, /pə́rmĭt/ (noun) : /pə̆rmít/ (verb) *permit*. The logical conclusion is that /′ ˇ/, /ˇ ′/, and various others must be considered as morphemes.

Do these morphemes have meanings? In pairs of nouns and verbs like *permit, index, present,* etc., they seem to. But in most instances this is not so clear. They are, however, comparable to *to* in *I want to go.* In both cases (*to* and /′ˇ /) the structure demands these not obviously meaningful elements. Their function is to mark the internal structure of the utterance in which they occur. *To* indicates the relationship between *want* and *go;* /′ ˇ/ indicates that between /riyd/ and /–iŋ/. Both are morphemes for the reason that they form part of the morpheme system of the language; without them the system (as presently constituted) would be inoperable.

8.25 The significance of stress morphemes is nowhere more evident than in compounding. At first sight this type of stem formation consists of nothing more than the juxtaposition of two stems; thus, *green* and *house* may be put together to form *greenhouse* 'a glass house for growing plants.' But this is certainly not the whole truth, since the same items can be put together in the same order to produce *green house* 'a house that is green.' The difference is one of stress: /gríyn+hàws/ has a morpheme /′+`/ which is characteristic of compounds; /gríyn+hâws ∼ grîyn+háws/ has one of the morphemes /′ +^ / or /^ + ′/, which are characteristic of such constructions as adjectival plus noun or verb plus object. Many other instances of this contrast can be cited: *bláck-bìrd : blâck bírd, spít-fìre : spît fíre* (as in *It began to spit fire.*), *gréy hòund : grêy* *hóund.* There are also many cases of compounds with this $/\,'+\,`/$ morpheme for which there are no such minimal pairs: *bírd-càge, báth tùb.*

An English word characteristically consists of a root and a stress morpheme, with or without derivational and inflectional affixes. Rather exceptionally there may be two or more roots, but there may be several derivational affixes. With very few exceptions, no word has more than one inflectional suffix. Every word said in isolation normally has one and only one stress morpheme, though in context the stress morphemes may be altered in certain regular ways.

These statements will not serve as a definition of a word, unfortunately, because of certain complications which occasionally arise. The word is one of the most difficult concepts in English morphology to define, though in the vast majority of cases little question can arise as to whether a given sequence of morphemes is or is not a word.

Some Types of Inflection

9.1 A monolingual student expects that a second language will differ from his native speech in many details, but he is seldom prepared for the differences in basic structure which are commonly found. Most Americans who have studied some language in high school or college are only slightly more aware of the possibilities. French, Spanish, German, and Latin are all closely related to English and quite similar in many features. Moreover, they are commonly taught in such a way as to emphasize the similarities and suppress the differences. Were Chinese, Swahili, Aztec, or Navaho taught in our schools, they would serve much better to deepen the student's linguistic perspective. Even a brief introduction to these or any other non-Indo-European language will demonstrate that the languages of the world show remarkable variation in the most basic features.

The diversity in languages is so great that it would hardly seem possible to say anything at all about the structure of languages in general. Yet, while very few features can be found which are common to all languages, a much larger number will be found to be very widespread. Throughout this chapter you must bear in mind that the features described are not necessarily universal. They are presented as indicative of the possible range of variation and as illustrative of frequent types of structure.

9.2 The most generally useful method of describing the structure of words is by analysis into morphemes and the description of the ways in which the morphemes can be combined. Always there are restrictions of various kinds on the combinations which can occur. These restrictions may affect the order in which the morphemes can be arranged; or there may be sets of morphemes which can never occur together in the same word; or certain classes of morphemes may be required to occur in certain circumstances. In addition there are frequently complex patterns of selection of allomorphs.

In some instances the number of affixes used in a single paradigm is very large; or a single word may consist of a rather long series of morphemes. It is necessary to have some simple way of stating the complex combinations which can occur. This can often be done by classifying the morphemes into groups known as **orders** which are most conveniently designated by numbers. Thus, order 1 consists of all those suffixes which can occur only immediately after the root. Order 2 consists of those which can occur immediately after a morpheme of order 1, or immediately after the root if no morpheme of order 1 is present, but never farther from the root than this. Order 3 consists of those which can occur only after roots or members of orders 1 or 2. Similarly, prefixes can be classed into orders. If both prefixes and suffixes occur, prefixes may be distinguished by the use of negative numerals. Thus, order −1 would include those prefixes which occur only immediately before the root. Order −2 would consist of those which can occur only immediately before the root or a member of order −1.

Only one affix of a given order can occur in a given word. If, for example, two members of order 1 should occur, then one would have to follow the other. By our definition, a member of order 1 can only follow a root. Our classification of affixes into orders would be shown to be erroneous, and we would have to revise it to accord with the facts of the language. **Orders** are, therefore, mutually exclusive classes of morphemes occupying definable places in the sequence of morphemes forming a word.

9.3 The utility of this method can be illustrated by the following brief description of the Turkish verb. Turkish has very few prefixes, but a very extensive series of suffixes. The following list includes only the most important of those used with verbs. As it stands, it illustrates the salient features of Turkish verb structure;

to make it complete would add further complications and little of illustrative value.

Order 1:	/–il–/	'passive'
	/–iš–/	'reciprocal'
	/–in–/	'reflexive'
Order 2:	/–tir–/	'causative'
Order 3:	/–ma–/	'negative'
Order 4:	/–ir–/	'habitual action'
	/–iyor–/	'continuous action'
	/–aȷak–/	'future action'
	/–mali–/	'obligatory action'
Order 5:	/–di–/	'past'
Order 6:	/–lar–/	'third person plural actor'
Order 7:	/–sa–/	'conditional'
Order 8:	/–m–/	'first person singular actor'
	/–k–/	'first person plural actor'
	/–n–/	'second person singular actor'
	/–niz–/	'second person plural actor'
Order 9:	/–mi–/	'interrogative'
Order 10:	/–im/	'first person singular actor'
	/–iz/	'first person plural actor'
	/–sin/	'second person singular actor'
	/–siniz/	'second person plural actor'

9.4   There are various restrictions on the occurrence of some of these affixes beyond what is expressed by the classification into orders. These additional restrictions must be explained in notes: Only one of orders 6, 8, and 10 can occur. That is, these three orders are mutually exclusive. They cannot, however, be treated as a single order because of different arrangements when orders 7 and 9 are also involved. Order 10 cannot occur with either order 5 or order 7. Conversely, order 8 can occur only with either order 5 or order 7 or both.

Various other types of mutual relationships between orders of morphemes occur in other languages. Not infrequently, if a certain morpheme or any one of a certain class of morphemes occurs, it is obligatory for one member of some order to occur. This restriction is the converse of the mutually exclusive relationship which occurs between orders 6, 8, and 10 in the Turkish verb. No one of the orders of affixes in the Turkish verb is required. A single word can have affixes from a considerable number of them, or no affix at all.

9.5 In the absence of any morpheme of a given order, some specific type of meaning may be implied. Thus, in Turkish, in most circumstances, the absence of any member of either order 8 or order 10 implies 'third person actor.' This may be either singular or plural, unless /–lar–/ (order 6) is present, in which case it is necessarily plural.

9.6 The following forms will illustrate the operation of the system just described. The affixes are arranged in columns to show their assignment to orders. At the top a list of the morphemes in each order is given for reference.

	0	1	2	3	4	5	6	7	8	9	10
	kir	il	tir	ma	ir	di	lar	sa	m	mi	im
	čališ	iš			iyor				k		iz
	etc.	in			ajak				n		sin
					mali				niz		siniz
a kirdi 'it broke'	kir					di					
b kirilmadilarmi 'were they not broken?'	kir	il		ma		di	lar			mi	
c kirajaksan 'if you are going to break'	kir				ajak			sa	n		
d čališajakdim 'I was going to work'	čališ				ajak	di			m		
e čalištirmalisin 'you ought to make [somebody] work'	čališ		tir		mali						sin
f *kirilišdi	kir	{il / iš}				di					
g *kirajaklarim	kir				ajak		lar				im
h *kirdisin	kir					di					sin
i *kirsamali	kir				mali			sa			

The last four forms (with asterisks) are impossible. They are given only to illustrate the operation of the restrictions mentioned above. Because they are impossible, they are meaningless, so no glosses are given. Example *f* has two morphemes of the same order. These are by definition mutually exclusive. If a word such as that given could occur, it would require assignment of /–il–/ and /–iš–/ to different orders, but such words do not occur. (Note: /*kirilišdi/ is not said to be impossible because /–il–/ and /–iš–/ are of the same order; rather, these two morphemes are described as belonging to the same order because, among other things, such a form as /*kirilišdi/ does not occur. Orders are a device to state restrictions rather than rules determining what forms are to be prohibited or allowed.) Example *g* contains two morphemes which, though in different orders, are mutually exclusive. (Note: The difficulty does not occur because the meanings seem incompatible, but because of the nature of Turkish structure. Example *d* contains affixes glossed 'future' and 'past.' These might seem at first sight unreconcilable. But forms like /čališajakdim/ do occur and are meaningful. In any case, it would be very dangerous to rest our analysis so thoroughly on glosses; they certainly do not give a full idea of the meanings of these affixes.) Example *h* is impossible because with /–di–/ (order 5) the actor is expressed by a morpheme of order 8 (perhaps /–n–/) rather than one of order 10 (as /–sin/). In the example *i* the morphemes are all compatible, but a member of order 7 precedes a member of order 4. The same morphemes in the arrangement /kirmalisa/ would be acceptable and might be glossed 'if he ought to break.'

9.7 Even with the abridgment which was made in this statement, something over three thousand verb forms are mathematically possible from any given root. It is obviously inefficient to try to present a full paradigm; moreover, it is completely unnecessary, and it would be quite misleading if it were done. Some of the possible forms are quite common; others are used very rarely, if at all. But these forms, though rare, are possible, and would be understood when used. When the need for one of them arises, a Turk produces the proper form without realizing that he may never have heard that word before. Another Turk will understand it with equal readiness. The type of description just given is a formalized statement of the way a native speaker constructs needed verb forms in the Turkish language. A paradigm giving a fixed repertoire of prefabricated verbs is unsuited to such a language.

9.8 This statement of Turkish verb forms is seriously inadequate in one respect. It mentions only one of the often numerous allomorphs of each affix. A full statement would have to list all the allomorphs and give rules for the correct selection under any possible conditions. Many of the morphemes have parallel sets of allomorphs with similar conditioning. It is, therefore, possible to make certain general morphophonemic statements which apply quite universally in the system. For example, the affixes of order 10 have the following allomorphs conditioned by the vowel of the preceding syllable:

	1 sing.	1 plur.	2 sing.	2 plur.
after /i e/	/–im	–iz	–sin	–siniz
after /ü ö/	–üm	–üz	–sün	–sünüz
after /ɨ a/	–ɨm	–ɨz	–sɨn	–sɨnɨz
after /u o/	–um	–uz	–sun	–sunuz/

Similar sets of allomorphs occur in all the other affixes which were listed in 9.3 as having the vowel /i/. (Some of them have other types of variations also.) This is an instance of **vowel harmony.** The whole system can be summed up in two quite general **rules:** Suffixes containing high vowels have —

/i/ if the preceding syllable has /i e/ (front, unrounded)
/ü/   /ü ö/ (front, rounded)
/ɨ/   /ɨ a/ (back, unrounded)
/u/   /u o/ (back, rounded)

Suffixes containing low vowels have —

/e/ if the preceding syllable has /i e ü ö/ (front)
/a/   /ɨ a u o/ (back)

Exceptions are not numerous. One is indicated in the listing. An affix in order 4 has the allomorphs /–iyor– ~ –üyor– ~ –ɨyor– ~ –uyor–/, with only the first vowel showing vowel harmony.

9.9 The situation can be quite different from the relatively regular structure of Turkish. A description of a small part of the verb system of Cree (an American Indian language of Canada) will illustrate a much more complex type of paradigm. In this language there are four classes of verbs. The following description is of part of the inflection of transitive animate verbs. These are verbs used with a subject and an object both of which are animate. (Animate is a gender class of nouns; every noun in Cree is either animate or inanimate.) A Cree verb exists in fifteen modes. The independent indicative and the conjunct indicative are two of the most frequently used. Complete paradigms of the endings for both these modes are given in the table on page 118.

Every transitive verb has both a subject and an object expressed in the ending. In the paradigm the meanings of these are indicated by code numbers. A hyphen follows the indication of subject and precedes that of object: e.g., 1–3 indicates 'I . . . him,' whereas 3–1 indicates 'he . . . me.'

1   first person singular, 'I'
2   second person singular, 'thou'
3   third person proximate singular, the chief person spoken of, or the first one mentioned, 'he,' 'she,' 'it'
3′   third person obviative, a person or persons spoken of, other than the chief character of the narrative, or other than the first one mentioned, 'he,' 'she,' 'it,' 'they,' 'the other'
3p   third person proximate plural, 'they'
2p   second person plural, 'you all'
12   first person plural inclusive, the speaker and the person addressed, 'we,' 'you and I'
1p   first person plural exclusive, the speaker and some person or persons other than the one addressed, 'we,' 'he and I,' 'they and I'

Blank spaces in the table represent combinations of subject and object which do not occur. For example, 'he . . . him' would have to be either 3–3′ or 3′–3. 3–3 is impossible because if there are two third persons they are distinguished, one as proximate and one as obviative.

9.10   These paradigms are formidable. The whole set would be even more so. For the learner they represent a considerable load of sheer memorization. For the linguist they fail to show clearly any recurrent regularities of structure. Some simplification and systematization would be desirable from both points of view. The

CREE VERB FORMS

Conjunct indicative

	-1	-1p	-12	-2	-2p	-3	-3p	-3'
1-				-itān	-itakok	-ak	-akik	-imak
1p-				-itāhk	-itakok	-akiht	-akihcik	-imakiht
12-						-ahk	-ahkik	-imahk
2-	-iyan	-iyāhk				-at	-acik	-imat
2p-	-iyēk	-iyēk				-ēk	-ēkok	-imēk
3-	-it	-iyamiht	-itahk	-isk	-itēk			-āt
3p-	-icik	-iyamihcik	-itahkok	-iskik	-itēkok			-ācik
3'-	-iyit	-iyiyamiht	-iyitahk	-iyisk	-iyitēk	-ikot	-ikocik	

Independent indicative

	-1	-1p	-12	-2	-2p	-3	-3p	-3'
1-				-itin	-itināwāw	-āw	-āwak	-imāwa
1p-				-itinān	-itināwāw	-ānān	-ānānak	-imānānāwa
12-						-ānaw	-ānawak	-imānawa
2-	-in	-inān				-āw	-āwak	-imāwa
2p-	-ināwāw	-ināwāw				-āwāw	-āwāwak	-imāwāwa
3-	-ik	-ikonān	-ikonaw	-ik	-ikowāw			-ēw
3p-	-ikwak	-ikonānak	-ikonawak	-ikwak	-ikowāwak			-ēwak
3'-	-ikoyiwa	-ikonānāwa	-ikonānāwa	-ikoyiwa	-ikowāwāwa	-ik	-ikwak	

Reconstruction of the independent indicative

	-1	-1p	-12	-2	-2p	-3	-3p	-3'
1-				-it-in-w (↑ 1 2)	-it-in-āwāw (↑ 1 2p) (1-2p used)	-ā-w (↑ 1)	-ā-w-ak (↑ 1 3p)	-imā-w-wa (↑ 1 3')
1p-				-it-in-ān (↑ 2 1p)	(1-2p used)	-ā-ānān (↑ 1p)	-ā-ānān-ak (↑ 1p 3p)	-imā-ānān-āwa (↑ 1p 3')
12-						-ā-anaw (↑ 12)	-ā-anaw-ak (↑ 12 3p)	-imā-anaw-wa (↑ 12 3')
2-	-∅-in-w (↓ 1 2)	-∅-in-ān (↓ 2 1p)				-ā-w (↑ 2)	-ā-w-ak (↑ 2 3p)	-imā-w-wa (↑ 2 3')
2p-	-∅-in-āwāw (↓ 1 2p)	(2p-1 used)				-ā-āwāw (↑ 2p)	-ā-āwāw-ak (↑ 2p 3p)	-imā-āwāw-wa (↑ 2p 3')
3-	-ikw-w (↓ 1)	-ikw-ānān (↓ 1p)	-ikw-anaw (↓ 12)	-ikw-w (↓ 2)	-ikw-āwāw (↓ 2p)			-ā-iw (↑ 3')
3p-	-ikw-w-ak (↓ 1 3p)	-ikw-ānān-ak (↓ 1p 3p)	-ikw-anaw-ak (↓ 12 3p)	-ikw-w-ak (↓ 2 3p)	-ikw-āwāw-ak (↓ 2p 3p)			-ā-iw-ak (↑ 3' 3p)
3'-	-ikw-ayi-wa (↓ 1 3')	-ikw-ānān-āwa (↓ 1p 3')	-ikw-ānān-āwa (3'-1p used)	-ikw-ayi-wa (↓ 2 3')	-ikw-āwāw-āwa (↓ 2p 3')	-ikw-∅ (↓ 3' 3p)	-ikw-∅-ak (↓ 3' 3p)	

full set of Cree verb paradigms would not appear at first sight greatly different in complexity from a full set of Turkish paradigms. It is, however, possible to present the structure of Turkish verbs in a way that is both simpler to learn and more revealing of structure. The same sort of analysis and reorganization seems to be needed in the Cree verbs.

Only a little experimenting is necessary to demonstrate that the problem is vastly different. Turkish verb forms can be analyzed rather easily in terms of a series of affixes. The Cree endings cannot be neatly dissected into morphemes. For example, we would expect to find a morpheme marking the independent indicative, or one marking the conjunct indicative, or both. That is, there ought to be some morphemic difference between the two. It should be possible to identify this difference by recurrent contrasts between each of the 42 forms in one paradigm with the corresponding forms in the other. However, when the forms are compared it is found that the differences are extremely various. The following is just a sample:

Differences of one phoneme:	3–1	–ik : –it	
	1–2	–itin : –itān	
	3–2	–ik : –isk	
Differences of two phonemes:	1–3	–āw : –ak	
	3'–3	–ik : –ikot	
Greater differences:	1p–3	–ānān : –akiht	etc.

Differences of this sort cannot easily be summarized in terms of a single morpheme or a contrasting pair of morphemes. Attempting such a summary would necessitate describing a very long and complex set of allomorphs. Certainly no simplification can be achieved.

9.11   There are some recurrent patterns that can be discerned. For example, comparison of all 3p forms with the corresponding 3 forms suggests that a morpheme with the tentative allomorphs /–ak ∼ –wak ∼ –ik ∼ –ok/ can be identified. It must be labeled "tentative" until the remainders of these forms can be analyzed satisfactorily. Unfortunately, such an analysis cannot be made, since most of the recurrent resemblances are limited to a part of one of the modes, or show such complications as to defy analysis. The paradigms as they stand are unanalyzable.

Analysis can be carried a bit farther if some preliminary reconstruction is done. There are a number of morphophonemic changes which are known to occur in Cree: For example, a final /w/ after a consonant is dropped. Final /w/ can be added to certain forms. /*wa/ and /*wā/ sometimes change to /o/. Some of the forms with /o/ can be reconstructed by substituting /*wa/ or /*wā/. /*āā/ can be substituted for /ā/ which might have been produced from /*āā/. 1p–3p independent /–ānānak/ can be reconstructed as /*–āānānak/, and 3p–1p /–ikonānak/ as /*–ikwānānak/; once this is done, they can be divided into /*–ā–ānānak/ and /*–ikw-ānānak/. /–ā–/ occurs in many of the forms in the upper right-hand half of the table of endings of the independent indicative; it indicates that the nearer of the two persons involved is the subject, and the farther is the object. For this purpose "nearer" means 1 rather than 2 or 3, 2 rather than 3, and 3 rather than 3'. Similarly, /–ikw–/ occurs in many of the forms in the lower left half of the table. It indicates that the farther of the two persons involved is the subject, and the nearer is the object. After /–ā–/ and /–ikw–/ are taken out, 1p–3p and 3p–1p are alike. /–ānānak/ must indicate that 1p and 3p are both involved in some way, but without specifying in what way. It may be further divided into /–ānān/ '1p is involved' and /–ak/ '3p is involved.'

9.12　On the basis of such a procedure, almost all of the endings of the independent indicative mode can be analyzed. The result is the following list of morphemic elements:

/–in ∼ –w ∼ –ayi/	'1 or 2 is involved'
/–ānān ∼ –ān/	'1p is involved'
/–anaw/	'12 is involved'
/–āwāw/	'2p is involved'
/–wa ∼ –āwa ∼ –iw ∼ ∅/	'3' is involved'
/–ak/	'3p is involved'
/–ā ∼ –it ∼ –imā/	'nearer is subject; farther is object'
/–ikw ∼ ∅/	'farther is subject; nearer is object'

There is never any overt indication that 3 is involved, so no morpheme can be set up for this meaning. We may consider it as implicit when there is no indication of other participants.

The following morphophonemic changes have been assumed:

/*ww/	becomes /w/
Final /*w/ after a consonant	drops
/*wa ∼ *wā/ after a consonant	becomes /o/
/*āa ∼ *āā/	becomes /ā/
/*āi/	becomes /ē/

A complete statement would have to describe the distribution of the allomorphs. These are all morphologically conditioned, and the distribution is not easy to state simply. How this analysis works is best seen by comparing the reconstructed forms given in the table with the unanalyzed paradigm. The reconstruction is divided into morphemes. Below each is written a symbol to indicate its identity.

9.13   There are three forms which are not analyzed. 3′–12 is identical with 3′–1p. We may assume that the distinction has been lost in this context, and that the 3′–1p form has been extended in meaning. Similarly, 1p–2p and 2p–1p seem to have arisen as extensions of use of 1–2p and 2p–1 respectively. To treat them in any other way would immensely increase the complexity of the statement.

9.14   We have already pointed out one major failing of the method of analysis into morphemes. Several others are evident. For example, we listed /–imā/ as indicating 'nearer is subject.' This is certainly the easiest way of treating it, if only the independent indicative is examined. But when the conjunct indicative is analyzed, /–im–/ must be treated as marking 3′. Such an analysis as has just been presented fails because it does not attempt to cover the totality of the data. This analysis is complex enough, but if it is extended to cover both modes, many additional and more intricate problems arise. Indeed, we may expect that the addition of still more of the fifteen modes will make the analysis still more difficult.

Even more serious than the difficulty of analysis is the inconclusive nature of the result. Even in the small part of the total system which was analyzed, there are numerous instances of very free conjecture. For example, /–ik/ '3–1' was reconstructed as /*–ikw–w/. There was little warrant for either /w/. In short, any attempt to analyze these forms will inevitably take the linguist out onto very thin ice. No one can be satisfied with the result.

The analysis of Cree verbs into sequences of morphemes has a very different sort of usefulness than the comparable analysis of Turkish verbs. It is of very little direct use to a learner. A full morphemic analysis would be much more difficult to learn than the paradigms. Nevertheless, a partial analysis can be quite useful even to the beginner in providing some understanding of the paradigm. He will be assisted by learning the more obvious morphemes like /–ak ∼ –ik ∼ –ok/ '3p,' or by understanding the contrast between 'nearer-farther' and 'farther-nearer' forms.

A detailed analysis does have both interest and value to a linguist. It gives a clearer insight into the structure than a list of forms ever could; it points out certain problems that may need further attention; it gives some basis for understanding some features of the history of the language. In short, it has more theoretical than practical value, though it does have some of both.

9.15   The verbs of Loma (of Liberia) are quite different. The total paradigm includes only four forms, but there are two entirely arbitrary subclasses:

	'tell'	'count'	'break'	'bend'
Base form	bó	dódò	gálé	kává
Continuous	bósù	dódòsù	gálézù	kávázù
Recent past	bógà	dódògà	gáléá	káváá
Far past	bónì	dódònì	gáléní	kávání

The continuous is formed by the suffix /–sù ∼ –zù/, and the recent past by /–gà ∼ –á/. Since the stems which take /–sù/ also take /–gà/, and those that take /–zù/ also take /–á/, it is possible and useful to set up paradigmatic subclasses.

9.16   A relatively short paradigm like this does not imply that Loma cannot express a number of distinctions of the sort that Turkish or Cree express through their larger assortment of verb forms. These four verb forms are used with various auxiliaries and with six sets of subject pronouns. Some of the distinctions which we might expect to be expressed in the verb form are expressed by the pronouns:

	I	you (s.)	he	we (exc.)	we (inc.)	you (pl.)	they
Present	gè	è	é	gé	dé	wò	tó
Future	gà	yà	tówàà	gá	dá	wà	tá
Progressive	gà	yà	tó	gá	dá	wà	tá
Dependent	gìe	yè	yé	gíɛ	díe	wìe	tíɛ
Negative	gè	è	ɛ́	gé	dé	wè	té
Habitual	gɔ̀	ɔ̀	ɔ́	gɔ́	dɔ́	wɔ̀	tɔ́

Loma is thus in very broad outline similar to English in that extensive inflection is replaced by a long series of syntactic constructions. The various combinations of pronouns, auxiliaries, and verb forms express a considerable number of different verbal ideas. In English, comparable forms are constructed of various verbal auxiliaries and verbs.

9.17 French has a moderately extensive paradigm of verb forms. The structure of many of the forms is such that analysis into morphemes, though possible, is not always simple and may not be very helpful. Four "regular" subclasses are traditionally recognized. There are in addition a large number of "irregular" verbs. Some of these differ from the "regular" verbs in only minor respects. In others the divergencies are extreme. The "irregular" verbs often fall into small groups that are inflected alike. If, starting with the four "regular" subclasses, we arrange all the groups of like inflection in order of size, a characteristic distribution becomes evident. This is shown in the figure.

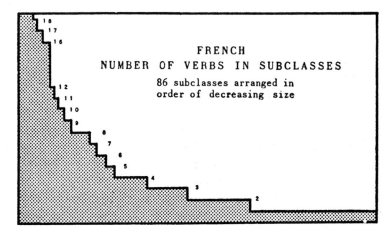

FRENCH
NUMBER OF VERBS IN SUBCLASSES
86 subclasses arranged in
order of decreasing size

This distribution is quite similar to that which was found in the English verbs described in Chapter 8. The largest of the French subclasses contains well over half of all the verbs of the language. More than one third of all the subclasses contain only one or two verbs apiece. From the point of view of the total VOCABULARY the "irregular" subclasses are quite unimportant.

This is, however, by no means the whole picture. Many of the irregular verbs are quite common, and conversely many of the common verbs are irregular. Of the commonest verbs in the language, about one third are irregular, and these include a disproportionate share of the most highly irregular. Among verbs of moderate frequency, only about one tenth are irregular. Among verbs which are rather infrequently used or distinctly rare, those with irregularities are a very inconspicuous proportion. The first subclass is the productive subclass of French verbs. That is, most new verbs fall into this paradigm, and there is some tendency for other verbs to be conformed to it. This class includes about half of the commonest verbs, about four-fifths of the verbs of moderate frequency, and a still larger proportion of the verbs which are more rarely used.

The practical effect of this is well known to any student of first-year French. The irregular verbs loom up as a major hurdle. There is one consolation; they will become less of a problem as he masters the commonest words and moves on. This same phenomenon is found in many other languages: the irregular forms are comparatively few in number, but often include many of the commonest words in the language. This is so, partly because the commonest words most successfully resist the pressure toward conformity with prevailing patterns.

9.18   The several verb systems just sketched briefly indicate something of the range of variation of types of inflection. Three variables require comment:

First is the number of forms in the paradigm. Turkish stands near one extreme with over three thousand. Cree is not far behind. English and Loma, with five and four respectively, stand near the other extreme. To complete the picture, it must be noticed that some languages have been reported as having no inflection at all. But in most languages there are at least one or two classes of words which are inflected.

Second is the complexity of formation. Turkish stands near one extreme in this matter; with only a few special restrictions, forms can be freely created by combination of affixes. Loma likewise has a very simple inflectional system, though here the short paradigm may be partly responsible. Near the other extreme is the verbal system of Cree. Here the combinations of affixes are so complex that it is hardly profitable, for practical purposes, to attempt to describe the formations. Fortunately, the division of words into stems and inflectional affix combinations is generally simple, so that a paradigm of one verb will serve readily as a pattern for the inflection of another. English, though it has a short paradigm, shows a relatively high degree of complexity.

Third is the number of inflectional subclasses. Turkish has only one. That is, the inflection of all Turkish verbs can be comprehended under one scheme of affixes and morphophonemic rules. Loma has only two; within each the inflection is quite simple, but it is necessary to know to which subclass any given stem belongs. English and French have more numerous subclasses; these are merely arbitrary divisions, classes of verbs having similar morphology. Cree subclasses are quite different. The verbs described were transitive animate verbs — that is, those which can and must have an object and whose object must be an animate noun. There are also transitive inanimate verbs, which must have an inanimate object; animate intransitive verbs, which have no object and whose subject is animate; and inanimate intransitive verbs, which have no object and whose subject is inanimate. The differences are not a matter of "meaning," but of usage. Frequently English translations will flatly contradict these distinctions and cannot, of course, be used to distinguish the verb classes. The subclasses depend on the syntactic patterns of the language, which are largely arbitrary, and on the two subclasses of nouns, which are also largely arbitrary.

9.19   With so much variation in the extent and nature of inflection in various languages, the form of analysis and description used must be suited to the language at hand. There is sometimes a tendency to force the description of a language into the pattern most familiar from past experience. For generations, Latin grammar supplied the pattern. Frequently, the familiar Latin parts of speech were recognized, whether they were there or not. Often the forms were fitted into the paradigmatic framework of Latin. Until

quite recently, English and American school children were required
to learn such paradigms as the following, which is given with the
Latin model:

Singular nominative	*the boy*	*puer*
genitive	*of the boy*	*pueri*
dative	*to the boy*	*puero*
accusative	*the boy*	*puerum*
ablative	*from the boy*	*puero*
vocative	*O boy!*	*puer*

and similarly through the plural.

The result of this sort of grammar is twofold. It gives the students the impression that grammar is essentially a specialized type
of formalized nonsense, of no practical value, though traditionally
part of the educational process. A direct consequence is the popu-
larity of foreign language courses that promise "no grammar."
This is, of course, ridiculous. A language is a systematic structure;
to learn a language is to learn this structure. Any description of this
structure is grammar.

A second result is to blind the observer to many features of the
language which are properly the concern of grammar, but which
are not usually treated in the traditional Latin grammar. In making the grammar of English as nearly like that of Latin as possible,
resort must be had to conflation as seen in the paradigm above, to
some measure of distortion, and also to the complete neglect of
features which cannot be made to conform. Because of the dominance of basically Latin concepts, the grammar of English has been
until very recently much less well known than that of many much
less used languages. The latter owe their superior descriptions to
the fact that the first approach had been made by linguists with
fewer prejudgments about grammar.

The bondage of English grammar to Latin patterns is being
broken, and with the break has come a period of rapid advance in
our understanding. Part of the credit for this belongs to modern
descriptive linguistics, which has brought to English a deeper
perspective gained from the examination of a wide variety of
language structures. But at least as much of the credit accrues to
students of the English language as such, who by closer attention

to the material they are studying have been led to much the same discoveries more or less independently.

The opposite, but ultimately identical, error has also been made. Some linguists have become so enamoured of a fixed pattern of analysis originating in revolt against Latin patterns that they have used it where it is no more appropriate than the other. Paradigms have been over-used by traditionalists and justly revolted against. But in some languages the listing of forms in paradigms is the most feasible and useful technique of description.

9.20 The wide variation in the number of forms in paradigms has led some into false conclusions about the functional adequacy of various languages. That Turkish has several thousand verb forms, while another has only one, does not imply that Turkish can express more different shades of meaning. There are other techniques by which a language can express fine differences of meaning. It would be necessary to examine the whole system of both languages before any such judgment could be made. But any reasonably close examination demonstrates immediately that it is senseless to make such a comparison: these two languages, like any two languages, may be expected to structure content in such different ways that direct comparison is quite meaningless.

It is, however, a safe generalization to say that all languages are approximately equally adequate for the needs of the culture of which they are a part. This is most particularly true when the cultures are relatively static. When they are not, all languages seem to be able to adjust with approximately the same lag, as culture changes impose new requirements on the communication system.

The evaluative comparison of languages can be a gross form of ethnocentrism and is usually utterly sterile. That some African language might be an inadequate medium to describe a World Series game is to be expected. Incidentally, Shakespeare's English would do little better. Nor, of course, is English satisfactory as a vehicle for the description of some intricate facet of African culture. Even with the highly developed special terminology of the anthropologist, difficulty is experienced; English must be eked out with numerous technical terms from the language of the community under scrutiny. But this proves little, since the most obvious deficiencies are in vocabulary, and new words can be created rapidly in any language as the need arises.

10

Immediate Constituents

10.1 Grammar is conveniently divided into two portions: morphology and syntax. **Syntax** may be roughly defined as the principles of arrangement of the constructions formed by the process of derivation and inflection (words) into larger constructions of various kinds. The distinction between morphology and syntax is not always sharp. In some languages such a definition of syntax is reasonably useful. In others it poses serious difficulties. But a more satisfactory discrimination cannot be found to cover languages generally. Nevertheless, in spite of the vagueness of the limits of syntax, the principles which will be discussed below apply very widely in languages and are often of great usefulness even where syntax is least sharply set off from the remainder of grammar.

10.2 Both the nature of the problem and the general approach to its solution are best presented through an example. For this purpose we will start with a sample of written English. Our first approach will be by rule of thumb, without the check of rigorously established method. This approach will serve primarily to indicate the nature of the problem. In this preliminary discussion, we will arbitrarily disregard those features of the language which are not indicated in the spelling (stress, pitch, and transitions), but we will make use of the indicated word divisions, thus sidestepping the issue as to what is a word. This will be adequate for a preliminary discussion, but will have to be amended at one point before any adequate final analysis can be reached.

10.3 *The old man who lives there has gone to his son's house.*

This utterance contains twelve words. We may, as a first hypothesis, consider that each of them has some statable relationship to each other word. If we can describe these interrelationships completely, we will have described the syntax of the utterance in its entirety.

As we attempt to do so, we will soon discover that the nature of the relationship varies widely from pair to pair. For example *old* and *man* have a clear, direct relationship which is relatively easily stated. *Old* and *house* present no such clear direct relationship, and any discernible connection is quite complex and seemingly less interesting. One might conclude that this is merely because *old* and *man* are near to each other in the utterance, whereas *house* and *old* are widely separated. This may have some truth in it, but it is certainly not the whole story, for we find no particularly close relationship between *there* and *has*, though they are contiguous, while a much closer relationship is sensed to exist between *man* and *has*. Since the pairs of words vary so widely in the closeness of relationship which a native speaker feels to exist between them, the description of the interrelation of each with each other would seem to be a very inefficient procedure. Moreover, it could be very cumbersome. This utterance of twelve words would require the analysis of 66 relationships; an utterance of one hundred, 4,950.

10.4 As a second possibility we might start by marking those pairs of words which are felt to have the closest relationship. We will also lay down the rule that each word can be marked as a member of only one such pair. Something like the following might be the result:

The old man who lives there has gone to his son's house.

At a second step in our procedure, let us assume that these pairs of words function in the utterance as single units. There is some reason to suggest that they do, since we can replace any of these by a single word and get a sentence which, though different in meaning, seems to be in some sense similar in structure. For example:

The	old man	who	lives there	has gone	to	his son's	house.
The	woman	who	sews	went	to	Mary's	house.

10.5   If this procedure is valid, there is no reason why it cannot be repeated as many times as may be useful. Something like the following might result:

These steps may be paralleled by the following series of utterances:

The	old	man	who	lives	there	has	gone	to	his	son's	house.
The	graybeard		who	survives			went	to		that	house.
The	graybeard			surviving			went	to		Boston.	
The			survivor				went			there.	
He							went.				

By this procedure we have reduced our example successively from twelve to eight, then six, then four, and finally only two items.

10.6   Much the same result can be attained by proceeding in the opposite direction. A native speaker might be asked to mark the most fundamental cleavage in the utterance. This would probably be between *The old man who lives there* and *has gone to his son's house.* (That this is so is involved in our earlier observation that *there* and *has*, though adjacent, seemed to have no very clear, direct association.) This process can be repeated with each portion, until the ultimate divisions consist of single words. (This is merely the limit of our present concern. The method could be extended by dividing at a still deeper level between, say *live* and *–s*. This would carry us out of syntax and into morphology.) The result would probably be something like this:

The | *old* ⦙ *man* ‖ *who* | *lives* ⦙ *there* ▮ *has* ⦙ *gone* | *to* ‖ *his* ⦙ *son's* | *house.*

This result is identical with that obtained before. However, with some other utterances, the two methods might lead to similar rather than identical results.

10.7   The procedure which we have just sketched will be useful to us, if it serves as a framework within which all the relationships of the utterance can be effectively and economically described. Let us consider that between *old* and *house*. We feel that the relationship here is not direct. Our analysis shows that they are, in fact, about as remote from each other in the structure as can be. Any relationship which exists between them arises from the fact that each participates in the formation of an item which ultimately is related in a definable way to that containing the other. We may symbolize it as follows:

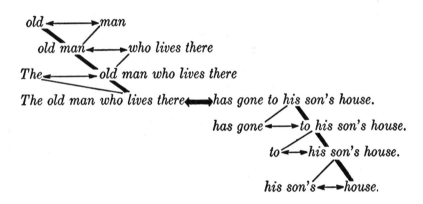

The heavier line is intended to indicate the most direct relationship between *old* and *house*. This is certainly complex and rather tenuous. It confirms our earlier impression that the interrelationships of the two words were hardly worth describing except for our desire to state the syntax of the utterance completely. This diagram, however, also established this important fact: the interrelationship of *old* and *house*, unimportant in itself, is nevertheless describable in terms of a chain of relationships each of which individually seems significant. We can, therefore, attain our objective of complete description by a proper selection of the relationships to be described.

10.8   When properly done, the method of describing the structure of utterances in terms of successively larger constructions and their relationships proves to be quite generally feasible and useful. In many instances it provides a simple framework within which everything significant can be effectively and efficiently described. In some instances where this is not so, it is found that this procedure generally disposes of most of the significant features efficiently, leaving only a small residue which must be treated by other methods.

As the demonstration above was carried out, the process of uniting items into larger items was somewhat haphazard. The whole procedure was based on the uncontrolled intuition of a native speaker. If several Americans had been asked to do the same thing, each working independently, the results would not necessarily have been identical. One person working with several utterances might analyze similar utterances in noncomparable ways. Such an erratic procedure might simplify description in some measure, but it could never be as effective as a procedure which would necessarily attain comparable results with comparable materials. Moreover, the method as sketched would be useless to a linguist confronted with a language for which he lacked a native speaker's "feel."

It should be possible to establish a method of finding the best possible organization of any given utterance and of insuring comparable results with comparable material. This is the basic problem of syntax. In the ensuing paragraphs some of the factors involved will be discussed briefly. Unfortunately, the methodology has not as yet been completely worked out in a generally applicable form. Moreover, some of the best approximations to a general theory are beyond the scope of an introductory text.

10.9   Further discussion will require certain definitions:

A **construction** is any significant group of words (or morphemes). Thus in the example we have been discussing, the whole utterance is a construction. So is *the old man who lives there* or *old man*. But *there has* is not, since the two words have no direct connection. Neither is *man*, since it contains only one word. On a syntactic level *lives* is not a construction; but on another level it is a construction consisting of two morphemes, *live* and *-s*.

A **constituent** is any word or construction (or morpheme) which enters into some larger construction. Thus, in the example we have been discussing, each of the words is a constituent. So likewise are *old man* and *the old man who lives there.* However, *there has* or *man who* is not a constituent. Neither is the utterance as a whole, since there is no larger construction of which it is a part.

Note that all but the smallest constituents are constructions and all but the largest constructions are constituents. The two terms apply equally to a very large number of items. Which term is used of a given item depends on our interest. If we are concerned with the item as a part of a larger whole, it is a constituent; if as a whole composed of smaller parts, it is a construction.

An **immediate constituent** (commonly abbreviated IC) is one of the two, or a few, constituents of which any given construction is directly formed. For example, *the old man who lives there* and *has gone to his son's house* are immediate constituents of the utterance. *Old man* is an IC of *old man who lives there*, but not of the utterance as a whole. The ICs of a given construction are its constituents on the next lower level. Those on any still lower level are constituents but not immediate constituents.

Of these concepts the most important is the immediate constituent. The process of analyzing syntax is largely one of finding successive layers of ICs and of immediate constructions, the description of the relationships which exist between ICs, and the description of those relationships which are not efficiently described in terms of ICs. The last is generally of subsidiary importance; most of the relationships of any great significance are between ICs.

10.10   The basic method for determining the ICs of any construction is that of comparing samples. For example, let us consider what are the ICs of *his son's house.* We will continue to operate with the written forms, assuming that the words are established constituents. Four ways of dividing our example are possible:

his | *son's house, his son's* | *house, his* | *son's* | *house* (with a discon-

tinuous constituent *his . . . house*), and *his* | *son's* | *house* (with three ICs). The problem is to select which of these is preferable and to establish a rule which will enable us to arrive at an equivalent result with all comparable samples.

If the construction being examined had only two constituents, only one method of division would be possible, and there would be no problem. This is the case, for example, with *old man.* We may find some two-word construction which is judged to be directly comparable with *his son's house*. This would be some construction which can occur in similar environments and which is alike in all those features which we shall see to be used to mark syntactic relationships. Such a one might be *John's house*. In such a case, the most obvious analysis is that *his son's* of the first example is equivalent to *John's* of the other. On this basis we will divide as follows:

his son's	*house*
John's	*house*

To base our conclusion on a single such comparison might be dangerous but for the fact that many others can be found, and the weight of evidence will clearly favor such a division as against any other possibility.

10.11   A procedure of this sort is by no means either automatic or infallible. At every step great care must be taken to insure that the constructions compared are in fact comparable. To be so, they must have the same constituents in the same constructional pattern. This is not a test, however, since it is precisely the constituents and constructional patterns that are sought. There is no one test that can be applied in all cases. Occasionally there is no test at all which will give a clear answer. It will take ingenuity and careful observation to select the proper constructions to compare. Syntactic analysis requires skill, not merely a well-laid-out program of operations.

In the last section *his son's house* and *John's house* were compared. Several things seem to justify this: the same word, *house*, and the same suffix, −'s, occur in both in the same position; they seem to native speakers of English to be implicitly comparable. But neither of these reasons is sufficient. Sometimes the speaker's notions about his language are erroneous or misleading; more often he is not able to state his correct feeling in any useful way. As we shall see, the occurrence of similar words does not guarantee comparability. The suffix −'s is better, since it is a construction marker, a morpheme whose primary function is precisely to mark relationships between ICs. But of course this cannot be known *a priori*, but must be discovered by observation of many instances.

It is characteristic of language that various words and other elements occur in several different construction types. Only a few examples are needed to show how various may be the syntax of apparently quite similar sequences. Consider *Green Bay Packers* : *green bay tree*. Here the first two words are alike, but the IC cuts are different: *Green Bay | Packers* : *green | bay tree*. Another example is *Old Light | Church* : *old | light house*. It is easy to say that this must be so because of a difference in meaning. But I doubt if anyone ever explained the meanings of these four expressions to me, though I do know the meanings. I must have gotten the feel for the difference in some other way, from some fact or facts about these and related sequences that I could observe directly, and from which I came to an understanding of the meaning. Rather than rest the analysis on meaning, it would be better to go behind meaning to the features from which it must ultimately be determined in the experience of a native speaker.

10.12   One of the systems which assists the native speaker in determining IC cuts is suprasegmentals. Very frequently pairs of the sort we have just instanced are distinguished by different stress or intonation patterns. This type of marking of syntactic relationships will be discussed in the next chapter. But without attention to the details, the point suggests one caution in procedure. In order to find comparable constructions, careful attention should be given to suprasegmentals. Only those constructions should be compared which have similar stress and intonation. Moreover, occasionally pairs of utterances of identical constructional type may be pronounced with different stress and intonation. Other checks also must be used, but it cannot be expected that any given one, nor any combination of checks, will always work.

10.13   Another test is that of freedom of occurrence. If we excise a portion of an utterance, we will generally find that it can occur in other utterances. Shorter portions occur more freely than longer ones, in general. And other things being equal, a sequence which is a constituent will occur more widely than one which is not. Thus if we cut *Old | Light Church*, as we would *old | light house*, we will find that *light church* occurs in very few contexts, such as *New Light Church*, whereas *light house* occurs in a considerable variety, including *new light house*, *pretty light house*, *lonely light house.* A more significant comparison would be that between *Old Light* and *Light Church.* The former does have much greater freedom of occurrence: *Old Light theology, Old Light movement, Old Light preacher,* and many others. This greater freedom of occurrence indicates that the correct cut is *Old Light | Church.* As a general principle (occasionally overridden by some other) that cut is best which gives constituents with maximum freedom of occurrence.

The native speaker learns the correct cut — hence the meaning — by hearing (or reading) the constituents in a number of contexts, preferably contexts which show the relevance of one occurrence to the other. *Old Light Church* was selected as an example because of its general unfamiliarity. The phrase is very likely to be a new one to any reader of certain treatments of American church history. In one such chapter where *Old Light Church* first occurs he will also find phrases like *old light zeal* or *the old light answer,* as well as nominal usage of *Old Lights* and *New Lights.* The only way to maintain the unity of the discourse is to read these taking *old light* as a constituent. In other instances the contexts from which the native speaker learns may be much more widely scattered, but the process is basically the same.

10.14   There are various situations where the criterion of freedom of occurrence will not work. Consider the phrase *light house keeping.* This may be cut either *light | house keeping* or *light house | keeping.* Either way there is considerable freedom of occurrence for the parts. In a particular occurrence, the unity of the discourse may suggest which is preferable in that instance. But in general and out of context, either seems perfectly acceptable. There are here two outwardly identical phrases with two different structures and two different meanings. It is necessary to know which of the two is at hand before it can be decided in which way to cut it into ICs.

This is a case of what is called **constructional homonymity.** This may be defined as the relationship between two or more constructions having identical ultimate elements, but in different constructional patterns, and commonly with different IC structures. Constructional homonymity is inevitably a source of trouble to an analyst and not infrequently to the user of the language. It is also the basis for many jokes, and a convenient medium for deliberate ambiguity. One task that can be set for a complete grammar is that of pointing out and accounting for all possible types of constructional homonymity.

10.15 Another check to be used in analysis for ICs is substitutability. When we match up *his son's house* with *John's house*, we are assuming that the constructional pattern is alike and that the constituents are the same. "Same" here cannot mean identical in form or meaning, or even similar in form or meaning, but only that they are alike in their potentiality for entering into constructions. If two elements are the same in this sense, they should enter into many otherwise identical constructions. That is, one should be **substitutable** for the other.

This is a comparatively easy thing to test. We may assemble a large number of utterances containing *his son's*, and try the substitution of *John's* into them. Or conversely, a large number of sentences containing *John's*, and substitute *his son's* into them. If the equation which we made above is to be sustained, most of the resulting sentences should be acceptable to a native speaker. There will be exceptions, so that absolute substitutability cannot be demanded. It will require a discriminating exercise of judgment to know how much difference can be permitted. If the analyst is too rigid, he will accomplish nothing. If he is too lax, he will very likely be led astray into all kinds of unwarranted conclusions. Some of the apparent exceptions may ultimately turn out to be explicable. If this is the case, it will be a confirmation of the analysis. One of the best supports for any theory is that it should explain what seemed at first to be exceptions to itself. But some anomalies will probably remain refractory to the end. Such exceptions can only be minimized; they cannot be eliminated.

For example, in the sentence *I saw Henry John's house.*, *his son's* cannot be substituted for *John's*. That is to say, if such a substitution is made, the result will not be normal English, and will certainly not be accepted by an informant. But in this sentence *his son's* can be substituted for *Henry John's*. The reason is simple enough — once the analysis is achieved: *Henry John's* is a constituent. Its ICs are not *Henry* and *John's* but *Henry John* and *–'s. John's* is not, therefore, a constituent in this sentence. Hence to substitute anything for it has a real probability of producing a monstrosity. This it does by leaving *Henry* as a fragment with no proper place within the sentence structure. Substitution can, ordinarily, work only with constituents.

What has just been illustrated is a very common phenomenon, much like constructional homonymity. In this case a construction is homonymous with a sequence which is not a construction. This causes less trouble to the native speaker, since he is usually able to recognize that one possible interpretation involves false constituents. But it can be extremely troublesome to the foreign analyst or the language learner. To guard against this difficulty every fragment must be accounted for; false constructions will usually show by leaving unassignable leftovers, like the *Henry* in the example above.

10.16   The concept of ICs can be made meaningful only in terms of two other concepts which are in many respects counterparts one of the other. These are **construction pattern** and **constituent class.** It is only by constant consideration of these that the ICs can be found and only by use of these that any useful statements about the ICs can be made.

A **constituent class** is any class of constituents which occur in the same constructional patterns, as shown by the fact that they have a very large degree of mutual substitutability. This is hardly a satisfactory definition. Both constituent class and constructional pattern are basic concepts not definable, and not operationally discoverable. But they seem to have enough intuitional reality that they can be exemplified so that another person can readily learn to identify them.

In terms of the concept of constituent class the significance of the second diagram in 10.5 can be stated more clearly. Vertical lines cut the diagram into portions. Every sequence of words limited by the same pair of vertical lines is of the same constituent class. Thus, *old man who lives there, greybeard who survives, greybeard surviving,* and *survivor* are all of the same constituent class, but *he* is not necessarily. *To his son's house* and *there* are of the same constituent class; *went* is not. Not all pairs of vertical lines mark out different constituent classes; the same class may occur two or more times in the diagram. The tabulation was, of course, set up to have this property, and is correct only if members of the same class have indeed been written in the proper spaces.

Put another way, it may be said that the IC structure of any two sentences in the tabulation is identical down to a certain level. For example, *He went.* and *The survivor went there.* are identical in that both have constituents of a certain class, *he* and *the survivor*, in exactly the same constructional pattern with constituents of a second class, *went* and *went there.* These two sentences are similar in only this way (as shown by the fact that only one vertical line cuts both). Every pair of sentences in this tabulation is similar in this respect. The top two sentences have in addition identical IC structures within each constituent, and in some cases within the constituents of constituents. Any description of any sentence in the set would apply equally and without change to any sentence above it in the diagram. This is true only if sentences are described in terms of constituent classes rather than specific constituents, of course. All syntax must be so stated. The constituent classes and the constructional patterns are the basic units in syntax.

Constituent classes have members of various lengths and of various internal structures. Indeed, it is precisely this that makes the notion useful. It allows us to describe comparatively long sentences in terms of construction patterns which are also useful in the description of short sentences. Without a concept such as this, it would be necessary to set up a description of two-word sentences, another of three-word sentences, etc. Moreover, many of these would be excessively complex. Indeed, it is found that most sentences are of like complexity at the top level — they are all two-part sentences — and the great variation in the length of the parts does not particularly matter. The parts in their turn can be described in terms of comparatively simple construction patterns, even when they are themselves of great length, by again focusing attention on one level of structure at a time.

10.17 If it is assumed that *the old man who lives there* is of the same constituent class as *he* (as was done in 10.5), then we might expect that *he* could be substituted into any sentence in which the former occurs, including *I saw the old man who lives there.* But when this is done, the result is **I saw he.*, a form which must be rejected. The same will often be the result if other constituents from 10.5 are substituted at random. One such substitution would give a sequence **I saw went.* That the latter is to be rejected is not surprising; there was nothing to suggest that it should be successful. But a native speaker might feel hesitant about rejecting both these "sentences" in the same way. The sequence *I saw he.* is wrong, but an easy correction suggests itself. Most informants will agree that it should be changed to *I saw him.* *I saw went.* is not only wrong, but so wrong that it fails to suggest a correction. It is much more thoroughly unacceptable.

This reaction may be interpreted as indicating that in some sense *he* and *the old man who lives there* are of the same constituent class, but in another sense they are not. There seems to be no sense at all in which *went* is of the same class as either of these. To give recognition to this conclusion a system of classes and subclasses may be set up. Once this is done, membership within the same class will state the similarities between *he* and *the old man who lives there*, and membership in different subclasses will account for the differences within that similarity, and for the partial correctness of some substitutions. *Went* belongs to a different major class, and this accounts for the total difference between it and either of the other two.

Another illustration will help to clarify the matter of subclasses. In sentences like *He saw., He heard., He went., He came.*, the pattern seems to be basically one, and we may set up a constituent class to include *saw, heard, went, came*. These we may label verbals. We also find sentences like *He saw the man., He heard the man.*, but not *He went the man., *He came the man.* This may be stated by recognizing within the class of verbals two subclasses, transitive verbals and intransitive verbals. The constructions in which verbals occur fall into at least two groups. In one group any verbal can occur; in another, transitive verbals but not intransitive verbals. The extensive overlapping in distribution of transitive and intransitive verbals, and the similarities which they show in various other respects make it much more effective to treat them as subclasses rather than wholly independent classes. The subclassification of verbals in English is, of course, a great deal more complex than this illustration would indicate, but it proceeds on the same principles.

Rather than a simple system of constituent classes, a language involves a system of classes, subclasses, sub-subclasses, and so on. Each successive subdivision operates within the framework of the last. Thus we have a **hierarchy** of classes and several levels of subclasses.

10.18 It is tempting to think of syntax in terms of words being joined together into sentences. In IC terms this would mean that all words would be constituents. This is not, however, always the case. We saw in 10.15 an instance where it seemed best to divide otherwise: *John Henry | –'s*. Such divisions seem to occur in many languages, possibly in all, although they may be uncommon in most languages. Yet a linguist should be prepared to find them, though he may expect word division to be syntactically significant in most cases.

One common instance in English is the suffix *–'s*. This quite commonly has a phrase for a partner in a construction. In 10.5 the structure was marked — tentatively — as

to	*his*	*son's*	*house*
to	*that*		*house*

This will all stand scrutiny except the line between *his* and *son's*. This was put there on the basis of a decision to mark off the relationships between words. This is an excellent preliminary procedure, but not necessarily wholly correct.

Subsequently it was found that in the case of *Henry John's* a cut *Henry John | –'s* would account best for the observed behavior. There is sufficient parallelism between this phrase and *his son's* that the same cut should certainly be tested here. Nothing except a preference for cuts between words is against it. *His son* seems a possible constituent, and probably has greater freedom of occurrence than does *son's*. Moreover, constructions like

The King of England's
The one who spoke to me's
The man I was telling you about's

are not at all infrequent. These also must be analyzed by a cut between *–'s* and the rest of the phrase. It is desirable to set up the smallest possible number of construction types. That analysis should be preferred which is possible for all constructions including *–'s*, and demanded by some. Otherwise it would be necessary to set up two different analyses: *his | son's : Henry John | –'s*.

10.19 In all examples given so far, the ICs have been continuous. This is the commonest case, but by no means universal.

In English **discontinuous constituents** occur. One common instance occurs in many questions: *Did the man come?* This is clearly to be cut *did . . . come* | *the man.* Another, of less clear status, occurs in sentences like *It is good to be home.* Here the ICs seem to be *it . . . to be home* | *is good.*

Another useful principle of analysis is that it is always preferable to cut into continuous ICs unless there is clear evidence forcing a different decision. But a linguist must be prepared for discontinuous ICs and recognize them when the evidence seems to indicate.

10.20   In analyzing a construction into ICs it is commonly found that it falls naturally into two parts. In the examples discussed so far, this has been the case at every level. But this is by no means inevitable. Occasionally a construction is found in which there are several possible ways of cutting into two, but no one has any clear advantage over any of the others. In such a case it may be desirable to divide immediately into three or more ICs. One of the clearest examples is the term *foot-pound-second.* While this might be cut *foot-pound-* | *second* or *foot-* | *pound-second,* there is nothing to particularly commend either arrangement, whereas cutting *foot-* | *pound-* | *second* seems quite natural.

Many linguists operate on the principle that cuts will be made binary whenever possible, but that cuts giving three or more ICs will not be excluded *a priori.* In the same way, they will make cuts giving continuous ICs whenever possible, but discontinuous ICs are not excluded on principle.

10.21   Under some circumstances there is some advantage in using a somewhat different technique, which gives an analysis similar to but not identical with that arrived at by strict adherence to the principles of IC analysis.

Suppose that there occur in the corpus such constructions as the following:

the boys	*old books*	*his books*
young men	*three new books*	*my two boys*
two girls	*the three men*	*two young girls*

The first step is to find which words in the corpus are mutually substitutable. For example, *boys* and *men* seem to be, i.e., *the men, young boys, the three boys, my two men,* all seem grammatical. However, *the* is not substitutable for *young* as *the boys* and *young men* might suggest. *Young boys* and *the men* are acceptable but **young three men* and **two the girls* (from *the three men* and *two young girls*) are not. Proceeding in this way, a tabulation of constructions is made, bringing substitutable items below one another:

the			*boys*
		young	*men*
	two		*girls*
		old	*books*
	three	*new*	*books*
the	*three*		*men*
his			*books*
my	*two*		*boys*
	two	*young*	*girls*

Having done this, we may condense the columns, eliminating duplications:

the	*two*	*young*	*boys*
his	*three*	*old*	*men*
my		*new*	*girls*
			books
(A)	(B)	(C)	N

The columns are now **order classes,** a special type of constituent class relevant to this type of structural statement. They may be designated by numerals indicating their position before the noun as were the prefixes in 9.2. In this example, however, only part of the system is shown and it will be better to use temporary labels A, B, C. Constructions of the type under consideration can be described by the formula (A)(B)(C)N, where the parentheses indicate that the order class may be represented in the construction, but need not be. The noun N is always present in this construction type; hence it is written in the formula without parentheses.

A statement of this sort differs from an IC analysis as described above in two important respects: (1) These constructions have been described as having four positions (actually there are several more, but they are left for the student to work out), whereas in an IC analysis most constructions would have only two ICs. (2) The structure of a construction may be stated in terms not only of the constituents which are actually there, but also of others which MIGHT have been there but are not. This is not to say that we assume they are "understood" or that we postulate zeros in the sentence, but only that there are zeros in our statement of its structure. A diagram of sentence structure on this basis might take the following form:

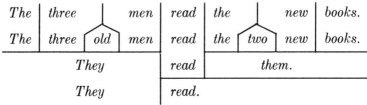

The first step is to supply the full form with all positions filled. Then, in one operation the whole phrase is reduced to one item. In pure IC analysis, the steps would be quite different:

The	three	men	read	the	new	books.
The	men		read	the	books.	
They			read	them.		
They			read.			

At each stage pairs of items are put together. Only occasionally would three be joined at one operation; very seldom four.

10.22 Suppose to the corpus discussed in the last section were added the following:

his son's books, three hundred and twenty-two men, very young girls

These would certainly complicate the picture. There are two ways to fit these into the analysis:

(1) The system of order classes might be expanded to provide a place for each element in these constructions. Something like the following would result:

his	the son's	three	hundred	and	twenty	two two	very	old young	boys girls

This increases the positions before the noun from three to nine. But the end is not in sight. The next items to be found might be *my wife's brother's child*, or *two thousand three hundred and twenty books*. Each of these would require the addition of further order classes. There would be no limit to this sort of thing, and the system of order classes would have to be gradually expanded into something so cumbersome as to be useless. Even the illustration given above with only nine places before the noun does not seem particularly useful. It is not only length that is troublesome; there are some complex restrictions on choices. No longer can any combination of classes be selected, provided only that they are kept in the correct order. For example *son's and very girls* is obviously to be rejected. Simply expanding the system of order classes inevitably leads to chaos.

(2) The basic principle of IC analysis might be followed. This is to recognize constructions within constructions. Certain sequences of words can be shown to be constructions structurally equivalent to single items in the simpler cases. The order diagram is not basically changed:

the	*two*	*young*	*boys*
his	*three*	*old*	*men*
his son's	*three hundred*		
	and twenty-two	*very young*	*girls*

Within each of the positions it would be necessary to work out another system to account for the complex constituents which occur. This might be another set of order classes. Consider the following: *his son's child, the two men's children, the oldest son's child*. These show a structure which exactly parallels that discussed above:

his			*son's*
the	*two*		*men's*
the		*oldest*	*son's*

If the structure (A)(B)(C)N is labeled as a nominal phrase, then to the list of items in the A position can be added nominal phrase plus *-'s*. This would suggest that the construction can be repeated within itself several times. *My wife's brother's child* is an example. Also possible, though much less likely, is *John's partner's wife's brother's child*.

In the C position occur not only a certain class of adjectivals, but also certain adjectival phrases. The structure of these phrases can be stated in terms of order classes, but with some complica-

tions. For example, the following are all possible: *more beautiful,
much more beautiful, very much more beautiful,* but not **very more
beautiful,* or **much beautiful.* If a system of order classes is to be
set up, there will have to be mention of a number of special restrictions, much like those described in 9.4. Moreover, not all
adjectivals work the same: in place of **more old* we find *older,*
but otherwise the structure is similar: *much older, very much older.*
It is such similarities which have led to applying the same label
"comparative" to both *more beautiful* and *older* in spite of an
obvious difference in internal structure. With these complications,
most of the possible advantages of the order-class description cannot be realized, and an IC description is probably better.

10.23   The contrast between the analyses resulting from the
IC approach and the use of order classes can be further seen by
considering another, more complex case: *my wife's brother's child.*
In terms of ICs the structure can be illustrated in the following
diagram:

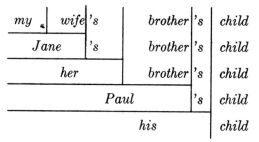

In terms of order classes the same phrase would be shown with
the following structure:

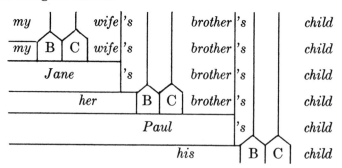

Certainly the second analysis is more complex. However, it has
the advantage that it will cover without any appreciable change

(except that the filled B and C positions must be opened to the top of the diagram) a longer phrase, such as:

my first wife's oldest brother's two small children.

In a pure IC analysis, each additional word would require one more level of structure in the diagram, and it would thus become the more complex of the two. Both IC analysis and order-class analysis have certain advantages and the one which should be used depends on the nature of the language and the purpose of the description.

10.24 If, however, the principle of constructions within constructions is rejected, no satisfactory description is possible. There are two lines of approach that suggest themselves. In 10.22 (1) one of these was briefly mentioned. Merely attempting to put in all the possibilities for nominal phrases led to an endlessly long formula. To do the same for whole sentences would be many times as complex. Only if the data are severely restricted is such a procedure possible. The result is a few formulae — possibly only one — but each of them very complex. Any sentence would be described as exemplifying one of these. But, of course, the overwhelming majority of the positions in the formula would be found to be unoccupied.

The other alternative would be to set up a large number of individual sentence patterns. Any sentence would then follow one of these exactly. Limiting ourselves to three-word sentences, at least the following would all have to be considered as of different patterns:

John saw him.	*John, go home.*	*Go home now.*
John came home.	*John, see him.*	*Take him home.*
John came now.	*John, look now.*	*Look at him.*
The boy came.	*Came the dawn.*	*Is he good?*
Two boys came.	*Who is that?*	*Is it water?*
Good boys work.	*Where is he?*	*Who saw him?*, etc.

The list is by no means complete. The limits cannot be stated unless there is first a definition of how detailed a system of classes and subclasses is to be used. It might run to several score. With four-word sentences, the count would be in the hundreds, not scores. Five-word sentence patterns run to thousands. Longer patterns are nearly incalculable. Certainly the total up to any reasonable sentence length is many millions — a number far too large to list in a grammar.

Some of these sentence patterns must be extremely rare, probably rare enough that many speakers of English never hear them in their lifetime. It is hard to imagine how they might be handed down from generation to generation if they had to be learned as such. And yet when a speaker of English does hear one of these very rare patterns — there are enough of them that this must be a frequent occurrence — they seem perfectly natural and even familiar. It is quite possible that Abraham Lincoln had never heard a sentence of the pattern on which he composed:

Fourscore and seven years ago our fathers brought forth upon this continent a new nation, conceived in liberty, and dedicated to the proposition that all men are created equal.

It would seem almost certain that a considerable number of the audience had not. Yet it appears that this sentence was accepted and understood as normal and familiar English. If such a thing can happen, it is only because this sentence was built out of familiar units. These might well be the various constructional patterns, some within others, which an IC or order-class analysis would find. Most of them are quite common, and necessarily familiar. What a grammar must describe, then, is not sentence patterns, but the smaller units of pattern of which they are constructed. Only thus can a language be described, a basis laid for understanding how it operates in human communication, or a foundation built for optimal language teaching.

11

Syntactic Devices

11.1 The meaningful structure of a sentence can best be stated in terms of a hierarchy of ICs. The immediately obvious structure of a sentence as spoken or heard is as a linear sequence of elements. Words or morphemes seem to come one after another, but they are not necessarily significantly related to the ones they precede or follow. They do, of course, have important relationships, but these may be to elements at some distance, and they may be of various kinds. To understand the sentence, the hearer must somehow identify what these relationships are. That is, he must deduce the IC structure, or something having many of the same properties. Otherwise the meaning will elude him.

Anyone who has studied a foreign language knows that this can happen. He has come upon a sentence in which he knows all the words. Yet it is not at all apparent what the sentence means. He does not know how the words fit together, and apart from these relationships they cannot form one meaningful whole. Such an experience merely shows that the student has not yet gotten control of the devices by which the IC structure of the sentence is signaled. It also demonstrates, as should be expected, that the structural signals may be very different from one language to another. The crucial task in learning a second language is precisely to master these structural signals.

11.2   What some of these signals are, and how they operate, can be seen by considering a sentence such as:

The iggle squiggs trazed wombly in the harlish goop.

Only three words of the nine are recognized. Nevertheless, to any native speaker of English the structure is clear, however obscure the meaning may be. It is almost unmistakably marked by these three words and by the four word fractions *–s, –ed, –ly,* and *–ish.*

Just how these seven items mark structure is not at all simple to describe. Their functions in the process differ somewhat from one to another. For the most part they do not mark structure either directly or decisively. But they do suggest certain facts about some constituents or hint at certain constructional patterns. Only part of the intricate web of evidence can be mentioned:

For example, *–ish* is commonly a derivational suffix forming adjectivals or words with similar functions. (Not always, of course, witness *starfish.*) This scrap of evidence is strengthened by the fact that *harlish* occurs in a position where such a word might be expected. This in turn, together with the position of *in the,* suggests that *goop* is most probably a noun. This would make *in the harlish goop* a construction of a quite common type. As the native speaker responds to such a sentence, it is probably not so formal a process, but perhaps effectively equivalent. These several clues might suggest to him that this portion of the sentence is comparable with some others that are familiar enough:

. . . . .	*in the harlish goop.*	
He lived	*in the red*	*house.*
I read it	*in the big*	*book.* etc.

Other comparisons are, of course, possible but for various reasons seem less likely:

He wandered   in the forest alone.
He gave everybody in the family money.

The first word in the sentence, *the,* signals in a somewhat different way. This must always be the first word (unless preceded by *all, both,* or *half*) of a nominal phrase. After *the,* perhaps separated by one or more adjectives and their modifiers, must usually be a noun. Thus the noun phrase must be: *The iggle,* or *The iggle*

squiggs, or *The iggle squiggs trazed,* or some longer sequence. There
is nothing that will surely identify the noun, though the ending *–s*
is certainly suggestive. There is a common noun suffix of this form,
and it is not at all common for adjectives to end this way. Thus
the iggle squiggs seems more probable as a nominal phrase than
does *the iggle squiggs trazed.* Following a nominal phrase, probably
a sentence subject, the most likely element would be some sort of
verbal phrase. This would normally consist of either a single verb,
or of a verb form preceded by one or more auxiliaries. If the latter
were present, they would be very helpful in signaling the beginning of the verbal phrase. Since no auxiliary is present, the verbal
phrase is most likely a single word, perhaps with one of the verb
inflectional suffixes. Either *squiggs* or *trazed* would qualify: both
have endings that look likely. But *wombly* looks rather unlikely
as a verb, though it would be risky to rule it out absolutely. Thus
we have two reasons, each a bit tenuous, to reject the following:

The iggle squiggs trazed	*wombly*	*in the harlish goop.*
subject	verb	

But taken together, they strengthen each other. We are left with
two possibilities:

The iggle	*squiggs*	*trazed*	*wombly*	*in the harlish goop.*
subject	verb	?	?	

The iggle squiggs	*trazed*	*wombly*	*in the harlish goop.*
subject	verb	?	

Which of these would seem best depends largely on the possibility
of identifying the elements marked with question marks. *Wombly*
in the second analysis looks like words such as *happily, daily.*
Like them it has the ending *–ly* and it occurs immediately after
the verb, a very suitable position. That is to say the whole sentence
might be comparable to:

The little pigs wallowed happily in the muddy puddle.

This is not the only possibility. The following will also fit:

The little boys threw gravel in the empty pool.

But somehow this seems less felicitous, and most people would prefer the first solution. To make *squiggs* the verb is also possible, but even less satisfying:

> *The boy throws gravel idly in the empty pool.*

It does not seem a happy solution to make *trazed* a noun, and the whole sentence seems a bit stilted, though possible. A choice must be made of the one solution that seems most probable, but at best errors will be made. The interesting thing is the generality (not usually unanimity!) with which Americans will agree on the structure of such sentences. Though hard to calculate formally, the probabilities are sensed in much the same way by many hearers.

11.3 If, starting with a sentence such as the one discussed above, the constituent classes of the words are given one by one, it is found that the analysis becomes very rapidly more certain. For example, if the only bit of additional information is that *trazed* is indeed a verb, the structure becomes quite unambiguous. Identification of the class of another constituent will strengthen the case a bit more. If the constituent class of every word is known, there is very little room for doubt, even in the most unusual sentence type. If the first bit of additional information is that *iggle* is an adjective, that will strengthen the case, but not as much as when *trazed* was revealed as a verb. Information as to constituent class is not equally valuable in all cases, but it is always of some help.

Suppose that, instead of revealing the constituent class of a word, a familiar word is substituted. Thus the first substitution might be:

> *The little squiggs trazed wombly in the harlish goop.*

and the second:

> *The little squiggs trazed happily in the harlish goop.*

and so forth. This would have much the same effect. After each substitution the structure becomes clearer. At the same time some meaning begins to emerge. But as far as structure is concerned, the analysis is just as clear when there is merely the information that *iggle* is an adjective as it is when *little* is substituted. The substitution of *little* can reveal nothing of structural importance which identifying *iggle* as an adjective cannot do. The only thing which is structurally revealing about a word like *little* is the constituent class to which it belongs. Not only so. If there is positive information that *iggle* is an adjective, more is known about the structure than if *little* is substituted. The best that can be said in the latter case is that *little* is very probably an adjective. English words have a habit of turning up in the constituent class where they are least expected! *Little* is about as thoroughly dependable as any word in the language. But it can occur as a noun very rarely.

Suppose instead that the first substitution has been for *squiggs.* Among the possibilities are:

> *The iggle pigs trazed wombly in the harlish goop.*
> *The iggle hogs trazed wombly in the harlish goop.*

These two give very different results. In the first, *pigs* is very probably a noun. In the second, *hogs* is probably a noun, but with a very appreciable possibility of being a verb. English words vary widely in the certainty with which they can, by themselves, be assigned to classes. Real ambiguity seldom occurs since only a coincidence of complementary uncertainties in several words will permit it.

Constituent class membership of various elements in a sentence is thus an important clue to structure. But like other clues discussed above, seldom definitive or decisive. It is not possible to deduce THE structure, only the MOST PROBABLE structure.

11.4   An example such as that just discussed seems like an excursion into unreality. One may well raise the question whether it does really have anything to do with the actual functioning of a language. The answer to this question must be that it does. Seldom do we see a sentence in which all the major words are unknown. But any student commonly sees sentences in which one or several words are unfamiliar. In a book used in some university courses is found the following:

> *The protonema is fixed to its substratum by rhizoids.*

Up to three words in this sentence may be unfamiliar (depending on the reader's background, of course). But the sentence structure is absolutely clear to any native speaker of English. The structural clues which might be yielded by the unfamiliar words are not needed; there are enough others.

Faced with a sentence of this sort, one might go to a dictionary for the meanings of the words. This is seldom done. Instead, the meanings are discovered from the context. The context consists of the whole discourse in which it occurs, the other words in the sentence, and particularly the sentence structure. If the sentence structure cannot be understood, there will be considerable difficulty in deducing the meaning of the hitherto unknown words. The ability to find the sentence structure without knowing the meaning of some of the words is an essential language skill.

The following sentences are not significantly more complex than that just given:

Die Gametangien entwickelnden Zweige unterscheiden sich bei den thallösen Jungermanien wenig von den sterilen.

Assez généralement, il est constitué par des graines mitochondriaux associés à de petits chloroplastes fusiformes ou lenticulaires privés d'amidon.

Unless you are a botanist, these will be good tests of your knowledge of German or French. If you really know these languages they should give you no more trouble than the English sentence above. Whether you know the meaning of *Gametangien* or *mitochondriaux* should not affect the matter at all. After all, very few Germans or Frenchmen know them either. If you cannot see the structure — easily — you will find great difficulty in discovering their meaning, with or without a dictionary. Indeed, some of these words are not likely to be in ordinary bilingual dictionaries at all.

One of the most serious weaknesses in American language teaching has been just here. Students are told in school that they must be absolutely sure of the meaning of every word. They learn rather well how to use a dictionary, but very poorly how to guess. In effect, they are being prohibited from learning to read German as the Germans do. Dictionaries are useful, of course, but they must be used properly. That means first guess, and then look it up. But the guess must be based on the sentence structure.

11.5   Throughout the argument in 11.2 and 11.3 was a constant appeal to word order. This is certainly one of the most fundamental of structural markers. Yet it is one which is easily overlooked or minimized. The significance becomes plain if the words are scrambled.

Goop harlish iggle in squiggs the the trazed wombly.

The native speaker sees no structure. This is not simply because the ICs are no longer adjacent. Such is not a necessary condition. Consider the utterance:

What are you looking for?

What . . . for and *are . . . looking* are constituents. They are not, however, merely discontinuous; they are discontinuous in a set and regular way. To make them continuous will just as surely destroy the intelligibility as to jumble the words in any other way:

*What for are looking you?

At first sight word order is simple enough. If there are two elements A and B, there are only two possible orders, AB and BA. Often enough one of these is required and the other excluded. Thus in English, articles precede nouns: *the man* not **man the*. But this sort of simplicity characterizes only part of sentence structure, and word order is often most difficult to describe meaningfully. Some constituents are positionally quite free. Thus either *Today I'm going to town.* or *I'm going to town today.* is acceptable. Sentence elements of the class of *today* show this sort of freedom in English.

Much more difficult are the cases where order is neither very rigidly fixed nor very free, but generally fixed with a very minor degree of freedom. In English the common order is subject—verb—object. It is also possible to have object—subject—verb. The latter is very much less frequent. Moreover, it seems not at all natural with many sentences. It is most common in a few rather stereotyped utterances: *This I must see.* The limitations are subtle and have not yet been satisfactorily defined. It is particularly difficult to determine what part of the restrictions are grammatical and what stylistic. Yet a satisfactory statement is contingent upon distinguishing these two clearly.

Word order may be affected by the presence or absence of some third element. Again the frequent and simple cases are easily stated. Thus in German the order is typically subject—verb, but this is reversed if certain elements precede. *Er geht* . . . . 'He goes.' but *Dann geht er* . . . . 'Then he goes.' The rarer and more complex situations can be puzzling. Worst of all are the instances where the presence of some other element merely conditions a change in the degree of freedom, or a change in preference, the order being somewhat free.

Word order and constituent class membership, the two basic structural markers, are of course completely interdependent. Constituent classes are defined by the ability of the members to occur in certain characteristic positions. These positions can be recognized or stated only in terms of relationships involving order. Word order can be defined only in terms of classes.

11.6   A recent newspaper carried the headline

Beethoven Works On Hess Program

Probably a number of other readers were startled as I was, taking *works* as a verb. Taking *works* to be a noun gives a less incongruous meaning, one which the article clearly confirms as the headline writer's intention. This kind of ambiguity is characteristic of a very special style of written English, largely restricted to headlines and telegrams. It arises, of course, from the omission of certain "small words," elements which contribute little or nothing to meaning, but function as pure structural signals.

These "small words" are commonly grouped as **function words.** The term is useful, but the concept is very difficult to define. There is a complete intergradation from items which are almost purely structural markers, to ones which have considerable lexical meaning and for which the function of marking structure is incidental. A function word is any word near one end of this continuum. How purely a structural signal it must be to qualify cannot be specified, and the limit of the group must be somewhat vague, and a matter of each linguist's opinion and convenience.

11.7   Perhaps the clearest examples in English are the **articles,** *the, a, some.* The greater number of nominal constructions contain one of these, almost always as the first member. They serve to signal the presence of a nominal and to mark one limit of the construction. In these functions, all three are equivalent. The differences mark either the subclass of the nominal phrase (see 14.4) or the position of the nominal in the discourse. In rather rare cases none of these grammatical factors exerts control, and the occurrence of one rather than another may signal a meaning difference. This is very much less common than it is popularly supposed, or than what the traditional grammars would lead one to believe. The pairs of contrasting sentences commonly advanced to illustrate the differences in meaning (*The man came.*: *A man came.*) are, for the most part, either artificial or cited out of context. Much of the grammatical control over the articles operates within stretches larger than single sentences, and so easily escapes the notice of grammarians.

Since articles are primarily structural devices, it is not surprising that languages show extreme variation in the matter. Many languages have none, others only one, others several. Apart from this the usages may be different not only in detail but also in broad outline. It is hardly ever safe to give, as many textbooks do, English articles as glosses for those of a second language.

The treatment of the articles of one language as equivalents of those in another has sometimes led to strange misunderstandings. For example, it has been said that Hebrew thought is less abstract than English, because, where an American would say *Gold is good.*, a Hebrew speaker would say /ṭóob hazzaaháab./, allegedly to be translated as 'The gold is good.', the latter being a less general statement than the regular English form. The fallacy is patently in equating the prefixed articles /haC-/ with *the,* so that /hazzaaháab/ must be 'THE gold' in contrast with /zaaháab/ 'gold,' and then reading the English distinctions into the resulting translation. The reason that there is no *the* in *Gold is good.* is that *gold* is a mass noun (see 14.4) and is signaled as such by the absence of *the.* With an English mass noun, *the* particularizes. In Hebrew there is no contrast of this sort. Therefore the argument about Hebrew being less able to generalize is irrelevant. Moreover, in a sentence of the pattern of /ṭóob hazzaaháab./, /haC-/ is used as a structural signal to mark the subject. It has nothing whatever to do with abstractness or concreteness in a context such as this. The whole alleged contrast fails, because /haC-/ is required by Hebrew structure in such a general statement, while the omission of *the* is required by English structure in an equivalent statement. Nothing which is required by the structure can signal any meaning.

Another instance in which the English article serves as a structural signal is seen in the contrast *a bowl or vessel*: *a bowl or a vessel*. The first implies that *bowl* and *vessel* are synonyms and no contrast between the two is intended. In the second, the intention is to contrast the two and imply that if the object is a *bowl*, it is not also a *vessel*. Such a contrast is not inherent in the *a* as such, but in the different structural relationships which the presence or absence of the *a* signals. Such a contrast may be marked by radically different means in various other languages.

11.8 Prepositions are another type of English function words. They most commonly occur as the initial word in prepositional phrases, and thus clearly mark this construction type. Prepositions differ markedly from articles in one very important respect. It is quite commonly the case that one preposition can be substituted for another with attendant change of meaning. That is to say, prepositions contrast very much more sharply with one another than do articles. For this reason they have a much greater part in signaling meaning.

It is, therefore, the mere fact that a word is a preposition which is structurally most significant. That is, the structure-signaling function is a property, not of any given preposition as much as it is of the constituent class of prepositions. In this respect a preposition is not greatly different from a noun. It may be no more significant structurally that a given word is a preposition than that another is a noun. This observation would seem to seriously weaken the distinction between function words and other word types.

There are, however, some other ways in which prepositions differ from nouns, and these may partially justify the distinction. For one thing there are comparatively few prepositions, in contrast to a very large number of nouns. Moreover, the stock of nouns in English is continually changing. Of the new words that flood the English language every year, most are nouns. New prepositions are rare. The probability of a new article in the next decade is entirely negligible. The distributions of nouns and prepositions are quite different. For example, *man* is a very common noun. Yet there are whole books in which the word does not appear at all. *In* is a common preposition. It would probably be possible to write a book without *in*, but it would be a very artificial exercise. Whether a given noun occurs in a book depends very largely on the subject matter. Not so with the prepositions. They have less meaning, and more direct involvement in grammar, and hence occur more uniformly through English texts of all sorts.

These remarks indicate the characteristics of the ideal function word. It should be a member of a relatively small constituent class with a fixed membership. Its occurrence in a corpus should be highly independent of the subject matter, literary type, or style. Any item approximating these qualifications is likely to be highly involved in structure signaling and easily recognized as such. They may conveniently be called **function words.**

11.9 In many languages there occurs a special syntactic device known as **government.** This means that certain inflectional forms are used primarily to signal the place of the word in a construction. When nouns are involved (the most familiar instance), these special categories are known as **cases.** In such a language, each noun occurs in a small paradigm of forms. Each form is restricted to a certain list of syntactic positions, and hence contributes to marking the structure. Each form in this paradigm is said to represent some case. There is considerable variation in the number of cases and the ways in which the several cases contrast within the system.

The minimum number of cases is, of course, two. This is found in many languages, among them Masai of East Africa. Both subject and object follow the verb, but are clearly distinguished by the case of the noun. The cases differ only in tone, and the morphology is quite complex with numerous inflectional subclasses, two of which are illustrated:

/ɛ́dɔ́l ɛmbártá/	'He sees the horse.'
/ɛ́dɔ́l ɛmbartá/	'The horse sees him.'
/ɛ́dɔ́l ɛntíto/	'He sees the girl.'
/ɛ́dɔ́l ɛntitó/	'The girl sees him.'

In Sanskrit there are eight cases:

	'love'	'goddess'	
nominative	/kaamas	deevii	subject of a sentence
accusative	kaamam	deeviim	direct object
instrumental	kaame ena	deevyaa	attributive to predicate or sentence

dative	kaamaaya	deevyaai	indirect object
ablative	kaamaat	deevyaas	attributive to predicate or sentence
genitive	kaamasya	deevyaas	attributive to a noun
locative	kaamee	deevyaam	attributive to predicate or sentence
vocative	kaama	deevi/	loosely connected to sentence

The uses listed are merely typical. Most of the cases have subsidiary uses of various sorts. Three, the instrumental, ablative, and locative, are used in very much the same syntactic positions (not identically!) but often contrast in the semantic relationship signaled. The instrumental is commonly translatable by English 'with,' ablative by 'from,' and locative by 'in,' but again, there is considerable variation in this.

Latin and Greek have case systems very similar to that of Sanskrit, but with fewer cases. In Latin the instrumental is lacking, and the locative is found in only a few nouns. In Greek the instrumental, ablative, and locative are missing.

In Finnish there are fifteen cases:

nominative	*talo*	'house'	subject
genitive	*talon*		'of'
accusative	*talon*		object
inessive	*talossa*		'in'
elative	*talosta*		'out of'
illative	*taloon*		'into'
adessive	*talolla*		'on,' 'at'
ablative	*talolta*		'from'
allative	*talolle*		'to'
essive	*talona*		'as'
partitive	*taloa*		'(part) of'
translative	*taloksi*		'(changes) into'
abessive	*talotta*		'without'
instructive	*taloin*		'with,' 'by'
comitative	*taloine*		'together with'

Such a system is different from that of Sanskrit in two very important ways. A great deal more of the contrasts between the cases seem to be semantic rather than merely structural. As a result it is easiest to describe the use of these cases in terms of positions of objects or the like rather than simply by the syntactic structure they signal. In this respect they are much like English prepositions: classes of cases signal structure, but the specific case signals something else. Moreover, it is comparatively simple to cut off the case endings in Finnish, and very much more difficult in Sanskrit. The Finnish case system seems in many respects intermediate between the Sanskrit system and the English system of prepositions. Indeed, we might think of the Finnish case-suffixes as essentially a system of postpositions ("prepositions" is usually reserved for elements which precede) lightly fused onto the noun. Case is thus very similar to certain kinds of systems of function words. If many languages are examined, various intergradations between systems of case and systems of function words may be found.

Hindi shows one kind of intergradation rather clearly. There are three patterns to consider: (1) Nouns occur in two forms, the selection of which is determined by the structure. /lərke/ 'boy' occurs before postpositions, /lərka/ in most other places. These are traditionally called oblique and nominative. (2) Certain postpositions occur directly after nouns: /mẽ/ 'in,' /se/ 'from,' /pər/ 'on,' /ko/ 'to,' /ka/ 'of,' /ke/ (not translatable), /ne/ (marks agent of past transitive verbs). These all have a large element of structure marking in their use. (3) A much longer list of postpositions, including /nice/ 'under,' /sath/ 'with'. . . occur after /ke/. /lərke ke sath/ 'with the boy,' /lərke ka bap/ 'the father of the boy,' /lərke ne kəha/ 'The boy said,' /lərka kəhta hæ/ 'The boy is saying.' The contrasting forms typified by /lərka/ : /lərke/ are clearly case, though they have very little signaling function, since a postposition is almost always present after the oblique, and never after the nominative. The set including /mẽ/, /se/, might be considered, with a bit less justification, also as case markers. Of these /ko ka ke ne/ have very nearly pure structure-marking function. Moreover, pronouns have fused forms: /mere sath/ 'with me,' not / *mʊjh ke sath/, /mera bap/ 'my father' not / *mʊjh ka bap/. The remaining postpositions, however, are very clearly not case markers but function words. It is relatively unimportant what labels we apply, of course; the important thing is that we must recognize that there are here three types of structure: One clearly case, one clearly a system of function words, and one intermediate between the two. If we call the latter "case," then we must be clear that there are two layers of case structure; if we call them function words, we must be clear that there are two very different systems of function words.

11.10 In English, case is restricted to pronouns. The difference between *I* and *me* or *he* and *him* is one of case. Thus in *I saw him.*, the form *I* and *him* rather than *me* and *he* assist in marking the structure. However, in English, word order alone is used for this purpose with most nominals. The sentence, *Paul saw Mary.*, is fully as clear, though there is one less structure marker. The result of this is that most Americans rely very little on the case forms, even when they are available. If a group of Americans are instructed to correct such sentences as **Me saw Paul.* or **Mary saw he.*, a majority will make them *I saw Paul.* and *Mary saw him.*, rather than *Paul saw me.* and *He saw Mary.* This may be taken to indicate that, when the facts of word order and case form are in conflict, native speakers of English will consider word order as the more significant. Case is a very marginal feature in English syntax.

The situation is quite otherwise in some other languages. In Latin, most nouns show case forms which mark the sentence structure much more clearly than do the cases of English pronouns. Moreover, they have much greater functional significance in Latin than in English. For example, 'Paul saw Mary.' might be expressed:

Paulus Mariam vidit.	*Mariam Paulus vidit.*
Paulus vidit Mariam.	*Mariam vidit Paulus.*
Vidit Paulus Mariam.	*Vidit Mariam Paulus.*

Any one of the six would be clear, since the inflectional suffix *–us* marks *Paulus* as subject, and *–am* marks *Mariam* as forming, with *vidit*, the predicate. Though all are intelligible, not all are equally "good." There are strong preferences for one as against the others, but at various periods in the history of the language these preferences have been different.

It is sometimes said that because of the highly developed inflectional system of Latin, word order was unimportant. This is a gross overstatement. In every language word order has important syntactic functions. The example just quoted is exceptional in Latin in allowing absolute freedom of word order. Every language has some definable instances of rigidly fixed word order and some definable freedom of word order. All that can fairly be said is that in Latin, word order is less important as a syntactic device than in English. It is still of great importance. Languages differ more in the relative importance assignable to various syntactic devices than they do in the inventory of such devices. Only the very specialized syntactic devices, such as government, are not essentially universal in languages.

11.11 Government is not restricted to nouns. In some languages other parts of speech occur in two or more forms which serve primarily to signal the place of that word in the sentence structure. Thus in Zulu, adjectives have different forms when attributive to a noun than when forming a predicate:

Umuntu omkhulu uzwa.	'The big man hears.'
Umuntu mkhulu. ·	'The man is big.'
Inkosi endala izwa.	'The old chief hears.'
Inkosi indala.	'The chief is old.'

Omkhulu and *endala* are adjectives in the attributive position following the nouns *umuntu* and *inkosi*. *Mkhulu* and *indala* are adjectives in the predicate position. There is a very similar contrast marking the position of a verb in a sentence:

Umuntu uyohamba.	'The man will travel.'
Umunto oyohamba uzwa.	'The man who will travel hears.'

Uyohamba is a form of the verb used as a predicate. *Oyohamba* is a form used attributively to a noun. Note the close parallelism of the verb forms with the adjective forms, and the very sharp contrast in the English equivalents. In English, predicate use of an adjective is marked by the function word *is;* attributive use of a verb phrase by the function word *who.*

It is not unusual to have special forms of verbs to indicate attribution of the verb or its clause to another verb. For example, in Kâte of New Guinea:

/nɔnɔ nɔpe valeve?/	'I ate, then he came.'
/nɔnɔ nɔme valepo/	'He ate, then I came.'

/valeve?/ 'he came' and /valepo/ 'I came' are main verbs; /nɔpe/ 'I ate' and /nɔme/ 'he ate' are subordinate verbs. The endings /–ve?/ and /–po/ signal not only the subject, but also the place of the verb in the sentence, and similarly with /–pe/ and /–me/.

11.12   Another device to indicate structure is **concord**. This means that certain words are required to take forms which correspond in specified ways with certain other words. There is very little concord in present-day English. The clearest instance is with the words *this* and *that*, which are required to show concord in number with any noun with which they are associated. Thus we say *that boy* but *those boys*, and similarly *this boy* and *these boys*. These are clear instances of concord, but they have relatively little functional value in English because they are isolated vestiges.

Latin has a much better-developed system of adjective-noun concord. Every adjective must agree with its noun in three categories: number, gender, and case.

filius bonus	'the good son'	(sing. masc. nominative)
filii boni	'of the good son'	(sing. masc. genitive)
puella bona	'the good girl'	(sing. fem. nominative)
puellarum bonarum	'of the good girls'	(plur. fem. genitive)

Moreover, Latin concord serves a syntactic function, since occasionally only the concord indicates the immediate constituents. Consider the following examples:

filius domini bonus   'the good son of the master'

filius domini boni   'the son of the good master'

Concord may involve various inflectional categories. In Hebrew, nouns in apposition must show concord in gender, number, and definiteness. The latter refers to the presence or absence of a prefix usually translated 'the,' or to certain equivalent conditions. For example:

/mélek gaadóol/	'a great king' (sing. masc. indef.)
/hammélek haggaadóol/	'the great king' (sing. masc. def.)
/malkáa gədooláa/	'a great queen' (sing. fem. indef.)

/məlaakíim gədoolíim/ 'great kings' (plur. masc. indef.)
/hamməlaakíim habbəruukíim/ 'the fortunate kings' (plur. masc. def.)

11.13 Concord of the head noun of the subject with the verb or other head word of the predicate is also common. By **head** is meant that constituent which seems to serve as the center of any construction. Here also, there is some trace in English. The $\{-Z_3\}$ form of the verb is a concord form indicating that the subject is third person singular. It occurs only in the present.

Latin shows a comparable type of subject-verb concord much more fully developed. All verb forms have distinct singular and plural forms:

> *Filius vidit.* 'The son saw.' (sing.)
> *Filii viderunt* 'The sons saw.' (plur.)

This type of concord differs from the adjective-noun concord of Latin in that gender and case are not involved.

Hebrew has a similar type of concord. In this instance both gender and number are involved:

/zaakár hammélek/ 'The king remembered.' (masc. sing.)
/zaakəráa hammalkáa/ 'The queen remembered.' (fem. sing.)
/zaakərúu hamməlaakíim/ 'The kings remembered.' (masc. plur.)

In Hebrew a predicate can be a verb, a noun, or various longer constructions. When the predicate is a noun, the same type of concord occurs as when it is a verb. That is, there must be agreement in number and gender. Since the subject is always definite and the predicate indefinite, a subject-predicate sentence is clearly distinguishable from a construction of two nouns in apposition, by the different type of concord:

/gaadóol hammélek/ 'The king is great.' (a sentence)
/mélek haggaadóol/ 'The great one is king.' (a sentence)
/hammélek haggaadóol/ 'The great king' (not a sentence)

11.14 Concord is one instance of a relationship which may exist between constituents other than those which are ICs of some construction. For example, in the Latin sentence *Filius bonus est.* 'The son is good.', gender concord occurs between *filius* and *bonus*. The immediate constituents of the sentence, however, are *filius* and *bonus est*. The relationship may be diagramed:

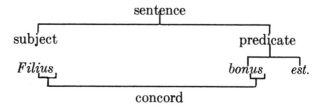

Government may also cut across IC structure in this way.

11.15 Both the English sentence, *The man carries.*, and the Latin sentence, *Vir portat.*, show concord between subject and predicate. But there is a very significant difference, which comes out if a longer series of sentences is examined:

Vir portat.	'The man carries.'
Viri portant.	'The men carry.'
Portat.	'He carries.'
Portant.	'They carry.'

The difference is that the Latin verb may stand alone, whereas the English verb must have an expressed subject. The reason for this is that the Latin verb contains within it an expression of the subject; the English does not. In a sentence such as *Vir portat.*, there are two indications of the subject: *vir* 'man' in the nominative, the usual case for the subject, and the suffix *–t* 'he.' The subject-predicate concord of Latin is a requirement that the two expressions of the subject must be consistent. The subject-predicate concord of English is merely a requirement that a third-person singular subject must have a certain verb form, but this form does not express the subject. Some consider this distinction sufficient that the two types should be differently labeled. In this case, the Latin type is called **cross-reference,** and the English type **concord.** But there is so much that the two have in common that it seems better to consider cross-reference as merely a special form of concord. The two are sometimes quite difficult to distinguish clearly.

11.16 The English examples discussed up to this point were deliberately presented in orthography rather than phonemic transcription. Enough structural signals are commonly present in spelled English to make sentences intelligible. But this is not always true. In an earlier draft of this text I wrote: *What thinking Americans do about language is* . . . . When I reread the script, this sentence seemed irrelevant until I realized that the written form is ambiguous. I had read it as meaning 'What is done about language by thinking Americans is . . . .' whereas I had written it to mean 'What thinking about language is done by Americans is . . . .' If this sentence is read aloud, there is no ambiguity. It can be read to carry either meaning, but not both simultaneously.

The ambiguity rests in different ways of organizing the words into constituents. The intention was that *Americans do about language* should be a constituent, not *thinking Americans*. There is nothing in the written form to signal this. But in speech these relationships are clearly marked by stress and intonation. Perhaps the most usual way of reading this sentence in either sense will be with two intonation contours, the first of which ends with /→/. The position of this /→/ will always mark a major division in the utterance. If the /→/ occurs at the end of *thinking*, only the intended meaning is possible. If there is no /→/ here but there is one after *Americans*, the other meaning is indicated.

We may see how this system works by considering again the sentence which was discussed so extensively in the last chapter. This can be read several ways. Probably the most usual would be

/²ðìy+ôwld+mǽn+huw+³lívz+ðêr²⁻²həz+góʜntuw+ìz+³sə́nz+hâws¹↘/

There are two intonation contours in this pronunciation. The terminal of the first falls at the major constituent break in the sentence. If the sentence were spoken more slowly, a different pronunciation would probably occur. One possibility would be

/²ðìy+³ówld+mǽn²⁻²hùw+³lívz+ðêr²↗²həz+³góʜn²⁻²tùw+ìz+³sə́nz+hâws¹↘/

In this pronunciation, the four intonation contours coincide with the four constituents at the second level in the hierarchy. Moreover, the terminal falling at the first cut is /↗/, while those at the second cuts are /→/. The intonation thus serves to mark the two top levels of IC cuts with precision.

We may arrange the English open transition and terminals in order of rank /+ → ↗ ↘/. In general, higher ranking cuts in the discourse are marked by higher ranked phonemes in this set. However, not only the terminals but also the pitch contours as wholes serve to mark structure. If instead of /232 → 232 ↗ 232 → 231 ↘/, the sequence of intonation contours had been /232 → 233 ↗ 232 → 231 ↘/ the structure would probably have been quite different. /233 ↗/ ordinarily occurs at the end of a sentence, whereas /232 ↗/ seldom does.

11.17   A system of transitions and terminals of this sort can often mark structure quite unambiguously. However, it is likely that there is no language in which such a system always does so. There are certain difficulties which must inevitably upset it. First, there are not enough kinds of markers. In English there are four ranked elements which might mark cuts. If the highest were to mark only sentence ends, then four levels of cuts could be marked within the sentence, the lowest being marked by the absence of any of these. But many sentences, even of moderate length, have more levels of IC cuts than this. Indeed, this is true of the sentence just discussed. In very complex sentences, of course, a very extensive system would be needed. Second, to mark the structure when some constituents are discontinuous requires something more than mere marking of cuts and their rank. Third, the contrasts between /↘/ and /↗/ in particular, and with /→/ to a lesser extent, are used for other purposes as well. In association with the preceding pitches, not only do they mark constituents; they also mark the kind of such constituents and the type of construction in which they are found. Thus sentences ending in /233 ↗/ are usually questions. Inevitably there must be conflicts between the use of terminals to mark rank of IC cuts and to mark other things. Fourth, there are occasional situations in which terminals or transitions are not used where the IC structure has a cut, or where one occurs but there is no cut.

For example, short sentences generally have at least /+/ between subject and predicate. In moderately long sentences there is usually a /→/ at this place, and in long sentences there may be a /↗/. Quite often this is the highest ranking cut within the sentence, and it is marked by the highest ranking of /+ → ↗/ within the sentence. However, if the subject is a personal pronoun and the first element in the predicate is *is, are, has, have, had, will,* or *would,* there is not even a /+/ in normal fast speech.

/²àyl⁺³gów¹↘/   *I will go.*   also spelled   *I 'll go.*
/²hìyz⁺³góʜn¹↘/   *He has gone.*   *He's gone.*

In both these sentences the cut marked by /+/ is of lower rank than the one before it without such a marker. The structure is clear enough, because the list of exceptions is familiar to every speaker of English and easily stated by a linguist. The converse is illustrated by certain words which are said with /+/, even some which seem to be best treated as single morphemes, e.g., /pléy⁺tòw/ *Plato.*

English stress and intonation is far from being an automatic marker of sentence structure. It is not possible to deduce the IC structure simply from the stress and intonation in all cases, though in a very large number of sentences it is possible. In many sentences these features are the decisive evidence for the structure. In most they lend support to and are supported by the various other markers. That is, stress and intonation function as part of a whole system of structure markers, and it is misleading to try to separate them from the others. In spoken English, however, these features are probably the dominant elements in the syntax-signaling system.

11.18   It is probable that all or very nearly all spoken languages have some sort of intonation or intonation-like system. In many, including some that are otherwise rather well known, we cannot even identify this system in speech. This does not mean that it does not exist, but probably only that it is so intertwined with other features of the structure that we have not as yet been able to sort the systems out correctly. In other languages intonation systems have been identified, but their functioning is not as yet understood. In spite of this, it would seem safe to assert that intonation or intonation-like systems are highly important structure markers in most languages, and more important than more obvious systems in many.

We have very little idea of the range of phenomena that will be found when more intonation systems have been studied. We would expect, *a priori*, that there would be some rather obvious differences from the type exemplified by English. Perhaps there may be some basic similarities, but we cannot at present identify what we may expect these to be. In short, we do not as yet know enough about intonation systems that any significant generalizations can be made. We may, however, feel confident that progress in the understanding of intonation systems, and the development of better methods of analysis of intonation, may have tremendous importance for the further development of descriptive linguistics, and particularly for syntax.

Transformations

12.1 A favorite exercise in public school English has been the changing of sentences from one form to another. Thus from a sentence like

> *John is writing a letter.*

may be formed, among others, the following:

> *John isn't writing a letter.*
> *Is John writing a letter?*
> *A letter is being written by John.*

Very little is ordinarily given by way of clearly formulated rules for these processes, yet students seem to learn the technique more or less readily. Given the same sentence to start with, and the same rather simple instructions (e.g., "Make this negative."), there will be a very high degree of agreement in the answer. All this would suggest that such exercises must reflect some significant structural relationships in the English language. If so, they are worth careful investigation and formal statement.

When such changes are discussed at all, it is generally in terms of the meanings of the sentences. But this cannot be very exact, and is seldom very helpful. For example, it is easy enough to label *Is John writing a letter?* as a question. But what is the meaning of a question? Indeed, we cannot even give a good definition of the word 'question.' There is, of course, nothing unusual in finding difficulties in describing meanings, or in making clear statements about language on the basis of meaning. But with questions, it seems particularly difficult and unsatisfactory.

On the other hand, a little examination will show that changes of the sorts illustrated above can be described structurally — that is, in terms of the addition of elements, the rearranging of elements, or the altering of the form of elements. What specific portions of the sentence are involved, and how, can be very exactly stated. This is done, not in terms of their meanings, but on the basis of their structural position within the sentence. Moreover, the descriptions so arrived at have very wide applicability. For example, almost any English sentence not already negative, may be made into a negative sentence in a way very similar to that shown. This can then be formulated into a rule of considerable power, precisely the kind of rule that we desire in grammars.

12.2   Not all changes are of this sort. Thus the same sentence might be altered to

John is penning an epistle.

Native speakers of English will recognize a very significant relationship between this sentence and its prototype. But they also sense that the relationship here is of an entirely different sort. The sentence structure is not changed; substitutions are made within the same structural framework. From a structural point of view

Mary is baking a cake.

is just as closely related to the original. There is a difference, of course. It lies in the fact that *penning* is a "synonym" of *writing*, whereas *baking* is not. Synonymy is not a precisely definable concept, nor indeed a structural concept. Changes of this sort are therefore not structurally describable. Moreover, they are of much more restricted scope. Clearly, not all operations of altering sentences to related sentences have the same linguistic interest. The ones involving structural changes stand apart from all the others. They will be called transformations.

12.3   A **transformation** is a statement of the structural relation of a pair of constructions which treats that relation as though it were a process. Hence, it is normally stated in the form of rules which may be applied to one of the pair — an **input** — altering it to produce the other — an **output**. Note that transformations are directional. Some can be described in either direction, though practically we must choose one. Others can be described effectively only in one way.

12.4   As an example we might consider the following set of sentence pairs. These are obviously a sample from a very much larger number.

1. *John is writing a letter.*   *John isn't writing a letter.*
2. *Jim has been trying to do it.*   *Jim hasn't been trying to do it.*
3. *James will come tomorrow.*   *James won't come tomorrow.*
4. *Ruth was a beautiful girl.*   *Ruth wasn't a beautiful girl.*
5. *Mary could have been there.*   *Mary couldn't have been there.*
6. *His father walked home.*   *His father didn't walk home.*
7. *My friends like chess.*   *My friends don't like chess.*
8. *The car runs well.*   *The car doesn't run well.*
9. *Sam started running im-*   *Sam didn't start running im-*
     mediately.   *mediately.*

If we can find a single clearly statable rule to cover all of these, we may describe these nine sentence pairs as examples of a single transformation. The sentences seem to fall into two groups. For sentences 1 to 5 a simple rule is immediately evident: *–n't* is added as a suffix to the first word in the verb phrase. This is true whether the verb phrase consists of a single word as in 4, or several as in 2 and 5. There is a minor complication in 3: *will + –n't* yields *won't*. We can easily show that this is quite regular, a fact about the language which would have to be described in any case. Pairs 6 to 9 seem to follow a different rule. Before the *–n't* is added, *walked* is changed to *did walk* and comparable changes are made in the other cases. If we try applying the pattern of the first five pairs without this intermediate step we get such very strange outputs as

* His father walkedn't home.

These two rules may be combined into one, if certain conditions can be met. The first of these is that we find a clear conditioning which determines which applies. This we can do: *–n't* is never added to words like *walked*. Which of the two rules applies is determined by whether or not the first word is one of the small list (*is, are, was, has, can, might* — an English-speaking student can easily complete the list) to which *–n't* can be added. If not, it is changed to a verb phrase which starts with *did, do, does*. A second condition which must be met is to find a clear statement as to how this change, *walked* to *did walk*, etc., is to be described.

12.5   The following sentence pairs may help with this problem:

10. *The boy ran away.*   *The boy didn't run away.*
11. *The boy did run away.*   *The boy didn't run away.*

These present no difficulty for the rules just mentioned for the negative transformation. In 11 the verb phrase begins with *did*, and *–n't* is added directly. In 10 *ran* is a word to which *–n't* cannot be added; it is therefore changed to *did run*. The interesting feature is that the outputs in the two pairs SEEM to be identical. Actually this is something of an illusion. There are a number of different pronunciations ·for a writing like *The boy didn't run away*. Only one factor, the position of the sentence stress, needs to be noted here. There are at least the following pairs:

10. a. *The boy ran awáy.*   *The boy didn't run awáy.*
     b. *The boy rán away.*   *The boy didn't rún away.*
     c. *The bóy ran away.*   *The bóy didn't run away.*
11.   *The boy díd run away.*   *The boy dídn't run away.*

This seems clearly the natural way to match them up. The sentences in each pair have the sentence stress in the same place. *Did run* occurs in the input only when the sentence stress falls on *did*. (A sentence like *The boy did run awáy.* sounds at best extremely archaic, and certainly cannot be considered normal modern English.) It follows, then, that *did* occurs in such sentences ONLY either when *–n't* is suffixed or when it receives the sentence stress. There are other uses of *did*, but most of them fit into the same pattern. The auxiliary *did* occurs in English only where sentence structure demands it. It is never required by the meaning, and it never means anything at all. The difference between *The boy ran awáy.* and *The boy díd run away.* is not a matter of the presence or absence of *did*, only of the stress position. *Did* is there only to provide a meaningless carrier for that stress in the required position. If anything else were available, *did* would not occur. Compare

    The boy will run awáy.   *The boy wíll run away.*

Did, do, does, done (the verb *do* in all its forms) as auxiliaries are always completely meaningless — mere position makers. *Do* may also occur as a main verb, in which case it does have meaning: *I díd do my homework.*

The morphemes $\{-Z_3\}$ and $\{-D_1\}$ can occur only in the first word of a verb phrase. If that word ceases to be first by addition of $\{do\}$, these morphemes must shift to the new first word. Thus

walked (= $\{walk\}$ + $\{-D_1\}$) becomes *did walk* (= $\{do\}$ + $\{-D_1\}$
                                                 + $\{walk\}$)
like   (= $\{like\}$)   becomes *do like* (= $\{do\}$ + $\{like\}$)
runs   (= $\{run\}$ + $\{-Z_3\}$) becomes *does run* (= $\{do\}$ + $\{-Z_3\}$
                                               + $\{run\}$)

Both these rules (addition of *do* and position of $\{-Z_3\}$ and $\{-D_1\}$) are ones that will be needed anyway. They are not proposed merely to facilitate the definition of the negative transformation. This is, of course, the best possible recommendation of the result so far: All the rules are quite general. All the sentence pairs we have discussed can then be subsumed under one rule — the negative transformation — plus in some cases the operation of certain other rules, but these are also quite general.

12.6 We cannot speak of "the question transformation" in English, since there are a number of different ones, no one of which has any clear pre-eminence. But we can readily describe each of this rather heterogeneous family of transformations. Some are of considerable interest. Among them are

12. *John is writing a letter.*   *Who is writing a letter?*
13.   *Is John writing a letter?*
14.   *What is John writing?*
15.   *John is writing a letter, isn't he?*

Of these, number 12 seems the simplest. A question word (*who* or *what*) is merely substituted for the subject of the sentence. The intonation remains the same. This is a simple example of a transformation which can be described in only one direction. *Mary is writing a letter.*, *That old man over there is writing a letter.*, and many other input sentences all yield this same output. If the process is reversed, taking the question to be the input, how is the proper output to be selected from the multitude of sentences which are paired with it?

Number 13 is more complex. The first word in the verb phrase is transposed to the first position in the sentence. It must be one of the same list of forms as was found taking the suffix *—n't*. If it isn't, the verb phrase is first altered by the addition of a *do*, thus:

> *John wrote a létter.* → * *John did write a létter.* →
> *Did John write a létter?*

The intermediate stage is marked with * because it does not occur in that form in normal use. In pronunciation there is, of course, also a change in intonation. Commonly it is from /231↘/ to /233↗/.

Number 14 is also best described as involving a series of changes. First, the first word in the verb phrase is moved, as in number 13. Then a question word is substituted for some sentence element, and this is transposed to the initial position:

> *John is writing a letter.* → *Is John writing a letter?* →
> **Is John writing what?* → *What is John writing?*

This illustrates another very common characteristic of transformations. When two or more apply in one sentence, it is usually easier to describe them in one fixed order; sometimes it is extremely difficult or impossible to use another order. Almost always the form in which the rules are stated must be changed if they are not applied in the same order.

Number 15 involves both change of the intonation (commonly to /232 →/) and the addition of a second clause. This consists of only two words. The first is identical with the first word in the input's verb phrase, except that only one of the two must have the suffix *—n't*. The other word is the proper pronoun to substitute for the subject. This is pronounced with the intonation /233↗/.

12.7   Describing various types of questions in this way does not merely elucidate their structure. It also provides a good basis for understanding some of the dialectal or stylistic variations which occur. The following two outputs from a single input will illustrate:

16. *John is writing to his mother.*   *To whom is John writing?*
17.   *Who is John writing to?*

Examined as they stand, these two results have quite different sentence structure. But looked at in terms of transformations, they are seen to be very much more similar. The intermediate steps are something like the following:

John is writing to his mother. → *Is John writing to his mother?*

→ **Is John writing to* $\begin{Bmatrix} whom \\ who \end{Bmatrix}$ → $\begin{cases} To\ whom\ is\ John\ writing? \\ Who\ is\ John\ writing\ to? \end{cases}$

In the last stage they differ as to how much of the sentence is transposed. The transposition of a whole phrase, *to whom*, is found almost exclusively in literary and quite formal English. Colloquial usage very seldom transposes more than a single word. (Colloquial usage, including informal writing, is also much more likely to use *who* than *whom*, particularly when separated from its conditioning context.) The result is sentences with final prepositions and various other "errors." As is often the case, these "errors" are not the result of "loose grammar," but of very rigid and explicit patterns. Most colloquial English usage calls for transposition of the single question word, result what may.

In this discussion there is no desire to evaluate either pattern. The intention is rather to point out that much of our prescriptive grammar, and equally much of the rebellion against it, is vitiated by bad diagnosis. Linguistic description is neutral in such questions. Its task is to give a clear and significant description of usages which actually occur, and when usages differ, to make clear and significant statement as to how they differ. That is, descriptive linguistics can provide the diagnosis on the basis of which an evaluation can be made. Every thoughtful speaker must evaluate conflicting usages; he will do so more effectively with a clearer understanding of the facts. One of the strengths of a transformational description of this type of question is the clarity with which it sets forth this particular difference in usage.

12.8 In the process of operating these transformations we find that not only are words shifted around in sentences, but even affixes are moved from one word to another. Not infrequently this causes rather complex changes in forms. For example, applying two of the transformations we have just discussed in succession:

John will go. → *John won't go.* → *John won't go, will he?*

With the addition of *–n't*, the form of *will* was changed. Then in the second operation the *–n't* had to be removed, restoring the original form of *will*. This constant shifting of forms is awkward and wasteful. As long as every stage in our description is plagued with these operations, many of them only to be later undone, transformational description is unnecessarily complex.

One way around this difficulty is to operate not with sentences but with "strings" of morphemes, leaving the adjustment to the proper form to the last:

{John} {will} {go} → /²ĵâʜn⁺wìl⁺³gów¹↘/ *John will go.*

↓

{John} {will} {–n't} {go} → /²ĵâʜn⁺wòwnt⁺³gów¹↘/ *John won't go.*

↓

{John} {will} {–n't} {go} {will} {he}
　　→ /²ĵâʜn⁺wòwnt⁺³gów²⁻²wíliy³↗/ *John won't go, will he?*

So described, there are two quite distinct sets of operations. The vertical arrows indicate transformations. They carry one string of morphemes into another. The horizontal arrows represent **morphophonemic** operations. They give any string of morphemes a phonemic shape. (Or, if a written language is being described, a comparable set of operations gives it a graphic shape.) Morphophonemic operations are described as applying only after all transformations have been completed. This, of course, will require some restatement of the transformational rules discussed above. It will also require a slight redefinition of transformation, since transformations do not alter one sentence into another, but one string of morphemes into another. These strings may be said to underlie the sentences which we used in the presentation above.

12.9 The word "string" might easily be misleading. We must certainly mean more than merely some assortment of morphemes arranged in some linear order. Several reasons for this should be apparent from the discussion above. Many of the transformations must be stated in terms of an operation performed on a certain element in a certain position in the string. For example, many of these we have discussed involve the first word in the verb phrase. But if a string were merely a sequence of elements in linear order, the only position we might define would be something like "second element" or "third from the end." Some of the question transformations involve substitution of a question word for a constituent. This might consist of a single morpheme, or of a considerable number. If transformations are to apply to strings, strings must be assemblages of elements having constituent structure. When used in description in terms of transformations, "string" must mean a special sort of sequence of elements, which, because it is characterized by a constituent structure may be called a **structured string.**

Since transformations operate on structured strings, a grammar which is to describe transformations must first describe the construction of a set of structured strings. This can best be done in terms of very much the same concepts as have been described in Chapter 10.

12.10 When carried out consistently, the ideas just sketched result in a grammar quite characteristic in its organization and form of statement. Such a description is called a **transformational grammar.** It is claimed by some linguists that this type of statement can attain to a degree of precision, completeness, and conciseness not possible in any other way — in fact, that this technique can overcome certain limitations which are inherent in any other known form of description. Needless to say, these claims are not universally accepted. Both the technique and the claims imply a certain distinctive general theory of linguistics. This differs from other descriptive linguistic theories in certain ways that produce characteristic features in grammatical statements. Certain of these should be pointed out:

1. A transformational grammar is organized in three sections. The first of these describes certain strings of comparatively simple structure. The basic theory here is similar to that underlying all descriptions in terms of immediate constituents (see Chapter 10). For this reason, it is called the **constituent structure,** or by others, the **phrase structure,** segment of the grammar. The second, or

transformational section, describes all the transformations by which the output strings of the first section of the grammar are carried into **terminal strings,** sufficient in number to underlie all of the sentences of the language. The third is the **morphophonemic** section. Here are described all of the processes by which terminal strings are given shapes which can be identified as utterances or portions of utterances. Any transformational grammar must have all three, but some individual sentences may involve no transformations. That is to say, the transformational section may be by-passed in some sentences; the other two cannot.

2. Since in such a scheme, no matter of phonemic (or orthographic) form comes in until the third, morphophonemic, portion of the grammar, the greater part of the statement, is properly in terms of quite abstract symbols. If the symbols used should have a form reminiscent of a familiar spelling or of a phonemic transcription, this is of no particular significance. In most instances the symbols are more or less arbitrary letters representing classes of structures, often with subscripts representing subclasses. Some of these symbols bear no obvious meaning, being selected merely for convenience. The use of such abstract symbols gives a thoroughgoing transformational grammar an algebraic appearance. This. is often enhanced by the fact that the terminology and phraseology used in such grammars has been strongly influenced by that of mathematics. However, a transformational grammar is not properly any more mathematical than any other type of grammar in its basic features.

3. The statement is largely in the form of a set of rules. These are of two kinds. The first is of the form "X → Y + Z." This should be read as "X is to be rewritten as Y + Z." Such rules are referred to as **rewrite rules.** They have the effect of changing a symbolization, generally in the direction of making it more specific and explicit. For example, in one formulation of English grammar the starting point is the symbol S, roughly to be read as "sentence." The first rule is S → NP + VP. This substitutes for the very general representation, S, the more specific and explicit representation, NP + VP, roughly to be interpreted as "noun phrase plus verb phrase." This is not a statement that a sentence CONSISTS OF a noun phrase and a verb phrase. Many do, of course, but not all: e.g., *Come here!* lacks the noun phrase. Rather it is a

statement that all sentences (or only one set if there is another rewrite rule that starts from S) must be DESCRIBED IN TERMS OF a noun phrase and a verb phrase. Subsequent rules may have the effect of cutting out some of these structures.

The rewrite rule applies to any string wherein the proper symbols are found. The second type of rule, the **transformational rule,** is similar in many respects, but operates only on certain symbols in certain places within a constituent structure. Thus a rewrite rule applying to NP, will apply to any NP. But a transformational rule may apply to certain NPs only. For example, a transformation involving the moving of an NP in object position relates the following pair of sentences:

18. *I saw John yesterday.*   *John I saw yesterday.*

But cannot apply to an NP in some other position:

19. *I gave the money to the man with John.*
    *John I gave the money to the man with.

4. Transformational grammars are generally very explicit about the conditions under which any given rule can be applied. Careful attention is given to the order of application of rules. An effort is made to distinguish clearly between **optional** and **obligatory** rules, and between **recursive** rules (ones that can be applied repeatedly) and **non-recursive** rules. Properly, this is not a peculiarity of transformational grammars as such, but of all grammars which attempt to be thoroughly rigorous in their description.

5. A key word in all transformational grammar is **generate.** This is used in a sense taken from mathematics.

$$(x - a)^2 + (y - b)^2 = c^2$$

may be said to generate a set of circles in a plane defined by x and y. That means that for any given a, b, and c this equation defines one specific circle. For all possible values of a, b, and c it defines all possible circles in the plane concerned. In the same way, a transformational grammar consists of a set of statements which generate all possible sentences in a given language. Depending on the choices made wherever a choice is possible (whether to apply a certain optional rule, or which alternative to select when several are offered), it defines each specific sentence. In this sense, a particular running through of the grammar is not to be considered as CREATING a sentence, but more nearly as SELECTING a sentence from a pre-existing stock (the language) of all possible sentences. Thus the grammar might start with the symbol S and in a particular application of it end with /²ĵâʜn⁺wìl⁺³ɡów¹↘/. But the last expression does not represent anything not represented by the first. Rather S stands for ALL sentences in the language, and thus represents, among others, /²ĵâʜn⁺wìl⁺³ɡów¹↘/. The process of running through the grammar and making the required choices is a matter of singling out a specific sentence to replace the general symbol S. Nothing is created, increased, or added to; the meaning is instead very much narrowed. In much the same way $(x - 2)^2 + (y - 5)^2 = 3^2$ represents nothing not already completely covered by $(x - a)^2 + (y - b)^2 = c^2$, but only one specific instance out of the total set of circles. The selection is made by choosing values 2, 5, and 3 for a, b, and c.

12.11 At the beginning of this chapter a few transformations were described in terms of familiarly spelled sentences. Later it was shown that it would be preferable to work, not with sentences, but with structured strings. In the last section it was suggested that a transformational grammar, when formally stated would be quite different from the non-rigorous description above. Here will be given a more formal description of the pair of sentences with which the discussion began. Not all alternatives are stated at every step, but some are mentioned so that it will be clear where choices must be made and how it is that more than one sentence might come out. At each step the rule being applied is listed at the left and the form resulting from its application at the right. Braces around morpheme symbols have been omitted.

The description starts, of course, with the general expression for a sentence.

STEP 1.   S

The first rewrite rule is generally described as obligatory, that is, there is no other choice at this step:

STEP 2. S → NP + VP   NP + VP

There are a variety of ways in which the VP might be developed leading to a variety of sentence patterns: . . . *ran.*, . . . *is good.*,

... *saw him.*, etc. At this point a choice of rewrite rules will determine which type, in the broadest sense, will result.

STEP 3. $VP \rightarrow Verb + NP$ $NP + Verb + NP$

At the next step there are two alternatives, between which a choice must be made. In such a case a rewrite rule giving the alternatives can be stated in the following form:

STEP 4. $NP \rightarrow \begin{Bmatrix} NP_{sing} \\ NP_{pl} \end{Bmatrix}$ $NP_{sing} + Verb + NP$

The import of this rule is to demand a choice between singular and plural for each NP. It must be applied twice, since there are two occurrences of NP in the form resulting from step 3. These must be considered as two separate steps, since they are quite independent of each other. Moreover, one basic principle of this sort of grammar is that each rewrite in the constituent structure must replace just one symbol.

STEP 5. $NP_{sing} + Verb + NP_{sing}$

STEP 6. $Verb \rightarrow Aux + V$ $NP_{sing} + Aux + V + NP_{sing}$

STEP 7. $Aux \rightarrow C(M) + (have + en) + (be + ing)$
$$NP_{sing} + C + be + ing + V + NP_{sing}$$

The parentheses in this rule mean that a choice may be made. C must be used, M (which stands for *can, may, shall*, etc.) may be omitted, have + en and be + ing can be omitted. Of the optional elements only be + ing was selected. The next rule also presents some choices, but these are partly controlled by the context.

STEP 8. $C \rightarrow \begin{Bmatrix} Z_3 \text{ in the context } NP_{sing} \\ \emptyset \text{ in the context } NP_{pl} \\ \text{past in any context} \end{Bmatrix}$
$$NP_{sing} + Z_3 + be + ing + V + NP_{sing}$$

Next there are several alternatives for the rewriting of NP_{sing}, of which only two are listed here.

STEP 9. $NP_{sing} \rightarrow \begin{Bmatrix} D + N + \emptyset \\ N_{prop} \\ \text{etc.} \end{Bmatrix}$
$$N_{prop} + Z_3 + be + ing + V + NP_{sing}$$

STEP 10. $N_{prop} + Z_3 + be + ing + V + D + N + \emptyset$

The $\emptyset$ in the last rule points out the lack of an inflectional suffix in contrast to $NP_{pl} \rightarrow D + N + Z_1$.

The result of step 10 is an expression consisting of some symbols for specific morphemes, either affixes like Z_3 or stems of function words like *be*, and some symbols standing for classes of stems or words. The next four steps consist of substituting an actual member of the class for each class symbol:

STEP 11. $N_{prop} \rightarrow$ Mary, John, Henry, . . .
$$John + Z_3 + be + ing + V + D + N + \emptyset$$

STEP 12. V $\rightarrow$ write, read, take, . . .
$$John + Z_3 + be + ing + write + D + N + \emptyset$$

STEP 13. D $\rightarrow$ the, this, a, . . .
$$John + Z_3 + be + ing + write + a + N + \emptyset$$

STEP 14. N $\rightarrow$ ball, man, letter, . . .
$$John + Z_3 + be + ing + write + a + letter + \emptyset$$

The result of step 14 is a possible terminal string. Two courses of further development are open. We may apply certain transformations, or we may pass to the morphophonemic section of the grammar immediately. In the latter case there will be a variety of rules which must be applied, and no attempt will be made to give them in detail here. However, one type needs to be noticed. Certain affixes will regularly be combined with the following verbal element. In spelling the effect is as follows:

$$John + \underbrace{Z_3 + be} + \underbrace{ing + write} + a + \underbrace{letter + \emptyset}$$
John   *is*   *writing*   *a*   *letter.*

Or we may apply to the result of step 14 a transformation:

STEP 15. $NP + C + \begin{bmatrix} M \\ have \\ be \end{bmatrix} \ldots \rightarrow C + \begin{bmatrix} M \\ have \\ be \end{bmatrix} + NP \ldots$

$$\underbrace{Z_3 + be} + John + \underbrace{ing + write} + a + \underbrace{letter + \emptyset}$$
Is   *John*   *writing*   *a*   *letter?*

Again, the morphophonemic steps are not given in detail, but only suggested by showing the final result in spelling. Much the same set of rules applies, however, as did above.

12.12   At first reading, the last section seems to be a very elaborate and complex way of describing a pair of quite simple sentences. But such an evaluation is not entirely appropriate. To be sure a very much more simple description is possible: In *John is writing a letter.*, the first word is *John*, the second word is *is*, the third word is *writing, ...* But such a description tells us very little if anything about the sentence. It might be possible to make a somewhat more sophisticated description of the same anecdotal sort, but however detailed this might be, it would tell nothing whatever about the grammar of the sentence. A sentence has a grammar only as it stands in relation to other sentences as part of a language. Any speaker of English immediately sees something of the grammar in a sentence like *John is writing a letter.* This is only possible because he knows the language, and can fit this sentence into its place within the language. The sentence *apko kya cahɪye.* 'What do you want?' is just as grammatical, but the grammar is inaccessible to most readers of this book, simply because they cannot relate it to other sentences in Hindi. A grammatical description must place any given sentence in a framework which can be used to describe any sentence in the language, even though this requires making some statements which do not seem, superficially, to be of any great pertinence to the sentence at hand. Many features of the statement in the last section are not demanded by anything in the sentences being discussed, but by things in other (perhaps very many other) English sentences. At every point where a choice was presented, these two sentences were related to, and set off from, a host of other sentences. The statement did not merely describe the sentences in themselves, but rather put the two sentences into their place within the whole structure of the English language. The English language is an immensely complex thing, ramifying in many directions, and a description which does actually relate a single sentence to this complex structure cannot be very simple. One of the marvelous things about language is that any statement as short as that just given could in fact approach adequacy in relating these two sentences to the billions of billions of other sentences in the language.

In a statement of this sort, given with just two sentences in focus, the reasons for some of the features of the statement could not be made clear. To understand them, it would be necessary to trace out some of the consequences of other alternatives. An excerpt from a grammar cannot be as meaningful as a full grammar. To have given a full grammar of English, even if very much lacking in detail, would have been impossible here. What was given is a little like a full recounting of all the moves of the king's bishop in a championship chess game, mentioning the other pieces only when they fall directly in the path of the bishop.

There is another very important reason why the statement may seem unduly cumbersome. It attempted to state explicitly a number of things which are quite easily taken for granted. Every grammar leaves a great deal unsaid which the user must supply somehow from his "common sense" or "Sprachgefühl" or some other undefinable source. Much of this seems so obvious that to state it seems gratuitous. But research consists very largely of attempting to state the phenomena as explicitly as possible. Thus, Newton's law is traditionally said to have been found through dissatisfaction with treating the fall of an apple as simple and obvious, and was nothing more than an attempt to explain explicitly how it falls. Progress in linguistics must come largely by raising questions about the unstated phenomena, probing into them and attempting to make explicit statements in places where it had not previously been done. An explicit statement is not necessarily an acceptable statement. But it is often a testable statement. It always calls the attention of investigators to the question, and often provides a starting point toward a better formulation. Work on a transformational grammar of English has forced explicit statement at some points in the structure of the language and in general linguistic theory which had previously been passed by.

12.13 The introductory sections of this chapter centered around a small selection of sentence pairs related through a few transformations. The rules were not explicitly stated. Indeed, it would have been rather pointless to have given an explicit statement of the transformations without building this on an explicit statement of the underlying constituent structure. It should be pointed out, however, that a formal statement is possible. None of the sentences discussed would require the use of any very complex rules, and most of the rules would be quite general in application. Indeed, a proper writing of the rules might lead to a further step in generalization. For example, pairs 12 and 14 were described differently. But this is not necessary. Instead, the same sequence of transformational rules can be applied to produce both. The first fifteen steps in the generation are identical with that described in 12.11. Step 14 gives the string which, if taken directly through the morphophonemic rules, would give *John is writing a letter*. In the same way, the product of step 15 would yield *Is John writing a letter?*. As a string it is of the form:

STEP 15. $Z_3 + be + John + ing + write + a + letter + \emptyset$

The next step replaces an NP by a question word. There are two NPs in this string, *John*, and *a letter*. They belong to different classes, one which requires *who* as a substitute, and one that requires *what*.

STEP 16. $Z_3 + be + who + ing + write + a + letter + \emptyset$
      OR $Z_3 + be + John + ing + write + \quad what$

This is followed by an obligatory transformation which shifts any such question word to the initial position:

STEP 17.   who $+ Z_3 + be +$ $ing + write + a + letter + \emptyset$
      what $+ Z_3 + be + John + ing + write$

To these the same morphophonemic rules would apply. They would have the effect of taking them into a phonemic form familiarly associated with the spellings of examples 12 and 14:

| *Who* | *is* | | *writing* | *a letter?* |
| *What* | *is* | *John* | *writing?* | |

The other transformations discussed can be formally stated in much the same way.

A complete transformational grammar of English would, of course, list many more transformations than this small sample. Some of them would be rather different in general form and effect. In the following sections a few more will be mentioned in order to show the range of possibilities. All are, of course, capable of formal statement. But for the present purpose, it will be better to revert to the less rigorous style of discussion in which sentences are compared rather than strings, and in which only certain outstanding features are mentioned.

12.14 One type of transformation uses two or more inputs, combining them into one output. A very simple case is the following:

20. *The car stopped suddenly.*   *The car stopped suddenly and I*
    I was thrown against the   *was thrown against the wind-*
    windshield.   *shield.*

This particular transformation can be described in terms of nothing more than concatenation, the addition of a marker *and*, and appropriate adjustment of the intonation (or in writing of the punctuation). But the situation can be more complex:

21. *You have some bananas.*   *If you have any bananas, I*
    I would like about a dozen. *would like about a dozen.*

At first sight, sentence 21 would seem to come from **You have any bananas.* and *I would like about a dozen.* But the first of these two sentences seems quite unnatural. A little investigation will show that there is a very special relation between *any* and *some*. The one occurs in certain types of sentences, the other in other types. An adequate set of transformational rules will have to include a rule which has the effect of substituting *any* for *some* to produce sentences like that in 21. This is not as special a rule as it might seem. Very much the same relationship is seen in other pairs of sentences, so that the same rule can be applied in the series of transformations which connect them.

22. *I have some bananas.*   *I haven't any bananas.*
23. *You have some bananas.*   *Have you any bananas?*

Another somewhat similar phenomenon is illustrated in the following:

24. *I will come.*   *He said he would come.*

Only one of the two input sentences is shown here; the other will be discussed in 12.15. There is a change of *will* to *would*, and of *I* to *he*. These changes are conditioned by the occurrence of *said* and *he* in the first part of the sentence, as may be seen by comparing the set of sentences in 25, all having the same input:

25. *I will come.*   *He says he will come.*
                       I said I would come.
                       I say I will come.

Transformations which have the effect of putting two or more inputs together into one output involve a number of rules. There is the addition of various construction markers, *and, either . . . or, because, therefore, if . . . then,* etc. There may be changes of certain specific items, *some → any, sometime → ever,* etc. Verb forms may be changed to bring them into the proper relationship. (Traditional grammar gives a partial treatment of these phenomena under the rules of "sequence of tenses.") Pronouns may undergo various changes. As all of these can be structurally defined, they belong in a grammar and can be formulated in transformational rules.

12.15   Example 24 illustrates another feature of some transformations. The other underlying sentence cannot easily be *He said.* Such a sentence does occur, but rather infrequently, and in a quite specialized situation. Rather it must come from something like *He said it.* In the transformation, *it* is replaced by *he would come.* This sort of transformation does not merely connect strings; it inserts one into another so that it becomes an element in the structure of the other. In doing so it removes and replaces some element. Sometimes it is fairly obvious what this replaced element must be. In other cases it is not clear from the final result what such an element should be considered to have been in the input. In this respect, such a transformation is exactly like some of the question transformations. In example 12, the transformation involved the substituting of *who* for *John.* Looking at the output alone, it would not be clear what nominal was involved. It might have been *Mary, the man, my neighbor who grows daffodils,* or innumerable other possibilities. But it could not be *the pen* or *that typewriter,* or many others, which would require the substitution of *what* rather than *who.* Perhaps it is just this uncertainty which lies behind calling a sentence like *Who is writing a letter?* a question. It is not possible to go from the output sentence backward and reconstruct in detail every step of the generation. But it is possible to know that *who* substitutes for an NP, and equally to know that *he would come* must substitute for an NP.

Another type of transformation which inserts one input into another is exemplified by the following two sentences:

26. *The man who drives the yellow Cadillac hit a lamppost yesterday.*
27. *The man who hit a lamppost yesterday drives the yellow Cadillac.*

Both these sentences can be generated from the same pair of inputs.

> *The man hit a lamppost yesterday.*
> *The man drives the yellow Cadillac.*

To be usable in this transformation, the two inputs must have some part in common, in this case, *the man*. For this constituent in one input may be substituted *who* or *which*, whereby the whole S becomes attributive to the matching noun in the other, and is inserted in the position after the noun. When the NP replaced by *who* or *which* is not initial, then additional changes have to be specified.

By means of various transformations of these types, it is possible to take care of all those sentence types which are traditionally labeled as "compound" or "complex." So conceived, the phrase structure sector of the grammar generates certain clauses, and the transformational sector unites these into sentences. In the light of this, it is not, strictly speaking, correct to read the symbol S at the start of 12.11 as meaning "sentence" as used in traditional grammar. Nor indeed is it necessarily much better to read it as meaning "clause" in the sense of traditional grammar, since some transformations will carry an S into some structure other than what is traditionally called either a "clause" or a "sentence." But this does not mean that S does not designate some real and significant unit, only that it is not a unit identical with any one of those defined in traditional grammar. It is better to consider S as a designation for a unit which is basic to English grammatical patterns as described by a transformational grammar. If read as "sentence" it means only "sentence" as understood in this kind of grammar. It should not be expected to match precisely any unit in any other statement of English grammar. A transformational grammar is not merely a restatement of, or a minor amendment to, a traditional grammar or an immediate constituent grammar, but a basically different approach to language structure. It must find different units.

12.16   Once it is recognized that transformations can be applied to a pair of input strings to reduce one to the status of an element within the other, a vast panorama of possibilities opens up. Certain types of what are traditionally labeled "phrases" seem quite similar in important ways to "subordinate clauses" and suggest that a similar treatment is possible. As examples the following sentences will serve:

28. *His coming and going like that gives me the willies.*
    from   *He comes and goes like that.*
29. *His continual drumming on the table makes me nervous.*
    from   *He continually drums on the table.*

These both have a great deal of the underlying sentence pattern still remaining, and therefore have a great deal that commends such treatment.

If it is permissible with sentences like 28 and 29, why not also with similar phrases with less of the sentence elements preserved? The following all seem to be related in some way to example 29, and should perhaps be treated as having the same origin:

30. *His continual drumming   makes me nervous.*
    His   drumming on the table makes me nervous.
    Continual drumming on the table makes me nervous.
    His   drumming   makes me nervous.
    Continual drumming   makes me nervous.
    Drumming on the table makes me nervous.
    Drumming   makes me nervous.

but not

   *His continual   on the table makes me nervous., etc.

All of these differ from 29 only in the omission of certain parts. Any element or combination of elements can be omitted except *drumming*. They might accordingly be described in terms of a special type of transformation which merely deletes certain statable constituents.

This sort of transformation has a very wide usefulness, but it requires caution. It would be quite possible to generate 29 by a series of deletions from something like:

31. *His continual drumming on the table with his knife and fork while the toastmaster is introducing the speaker of the evening makes me nervous.*

But this is quite unnecessary. There seems to be no reason to start from the longer sentence. *He continually drums on the table.* is sufficient as an input. But if so, why not merely *He continually drums.* for the first sentence in 30? In this case a deletion transformation would be unnecessary. But this is not true of all these sentences. The input may be *He continually drums.*, or *He drums on the table.*, or simply *He drums.*, but it must have *he* or some other NP in the subject position. Those sentences in 30 without *his* must be derived by the use of a deletion transformation if the *drumming* is to be gotten from the VP of an S. Unnecessary deletions are not justifiable, but some deletions are necessary in a transformational grammar of English.

12.17   One of the commonest criticisms of traditional school grammar has been directed at the use of "understood" sentence parts. For example, an imperative sentence like *Come here!* is commonly described as having as subject "*you* understood." *You* in such sentences is quite rare and exceptional. Some linguists reject the use of such "understood" elements in a grammatical statement. Here, as in many other instances, a transformational grammar parallels traditional grammar in some respects. This sentence can be derived by the same first rewrite rule as used in 12.11, S → NP + VP. If so, at a later point in the grammar, a deletion transformation must remove the NP. The question is, then, is it necessary to have the NP in the derivation? There is some evidence that it is. *Myself* occurs, generally speaking, only in sentences in which *I* occurs in subject position. *Yourself* occurs commonly in two kinds of sentences, those with *you* for the subject, and imperatives. All these facts can be brought under one rule if *you* could be the subject of imperative sentences at the point in their generation at which the rules introducing *yourself* apply. That is, if something like **You go chase yourself!* were one stage in the generation of the imperative sentence *Go chase yourself!*

Within the framework of a transformational grammar deletion transformations seem to have a place when they are required to explain existing patterns. Unnecessary deletion transformations have no such place — no unnecessary rule of any kind can be tolerated. In other types of grammars the use of "understood" elements may be less easily justified, and whether they will be used or not is a decision which the linguist must make, just as he must decide which of several possible forms of statement he will follow. There is, however, one special danger in "understood"

elements which explains, and at least partly justifies, the condemnation of many linguists. This is the use of "understood" elements in field linguistics. It requires a very profound knowledge
of a language to be able to assess when such a device is justified
by the structure of the language itself. The temptation in preliminary stages is to supply "understood" elements in order to
bring the structure into line with that of some other language.
For example, in Hebrew /ṭóob haaʔíiš/ 'The man is good.,'
/ṭóob/ means 'good' and /haaʔíiš/ means 'the man.' There is no
direct equivalent to 'is,' though of course the sentence structure
as a whole is in some way equivalent to the structure of the English sentence as a whole. Some grammarians have stated that 'is'
is understood, or even that /haayáa/ is understood. (This is
glossed in some dictionaries as meaning, among other things,
'to be.') But it is difficult to see how /haayáa/ can be "restored"
to this sentence without utterly changing it. In no instance can
there be any justification for "understood" elements or deletion
transformations except in the STRUCTURE of the language. That
"the meaning requires" — or the exigencies of translation, or any
other non-structural indication, real or imaginary — is totally irrelevant.

12.18 If individual words can be introduced into a sentence
by means of a transformation combining two structured strings,
it would seem possible to give a similar treatment to a great deal
more of what has in the past been taken care of in the IC structure, or handled by traditional grammatical devices of various
kinds. For example, it has been proposed that attributive adjectives can be introduced into noun phrases by this means.

32. *I see the house.* ⎫   *I see the red house.*
   The house is red. ⎭

In favor of this suggestion is the fact that *I see the red house.* does
seem to be related in some way to *I see the house which is red.* The
latter clearly can be gotten from the inputs of 32. It is claimed
that this procedure does result in a considerable simplification of
description, but some linguists are less convinced of the value of
such transformations than of those described earlier in this
chapter.

Such a proposal seems to be pointing in the direction of making all of sentence structure a matter of transformations. But this is not the case. While it is easy enough to derive *red house* from an input *The house is red.*, it does not seem possible to generate *the house* in this way. Certainly it cannot be done in a strictly parallel way, since there is no sentence of the form **House is the.* In any case, it would seem that there must be at least a small collection of sentences in the derivation of which no transformations are applied. Nevertheless, one of the important issues in regard to transformational grammars is determining the proper apportionment of the task of description between the phrase structure sector and the transformational sector of the description. Some would push the use of transformational description much farther than others.

The use of transformations in grammar, in any rigorous sense, has been a new development in the decade of the 1950's. Involving as it does a reorientation of linguistic theory and a significantly different technique of description, it has necessarily been the center of a vigorous controversy. At the time of writing, several of the issues are not as yet clearly defined. Not enough has been published in the way of transformational grammars of a variety of languages. It is, therefore, not yet possible to evaluate its potentialities adequately. It may be expected, however, that the theory will continue to play a significant role in the development of linguistics by virtue of having raised some important, previously overlooked issues, and perhaps by contributing to their solution.

chapter

llllllllllllllllllllllllllllllllllllllllllllllllllllllllllllllllllllllllllllllll

◇◇◇◇◇◇◇◇◇◇◇◇◇◇◇◇◇◇◇◇◇◇◇◇◇◇◇◇

13

Language and Grammars

13.1 A linguist doing field work on a hitherto undescribed language gathers a **corpus** of material from an informant or a few informants. This may consist of only a few thousand phrases and sentences, perhaps only a small portion of it in connected discourse. On the basis of this limited amount of material he will write his description. Inevitably the question arises as to just what he is describing and how he can justify his work.

It would seem comparatively simple to produce a description of the corpus. But this would very seldom serve any significant purpose. The corpus usually has very little intrinsic value. It is too fraught with the personal peculiarities of the informants and the investigator. It is colored by the artificiality of the situation in which it is produced and recorded. It has little or no internal coherence. Much of the subject matter is trivial. If such a corpus has any value, it is largely—often solely—because it is a sample of the language. The only worth-while description is one of the language, not of the corpus. The linguist's problem, then, is to get from his sample to the characteristics of the whole. This is, of course, a problem common to all empiric sciences, and always a difficult one.

Behind this is another problem, also with close parallels in all sciences: that of obtaining a corpus which will have a maximum usefulness for analysis. It must be representative. That is, it must exemplify the full range of structural features in such a way that they can be identified, characterized, and related to other parts of the system. If the sample is not representative, the results may be vitiated; the description will not be of the language, but of a more or less similar pseudo language. A sufficiently large corpus of randomly gathered material would seem to meet this need. But there are difficulties: Some grammatical features are quite infrequent; an unplanned corpus may have to be extremely large to include adequate representation of these. Others are very common; even a moderate amount of material may exemplify these far beyond what is required to establish or confirm an analysis. Vast amounts of unneeded data can only complicate recording, filing, searching, and all the other processes involved in analysis. An adequate supply of needles is not assured simply by building a big enough haystack. A linguist, therefore, strives to obtain a corpus that will be representative in the minimum total bulk.

Obtaining a representative corpus can also be a very difficult matter. The field linguist must be continuously aware of all the factors which might affect the representativeness of his sample. It may be biased by the method of collection. It may be seriously distorted by the bilingual situation, or by the cultural abnormality of the linguist's intrusion. It may be compromised by his, or the informant's, prejudices about the language. Limitations of subject matter may exclude significant parts of the structure. Not only must the linguist be aware of these possibilities, but he must take specific steps to minimize the biases, both in his gathering and in his analysis.

Linguistic field work is, therefore, an art requiring skill and experience. No predetermined program can be followed successfully. The investigator must improvise, adjusting his further elicitation to his evaluation of the materials already gathered. A preliminary analysis must be carried along with the work of gathering a corpus. This analysis will point out deficiencies and suggest ways of removing them.

13.2   The difference between a description of a corpus and of a language is partly a matter of scope. A corpus consists of a few thousand sentences. A language might be considered as consisting of a very large number of sentences — all those, either already spoken or not yet used, which would be accepted by native speakers as "belonging" to that language. Even the largest corpus can be only an infinitesimal portion of the language.

A description of a corpus would be under obligation to cover all the sentences of the corpus, but only these. It would classify them and relate them to one another. A description of a language would similarly cover all the sentences of the language and no others. These it would classify and relate. Since it would necessarily cover many sentences which the linguist had not observed, the description would constitute a prediction of sentences which could reasonably be expected to occur, given the proper stimulus.

Obviously, the linguist cannot know in advance what he is to describe. Nor can he define in advance what a sentence is. Only the grammar itself can do that. But he must have some general idea of what is meant when a sentence is assumed to "belong" to a language. Otherwise he would have no basis on which to proceed with his work.

13.3 The occurrence of a sentence in a carefully elicited corpus is prima-facie evidence that the sentence does "belong" to the language, but nothing more. Informants do make mistakes. Occasionally very bad sentences will occur. Most of these will not be accepted by the informant when checked at another time and in another context. Sometimes the informant will voluntarily correct himself. But almost inevitably occasional ungrammatical sequences will get past the linguist's vigilance into his corpus. The analyst will have to bear constantly in mind the possibility of error. But he cannot afford to be too free with this as an explanation of seeming irregularities. To exclude a sentence from a corpus as non-grammatical is a serious matter, never to be taken lightly. And, of course, when errors do occur, they are very much more frequently the responsibility of the linguist than of the informant.

It is hardly possible to proceed merely with the knowledge that certain sentences — the sentences of the corpus — are grammatical. (Or more realistically, that the sentences of the corpus are very largely grammatical.) There is needed also some idea of the sort of sequences that are not grammatical. The linguist must get this also from his field work. As he gets some knowledge of the language and the culture, he can set up situations where it seems entirely reasonable to expect a certain sentence or type of sentence. If he finds it impossible to obtain, this is a hint that it is in some way out-of-bounds. Or he may suggest a form and find that the informant rejects it. Or he may have tried to communicate by use of the language and failed. Or he may note the instances where the informant corrects himself. The canceled "sentence" may be more valuable for analysis than the "correct" form which is substituted for it. The linguist's feeling for what is non-grammatical is commonly inchoate, but it is essential, one of the seldom recognized results of good field work.

13.4   However, it cannot simply be assumed that if the informant rejects a sentence it is non-grammatical. There are several other possibilities. It might be **non-sensical,** the sort of sentence for which there is no conceivable occasion. *Boiling ice danced across the leaf.* may be taken as an example of a non-sensical sentence. If asked specifically what is wrong with it, a native informant might launch into an explanation that ice doesn't boil, etc. This would be a diagnosis not so much of linguistic faults as of semantic inappropriateness. *The of was could.* might, by contrast, be an example of a non-grammatical sentence. A critique might mention that there is no noun, whereas *the* normally occurs only before nouns, etc. A less sophisticated informant might merely say, "Well, we don't talk that way." or something which could at least be construed as meaning that in some way which he cannot necessarily explain he feels that the sentence is put together wrong, i.e., that the trouble is linguistic. A non-sensical sentence may be quite grammatical. If so, this merely means that, should the occasion arise, the sentence in question might well be said, and in that situation might seem quite natural, even usual. A non-grammatical sentence cannot be used unless the language should change. If the distinction between grammaticalness and sensicalness can be drawn, the task of a grammar is to describe the grammatical sentences, sensical or non-sensical, clearly distinguishing them from the non-grammatical. The fact that some grammatical sentences do not occur is a separate problem, part of it, at least, falling in the domain of semantics.

To be non-sensical does not mean the same as to be **untrue.** *The* *moon is made of green cheese.* is presumably untrue, but it is sensical, since there have been repeated occasions to say it, and, indeed, it probably has been said many times more often than certain quite true sentences. Moreover, it is possible to lie in every language (in what situations and how frequently varies, and is culturally controlled; e.g., it is conventional in America to tell mothers that their babies are beautiful), and a grammar must cover such usages. Nevertheless, some of the sentences which the informant rejects are merely untrue. They may be common enough as sentences, either in different situations where they are true, or under different circumstances where an untruthful sentence seems in order. Or again, many sentences will be rejected by the informant merely because they are **tabooed.** Tabooed sentences not only can be said, they are said. But in certain, perhaps quite general, situations they are scrupulously avoided.

An informant may, therefore, reject a sentence because it is non-grammatical, non-sensical, untruthful, or tabooed, or for some combination of these reasons. The linguistic significance of his rejection depends on the reason for rejection. It may be extremely difficult for the linguist to identify this. Sometimes the informant's remarks, or the mode of his rejection, will give a hint. He might say something like: "We wouldn't say it that way." or "Well, I suppose you could say that, but we wouldn't." or "Nice people don't say that." In any case, such remarks are difficult to interpret, requiring considerable knowledge of the culture. With some informants, comments can be of little direct help. It may take a very sophisticated chain of reasoning and considerable ingenuity to draw these distinctions satisfactorily.

13.5 If the discrimination between grammaticalness and other qualities of "sentences" is so difficult, it might be possible and desirable to sidestep the issue entirely. A "grammar" might be written to account for what people actually do say or might be expected to say in probable situations. But this would not really be a grammar at all, but a complete account of the environment and culture of the people. For example, to account for certain otherwise possible sentences not occurring, it would have to cover all the details of the taboo system. Then it would have to cover the people's whole understanding of the world of nature, since this clearly bears on their saying certain things and not saying others.

It would, of course, be desirable to have a total description of a people's culture (including language) and environment. But any such approach as that suggested in the last paragraph would produce not a systematic structural statement, but only an anecdotal account. No amorphous and unorganized recounting of facts is of much value. Only organized knowledge is usable. Organization can come only as a result of two operations: observed facts must be sorted out into appropriate systems of interrelated phenomena. Then perspicacious generalizations must be made about each such system. If the totality of speech behavior is to be described, it will be necessary first to segregate it into several aspects, each consisting of those matters which can be studied together. One of these will include all questions relating to grammaticalness of utterances. This is the proper domain of descriptive linguistics. A number of other aspects may also be distinguished, each capable of being studied by the appropriate discipline. If the total picture is required, it will be necessary to seek separate systematic statements from each relevant discipline, and then relate the several statements.

13.6   To say that a language is a very large set of sentences is a highly suspect way of speaking. If it were just this, no one could ever learn a language, and as a result, no language would exist. Nor can it be a set of sentence patterns. As pointed out in 10.24, these also are entirely too many to be learned. Moreover, no description of a language in terms of sentence patterns — if it were possible — could ever account for the fact that people can produce sentences or understand sentences on patterns which they have presumably never heard. This ability to produce new sentences and new sentence patterns is precisely the most important feature of any speaker's command of a language. A language, therefore, is not so much a set of sentences, or of sentence patterns, as a set of much smaller patterns of formation which in combination enable a speaker to produce sentence patterns. Sentences are made up of constructions within constructions. Underlying these constructions are the patterns which the speaker learns and which therefore constitute the language. The task of a grammar is to describe these constructional patterns, giving a statement, perhaps in the form of a rule, to cover each. As sentences are built of these constructions, so a suitable selection of rules from the grammar will describe each sentence. It is only in some such sense that a grammar may be said to describe all the sentences of a language.

A corpus is representative of a language to the extent that it includes adequate exemplification of these constructional patterns. Their number is small enough that a carefully gathered corpus can feasibly be expected to attain a very high degree of representativeness. A second corpus of roughly comparable scope should also exemplify a similarly high percentage of the pertinent constructional patterns. This being the case, the greater part of the grammatical features of either corpus should be shared by the other.

This gives a test for a grammar. It is only necessary to elicit another sample, independent of the first. If the grammar fits the new corpus equally well, it is highly probable that it is correct. In this elicitation it is very desirable that the biases in the samples (since they cannot be wholly eliminated) be as different as possible in the two. That is to say, it might be useful to obtain texts dealing with different subject matters, elicited under different circumstances, or from different informants.

Not only will this test tell us whether we have a representative sample and have analyzed it correctly; it will also justify or correct our distinction between grammaticalness and other controls over the occurrence of sentences. These different factors operate in very different manners. Sensicalness is more specific; when patterns occur, they are of a different sort. They may involve classes of words, but they are not, in general, the constituent classes that figure in grammatical description, but more often have a strong semantic component. Patterns of sensicalness (as also of truth or taboo) more often differ from one type of subject matter to the next, and they more often differ from one situation of elicitation to the next. If the optimum distinction between grammaticalness and other controls is not made, there will be much greater difficulty in finding a grammatical statement that will hold as it is tested on a variety of additional corpora. Mixing into one statement restrictions associated with grammaticalness and with sensicalness will in some measure (perhaps small if the mixture is not extensive) produce the same sort of chaos which would be produced if the distinction were completely by-passed.

All this is to say that generalizations about culture and the environment must be made in a different way (or a different set of ways) from those about language. The methodologies of the several sciences are necessarily different. The subject matter of descriptive linguistics — grammaticalness of sentences — determines its method, and is in turn defined by the applicability of its method. Those restrictions which are studiable by the methodology of descriptive linguistics are the restrictions of grammaticalness. A grammar is merely a systematic statement of those controls.

13.7   If the linguist succeeds in generalizing properly from his corpus, he produces a **descriptive grammar.** This is a systematically organized set of statements about the constructional patterns that characterize grammatical statements. Properly speaking, a descriptive grammar is nothing more than this, though in practice there are commonly added some incidental introductory remarks, and scattered through the text may be numerous illustrative examples. A successful descriptive grammar provides, for any given sentence in the language, a description. Such a description is a selection of rules which, properly combined, define a sentence pattern which may be considered as exemplified by a given sentence.

For example, a suitable descriptive grammar of English will include statements which will form a sentence pattern SUBJECT–VERB–OBJECT. This is exemplified by such a sentence as *John saw James*. Given this sentence and the grammar, it should be possible to find the proper rules, combine them into this sentence pattern, and thus provide a description for the sentence. But to do so, one must have some understanding of the operation of the grammar and some knowledge of English. That is, while the grammar asserts that sentences on the pattern SUBJECT–VERB–OBJECT exist in English, it is the linguist that identifies *John saw James.* as an exemplification of this pattern.

But how does he do this? Why did he select this particular sentence pattern of all the many that he might have taken? Among these are ADJECTIVE–SUBJECT–VERB (as *Good boys behave.*), AUXILIARY–SUBJECT–VERB (as *Did John go?*), etc. Obviously no informed speaker of English would match *John saw James.* with any of these other descriptions. But a stranger to the language might. A very important link in the operation is the speaker's feeling about his language, or a linguist's ability to sense language structure. These things are not in the grammar, but in the user of the grammar. The grammar might provide some tests to ascertain, once the match has been made, whether it has been made correctly, but it cannot, of itself, lead a user to the proper description for any sentence.

13.8   A grammar, even a very good one, of a language only partially known can be a very frustrating thing. Faced with a sentence which is not understood, one turns to the grammar for help. It cannot give this help directly. The user is thrown back on "common sense" or some other undefined quality to guide him through it and lead him to the description he needs. Often this works; frequently enough, it does not. A grammar that would lead a user directly to the correct description for any given sentence would be far more useful for many purposes. Such a grammar may be called a **sentence-interpreting grammar.**

A sentence-interpreting grammar would seem at first sight to be quite easily possible, since it would only be accounting for — or describing — a normal, everyday occurrence. Language users identify sentence structures with apparent ease, and seem to be highly successful. Yet the way they do this is probably the least understood of all language skills. We have very little idea of how it is done, so the hearer's reactions can give very little help as a model for a sentence-interpreting grammar.

A large part of the discussion in Chapter 11 was phrased in a way suggestive of a sentence-interpreting grammar. It will serve to point out one of the difficulties. In discussing how structure was marked, repeatedly statements had to be made in terms of probabilities. Description in terms of probabilities is legitimate enough; indeed, it is very nearly standard practice in many sciences. But it is quite foreign to descriptive linguistics as currently developed. The descriptive linguist commonly works with a corpus elicited in such a way as to make observations of probabilities impossible or invalid. To handle a sentence-interpreting grammar rigorously, a totally new method of approach both in data collection and in analysis will be needed.

There are many other problems. One of the most obvious is that of constructional homonymity (see 10.14). This is not simply an occasional freakish situation, but something pervasive and recurrent in language. Even more serious is the problem of environment. Each part of an utterance has a relevant environment, and it cannot be understood without reference to this. A sentence-interpreting grammar will have to take environment into consideration at each step. The difficulty is in defining what is the RELEVANT environment. It cannot be simply everything within so many units on either side. For some items the relevant environment is very restricted; for others, very wide. It may be immediately adjacent, or separated by a mass of non-relevant material. That is to say, it is impossible to define the relevant environment for any linguistic unit in advance and without any knowledge of the utterance in which it occurs. Once the structure is known, the environment can be identified for each unit. In default of a definition of the relevant environment, an arbitrarily defined environment might be used. But this will either be so broad as to bring in a vast quantity of non-pertinent material, or so narrow as to miss much of importance. Either choice may make systematic treatment difficult or impossible.

13.9   Rather than ask that a grammar give rules by which the proper description can be found for any given sentence, we might require that it provide rules to construct a sentence to fit any given specifications. Such a grammar may be called a **sentence-producing grammar.** At first sight a transformational grammar such as was discussed in Chapter 12 would seem to be just this. Starting from S, which for this purpose can be thought of merely as a conventional starting point, each running through of the rules in proper sequence ends with a fully formed sentence. And with proper choices, it may lead to any sentence in the language.

This is not, however, sufficient to meet the requirements as a sentence-producing grammar. All the rules may be there, and all that is required may be to make the proper choices. But making them is far from a simple matter. A linguist can, indeed, show how any given sentence might be generated. But to do so he must use something additional to the grammar. The grammar does not give much help as to how the choices are to be made in order to meet the specifications. Often enough, this is obvious — so obvious that it seems almost ridiculous to pose this as a problem. But occasionally it is not at all obvious what choices should be made to produce a desired sentence. A deep understanding of the language and the grammar may be required, and even in the "obvious" cases the choice is largely dependent on the user's "feel" for the language. The choices are obvious simply because of this "feel" and possibly very obscure to an outsider.

A descriptive grammar, particularly one which is phrased in terms of generating sentences, may be thought of as analogous to a system of branching highways leading out from a central point to all the cities and hamlets in the land. An observer flying over in an airplane can see how the system ramifies and choose a suitable route to any given point. But a motorist on the ground can see little beyond the road fork immediately before him. He must have road signs telling him the destinations of each road — the consequences of each choice — and not merely the immediate way-stations, but all the places, big and small, down each road. What is required, then, to construct an operating sentence-producing grammar is to provide a set of additional rules that will point out in detail the consequences of any choice, and do this at the place where the decision must be made. The linguist's panoramic view of the language structure, on which he relies in applying a descriptive grammar, must be replaced by a set of explicitly stated rules.

A sentence-producing grammar is not merely more explicit than a descriptive grammar; it is explicit in an additional way. This means that it will require an additional type of rule, rather than merely more rules of the familiar types. It is not, then, simply a natural development of a descriptive grammar, but a new type of grammar, the properties of which are not yet understood.

13.10 Wholly adequate sentence-interpreting and sentence-producing grammars would contain within themselves all the rules necessary for their operation. If such could be developed, and further, if some method of linking the two could be found, there would result a device which could translate texts from one language to another. It has become something of a commonplace that, if the rules can be stated explicitly and completely, a machine can be programed to carry them out. The translation device could, then, be embodied in a machine. This machine would accept an input text in one language and produce an output of corresponding text in another. The expense, and more particularly the scarcity, of competent human translators makes this prospect an attractive one.

In the last decade or so, considerable interest has been aroused in the possibility of building such a translation machine. Many large engineering projects are underway in this field, both in the United States and abroad. A certain measure of success has been attained, and the construction of a practical machine does not seem remote.

There are two possible approaches. If certain restrictions and conditions are imposed, the problem is comparatively simple. For example, the machine might be limited to a certain finite number of vocabulary items and a finite number of sentence patterns. (Both are, of course, infinite in a real language.) Or it might be agreed to accept some degree of success short of 100 percent. (After all, perfection can hardly be expected of human translators either.) If these limitations are severe enough, building a machine presents hardly any challenge. Then, if the scope is broadened a bit, all that is needed is to add more hardware. A bigger vocabulary calls for a bigger storage capacity; more complicated sentence patterns for more switching equipment. If a simple machine can be built, a more complex one can too, given more space, more parts, more time. The question is not, therefore, whether a translation machine can be built, but only whether one can be built that is practical. That would mean one with sufficient capabilities to be useful with real material, and cheap enough to be feasible. ("Cheap" here means, of course, a reasonable number of millions of dollars, rather than a very large number of millions.)

The second approach would be to concentrate on the basic research task of developing more and more refined sentence-interpreting and sentence-producing grammars and a more powerful general theory of linguistics. If successful, this might lead to a comparatively elegant solution and perhaps to a much more adaptable and compact machine. But, equally, it might produce nothing practical for a considerable time, and perhaps never develop a translating machine. It would almost certainly discover something of interest and significance to linguistics as an academic discipline, and would be very likely to contribute in unforeseeable ways to other aspects of knowledge.

When the work on machine translation first began, linguists were hopeful that there would be important theoretical advances coming out of the very extensive research programs. On the whole, expectations have not been fulfilled. In general, the emphasis has been on the first approach. Problems have been met, not so much by basic research on language, as by more and better hardware. The tendency has been to by-pass some of the more complex linguistic problems, relying on rough-and-ready approximations. This has been possible because the development has centered on German and Russian, languages which share a great deal more with English than do, say, Chinese and Tagalog, and because within these languages the focus has been on scientific literature, probably the easiest type in which to find equivalences from language to language.

13.11 If instead of a sentence-interpreting and a sentence-producing grammar, descriptive grammars of two languages are tied together, the result is known as a **contrastive grammar** or **transfer grammar.** This does not provide for the automatic selection of a correct sentence in a target language for any given sentence in the source language. But it does tell what construction patterns may be expected in one for any given set of construction patterns in the other. Such a grammar might assist a translator, but it would not itself translate, and it is not for this purpose that it is of interest.

Contrastive grammars are most useful in setting up second-language teaching materials. They enable an experienced teacher to predict with reasonable success what parts of the language structure will present the greatest difficulties to learners. Moreover, they commonly define rather precisely the exact nature of those difficulties. This gives the teacher or lesson writer the basis for selecting a strategy to meet or minimize these difficulties. By clearly defining the problems, contrastive grammars make possible the accumulation of a body of experience dealing with second-language teaching. Without this framework, there can develop, say, a body of experience in teaching French to speakers of English, but there is no way to correlate this with experience in teaching Italian to speakers of German.

Like many other modern ideas in linguistics, contrastive grammar is not wholly new. There was always a great deal of it in traditional grammars. This often arose from the fact that the grammar writers were successful practical language teachers. Their success had arisen in part from their intuitive grasp of the contrastive grammar involved in their teaching. The important thing that was not generally seen before is that contrastive grammar must be clearly separated from descriptive grammar, and that the former must be based on the latter, and not vice versa. A suitable transfer grammar can be prepared only by bringing together adequate descriptions of the two languages contrasted. These descriptions must each be in terms proper to the languages being described.

A contrastive grammar is not a teaching device. It is rather a tool in the preparation of teaching materials, or a guide for the teacher in their use. A contrastive grammar should be systematically arranged, convenient for reference, and designed to show the significant structural contrasts in proper proportion and interrelationship. A beginning language textbook is a quite different matter. It may cover the same material, or a selection from it, but it is arranged in a different way, taking account of many non-linguistic factors. Chief among these are learning theory and practical classroom necessities.

13.12 A descriptive grammar merely records the structural patterns discernible in the corpus on which it is based, and therefore assumed to be features of the language. It does not evaluate them in terms of any non-linguistic factor. Yet not all patterns or combinations of patterns that are actually used have the same social significance. This dimension of language is of great importance and worthy of careful study. To be realistic, such study must be based on the definitions of usages provided by a good descriptive grammar. The problems of identifying language patterns and evaluating their social significance must not be confused; entirely different methods are required.

To include social valuations in a grammar so alters its nature that it cannot properly be labeled simply as "descriptive." Most often the grammars which take note of social values do so by specifying certain usages as "good" and rejecting others as "bad." They tend to assume the form of rules to assist in following one and avoiding the other. Such statements are called **prescriptive grammars.** The term can also be extended to cover statements which discriminate between patterns in terms of appropriateness to an assortment of social situations.

Many linguists have very decidedly rejected prescriptive grammars as pernicious distortions. In many specific instances this is fully justified. However, the fault is not that these grammars are prescriptive, but that they are based on inadequate or false description. The usages which are condemned are often quite obviously neither understood nor correctly diagnosed. There is a temptation to prescribe patterns which seem somehow attractive, even if not in actual use and perhaps incompatible with established and approved constructions. When a classical language has prestige, there is a tendency to use it as a standard of comparison, and this may encourage wholesale importations of new and sometimes quite inappropriate patterns. The ultimate development is to reject usage altogether, and to condemn "even the best writers" for "frequent solecisms." Traditional school grammars of English exhibit all these faults.

However, none of these fallacies is inherent in prescriptive grammars as such. If such a grammar were based on good descriptive grammar and on accurate observation of social value, it would not be open to any such easy condemnation. Moreover, a prescriptive grammar does have a usefulness, particularly in teaching or in editing. If the schools are to teach Standard English, there must be rules discriminating patterns acceptable within Standard English from those which are not, and thus clearly defining the usage which is to be encouraged in situations calling for this form of the language. But it is wasteful, if not much worse, to use a prescriptive grammar which shows obvious ignorance of English structure and which attempts to teach a form of the language in conflict with the accepted speech that the student hears around him.

13.13   In the last several sections six types of grammars were mentioned. Of these, the descriptive grammar clearly occupies the central place. Not only is it the first product of analysis, but it is also the least specialized. All others are derived from it by the addition of other sorts of rules, or by the combination of two grammars. Moreover, all the more specialized grammars require the observation of additional kinds of data, often by different methods of observation. In view of these facts, it is not surprising that the descriptive grammar has been more highly developed than any of the others.

During several decades of the modern development of linguistics, efforts were concentrated almost entirely on the descriptive grammar. It has only been since 1950 that many linguists with backgrounds in descriptive techniques have ventured seriously into some of these derivative types. By the end of that decade, however, the production of a contrastive grammar was becoming an accepted activity for such linguists, though the body of experience had not yet become sufficient for the technique to be thoroughly understood. Interest in rigorously produced prescriptive grammars (other than introductory second-language textbooks) had not yet appeared. In the past, too many prescriptive grammars had been based on utterly inadequate or incorrect descriptive work, and this stigma had not been dissipated, though there were very small indications that a change of attitude might be on the way. Through much of the decade machine translation had been a major research activity, receiving funds that were, for linguistics, totally unprecedented. The linguistic aspects of this effort touched the problems of producing rigorous sentence-interpreting and sentence-producing grammars. By the end of the decade some of the problems were beginning to be clearly visible, but techniques that might meet these problems in any general way had barely begun to emerge. Thus even after a decade of work, these several derivative grammar types could hardly be considered as having a firmly established status within linguistics. By far the larger part of the grammars published were still of the descriptive type. For many linguists, this remained the ultimate goal of their work. For some of them, the writing of a contrastive grammar was merely a permissible side activity for a descriptive linguist rather than any legitimate part of his central task.

But if descriptive grammars have been more highly developed than any of the derivative types, this must not suggest that their development has reached the end, or that their properties are adequately understood. Indeed, one important reason for the slow development of derivative grammar types has been the inadequate base from which it might proceed.

The problems of analysis and statement behind a descriptive grammar are a great deal simpler than those behind, say, a sentence-interpreting grammar, and, because of a much longer period of intensive research, are far better met. But much remains to be done. It cannot be claimed that the typical descriptive grammar produced today serves adequately all the functions which might legitimately be expected of it. And it should be a source of humility to modern linguists to recognize that the most successful and complete description is very probably still the Sanskrit grammar of Pāṇini and his associates — antedating modern descriptive linguistics by millennia. The descriptive linguist's skill in writing grammars is not yet fully adequate; but his understanding of the nature and properties of the grammars he writes is even less adequate. The rise of interest in some of the specialized types of grammars during the fifties has raised new and important questions about the descriptive grammar. Its properties will become much better known as they can be contrasted with those of other types. Thus the new grammars may be of great importance to descriptive work, even in its most narrowly restricted form.

13.14 Even within the relatively narrow circle of American descriptive linguistics, viewpoints have been far from homogeneous. There have been three great classic formulations: Boas' introduction to the *Handbook of American Indian Languages* (1911), Sapir's *Language* (1921), and Bloomfield's *Language* (1933). These show wide differences together with important shared basic convictions. All three have been tremendously influential. However, they have tended to pull American linguistics in different, occasionally conflicting directions, and there have been sharp tensions between individual linguists as they have been influenced in different ways by these three. The history of descriptive linguistics in America has been one of continual interplay between diverse opinions, most, but not all, of which can be traced to one or the other of these three sources. Boas, Sapir, and Bloomfield were all excellent field linguists, and they gave field work a prominent, almost dominant place in their discipline. Here also they showed differences. Their followers have experimented with a wide spectrum of analytic methods and forms of statement. Inevitably this diversity in theory and practice has produced a certain degree of diversity in terminology and professional conventions. Much of this is unfortunate. But it should be remembered that it was precisely the same diversity of background and interest which brought about the productivity that has marked the relatively short career of descriptive linguistics in America.

More regrettable has been the isolation of American descriptive linguistics from parallel developments in Europe. Partly this is the result of differences in the academic roots. American linguistics has been closely associated with anthropology. Boas' part in forming American anthropology is as great as his contribution to linguistics. Many of his colleagues and students worked in both fields, but most of them considered themselves primarily anthropologists. Bloomfield's background was in Germanic languages, but as he turned to Algonquian, he entered into the same anthropological heritage and found much of it congenial. European linguistics has had much less close connections with anthropology, and its molders have been largely trained in Indo-European historical linguistics, classical and modern European languages, or literary criticism. European linguists are puzzled by the common American practice of identifying linguistics as a social science, and some Americans are discomforted by the overwhelming orientation of much European linguistics toward the humanities. Another factor in the isolation has been the heavy concentration of American work on North American Indian languages. European workers have been more concerned with Old World languages, with the heaviest concentration on those of Europe and classical antiquity. Working on the same or closely related languages can be a strong force to bring linguists together. But workers in different language groups often have little occasion to read each other's papers. Moreover, the problems encountered by the two groups have been quite different. American linguists have been faced largely with unwritten languages where the field worker has had to do the initial analysis on the basis of elicitation from informants. European linguists much more frequently have been reworking languages which have long been written and on which a great body of linguistic literature has already been published.

All these differences were aggravated by the fact that important formative years for the discipline came in a period of growing international tension, when scholarly contact was difficult and finally completely cut off in many instances. The linguistic community has, therefore, been deeply fragmented into schools, having their own theories, terminologies, and conventions.

There are a number of European schools of linguistics, and the differences between them are in some instances quite great. Limitations of space prohibit presentation of the theoretical positions of these schools, but references in the bibliography will give an introduction to some of them. Three might be mentioned. One of the most important is the so-called Prague School, whose classic formulation is Trubetskoi's *Grundzüge der Phonologie* (1939). This has been widely influential in many European linguistic circles, and many of the basic ideas of the school have diffused very widely, far beyond the group that originally came together around Trubetskoi. At the same time the linguistic theories which they hold in common have been developed in a variety of ways, so that the movement is no longer either as homogeneous or as sharply marked off as it once was.

Another group of considerable importance is that gathered around Louis Hjelmslev of Copenhagen. They prefer to call their science **glossematics** rather than linguistics, reflecting what they consider to be a very definite departure from previous approaches. They are attempting to build a theory of language of great generality and abstractness. American linguists, with their immediate concern with analysis, tend to be impatient with such an approach, feeling that much of the discussion is too far removed from real language systems and actual field data.

Probably the most profoundly different from any American point of view is the so-called London School, the followers of Professor J. R. Firth. Not only is their view of language basically different; their terminology contrasts sharply with that used by most other linguists. As a result, Americans find great difficulty in reading their papers, and so fail to profit by their insights. Unfortunately this causes a large body of descriptions of otherwise poorly known languages to be difficult of access.

In the forties American ignorance of European linguistics was profound, and there were many misunderstandings, often very ill-founded. There were also real and significant theoretical differences, and some of these were sharp. Gradually the prejudices have been dispelled, understanding has increased, and some of the differences have been blunted. This was easiest with the "Prague School" because of the fundamental similarities of the positions held. More and more evidence can be seen of "Prague School" influence in American papers. American linguistics has certainly profited from this. We may assume that many Europeans have also found the exchange to their benefit. It seems that the barriers which have isolated one group of linguists from another are breaking down, making available to all the whole range of theory and practice.

13.15   With this diversity of viewpoint within descriptive linguistics, it is not surprising that the descriptive grammar is not, as a type, uniform. There are a number of varieties, even within American practice. Some of them differ merely in stylistic conventions of statement, in terminology, or in other basically inconsequential matters. Puzzling as these may be to the beginner, they have no real significance. Sometimes grammars differ in the view of language that underlies them. It is therefore important that anyone working at all regularly in the field of linguistics should come to understand something of the range of theory that is or has been held. Some grammars differ in the degree of explicitness which is sought after or attained. In connection with the development of transformational grammars it has been pointed out that some familiar types of descriptive grammars are far from completely explicit. Efforts have been stimulated to develop more rigorous statements, not only on the transformational model, but also of other kinds. Grammars also differ in the thoroughness with which the writer is committed to descriptive principles, many showing — consciously or unconsciously — some compromise with non-empiric linguistic tradition. In any discussion of types of grammars some account must be taken of several of these dimensions of variation. For the most part these do not divide descriptive grammars into sharply distinct subclasses. Rather there is variation in many directions, with intergradations in most.

13.16   One fundamental cleavage between different types of descriptive statement rests in the entities which are made the basis of description. In most of the discussion in this book, structure is described in terms of elements of various sorts, morphemes, words, phrases, etc., and the arrangements in which they are joined. Thus, the English past verb is described as a construction of a verb stem (e.g., *walk*) plus an affix, $\{-D_1\}$, which in this particular case is pronounced $/-t/$ and spelled *-ed*. Every statement in one kind of descriptive grammar would be of the same general form. Each construction is described as composed of two or more elements, each usually specified as any member of a certain constituent class (in the example just cited, "verb stem"). This technique may be called the **element model.**

A second basis for description is the **process model.** This must also start from elements, to be sure, but typically the statement is in terms of one element and one process. Thus the English past verb might be described as resulting from the application of a process (perhaps acceptably labeled as "preteritization," or something of the sort) to a verb. With an example like *walked* this seems a bit awkward; nothing seems to be gained by describing *walked* as *walk* having undergone preteritization, which in this instance takes the special form of suffixation. But with an example like *ran*, the impression is more favorable; this seems quite appropriately described as *run* having undergone a process of preteritization, which in this instance takes the form of vowel change. The process model seems more satisfying than an element model for words like *ran;* and indeed the element model is necessarily stretched in some barely satisfactory way to cover such cases at all. In 6.19 this was done by treating a change as if it were an element; a replacement (process) becomes by fiat a replacive (morpheme). Neither model seems wholly satisfactory for universal application.

The element model has two interesting varieties. These differ in the way in which variations in morpheme shapes are accounted for. In one variety a morpheme is stated in such a form as

$$/\text{-d} \sim \text{-t} \sim \text{-id} \sim \ldots /.$$

($\{\text{-D}_1\}$ is only a convenient abbreviation for the full expression.) A construction is then described in terms of selection of a morpheme from each of the constituent classes which are required, and then further selection — or subselection — of the proper allomorph from the total roster that constitutes the morpheme. For example, if in the past construction the morphemes /wɔʜk/ and /-d $\sim$ -t $\sim$ -id $\sim$ .../ are selected, then the allomorph /-t/ must be subselected. This form of statement may be called the **subselection model.**

In the second variety of the element model, each morpheme is stated in a base form. Thus the past suffix in English might be stated as having the form /-d/. The past *walked* is described as a construction of /wɔʜk/ and /-d/ and subsequent adjustment of the resulting form as required by certain rules (often called morphophonemic rules) to yield the shape /wɔнkt/. This form of statement may be called the **adjustment model.**

The adjustment model is easily confused with the process model. The difference, however, is profound. In the one, the process is the basic unit in the grammar; it is meaningful in itself, either grammatically or semantically. In the adjustment model there is also a process, but it is not basic in the description; it is meaningless, the automatic result of a certain element being in a certain environment.

13.17   One trend that has characterized the modern development of descriptive linguistics has been the search for consistent bases of statement, for grammatical models that might be applied uniformly throughout a description. During the thirties this took the form of widening the application of element models and eliminating process statements from grammars. Adjustment was in general the favored variety, though it was commonly mixed more or less with subselection statements. Early in the forties the trend moved toward more consistent use of subselection statement and the elimination of adjustment techniques. During the fifties process statement has been revived in the form of transformational grammar. A transformation is, of course, a special type of process. It is not something which is added, but a change which a structured string undergoes. When a transformation does, in fact, add an element, the emphasis is on the addition (the process) rather than on the morpheme or word (the element).

It is, however, too simple to consider grammars as exemplifying one or another of the pure models just described. The actual models are more complex, often involving more than one form of statement, preferably in some discernible pattern. The transformational grammar is an excellent example, since its structure is unusually clear. As shown in 12.10.1 it has three parts. The first of these is built on an element model; the second on a process model. One of its most original features is that all matters of morpheme variation are deferred to the third part. Here an adjustment model is used, suitably modified to allow the separation of the third part of the grammar from the first. Part of the rationale for the sharp separation of parts one and two is the use of different forms of statement in the two.

Underlying the experimentation with different forms of statement and the shifting of interest from one model to another seems to have been a largely tacit assumption. This is that the ultimate efficiency of description is served by consistency in the form and bases of grammatical statements. A grammar which mixed indiscriminately statements of an element model with those of a process model was suspect as soon as it was found that this mixture could be avoided. As soon as the contrast between adjustment and subselection became clear, mixture of these two began to be avoided.

The **paradigm model,** long a favorite with traditional grammarians, is another familiar practical model. It has generally been in disfavor with descriptivists. This can certainly be ascribed, in part, to its frequent abuse. Uninflected languages were forced into a Latin-like system of declensions and conjugations. Moreover, the paradigm model has been too closely associated with nonempiric approaches to language. But perhaps as important has been the fact that, as now known, it is a mixed model — process, adjustment, and subselection meeting in apparent disorder. Nevertheless, the paradigm model does show interesting possibilities of development if some basic work can be done on it. Cree was described in 9.9–9.14 as an instance in which familiar element models present great difficulties. It may well be an example of a language for which a formalized paradigm model would offer great advantages.

13.18 A special form of the descriptive grammar is the **structural sketch,** a short, concise statement with a minimum of exemplification and avoidance of any incidental remarks on side matters. This is the linguist's grammar. It is written in his jargon, and in his style. The reading of it requires familiarity with descriptive linguistics. It is designed to bring out in high relief those structural features of special interest, and to give a linguist a clear picture of over-all structure.

With this contrasts the **reference grammar.** This is written primarily for the non-linguist. It is intended for casual or occasional reference. For this reason individual sections are made as nearly self-contained as possible. The intention is that anyone with a basic understanding of the language can refer to any part of it independently and obtain the information he needs. A reference grammar must avoid the tight reasoning that is the pride of the writer of a structural sketch. Some measure of redundancy must be permitted, though in a structural sketch it is assiduously avoided. Exemplification should be full. Access must be made as easy as possible through full indexing and copious cross references. But when all this has been said, it remains that a reference grammar may differ from a structural sketch only in style of writing, this being in each case adjusted to the audience and the intended use.

13.19   There is another much more disturbing dimension of difference between grammars. This is the matter of size. This may vary from a very short paper in a journal to a grammar running to many volumes. Even after making all due allowances for the prolixity of the reference grammar compared to the conciseness of the structural sketch, the range of size and scope may be extreme. This raises the question: How is it possible to have descriptions ranging from a few pages to several volumes? If the longer treatment is useful, how can the shorter be valid? Or if the shorter is useful, why is the longer needed?

The easy answer might be that the longer treatment gives greater detail, and that a grammar writer might give as much or as little as he chooses. But the linguist is convinced that a language is a system, not merely a collection of individual rules. If this is so, the fact should severely restrict any freedom to choose more or less at random what to include and what to omit. The only grammar that would be acceptable would be one that presents the whole integrated system of structure in its entirety. Less would be mutilation; more, gratuitous; anything else, a mere incoherent assemblage of "facts."

In 10.17 it was shown that a language involves not merely a system of constituent classes, but a system of classes, subclasses, sub-subclasses, and so on — a hierarchy of classes. Some of the structural patterns are statable in terms of constituent classes, some only in terms of elements farther down the hierarchy. There is thus a hierarchy of structural patterns. The assertion that language is an integrated system must mean that it is integrated on several levels. That is, language is not merely a system, but a hierarchy of systems.

If this is indeed the case, then it should be possible to construct a grammar which sets forth the facts of the system at any level at which it is integrated. Grammars of several different sizes would thus be possible. These several grammars would not be independent of each other, but there would be very special relationships between them. Since one would be written in terms of classes, and another in terms of classes and subclasses, and since the subclasses are set up within the framework of the classes, one of these grammars should work out to contain the other. Each grammar would be a synopsis of the next, or an expansion of the preceding. This implies that for any language there is not merely one grammar, but a HIERARCHY of grammars.

Each grammar would define certain sentences as grammatical. Some sentences would be grammatical in terms of all the grammars. Others would be grammatical by the rules of some but not all of the grammars. There would thus be different **degrees of grammaticalness.** Some sequences would be grammatical by none of the grammars; these would be totally non-grammatical.

For example, a very basic grammar of English might include a statement to the effect that a noun with or without an article can occur as the subject of a sentence. By this grammar sentences such as *James came.*, *The boy came.*, *A boy came.*, *Boys came.* would be grammatical. Presumably they would be also by other grammars; they are grammatical to a high degree. By the same very basic grammar sentences like **A James came.*, **Boy came.*, **A boys came.* would be grammatical. But they would be excluded by higher grammars; they would be grammatical to a low degree. **The came.* would be excluded by all grammars; it would be non-grammatical. The simplest grammar operates only with the classes, including nouns and articles. A higher grammar would discriminate between several subclasses of nouns, and treat *a* and *the* in different subclasses of articles. It would have a set of rules about sequence of articles of various subclasses with nouns of various subclasses. Statements of this sort would exclude **A James came.* and various other sentences which would be acceptable under the coarser rules of the simplest grammar. Probably the very simplest of these grammars would have little value, which is only to say that no one has much interest in sentences of the minimum degree of grammaticalness. Higher degrees of grammaticalness and their associated grammars might be of real value for various purposes.

Part of the art of linguistic analysis — a part which has never yet been formalized at all — is finding the scope or size at which an integrated description can be written. There is more than one such. But there are also many intermediate sizes at which grammars will be less successful, perhaps even confused or partially incoherent. Involved in finding a suitable scope is the finding of compatible levels of subdivision within each of the various classes. It may be presumed very inefficient to describe an intricate system of subclasses and sub-subclasses of, say, English verbs without setting up any subclassification in the nouns. No part of the total structure can be effectively described in greater or lesser detail than is appropriate to the level of complexity selected for the whole.

13.20   At the beginning of this chapter it was assumed, tentatively, that the function of a grammar is to describe the sentences of a language. This has been a common conviction of linguists, and an even commoner working limitation. As an arbitrary working limit it is quite proper; as an absolute upper bound to the domain of linguistics it is certainly unjustified. In every language there are formal, structural features operating at a level higher than that of the sentence. As an example, we might cite the restrictions on the use of pronouns such as *he* and *she*. These restrictions differ from one sentence to another in a discourse, depending on the place of the sentence in the discourse and the relationship to other sentences. At first sight this might seem to be merely a matter of "logic," the controlling factor being whether the reference is sufficiently clear from the context. But anyone who has done much translating knows that the rules differ from language to language. The control is, therefore, at least in part, a matter of language structure, rather than any universal or nonlinguistic system of logic. If the use of pronouns is a formal property of utterances, it is in the province of grammar.

It is, however, legitimate and feasible to describe the grammar of a language only up to a certain level of complexity in the constructions. In some languages, perhaps in all, the sentence or some very similar construction is a convenient and structurally valid stopping point. In some the word is another, smaller one. Thus there may be grammars describing only word formation, or only sentence formation, or going beyond the sentence level. All of these may be equally valid within their own frames of reference.

Supra-sentence grammar is even more difficult than sentence grammar, just as sentence grammar (traditionally "syntax") is more difficult than word grammar (traditionally "morphology"). The reason is much the same. As constructions become larger, the number of possible forms increases very rapidly. A great deal larger corpus is required in order to obtain any appreciable amount of repetition, or of good minimal pairs. Moreover, more of the rules contain options, and it becomes ever more difficult to separate grammar from style or accidental differences. Recurrences become not only harder to find, but very much harder to assess. The analytic problem of extrapolating from a limited corpus to an unlimited language becomes rapidly more complex. The upper limit comes when the analytic problem becomes so involved that the child in learning his language cannot handle it. At this point no language patterns can be said to exist. It is not yet certain, however, that the linguist in his analysis has approached this upper limit very closely. At present very little precise supra-sentence grammar seems immediately practicable in any language, though material for such does seem to be present in many languages.

14

Some Inflectional Categories

14.1 Expression and content are equally fundamental aspects of language. The last six chapters have sketched some of the phenomena of grammar, that part of the expression system directly related to content. Throughout the discussion, occasional reference was made to the content categories expressed. In this chapter we will discuss some of these more explicitly and attempt to point out some of the more important characteristics of such units in language structure. The topics discussed have been selected because they are commonly associated with the inflectional systems of languages, and the illustrations will be drawn mostly from use in this connection. This must not be taken to imply that any one of the categories mentioned will necessarily have anything to do with the inflectional system of any particular language. Languages differ as widely in the categories expressed in inflection as they do in the morphologic structure by which they are expressed.

14.2 In some languages inflectional categories very familiar to speakers of European languages are entirely lacking. For example, in many languages nouns or noun-like words are characterized by inflection for number. This is by no means either universal or necessary, though our English background leads us both to assume it to be normal and to be puzzled that a language can exist without it. But many do, the most familiar example being Chinese. Words semantically equivalent to numerals, or other terms for quantity, do exist in Chinese and can be used when called for. English likewise has similar words which can be used whenever the number is particularly significant. The difference between the two languages is that the expression of number in Chinese is optional; in English it is compulsory. Every English noun is required by the language structure to be either singular or plural. In many cases this is informationally unimportant. In a large part of the instances where number is significant, numerals or other expressions of quantity are added, making the singular-plural distinction in the noun itself redundant.

Many have said that the lack of number inflection in Chinese was a mark of inadequacy of the language. With perhaps more justification one could say that the distinction in English is of little value, being in most instances either irrelevant or redundant. Neither conclusion is defensible. Number has a significant function in English grammar, whereas Chinese has a grammatical system in which number has no such part. Both languages are workable and each has its own systematic structure composed of just such details, most of which cannot be individually justified. When a brick house is to be built, it does not matter whether this brick or that brick is used, but some brick must be used. Number is one of the bricks in English structure; Chinese uses others.

14.3 Number is familiarly thought of as a contrast between one category indicating a single individual and another indicating two or more. These are traditionally designated **singular** and **plural**. These names are intended to suggest the "meanings" of these categories.

Probably the category of number has a more obvious and direct connection with demonstrable contrasts in the world of experience than any other inflectional category of English. Because of this seeming objectivity, number is an ideal example to demonstrate that all such categories are, at least in part, arbitrary. Some others are very highly arbitrary with very little demonstrable connection with observable phenomena. English number (in the singular-plural sense) is a structuring imposed on experience by English patterns; it is part of language, not of nature.

There is an old story of a man who was asked, presumably by a grammarian, whether *pants* was singular or plural. His reply was, "Well, mine are plural at the bottom, and singular at the top." Ultimately, the confusion, which many others have also felt, rests not so much in the shape of the garment as in the grammar of English. The object named is as clearly one entity as, say, a shirt or a coat. This does not matter; by a convention of English, *pants* is plural. Interestingly enough, this is not an isolated case; compare *trousers, breeches, shorts, slacks*, etc. This whole group of words are grammatically plural with no evident semantic justification.

14.4   English nouns fall into two major classes with regard to the semantic value of number. They may be referred to as **count nouns** and **mass nouns.** No discussion of the meaning of singular and plural can be realistic without carefully distinguishing between these. The two classes are also syntactic subclasses of nouns, since they differ markedly in the use of the articles. In general, singular mass nouns use the articles in the same way as do plural count nouns. For example, singular count nouns can be freely preceded by *a*, whereas mass nouns can be only in very special contexts. Singular mass nouns can be preceded by /sə̌m/ *some* 'a quantity of'; this word is only used before plurals of count nouns. (/sə̌m/ *some*, though spelled the same, is a very different word meaning 'a certain' or something of the kind. It can be used much more freely.)

The concords of verbs and of *this* and *that* depend solely on number, without regard to the contrast of mass and count nouns. The distinction between these subclasses of nouns is purely arbitrary. Consider *rice* and *beans*. Both refer to articles of food consisting of numerous small particles. Yet one is a mass noun and the other a count noun. The contrasts and resemblances in usage may be seen in the following examples:

Mass noun:	Count noun:
Rice is good for you.	*Beans are good for you.*
This rice is good.	*These beans are good.*
I choked on a grain of rice.	*I choked on a bean.*
*A rice . . .	**A grain of beans . . .*
/sə̌m ráys/	/sə̌m bíynz/

Not only is the distinction between words like *rice* and *beans* arbitrary, but various dialects of the language differ at some /sŏm/ points. *Molasses* in standard American is a singular mass noun like *rice*. In some other dialects it is a plural count noun like *beans*. Compare the following:

Molasses is good for you.   *Molasses are good for you.*
(standard)   (some colloquials)

I have never heard a singular **a molass*, but this does not affect the case. I suspect that if a situation should arise which would elicit it, speakers of certain dialects would readily use it.

14.5　Moreover, in all dialects certain words are used either as count nouns or as mass nouns, always with a difference of meaning. In these cases, the difference is frequently signaled by the use of *a* before the count noun. Compare:

A piece of iron   *A piece of an iron*

The mass noun refers to a material, the count noun to a tool. The difference is perhaps most clearly seen in such an utterance as:

That piece of an iron is not a piece of iron; it's the wooden handle.

The semantic relationship between the two may be rather obscure. Soldering irons are customarily made of copper; we have had coppers made of iron-zinc alloy; and nickels contain almost no nickel. Even when such apparent contradictions do not need to be reckoned with, there is no way of predicting one meaning if the other is given.

14.6　The singular of a mass noun, in the simplest case, refers to some quantity, usually undefined and frequently not countable, of some substance. The plural of a mass noun usually refers to a number of kinds or species of the substance. Thus *metals* does not imply several discrete occurrences of objects, but of a number of kinds of substances. In other instances, this formulation does not fit so clearly, but the meaning seems to be more nearly this than the traditional statement of the meaning of singular and plural. Consider *the beauties of poetry*. This certainly does not refer to any collection of discrete occurrences of things. It can be debated to what extent it has any sense of a number of kinds of beauty (that is, to what extent *beauties* parallels *metals* in meaning). These details need not detain us. Their full discussion can be either very involved or very profitless or both. What is important to note is that the category of plural in English gathers together a rather diverse assortment of concepts. All these have one thing in common; they contrast with another assortment of concepts which we call "singular." That is, the unity within the category is purely a feature of the linguistic system of the language which arbitrarily sets these two in contrast and imposes the requirement that every noun be assigned to one or the other. The singular-plural contrast is common in languages. We must, however, expect that there will be considerable differences of detail or even of rather broad outlines between the assortments of concepts which various languages bring together into each of these categories.

14.7   The possibilities of number distinctions are not exhausted with singular and plural. Some languages distinguish two or more plurals on the basis of distinctions which are not inflectionally significant in English. For example, Kru, a language of Liberia, has a singular and two plurals. One of these refers to any chance assortment of two or more of the objects referred to. The other refers to a group of objects which are in some way related. Thus the English term *men* might be translated in two different ways. One would refer to a chance group, the other, perhaps, to a number of men from the same tribe. One form to be translated 'books' might mean any odd assortment, the other a number of volumes from a set.

Other languages make distinctions of the same sort that English does, but in greater detail. Many languages have three numbers: singular, dual, and plural. **Dual** refers to two of a kind. In such a system, plural applies to three or more. Less frequently there may be singular, dual, trial, and plural.

Finally, there may be a system that combines some aspects of several types of distinctions. At one stage in Hebrew there were singular, dual, and plural. Dual referred to two objects which were members of a pair. Plural referred to three or more, or to two objects which were not members of a pair. Thus /yaadáyim/ 'hands' would refer to the two hands of a single person; /yaadíim/ 'hands' would refer to any three or more hands, or to, say my hand and your hand, but not to my two hands.

14.8   **Gender** is another category which is quite common in nouns. In English it is not richly developed. The gender of an English noun is defined solely in terms of the pronoun substitute, *he, she,* or *it,* which may be used in its place. Typically, gender involves not only substitution but also concord. Indeed, probably the best definition of gender is as a set of syntactic subclasses of nouns primarily controlling concord.

Languages which have gender as a grammatical category vary widely as to number of genders. French, Hebrew, and Hindi have only two. Latin, Russian, and German have three. Some languages have more than a dozen.

In European languages there is some correlation of gender with sex. This is reflected in our traditional labels, masculine, feminine, and neuter. However, the correlation may be exceedingly loose. The names of many sexless objects are assigned to either masculine or feminine, even in those languages which have a neuter. Of course, in a two-gender language like French, every noun must be assigned to either masculine or feminine. Rather more frequently than is commonly realized, male or female beings are referred to by neuter nouns, and occasionally male beings are named by feminine nouns and female beings by masculine nouns. Gender is in large part a linguistic classification of nouns into arbitrary groups for syntactic purposes. Nevertheless it is not wholly arbitrary. This is shown by the high degree of agreement that will be found if, for example, monolingual speakers of German are asked to assign genders to loan words. The content structure of the language seems to gather a number of disparate semantic categories together into three genders. It does so in a way that is in part arbitrary and in part systematic, at least to the extent that the native speaker can sense a proper place for a new word which will coincide with that selected by a fellow speaker.

In many languages gender categories have nothing whatever to do with sex. A common type is that which distinguishes between **animate** and **inanimate.** This is the case, for example, in the Algonquian languages such as Cree. (Compare the verb inflection discussed in 9.9ff.) The animate class basically includes all persons, animals, spirits, and large trees. But the following are also arbitrarily animate: tobacco, corn, apple, raspberry (but not strawberry), feather, kettle, snowshoe, smoking pipe, etc.

Many African languages have highly developed gender systems

controlling concord. An example is Bariba, a language of Dahomey and southwestern Nigeria. The following noun classes are found (each example is given with an adjective to show the concord):

1. /dum baka/   'a big horse'
2. /kpèè bakaru/   'a big stone'
3. /boo bakɔ/   'a big goat'
4. /dɔnɔn bakɔ/   'a big fire'
5. /yam bakam/   'a big space'
6. /tam bakasu/   'a big yam'
7. /gáá bakanu/   'a big thing'

Classes 3 and 4 have the same forms of the adjective. They can, however, be clearly distinguished by the concord forms of the 'that': /gé/ with class 3 and /wí/ with class 4.

These seven genders are only very loosely connected with any discernible differences in meaning. For example, all nouns referring to persons are in class 4, but so are also such words as 'fire,' 'ulcer,' 'mouth.'

14.9 Genders are primarily syntactic categories, but they may also have inflectional significance. In Bariba there are a number of different allomorphs of the plural affix. In some instances the plural can be predicted if the concord class (gender) is known. For example, all nouns of class 2 form the plural by adding /-nu/. Conversely, if the plural is known to be formed by /-nu/, it may be predicted that the noun belongs to gender 2 or 3. Class 3, however, includes nouns that form their plurals by adding /-nu/ or /-su/. There are a few nouns, mostly in class 1, which are irregular.

A similar situation is familiar to students of Latin and Greek. For example, in Latin the first declension (a paradigmatic subclass) is largely composed of feminine nouns. There are, however, a few masculines, including *agricola*, 'farmer,' *poeta* 'poet,' and *nauta* 'sailor.' The second declension is largely composed of masculine and neuter nouns, but contains a number of feminines, including *fagus* 'beech,' *pinus* 'pine,' and *taxus* 'yew.' That is, in spite of numerous exceptions, there is a positive and significant correlation between gender and inflection.

14.10 In nouns, gender is commonly an inherent feature of each stem. That is, nouns are not inflected for gender, but each noun has a characteristic gender. In those languages with a well-developed concord system, adjectives are usually inflected for gender; that is, no adjective has an inherent gender, but may be inflected to produce a form for each gender. In many instances this is a useful basis for distinguishing between these two parts of speech. It can be conveniently used in Latin and Swahili and many other languages.

Content categories are not inherently either inflectional, derivational, or associated with the roots, even in a given language, but may be associated in different ways with the different parts of the expression system of the language.

14.11 Person is a common category in verbs and pronouns. English verbal inflection for person is very rudimentary, so we will start our discussion from a consideration of the pronoun root forms. Eight sets of forms were listed in 8.18 as personal pronouns. Of these, *who* is a special case and will not be discussed here. The remaining seven are ordinarily thought of as belonging to one of three persons, each of which is said to occur in both singular and plural. Actually, some questions can be raised about this interpretation.

The **third person** certainly has a singular and plural in English. These forms have much in common syntactically and semantically with singular and plural nouns, and can often be directly substituted for them. The usage of pronouns parallels all the vagaries of the noun plurals. *Where are my pants? They were right here. : Where is my shirt? It was right here.* In some situations *they* can substitute directly for a construction composed primarily of third person singular pronouns. *He and she came. They soon went.* All these considerations support treating *they* as the plural of *he she it* in much the same sense as *dogs* is the plural of *dog*.

The **second person** presents a different situation. In most dialects there is absolutely no distinction whatever between the so-called singular and the so-called plural. *You* is used indiscriminately and always with the unmarked form of the verb. This is in contrast with the third person, where the differentiation between singular and plural pronouns is paralleled by concord forms of the verb (in the present). With no structural basis whatever, it is questionable procedure to use two labels, "second person singular" and "second person plural." Such labels are justified in those dialects which do actually have two forms, frequently something like /yúw/ : /yúwɔнl/.

In the **first person** the situation is even more complex. Two forms occur in all dialects. However, the distinction between them is seldom comparable to that between singular and plural in nouns, or to the distinction in the third person pronouns. *I* means, roughly, 'the speaker.' If it had a plural it would be expected to mean 'the speakers.' This is certainly not an ordinary meaning of *we*. It might occur in a choric reading, but this would be unusual and artificial. I do not remember ever having heard *we* used as a plural of *I* in any instance that was spontaneous and unrehearsed. While it is probably convenient to continue familiar terms, it is important to realize that "first person plural" can be nothing more than a convenient designation for *we;* it is not a description.

14.12   The commonest meaning of *we* is 'the speaker and somebody else.' In English the "somebody else" is literally anybody. In some other languages a distinction comparable to that which English makes between second and third persons is made in the "somebody else." In the Cree paradigms of 9.9 one category refers to the speaker and the hearer; this is usually called the **inclusive first person.** Another refers to the speaker and someone other than the hearer; this is usually called the **exclusive first person.** Such a distinction occurs in many widely scattered languages, though, of course, there are differences of detail from language to language.

In Cree, both forms of the first person plural are secondary, however. They are formed by combinations of the following categories. (The forms cited are used in noun inflection to indicate the possessor.)

/ke–/   'the hearer is involved'
/ne–/   'the speaker but not the hearer is involved'
/o–/   'neither speaker nor hearer is involved'

Alone these will be translatable by 'your' (singular), 'my,' and 'his.' The latter involves no distinction of sex-gender, but is animate rather than inanimate.

/–enān/   'the speaker and someone else are involved'
/–wāw/   'two or more but not the speaker are involved'

In combination the following meanings are expressed:

/ke-	−enān/	'our (inclusive)'
/ne-	−enān/	'our (exclusive)'
/ke-	−wāw/	'your (plural)'
/o-	−wāw/	'their'

14.13 The same Cree paradigm includes forms illustrative of another type of person distinction, that between **proximate** and **obviative** third persons. Both refer to someone other than the speaker or hearer, but they distinguish between two such persons. Roughly, the proximate refers to the nearer one, the main character in the narrative, or the one mentioned first. The obviative refers to the lesser character or to the one mentioned second. This is an inflectional category in both nouns and verbs, and the references are kept more or less clear by concord. For example:

/kitotēw/	'he (prox.) talks to him (obv.)'
/kitotik/	'he (obv.) talks to him (prox.)'
/okimāw/	'chief (prox.)'
/okimāwa/	'chief (obv.)'
/iskwēw/	'woman (prox.)'
/iskwēwa/	'woman (obv.)'
/okimāw iskwēwa kitotēw/	'The chief talks to the woman.'
/okimāwa iskwēw kitotik/	ditto
/okimāw iskwēwa kitotik/	'The woman talks to the chief.'
/okimāwa iskwēw kitotēw/	ditto

The sentences translated alike are of course not identical in meaning, since they may imply some difference in the place of the two individuals in the total narrative. Nevertheless, the primary function of the distinction is to identify the relationships between nouns and verbs. This is shown clearly in these sentences, which, though admittedly artificial in some respects, do illustrate the Cree method of marking certain syntactic relationships. There are numerous complexities in the uses of these distinctions, which, though presumably clear to a Cree, can be very perplexing to a learner.

14.14 English makes limited use of contrasts comparable to that in Cree between proximate and obviative. One common case is the use of *the former* : *the latter*. Frequently the use of *this* : *that* parallels the Cree system in some respects. Both these devices are used with the same rather erratic shifting from one form to another which the student thinks he observes when he starts reading Cree. An American seldom has any difficulty following the story through a tangle of *this* and *that* because the usages follow established English conventions.

The significant difference between these devices and the contrast in Cree between proximate and obviative is that, while English can distinguish in various ways between two characters in a narrative, it is not necessary to do so. In Cree, however, the proximate : obviative dichotomy is compulsory. This sort of nonconformity between the categories of languages imposes one of the major difficulties in translation. Consider the following sentences.

James and John had a fight. He got a black eye.

To translate this into Cree, one would have to decide who got the black eye. One of the two names 'James' and 'John' would have to be marked as obviative, since there cannot be two proximates in one context. Then 'he' would have to be marked as either proximate or obviative in accordance with our decision. In Cree it is difficult to be ambiguous or to dodge the issue. In English ambiguity at this point is possible, though one can be as specific as he likes. If, however, the sentence were *James and Mary . . .*, English could not easily be ambiguous, but would identify the reference of the pronoun by using either *he* or *she*. Cree would have to distinguish here also, but by the same device as before. But in certain other contexts, Cree could be ambiguous where English could not. Languages differ not as much in what they can express as in what they regularly do and must express. Translation must frequently add to the meaning by making distinctions which are required by the structure of one language but not specified in the text being translated.

14.15 Most languages have words or affixes which are used to specify the particular instance intended; these are sometimes called **demonstratives.** In English there are two, *this* and *that*. The basic distinction between the two is a matter of proximity. *This* points out the thing which is nearer. *That* refers to the one which is farther away. The same contrast is found in the adverbials *here* and *there* and in the obsolescent words *hither : thither* and *hence :*

thence. Of course there are numerous complications in the way this distinction is actually applied, but whenever the two are in contrast, some form of this difference can be found.

Other languages have similar contrasts but distinguish more degrees. This is the case in some English dialects which have a three-way contrast between *here, there,* and *yonder,* and between *this, that . . . there,* and *that . . . yonder.* Instances have been reported of several more gradations of this sort. Latin has three demonstratives, but the distinction involves another contrast. *Hic* generally means 'near the speaker,' *iste* can mean 'near the hearer,' and *ille* 'remote from both.' Translation difficulties can easily arise. *Hic* is usually translated 'this' and *ille* 'that,' but *iste* must be translated 'this' or 'that' depending on the context. In addition, of course, differences in the details of application of these contrasts in the two languages can produce other complexities.

Another type of distinction which is commonly made is that between objects which are visible and those which are not visible. Since visible objects are frequently nearer than invisible ones, the distinction is usually translatable by 'this' and 'that.' But such a translation may badly obscure the sense that was intended or even be contradictory to it.

These examples will serve to indicate that demonstratives cannot be satisfactorily defined by translation glosses. This is, of course, true of many other linguistic contrasts, but is particularly troublesome with items of this sort. Only copious illustration of usage can ever convey the meanings of such words or morphemes. To be most effective these illustrations must be chosen with great care, and preferably should include examples of contrasts.

14.16 There are a number of categories which are associated with the verb in Latin, including active, future, imperfective, imperative, indicative, passive, past, perfective, present, subjunctive. However, such a random listing, even if full definition were given, presents no significant picture. The several categories are not independent entities, suitably presented by mere listing, but components in a system with significant interrelationships, meaningful only within the system. Those listed are organized into four sets: past, present, and future are the categories of **tense;** perfective and imperfective are those of **aspect;** indicative, subjunctive, and imperative are those of **mood;** and active and passive are those of **voice.** The members of each set contrast with one another, but they combine with members of the other sets. In fact, every Latin finite verb must exhibit one category from each of these four sets. However, not all combinations are possible, and only the following occur (the second person singular of a verb meaning 'rule' is given):

		INDICATIVE		SUBJUNCTIVE		IMPERATIVE	
		Active	Passive	Active	Passive	Active	Passive
IMPERFECTIVE	Pres.	regis	regeris	regās	regāris	rege	regere
	Past	regēbās	regēbāris	regerēs	regerēris	—	—
	Fut.	regēs	regēris	—	—	regitō	regitor
PERFECTIVE	Pres.	rēxistī	rectus es	rēxerīs	rectus sīs	—	—
	Past	rēxerās	rectus erās	rēxissēs	rectus essēs	—	—
	Fut.	rēxeris	rectus eris	—	—	—	—

Of 36 possible combinations only 24 occur; of these 19 are expressed morphologically and 5 by syntactic constructions.

Each of these sets of categories is in some ways comparable to a set of color terms as described in 1.5. For example, the tenses divide the continuum of time into three portions. The division does not accord strictly with logic, however, and there are occasional usages that complicate or confuse the pattern. But in general, every temporal circumstance is assigned by the content structure of Latin to one of these three tenses, much as every physical color is assigned by the content system of English to one of eleven basic colors.

14.17   The English system of verbal categories is quite different. For example, there is a **passive** marked by {be} + {$-D_2$}. It is in many ways similar to the Latin passive, and indicates that the grammatical subject is not the doer of the action but the undergoer. E.g., *The car is driven frequently. The box was opened with difficulty. The ball was thrown to third base.* All these sentences have passive verbal phrases, and *car, box,* and *ball* are thereby clearly shown to be the recipients of the actions. There is, however, nothing like the Latin active to indicate that the grammatical subject is the doer of the action. Rather there is in English what can at best be called non-passive. It can be used in various ways: *The man drives the car. The boy opened the box. The shortstop threw the ball.* In all these sentences the grammatical subject is the doer of the action. *The car drives easily. The box opened at the top. The ball threw straight.* In none of these is the grammatical subject the doer, but rather the undergoer. In spite of quite opposite implications with identical verbs, none of these sentences is really ambiguous; in each it is clear what semantic relation exists between the subject and the verb. But this is NOT signaled by the form of the verb; some other feature of the sentence must tell what part the subject has in the action. Verb forms like *drives, opened, threw* do not specify anything like Latin voice. The English passive category does not contrast with an active category, but only with non-specification (in the verb) of voice.

There are four basic categories in this sector of the English verbal system, and all have this same characteristic. None of them contrast with any other category, but only with their own absence. The absence of a category does not signify the presence of its opposite, but only leaves the matter unspecified. For another example, the English **past** (marked by $\{-D_1\}$) specifies that the action took place at some earlier time. Verbal phrases without past indication merely say nothing about time, and hence may be used of any time. *The train goes at five o'clock tomorrow. Yesterday he comes to me and says . . .* (quite colloquial, of course, but very frequent in speech) *He sees something over there.* These are respectively future, past, and present in time reference, but the verb forms are all comparable. The time is signaled by something else, including such items as *tomorrow* and *yesterday* and various contextual and situational matters. This particular type of verb form is most often used in English in situations where the time is not only unspecified but actually irrelevant: *The earth rotates on its axis. Two and two is four. Barking dogs don't bite.* These are statements of real or imagined universal timeless truths. *Mr. Smith teaches school. Father plays tennis every day.* These are habitual activities where temporal limitations are not under consideration.

If temporal limitations were of concern, a different form (marked by $\{be\} + \{-ing\}$) would be used: *Mr. Smith is teaching school this year, but will retire in June. After being away for a year, Mr. Smith is teaching school again. Father is playing tennis every day while his vacation lasts.* The meaning of this form is very complex, sometimes emphasizing duration, sometimes limitation, but always some aspect of extent in time. It can be labeled as **limited duration.**

The fourth of these categories may be labeled **current relevance.** It is marked by {have} + {–D₂}. It indicates that the action or its results are still pertinent in some way. As with the others its absence merely leaves current relevance unspecified. The contrast may be seen in pairs like *I have been in America for three years.; I was in America for three years.* In combination with the past, this marks that the fact was currently relevant at some past time. *I had been in America for three years when I started to college.*

These four categories combine with one another in every possible way. The sixteen combinations may be illustrated with the verb *give*, here in the forms appropriate to a plural subject *they.*

None of the four specified:	*give*
One category specified:	
Past	*gave*
Current relevance	*have given*
Limited duration	*are giving*
Passive	*are given*
Two categories specified:	
Past + current relevance	*had given*
Past + limited duration	*were giving*
Past + passive	*were given*
Current relevance + limited duration	*have been giving*
Current relevance + passive	*have been given*
Limited duration + passive	*are being given*
Three categories specified:	
Past + current relevance + limited duration	*had been giving*
Past + current relevance + passive	*had been given*
Past + limited duration + passive	*were being given*
Current relevance + limited duration + passive	*have been being given*
All four categories specified:	*had been being given*

14.18   The Latin and English systems of verbal categories are different in very fundamental ways. Latin has a number of sets of categories that contrast, one from each set being (in most instances) obligatory. English has a group of categories which merely specify matters that might otherwise be left unspecified, and which are not obligatory in any way in most contexts. This is paralleled by the fact that all Latin verb forms have complex sequences of often highly fused affixes, whereas English verb phrases may have any number of grammatical markers from zero to four (or more if those of some other systems are included). It is tempting to think that the difference in the content structures is simply a counterpart of the difference in morphologic structures: obligatory categories are merely concomitants of obligatory morphemes, and optional non-contrasting categories, of optional and compatible markers. But it is not as simple as this. In English nouns the morphology is similar (though much simpler) to the situation in English verbs. Noun stems are found either with or without a plural suffix. But the two categories singular and plural contrast in the way Latin verbal categories contrast. *Man* is singular; *men* is plural. We feel that there is something strange about either *one or more man* or *one or more men*. To leave number unspecified in English we must resort to a circumlocution, *man or men*. The system of inflectional categories (part of the content system) is not simply a reflection of the morphology or syntax, but a separate, parallel system with its own peculiarities.

14.19   Throughout the discussion in this chapter certain categories have been treated in such a way as to imply that they are associated primarily with certain parts of speech. While it is probably true that number, for example, is most often basically a category of nouns, this is not necessarily the case. For example, in Quileute (Oregon) both nouns and verbs have plurals. /aʔt'šit/ 'chief' (singular) : /aʔaʔt'šit/ 'chiefs' (plural), /éla·xali/ 'I leave him' (singular) : /éʔela·xali/ 'I leave him often' (plural), /ó·xwal/ 'he carries water' (singular) : /ó·ʔo·xwal/ 'he carries water often' (plural). The two verbal examples are exactly comparable in their formation to the noun cited. All three are formed by the infix /-ʔV-/. The latter two are not plural verbs in the sense that they are verb forms used with plural actors. Instead, they indicate the plurality of the action expressed.

There is no grammatical category that is necessarily associated with any particular type of word. Each language has its own patterns. As between closely related languages (like most European languages) the patterns may be quite similar, and the similarities may be reinforced by conventional grammatical statements. As a result we are accustomed to think of certain categories as "always" expressed in certain ways. But languages of other relationships, associated with other cultures, may be fundamentally different, not only in how they express things, but in what they express and how they associate in a sentence structure the various concepts which are mentioned. No single pattern can be taken as normative. One must carefully avoid the tendency to think of the conventions of his own language as logically necessary or as inherently more reasonable or convenient than those of others.

||||||||||||||||||||||||||||||||||||||||||||||||||||||||||||||||||||||||||||||||||

◇◇◇◇◇◇◇◇◇◇◇◇◇◇◇◇◇◇◇◇◇◇◇◇◇

15

Articulatory Phonetics

15.1 The science of linguistics depends on various other disciplines for certain basic concepts and methods. One of the most important contributions is made by phonetics, particularly the older branch known as **articulatory phonetics.** This branch is concerned with the study of sounds usable in speech in terms of the mechanisms of their production by the human vocal apparatus. It has provided linguists with the greater part of their technique and terminology in handling sounds.

Phoneticians at one time set as their goal the exact and detailed description of every sound. As work proceeded, it soon became evident that this objective could never be reached. The human vocal apparatus can produce an infinity of sounds. The only limit on the number which can be identified is the instruments used. Nor can the field be feasibly restricted by excluding some on the basis that they do not figure in speech. Certainly some are rarely so used, but some languages use sounds which from our ethnocentric viewpoint seem very odd. A linguist must be prepared to find any vocal sound in use in speech. General phonetics has accordingly come to seek after a comprehensive description of classes of sounds and of the general mechanisms of speech production. One objective is to provide a means by which any given sound can be classified and described with whatever degree of precision may be necessary. This provides the linguist with the tools needed to handle the phonetic systems which he finds in his work.

15.2   Speech production is an incidental activity of the respiratory system. Most of the time, air passes into and out of the lungs more or less silently; only when there is some obstruction is appreciable sound produced. Speech further requires that there be easy and effective control of these sound-producing obstructions. This limits the mechanisms of interest to linguists largely to movements within the mouth, pharynx, and larynx. While these have always received the greater attention from phoneticians and linguists, it must not be forgotten that the motive power for sound production arises largely in the activity of the thorax, which therefore has an important, though quite different, effect on speech production.

The traditional phonetic classification of speech sounds is based primarily on three variables, each of which will receive separate discussion. These are: (1) the activity, if any, in the larynx, most familiarly thought of in terms of the dichotomy between voiced and voiceless sounds; (2) the place of maximum constriction in the mouth or pharynx, usually referred to as the **point of articulation;** (3) the type of sound-producing or sound-modifying mechanism in the mouth or pharynx, often referred to as the **manner of articulation.** While these three provide a basic classification, alone they are inadequate to specify sounds with sufficient precision for all linguistic work. Not infrequently it is necessary to mention some **secondary articulation,** that is, some other feature or features which can be conceived as modifications imposed on a basic speech sound defined in terms of the three classical phonetic variables.

15.3   The **larynx** is a cartilaginous structure at the summit of the trachea. Its chief importance in speech is that it contains the vocal cords, which are two horizontal folds of elastic tissue, one on either side of the passage. They may be opened so as to cause no obstruction (as in normal breathing), completely closed, or partially closed so as to produce various sorts of audible sounds. Since they are elastic they may be caused to vibrate if brought together while air is forced between them. The resulting sound is **voice.** Though voice may be produced by other elastic organs, voice produced by the cords is by all means the most important type and is usually referred to as "voice" without qualification. Voice is characterized by a definite pitch, which is controlled, in large part, by adjustment of the tension on the cords. Many speech sounds are basically glottal voice modified in various ways by the shapes of the respiratory passage above the larynx.

The passage of air through a narrowly constricted opening produces a second fundamental type of sound known as **friction.** Friction differs from voice in that it has no definite pitch. If the vocal cords are incompletely closed, glottal friction may be produced. This substitutes for voice in **whisper.** The exact quality of the whisper is determined by the shape of the passages above in ways that parallel closely the control of quality of voiced sounds. No glottal sound can escape modification by the position of the vocal organs in the mouth and pharynx.

Nevertheless, it is customary to list in an inventory of sound types at least three glottal sounds, each of which is provided with a phonetic symbol — [h ɦ ʔ]. They may be taken as cover symbols, useful primarily in situations where the articulatory modification does not particularly need to be noticed.

The **glottal stop** [ʔ] is produced by the closure, opening, or closure and opening of the vocal cords. It is, of course, not possible to have a voiced glottal stop similar in mode of formation to another voiced stop. Glottal stop frequently accompanies various articulations, producing **glottalized sounds.** Most common are glottalized stops, but glottalized fricatives and resonants also occur.

Customarily, [h] and [ɦ] are listed as "glottal fricatives," voiceless and voiced respectively. For [h] this description is generally adequate, since the mechanism of formation is quite comparable to that of [f θ s x], etc. But for [ɦ] it is nothing more than a convenient label, since a mechanism such as that for [v ð z ɣ] is obviously impossible. A rapid change in the pitch of the voice seems to be involved in [ɦ], as the cords are relaxed or tightened in passing from voice to an [h]-like position, or the reverse. The pitch change is so rapid that it is not heard as such, but produces an acoustic effect very similar to [h].

Since during the pronunciation of [h] or [ɦ], the mouth may be in position for almost any sound, these two may be considered as existing in a number of varieties, each of which can be alternatively considered as a variety of some vowel or other speech sound defined by that articulation.

Other adjustments of vocal cords produce falsetto, ventriloquistic voice, and various other phenomena of lesser importance.

The mechanism of most of these is poorly understood, and they are only rarely of linguistic importance. The diagrams illustrate

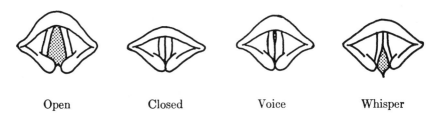

| Open | Closed | Voice | Whisper |

The Vocal Cords from Above and Behind

the appearance of the cords as seen from above in four of their most important positions.

15.4   The passages may be partially or wholly obstructed or altered in shape by various organs known as **articulators.** Often the obstruction is formed by two organs, one of which is movable and approaches the other, which is immovable.

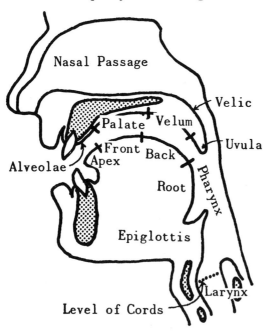

The roof of the mouth is divisible into four portions. Just behind the front teeth is the tooth ridge or **alveolae,** the portion of the roof of the mouth which is convex in shape. Behind the alveolae is the **palate** (or hard palate), which is a plate of bone thinly covered with other tissue. It is immovable. Behind the palate is the **velum** (or soft palate), which is muscular and movable and may be raised to close off the nasal passage. This is called **velic** closure in contrast with **velar** closure, which is the closure of the oral passage by the tongue against the lower surface of the velum. The **uvula** is a small, flexible appendage hanging down from the posterior edge of the velum.

Around the alveolae and palate are the **teeth.** In many articulations the edges of the tongue lie against the molars closing the oral

passage at the sides. This, however, is not independently variable, but seems to be largely incidental to the height of the tongue, so that the molars are of little significance in phonetics. The term **teeth,** when unqualified, refers to the upper front teeth only. The lower teeth are much less often significant, but do play some part in speech formation.

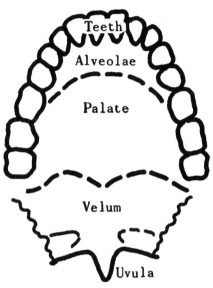

The **tongue** is conveniently divided into four portions. The **apex** is the portion that lies at rest opposite the alveolae; it may articulate against the teeth, alveolae, or palate. The **front** is the portion that lies at rest opposite the fore part of the palate. It may articulate against the alveolae, palate, or velum. The **back** or **dorsum** is the portion which lies at rest opposite the velum or the back part of the palate; it may articulate against the posterior part of the palate, or any part of the velum, or the uvula. The **root** of the tongue forms the front wall of the pharynx. While not often listed as an articulator, this portion of the tongue contributes to sound formation in altering the size and shape of the pharynx.

Both the lips are movable and of importance in speech. However, the lower lip is more flexible and more variously used. Therefore, when used without qualification, the term **lip** refers to the lower. It may articulate against the upper lip or the teeth. The spreading and rounding of the lips, and their protrusion, are among the most important secondary articulations. The lips have the advantage of being visible and hence should be visually observed, as should any other feature which can be seen. One of the commonest failures of students in phonetic work is to neglect the visual evidence of sound formation.

15.5   The articulators taken in pairs serve to define the basic **points of articulation.** Intermediate points of articulation are common, but the following terms do, however, serve to classify sounds with sufficient precision for most linguistic purposes:

	LOWER ARTICULATOR	UPPER ARTICULATOR
Labial		
Bilabial	(lower) lip	upper lip
Labiodental	(lower) lip	(upper) teeth
Apical		
Dental	apex of tongue	(upper) teeth
Alveolar	apex of tongue	alveolae
Retroflex	apex of tongue (see below)	palate
Frontal		
Alveopalatal	front of tongue	alveolae and far front of palate
Prepalatal	front of tongue	front of palate
Dorsal		
Palatal	back of tongue	back of palate
Velar	back of tongue	velum
Uvular	back of tongue	extreme back of velum or uvula

Extreme forms of dental sounds in which the apex of the tongue actually protrudes beyond the teeth are sometimes distinguished as **interdental.**

In **retroflex** articulation the tip of the tongue is turned back so that the closure is relatively far back on the palate. Because of this turning back, the closure may be made with the underside of the tip.

Alveopalatal sounds are, as the term indicates, intermediate between alveolar and palatal. Both the alveolae (or perhaps only the back portion) and the front part of the palate are involved. The apex of the tongue is not involved in alveopalatal or palatal sounds and should be kept down. Close attention to this will help avoid one of the common errors of Americans with some of these sounds — that is, the tendency to substitute an alveolar sound followed by [y].

In uvular sounds the articulation is as far back as possible. American English velars vary from palatal to true velar. Prepalatal and uvular sounds may be considered as just beyond the limits of variation of velars in normal American speech.

In **labiovelar** stops there is a simultaneous closure at two points, bilabial and velar. These sounds are often indicated by digraphs [kp] and [gb]. They are not, however, [k] followed by [p], or [g] followed by [b], but in a sense these two stops said simultaneously.

15.6 There are three basic general sound types: stops, fricatives, and resonants. The vast majority of speech sounds fall into one of these categories.

Any sound is modified by the shape of the air passages and cavities open to it. Thus, if voice is produced by the vocal cords, the sound will be quite different according as the oral passage, the nasal passage, or both are open to it, and according to the shape of the oral passage. (The shape of the nasal passage is not subject to controllable variation.) Thus a wide variety of voiced resonants are produced. **Resonants** are sounds in which the only function of the mouth and nose is to modify the sound already produced in the larynx. That is, there is no constriction in the mouth producing friction or other appreciable sound. Voiced resonants are generally more common than voiceless resonants. In the latter there must be some sound other than voice produced in or near the larynx — generally weak friction at the partially constricted vocal cords. Voiceless resonants are frequently not phonemically distinct from one another, and hence are commonly classed together as a glottal fricative [h].

If there is a constriction producing friction anywhere in the mouth, the resulting sound is a **fricative.** There may be simultaneous voice in the cords, in which case the sound is a voiced fricative, or the cords may be inactive, in which case the sound is a voiceless fricative.

Stops are produced by complete closure. Prolonged closure does not, of course, produce sound. It is only the act of closing or opening, or both, or glottal activity during closure (which cannot be long continued) that produces the sound known as stops. They therefore differ fundamentally from resonants and fricatives in that they cannot be indefinitely prolonged.

15.7   Fricatives vary not only according to the position of the constriction (point of articulation), but also according to its shape. Three kinds are shown in the chart, page 252. In **slit fricatives** the opening is relatively wide horizontally and shallow vertically. The tongue (if it is the organ concerned) is relatively flat. In **groove fricatives** the tongue is more or less grooved by a raising of the edges. The result is that the opening is much narrower horizontally, but may be deeper vertically than in slit fricatives. Groove fricatives all have more or less of an [s]-like quality, and are for this reason sometimes called **sibilants**. In both of these types the opening is **median,** that is, it includes the mid line of the mouth. A

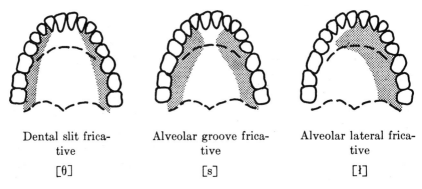

Dental slit frica- tive	Alveolar groove frica- tive	Alveolar lateral frica- tive
[θ]	[s]	[ɬ]

lateral fricative has the opening on one side of the mouth only, or on both sides, but there is closure at the mid line. The differences between these types may be illustrated by the diagrams showing the areas on the roof of the mouth against which the tongue has contact for [θ], [s], and [ɬ]. Other types and many intergradations of these are possible.

15.8   There are numerous types of stops which can profitably be distinguished, and the mechanisms for many of them are relatively complex. The following descriptions of types of stops will be largely restricted to the opening phase (the closing phase is generally comparable, but variations are less frequently phonemically significant), and assumes that the stop will be followed immediately by a vowel [a].

A **voiced stop** is one in which the cords are in position for voice before the opening of the stop. The voice then starts as soon as the air stream starts. This may precede the opening by a short interval, so that if it is not held too long, voice may actually continue through the stop. A **voiceless stop** is one in which the cords are relaxed as the air stream starts, so that the start of the voice is delayed. The length of this delay may materially affect the perceived quality of the consonant. The air pressure necessary to produce voice for the following vowel will produce a strong puff of air in the interval between the opening of the stop and the closing of the vocal cords. The result is a **voiceless aspirated stop.** Since the puff of air (aspiration) is usually accompanied by glottal friction it may be represented by [h] and the sequence by [tha] or [tʰa], etc.

If the build-up of air pressure is delayed until the vocal cords are brought into voicing position, there will be no puff of air. Such a stop is a **voiceless unaspirated stop,** or **simple stop.** Unaspirated stops may be indicated, when the lack of aspiration is to be emphasized, by [t⁼], etc. Aspiration is a more or less relative matter. All intergradations are possible. The terms aspirated and unaspirated imply that only two values are considered significant. For some linguistic purposes much more precise specification is necessary.

Aspiration may usually be detected by holding a thin strip of paper in front of the lips. If aspiration is present, the strip will jump noticeably outward. Of course, the strip must be adjusted to the right degree of flexibility. Aspiration may also sometimes be felt against the back of the hand. These methods depend on the fact that aspiration involves a puff of breath, but this is usually closely correlated with the acoustic impression.

Voiced aspirated stops are much less frequent than voiceless aspirates. There must be voice or some similar sound at the moment of opening, followed by a puff of air. This is usually acoustically similar to [ɦ]. The sequence [dɦa] differs from [tha] in that there is voice or relatively strong glottal friction throughout.

15.9 Stops, and less often other types of sounds, may also be classified on the basis of the strength of articulation. **Fortis** sounds are those produced with relatively stronger articulation, **lenis** with relatively weaker. Voice, aspiration, and strength of articulation often combine in various ways. In English /p t k/ are generally fortis, voiceless, and aspirated, /b d g/ are generally lenis, voiced, and unaspirated. All three variables are relative, and various intergradations occur. Moreover some allophones of either set show different combinations.

Stops can be pronounced with more or less simultaneous glottal closure. Such sounds are said to be **glottalized.** Glottalized stops are most commonly very fortis, and glottalization is sometimes thought of as merely the extreme of the fortis : lenis dimension. However, glotallized lenis sounds are used in certain languages.

15.10 **Affricated stops** or **affricates** are produced by a relatively slower opening, simple stops by a relatively faster opening. As the stop is released it is necessary to pass through an articulation which, if held, would produce a typical fricative. For the time interval in which the articulators are passing through this position, friction is produced, and this contributes to the total acoustic impression which is heard as a stop. Affricates and simple stops differ in the prominence of this element of friction. An affricate is in some respects the same as a stop plus a homorganic fricative. Whether it is heard as a single sound or as a cluster depends on the phonemic patterns of the hearer.

15.11 There are as many types of affricates as there are fricatives. The chart shows two: **median** and **lateral.** The dental, alveolar, and alveopalatal median affricates are most commonly grooved. [¢] = [ts], [č] = [tš], [ǰ] = [dž]. Slit affricates such as [tθ] and [pf] also occur, though not given in the chart. The commonest lateral affricates are [ƛ] = [tł] and [λ] = [dl]. These may also be described as **laterally released stops,** since the distinction between [t] and [ƛ] rests as much on the fact that the latter is released first at the side rather than at the center as on any difference of speed.

15.12 Since an affricate differs from a cluster only in phonemic status, it might be thought that to discuss affricates in a treatment of phonetics is a confusion of phonemic and phonetic facts. In a sense this is so, but no more so in this instance than in any treatment of sound phonetically as a sequence of segments. The segmentation of speech is strongly affected by phonemic patterns. Phonetically there is no basis for the kind of segmentation which we customarily use.

Moreover, human hearing seems to be such that our impression of speech as a sequence of segments cannot be other than phonemic. In even the slowest affricate the fricative element is too short to be heard separately. The whole sequence is heard as one acoustic effect; it is interpreted on the basis of phonemic patterns either as one or as two sounds. This is not peculiar to affricates; it is just as true of aspirated stops. It is also true of most consonant clusters, or even of sequences of consonant and vowel. The shortest stretch of sound which can be heard as separate is longer than most of the segments which are heard as distinct sounds in normal speech. What is heard is a sequence of sounds each more or less smeared over its neighbors. The division of the stream of sound into discrete parts is a process of interpretation. There is no fundamental difference between the instances, like affricates, where the segmentation differs conspicuously from language to language, and other sound features which are generally interpreted much the same in many languages.

15.13   Variation in the manner of release of stops can be matched by variation in the manner of closure. Some languages have **preaspirated** stops. Perhaps more common are **prenasalized** stops. In these the oral closure slightly precedes the velic closure. The result impresses Americans often as a stop preceded by a short homorganic nasal [^{m}b], [^{n}t], etc. As with different types of release the interpretation of such sounds as single sounds or clusters depends on phonemic patterns of the language.

15.14   **Implosive stops** are made by drawing air into the pharynx by closing the cords and pulling the larynx downward, thus producing a slight vacuum above it. When the stop is released there is a very slight movement of air inward. This MAY be demonstrable by holding a paper strip before the lips; often, however, it is extremely weak. **Voiced implosives** result from an incomplete closure of the cords. In this case there may be no movement of air inward on release, because the vacuum in the pharynx and mouth has been expended in voicing.

15.15   **Resonants** are sounds in which the only function of the mouth and nose is to modify by resonance the sound which is already produced in the larynx. That is, there is no constriction in the mouth narrow enough to produce friction. There must be an unobstructed passage outward from the larynx. This may be through the mouth, through the nose, or through both. If only the nose is open, the sound is a **nasal.** The mouth is then a dead-end cavity, but its size and shape effect the resonance. Nasals are, therefore, best classified by the position of the closure in the mouth, a nasal being possible for any articulations for which a stop is possible, provided only that the closure is far enough forward to leave the velic passage open.

If both the nasal and oral passages are open, the sound is **nasalized.** This type is not provided for in the chart, since the sounds are conveniently considered as modifications of the corresponding oral sounds. They may be symbolized by [˜] written over the symbol for the corresponding oral sound. Any oral resonant can easily be nasalized; oral fricatives are sometimes nasalized, but stops cannot be, of course, since the opening of the nasal passage would immediately disqualify the sound as a stop.

15.16   If only the mouth is open, the sound is an **oral** resonant. These may be classified as median and lateral. **Lateral resonants** are closed at the mid line, and usually at one side. The other side is open enough that no friction occurs. Most laterals have an [l]-like quality to American ears, though there may be several contrasting laterals in some languages.

Median resonants include most vowels and various vowel-like consonants. The latter are commonly called **semi-vowels.** Whether median resonants are to be considered as consonants or as vowels is a matter of phonemic function in the particular language, not of phonetic nature. The three that are shown on the consonant chart are the three that occur in the consonant system of English. Only tradition and English background justify listing these in a general consonant chart. English /y/ is any mid or high palatal resonant functioning as a consonant; /w/ is any mid or high velar resonant with strong or moderate lip rounding functioning as a consonant; /r/ is in many dialects any median resonant with tongue-tip retroflexion. All three are difficult to describe phonetically because of numerous allophones and because the phonemic problem of the consonant : vowel contrast (which is phonetically irrelevant) looms so large in our thinking about them.

15.17   Before continuing with the discussion of median resonants in their aspect as vowels, it is convenient to sum up the description of consonants by presenting a chart showing some of the more common sounds classified on the two bases which have been presented in the last several sections. This chart is definitely not an inventory of all the consonant sounds possible, or even of all used in languages. Such a listing is not feasible, and probably would be of very little use if it were made. This is a skeleton chart in that most of the blank spaces represent possible sounds. (Not all! a glottal nasal, for example, is impossible.) It is also partial in the sense that many other sound types and other articulations are possible.

For example, the whole system of **clicks** is omitted. These are produced by closing the oral passage front and back, drawing the tongue downward to produce a vacuum, and releasing at some point. The most common are dental stop-like, alveolar affricate-like, and lateral. To include them in a phonetic chart involves more than merely adding a few more rows. They constitute a whole system of sounds coordinate with that exhibited in this chart. Clicks are phonemic in a few languages, but in many more are used in a few special words, as signals to animals, or as exclamatory expressions.

The chart also omits most types of **double articulations.** In addition to the main articulation on the basis of which sounds are classified in this chart, they frequently have one of several other constrictions, usually less close, which modifies the sound in some discernible way. One of the most important is **labialization** (the sound is said to be **labialized**), in which there is added lip rounding. Another is **palatalization,** in which there is an added constriction between the tongue and palate. Customarily phoneticians consider these sound types as produced by modification of some other sound type, and they usually transcribe them by the use of some sort of diacritic. In the examples and problems in this book we have marked labialized sounds by a raised [ʷ], e.g., [kʷ] and palatalized by a raised [ʸ], e.g., [kʸ].

The chart does, however, include two common sound types which do not easily fit into the basic division into stops, fricatives, and resonants. These are **trills** and **flaps.** A trill is a rapid alternation of two homorganic sounds, one being more open than the other. It is produced by the vibration of some flexible organ (lips, tongue, uvula), but the vibration is too slow to have an identifiable pitch. A flap is produced by a very rapid motion of an articulator. Often it is comparable to a single vibration of a trill. Sometimes it is best described as an exceedingly short stop.

PARTIAL SKELETON CONSONANT CHART

		Bilabial	Labiodental	Dental	Alveolar	Retroflex	Alveopalatal	Palatal	Velar	Uvular	Labiovelar		Glottal
Stops													
Simple	vl.	p	p̪	t̪	t	ṭ		k̟	k	q	k͡p		ʔ
	vd.	b	b̪	d̪	d	ḍ		g̟	g		g͡b		
Aspirated	vl.	pʰ			tʰ				kʰ				
	vd.	bʰ			dʰ				gʰ				
Glottalized	vl.	p'			t'				k'				
	vd.												
Affricated	vl.				ȼ		č						
	ɩvd.				ʐ		ǰ						
Laterally affricated	vl.				⋋								
	vd.				λ								
Prenasalized	vl.	ᵐp			ⁿt								
	vd.	ᵐb			ⁿd								
Implosive	vl.												
	vd.	ɓ			ɗ								
Fricatives													
Slit	vl.		f	θ					x				h
	vd.	ʋ	v	ð					ɣ				ɦ
Groove	vl.				s		š						
	vd.				z		ž						
Lateral	vl.				ɬ								
	vd.												
Resonants													
Lateral	vl.												
	vd.				l		ʎ						
Nasal	vl.	m̥			n̥								
	vd.	m	ɱ	ṉ	n	ɳ	ñ	ᶯ	ŋ	ɴ			
Median	vl.	ẘ					ẙ						
	vd.	w			r		ʝ						
Flaps	vl.												
	vd.				ř								
Trills	vl.				r̃								
	vd.				r̃				R				

vl. = voiceless   vd. = voiced.

This chart shows only some of the more important points of articulation and types of consonants. Symbols are provided for only a small part of those shown. Most of the blank spaces represent pronounceable consonants.

15.18   Median oral resonants are frequently referred to loosely as **vowels.** Properly the term should be reserved for use in phonemic description, but it is convenient to use the short term in phonetic contexts. Different qualities of vowels are produced by variations of the following types. Vowels may be described or defined in terms of these variables:

1) The height of the tongue
2) The position (front or back) of the highest part of the tongue
3) The position of the lips
4) The openness of the nasal passage
5) The shape of the upper surface of the tongue
6) The tenseness of the muscles of the tongue
7) Various phenomena in the pharynx and larynx

The first two of these seem to be nearly universally significant, and hence serve as the basis for the customary primary classifications of the vowels. The others are treated as producing modifications of the basic vowels. This is, of course, in part at least a reflection of the phonemic structure of European languages.

15.19   There is complete intergradation in all these characteristics by which vowels can be described and classified. As a result there is no possibility of complete agreement on certain vowels as basic. Various phoneticians and linguists have used different frameworks for the classification of vowels. The differences are generally more evident than significant, but can be puzzling to students. In any case, vowels can be precisely defined only by reference to some arbitrarily selected standard set of vowels. These cannot be specified by written description, but only by oral transmission, either by personal teaching of a phonetician or by recordings, carefully made and equally carefully played.

15.20   One such system is that proposed by Daniel Jones. This is a set of eight **cardinal vowels.** No. 1 is defined as the extreme high front unrounded vowel, No. 4 as the extreme low front unrounded vowel, and Nos. 2 and 3 are interpolated in such a way that the intervals between seem to be "equal" in terms of acoustic impression. The four back cardinal vowels are similarly defined, but all are rounded. The eight cardinal vowels are frequently indicated on a **vowel triangle** (actually usually drawn as a trapezoid).

The cardinal vowel system is frequently referred to in works by

British linguists. It can be used with precision only by one specially trained in it, but for others, the definition of vowels in terms of the cardinal vowels often serves to give a good rough idea. The vowel systems of languages are frequently presented in the

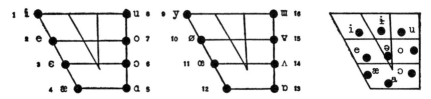

The Cardinal Vowels   English Vowels

form of such vowel triangles with the positions marked. This is done in the figure for the allophones of American vowels most frequently heard as simple vowels. (The allophones before /y w ʜ/ are generally different. Note that in no case do the American vowels coincide with the cardinal vowels.)

Not infrequently eight more cardinal vowels are listed. These have the same tongue positions as those defined above; however, the front vowels (9–12) are rounded and the back vowels (13–16) are unrounded. These are given with the symbols customarily used in Britain, the so-called IPA (International Phonetic Alphabet) symbols.

15.21 Another system, commonly used in America, employs most of the same symbols with very nearly the same values but with less claim to high precision. In addition a number of other symbols are added. This system also provides symbols for the central vowels, lacking in the British system of cardinal vowels, though provided for elsewhere in the IPA notation. In the chart on page 255 only those symbols are given which are used in this book or the workbook or are important for some other reason.

The lower high, mean mid, and higher low vowels are defined as being **lax,** that is pronounced with less tension on the muscles of the articulators. The remaining vowels are defined as **tense.**

15.22 Diphthongs may be considered either as vowels in which there is appreciable change of quality during the course of their pronunciation, or as sequences of vowels or of vowels and semivowels. Phonetically the first interpretation is generally best; phonemically they are often best treated as sequences, in other

	Front		Central		Back	
	Unrounded	Rounded	Unrounded	Rounded	Unrounded	Rounded
High	i	ü	ɨ	ʉ	ɯ	u
Lower high	ɪ		ɪ			ʊ
Higher mid	e	ö				o
Mean mid	ᴇ		ə			ꭥ
Lower mid	ɛ	ʒ	ɜ		ʌ	ɔ
Higher low	æ					
Low			a		ɑ	ɒ

instances as single phonemes. Thus there may be a marked difference in the phonetic and phonemic significance of such a term as
diphthong.

The stress may continue evenly through a diphthong, in which
case it is called a **level** diphthong, but more often it will vary
perceptibly. Those in which the stress is strongest at or near the
beginning are called **falling diphthongs.** (The stress falls.) Those
in which the main stress is at or near the end are **rising diphthongs.**
English /ay aw ɔy/ are falling diphthongs with the less stressed
element phonemically interpreted as a semivowel. /yu/ is phonetically a rising diphthong, though not usually treated as phonemically a diphthong in English. Most often, but not always, the
stress is strongest on the lower vowel and weakest on the high or
central vowel. However, some languages have phonemic contrasts
between rising and falling diphthongs that are otherwise quite
similar.

15.23 Phonetically, speech is always something more than a
linear succession of sounds. Since these are mostly produced by
air expelled from the lungs, the respiratory apparatus in the thorax
necessarily breaks the sequence up into portions. The most obvious
of these is a **breath-group.** This is the chain of sounds produced on
one breath. Its maximum duration is controlled by the necessity
of periodic inhalation. A breath-group does not, however, necessarily last as long as the air contained in the lungs might allow.

There are two partially independent mechanisms which control inhalation and exhalation of air. The first of these consists of the diaphragm and the abdominal muscles. These vary the volume of the thoracic cavity by moving its lower wall (the diaphragm) up and down. They seem to move more or less steadily throughout each breath-group, normally reversing their action between breath-groups for inhalation. This constitutes, therefore, the physiological basis of the breath-groups.

The second breathing mechanism consists of the intercostal muscles. These extend between successive pairs of ribs, and increase or decrease the volume of the thoracic cavity by moving the side walls (the rib-case). In speech the activity of the intercostal muscles does not continue steadily through the breath-group, but is subject to more rapid variation. This correlates in the simplest case with the alternation of vowels requiring relatively large amounts of air with consonants requiring less. Speech is, therefore, marked by a series of short pulses produced by this motion of the intercostal muscles. These pulses are the phonetic **syllables.** Typically a syllable centers around some vowel or other resonant and begins and ends in some sound with relatively closed articulation.

All speech consists of a sequence of such syllables and breath-groups, which are phonetically the basic framework of speech and the most clearly detectable segmentation. Their phonemic status is, however, another matter. In many languages syllables have no phonemic status whatever. They are merely part of the phonetic mechanism by which pronunciation is effected. In others, the relationship of sounds to these syllable pulses is phonemically significant, so that syllable division must be taken into account in a description of the language. Even in the latter case, however, it does not follow that phonetic and phonemic syllables are identical, and to assume that they are can be productive of serious error. In this as elsewhere, phonetics and phonemics must be kept distinct, though obviously they are intimately interrelated in many ways.

16

The Phoneme

16.1 In Chapter 2 the consonants of English were examined and found to be twenty-four in number. Among them was one which we chose to represent by the symbol /k/. This is heard, among other places, in the English words *key*, *sky*, and *caw*. This result was attained by two processes, one explicitly discussed and the other more or less implicitly assumed. The first was that of finding instances in which this sound in one of its occurrences was demonstrably in contrast with various other sounds. Thus the pair *key* and *tea* was put forth to establish /k/ and /t/ as contrasting phonemes. Some such pair can be found (not all were mentioned in the text) to establish /k/ as distinct from each of the other twenty-three consonants of English.

The implicit process was to assume that the sound which we have labeled /k/ in *key* /kíy/ is somehow "the same" as those which we labeled /k/ in *ski* /skíy/ or *caw* /kɔ́H/. This seems obvious enough to an American. But it is not necessarily obvious to a person of a different linguistic background. An Arabic speaker, for example, might object that the sounds in *key* and *caw* are quite different, though he would probably accept the identification of those in *key* and *ski*. Conversely, a speaker of Hindi would protest at the identification of that of *key* with that of *ski*, but would probably accept the identification of those in *key* and *caw*. This step in the analysis seems to depend heavily on the linguistic background of the observer. Obviously, if a linguist is to make an accurate phonemic analysis of any language, the procedure must somehow be freed from dependence on the native language patterns of the analyst.

The original method of Chapter 2 depended on a definition of the phoneme which was adequate for the purpose at that point. However, it provided only a criterion for determining when two sounds are different, and overlooked entirely the problem of determining when two sounds are alike. For this we relied on the feeling of a native speaker for his own language. We must therefore start by redefining the phoneme from a more comprehensive viewpoint. In this we will follow up the idea that was merely hinted at in 2.21.

16.2 A **phoneme** is a class of sounds. For example, the /k/ in *key* is easily demonstrated to be different from those in *ski* or *caw*, as the latter are from each other. But this is by no means the full extent of variation within one phoneme. Similarly, several other phonemes vary so widely that no significant phonetic description can be made without mentioning the variation. There is no English phoneme which is the same in all environments, though in many phonemes the variation can easily be overlooked, particularly by a native speaker. But since these patterns are not the same in any two languages, the foreigner is frequently struck by the differences that the native speaker does not hear.

16.3 Perhaps the clearest way to comprehend this aspect of the phoneme is through a brief (and somewhat superficial) description of the process by which a child learns to hear and reproduce the phonemes of his own language. The human vocal apparatus can produce a very great variety of different sounds differing from each other in numerous features. At first, the child attaches no significance to any of these and babbles randomly, using a very wide selection of these possible sounds. After a while he learns to distinguish between certain parts of his repertoire and discovers some utility in certain sequences of sounds. None of the latter are pronounced with any high degree of precision or consistency, but nevertheless some distinctions become established and at this point speech has begun. The process is not one of learning to produce sounds, but of distinguishing between sounds.

My daughter rather early learned to distinguish between labial and non-labial stops. Later she learned to distinguish between voiced and voiceless stops. However, the contrast between /t/ and /k/ was established much later. There was a long period when enough other phonemic contrasts were in use to make her speech intelligible, at least to her parents, but when /t/ and /k/ were not distinguished. [t]-like sounds were somewhat commoner than [k]-like, but the latter occurred, as did various intermediate varieties. Thus *cake* was usually something which impressed adults as /téyt/, but occasionally as /kéyt/ or /téyk/ or even /kéyk/. These several pronunciations sounded different to adults, but apparently were all alike to her. That is, from her own point of view there was one voiceless non-labial stop /T/ which might be pronounced as [t] or [k] or various other sounds, and *cake* was pronounced /TéyT/. Of course, *take*, *Kate* and *Tate* (all of which were in her vocabulary) were pronounced alike, that is, with the same range of variation, and hence all were confused. After some time she discovered the distinction and with increasing precision sorted out the four pronunciations and assigned each to its proper usage. When this had become as regular and consistent as it is in adult speech (we all make occasional slips!), her old phoneme /T/ had given way to /t/ and /k/. She had progressed one more step in acquiring the adult phonemic pattern of English.

Note that the process was merely that of dividing the total range of voiceless non-labial stops into two. Each continued as a range of variation, that is, as a class of sounds. Larger classes were replaced by smaller, but single sounds never entered into the picture. For this reason, if for no other, phonemes must be classes of sounds, but as we shall see there are other cogent reasons also.

16.4 The incentive for learning to distinguish between /t/ and /k/ was primarily the need to distinguish between such words as *cake*, *take*, *Kate*, and *Tate* and many other minimal pairs or sets. If such distinctions are not made, language serves as a less effective instrument than is otherwise possible. Use of the "correct" (from the adult point of view) pronunciation with improved success, often enough repeated, would assist in establishing the contrast firmly in the speech patterns of the child. However, /k/ would finally consist of a very wide range of sounds which will not be further divided since the stimulus which led, in this case, to differentiating /t/ and /k/ is missing: there are in English no minimal pairs for any two [k]-like sounds. The process of division therefore ceases, and the whole range of [k]-like sounds continues to produce the same reaction, that is, to remain as a single phoneme.

Had Arabic been the language the child was learning, the outcome would have been different. An Arab child might proceed through the same steps and emerge with a /K/ phoneme covering roughly the same range of sounds as the English /k/, but the process would not come to an end here. Arabic has numerous minimal pairs contrasting in two varieties of [k]-like sounds. These may be written /k/ and /q/. /k/ is rather far front: /q/ much farther back. Such pairs as /kalb/ 'dog' : /qalb/ 'heart' would force the child sooner or later to divide his juvenile /K/ phoneme into two ranges /k/ and /q/. Though narrower in their variation than English /k/, both these are, like all phonemes, classes of sounds.

An Arab listening to English may identify the consonant of English *key* with his /k/ since it is more or less fronted, and that of *caw* with his /q/ since it is more or less backed. (Actually the Arabic /k/ and /q/ are by no means identical with the two varieties of English /k/.) This may lead the Arab observer to object to the identification of the initial consonants in these words as identical. In short, in listening to English, he hears, at least in part, Arabic phonemes, not English ones.

The speaker of Hindi will be unlikely to hear any difference between the consonants of *key* and *caw*, because his language does not force him to establish such a contrast. There is, however, a contrast between aspirated stops such as /kh/ and unaspirated stops such as /k/. This may be seen from such a pair as /khiil/ 'parched grain' : /kiil/ 'nail,' and numerous others. Since the initial of *key* is regularly aspirated, he will equate it with his Hindi /kh/, whereas *ski* will be heard as containing his /k/. He may, therefore, object to the assumption that these two sounds are alike.

16.5 . The process of learning a second language involves, among other things, learning to make distinctions, both in hearing and speaking, that are phonemic in the new language, and learning to overlook those distinctions which are not significant, even though they may be phonemic in the mother tongue. Often the two languages will use very similar sounds but organize them into quite different phonemic systems. Learning new uses of old sounds is usually a larger and more difficult part of the problem than the mastering of wholly new sounds. Unfortunately, this part of the work is easily neglected. Few students of foreign languages are aware either of its magnitude or of its importance. Textbooks all too frequently aggravate the situation by describing the pronunciation in a most misleading manner. Thus French /i/ is frequently said to be pronounced as is the *i* in *machine*, which for most Americans would be /iy/. It is never so pronounced, though to most Americans French /i/ will sound much like their own /iy/. At the best, such pronunciation sounds like exceedingly poor and obviously foreign French; at the worst it may be wholly unintelligible. Phonemic systems are typically incommensurable. That is, no phonemic system can be accurately described in terms of the phonemes of another language, and very seldom can even a workable first approximation be so stated.

16.6   The definition of the phoneme in 1.10 will be inadequate when the observer cannot hear the language as a native does. To make it workable for a non-native it is necessary to add to it some objective criteria of the range of sounds that may be included within any given phoneme. There are two such criteria, and both must be met. (1) The sounds must be phonetically similar. An articulatory description such as that sketched in Chapters 2 and 3 is ordinarily a satisfactory basis for judging similarity — provided it is made sufficiently comprehensive to cover all the sounds concerned and sufficiently detailed to insure that nothing significant is overlooked. (2) The sounds must show certain characteristic patterns of distribution in the language or dialect under consideration. Two such patterns will be mentioned below. Basically both are types of distribution which make it impossible for minimal pairs to occur. The latter would of course make the two sounds members of different phonemes. Even the occurrence of two sounds in distributions which would permit minimal pairs (whether or not there are any such) will give some functional value to the distinction and hence suffice to establish the contrast as phonemic.

16.7   A **phoneme** is a class of sounds which: (1) are phonetically similar and (2) show certain characteristic patterns of distribution in the language or dialect under consideration. Note that this definition is restricted in its application to a single language or dialect. There is no such thing as a general /p/ phoneme. There is, however, an English /p/ phoneme. Likewise there is a Hindi /p/ phoneme. They are in no sense identical. Each is a feature of its own language and not relevant to any other language.

16.8 The simplest of the patterns of distribution is **free variation**. The human vocal apparatus operates with an incredibly high degree of precision, but still is far from exact. If the word *key* is pronounced, even by a single speaker, a hundred or so times and all the measurable features of each /k/ are measured, it will be found that no two are exactly alike. They will, however, cluster about certain average characteristics. That is, there will be an average duration of closure. Most of the instances will be found to be rather near this average, but a few will diverge farther. There will be an average degree of aspiration, and most instances will fall near the average, though a few will be appreciably more or less aspirate than the majority. And so forth. In each of these features there will be something like the familiar bell-shaped curve of statistics. These curves define the range and nature of variation in that one informant's pronunciation of /k/ in *key*.

For the most part the range of such variation is small — so small, in fact, that it is not ordinarily discernible except by instrumental measurement or by a highly trained phonetician operating under nearly ideal listening conditions. But occasionally the range of variation will be broad enough to be easily heard so that it must be given cognizance in phonemic analysis.

Obviously, any phonetic difference which cannot be consistently controlled is of no linguistic significance. Any two sounds which are always in free variation cannot be two phonemes, but only two points within the range that constitutes one phoneme.

16.9 In discussing free variation we deliberately selected as our example numerous repetitions of precisely the same word. If after studying a hundred instances of /k/ in *key*, we were to repeat the experiment on a hundred repetitions of the /k/ in *ski* we would find that the latter also shows variation in every measurable characteristic. But the ranges of variation found in the two experiments would not be alike. Some of the characteristics measured would differ both in the average values and in the scattering about the average.

Moreover, some of these differences are quite easily detected by either a moderately trained linguist or, as we have just seen, a

wholly unsophisticated speaker of Hindi. The most obvious difference is in the aspiration. In *key*, though there is variation in
aspiration, the range is roughly from moderate to strong; in *ski*
the range is roughly from none to weak. There is ample justification for considering these two as quite different ranges of variation.
Why then are the two not found separating minimal pairs?

To answer this question it is necessary only to obtain rough
estimates of the aspiration in a large number of /k/ phonemes in
many different words. Restricting our attention for simplicity to
initial position, we will find that /k/ following /s/ is always unaspirate or weakly aspirate, while /k/ not preceded by /s/ is
always moderately aspirate to strongly aspirate. If this is so,
minimal pairs are obviously impossible. The two [k] therefore
qualify as members of a single phoneme.

The distribution just briefly described is known as complementary distribution. This is the most important, practically at least,
of the types of distribution which fill the second criterion of our
present definition of the phoneme. Sounds are said to be in **complementary distribution** when each occurs in a fixed set of contexts
in which none of the others occur. In any discussion of phonology
the only kind of contexts which can be considered are phonologic,
never morphologic. Thus, English [k⁼] (unaspirated) and [kʰ]
(aspirated) are in complementary distribution since [k⁼] occurs
in consonant clusters following /s/ as in *ski* [sk⁼iy], in medial and
final clusters before another stop as in *act* [æk⁼tʰ], and when not
initial and preceding a weak stressed vowel as in *hiccup* [hík⁼əp].
(Note: There is some variation in the details of this pattern from
dialect to dialect. Some other speakers may have slightly different
distributions, but will be consistent in following their own patterns.) [kʰ] occurs in most other environments, but never in any of
those listed for [k⁼]. This is, of course, only a partial statement
of the whole pattern of variation in /k/; there are also other types
of differences besides aspiration which must be considered to give
a full picture.

16.10   Any sound or subclass of sounds which is in complementary distribution with another so that the two together constitute
a single phoneme is called an **allophone** of that phoneme. A phoneme is, therefore, a class of allophones. The ranges of sounds in
free variation such as were discussed in 16.8 are allophones.

16.11 Speakers of the same dialect ordinarily make the same phonemic distinctions and the same distribution of the allophones within each phoneme. A suggestion as to how a child learns to make the necessary phonemic distinctions and only these was given in 16.3. This does not serve to explain why two speakers have the same distribution of allophones, or even why one speaker should exhibit any consistency at all in his use of allophones. Without such consistency, complementary distribution would be a fiction. Even though that discussion was not integral to the development, it imposes the obligation to give some similar suggestions about the origin and significance of allophones.

In the first place some allophonic distributions are determined by physiological factors, or at least the latter make a strong contribution. For example, in English, front allophones of /k/ are used near front vowels, as in *key*, and back allophones of /k/ near back vowels as in *caw*. It would seem reasonable to assume that economy of motion might dictate such an arrangement. This is probably partially the case, but certainly not wholly so. By comparison, in Loma front vowels occur in central (backed) allophones after /k g ŋ/, which seem seldom to be as front as is /k/ in English *key*. For example, /e/, which is normally pronounced much like English /i/, is very similar to English /ɨ/ in Loma /ke/. (Note: I say "similar," implying an approximate description.) The other two front vowels, /i/ (higher than /e/) and /ɛ/ (rather similar to English /e/), have comparable central allophones. In Loma the vowels seem to accommodate to the tongue position of the /k g ŋ/; in English /k g ŋ/ accommodate to the tongue position of the vowels.

But economy of motion will not explain all the instances. There is no obvious reason to explain why unaspirated allophones of /p t k/ occur after /s/. This seems to be very largely just a matter of English conventional linguistic habit. It is learned by one speaker from another, and has apparently been handed down from speaker to speaker through a rather long history. The reason for learning it is not that it assists in the use of the language as a tool of communication. Its value for this purpose is at best very slight. Instead it is a matter of social conformity. If one sounds different from his companions he is understood linguistically but suffers socially. A person that says *key* [k⁼iy] or *ski* [skʰiy] sounds "funny." At least this is the case with [sk^{h}iy]. [k$^=$iy] might even cause linguistic troubles, as it is too easily confused with /giy/.

The use of the correct allophones is more important socially than it is linguistically. Though obviously of concern to linguists for many practical reasons, the allophones stand on the margin of his field of study and are in some respects external to language.

The use of correct allophones is obviously important to anyone learning a foreign language with intent to speak it. To make himself understood he must learn to pronounce all the phonemes and to use allophones which are sufficiently close to the normal in the language to avoid misidentification. Beyond that there is no need, if he is merely content to be understood, to worry about the allophones. But if he desires his speech to be socially acceptable — that is, to sound like that of a native — he must achieve the same use of allophones as is normal in the language. Contrary to the experience of many foreigners, it is quite possible to accomplish this. However, it seems that only exceptionally good mimics can attain such proficiency without being consciously aware of the problem in detail. An understanding of the phoneme principle is, for most adults, a *sine qua non* of successful language learning. It is certainly the most important single concept that a prospective language student can get out of linguistic training.

16.12   Of the two criteria for the classing of allophones into phonemes (16.7) the first, phonetic similarity, can be applied (at least in part) without reference to the actual use of the sounds in any specific language. Thus, voiced and the corresponding voiceless sounds can be said to be phonetically similar, irrespective of the language in which they occur. This does not make them the same phoneme; both criteria must be met. However, similarity is a relative matter. Sounds cannot be said to be either similar or dissimilar, but only more or less similar. Just how similar two sounds must be to fit the definition can only be determined by a consideration of the phonemic system of the language as a whole. If some phonemes are found to have both voiced and voiceless allophones, then any other pair of voiced and voiceless sounds are certainly sufficiently similar to qualify. If, on the other hand, voiced and voiceless sounds generally contrast, the chances are that another pair of voiced and voiceless sounds are heard as different in the language under consideration. This relativity introduces a certain measure of subjectivity into the approach. It is, however, of an entirely different kind from the subjectivity which limits the use of the method employed in Chapters 2, 3, and 4.

16.13 The second criterion for classing allophones into phonemes, non-contrastive distribution, has no meaning except in a particular language or dialect. It is often susceptible to much more objective application than is phonetic similarity. However, this criterion poses its own difficulty. The whole distribution of any given sound can only be determined by observing the whole language. This is obviously impossible. As a practical procedure, we must determine distribution within a sample. This always leaves the possibility that the examination of additional data may reveal additional features of distribution which can compel modifications of any earlier conclusions.

The larger the sample used, the less likelihood there is that more material would contradict our earlier formulations. It is, therefore, necessary to work with a sample large enough so that the probabilities of error are small. Or, stated another way: with a sufficiently large sample, conclusions can be drawn which have a high probability of standing as valid in the light of any additional evidence. It is also necessary that the samples used are representative of the speech form under analysis. Finally, once a satisfactory sample is obtained, it must be properly used. Nothing can be disregarded, however convenient it would seem to be to do so.

The techniques of selecting and appraising samples for linguistic analysis have received little attention from the point of view of the statistical problems involved. Linguists have instead relied on the use of very large samples (in most cases) — probably very often larger than necessary for their purposes. Most good phonemic analyses can be assumed to have appreciable (never absolute, of course!) statistical validity. The commonest shortcoming of linguists in this regard is to fail to recognize that their results ultimately rest on data of a statistical nature, and that the conclusions must be interpreted with this in mind.

16.14 In describing the English vowel system from an articulatory point of view we found that the nine vowels are describable in terms of two significant dimensions, and that in terms of these they are arranged in a neat 3 × 3 pattern:

i   ɨ   u
e   ə   o
æ   a   ɔ

This symmetry affects more than the phonetic base of the phonemes. There are various functional interrelations between the phonemes which seem to reflect the same pattern. Thus we can consider the phonemes not merely as contrasting entities, but as points in a system.

In some other languages, the phonemic system may show much more obvious interrelations. For example, the Turkish vowels differ among themselves in three dimensions. They are either relatively front or relatively back, relatively high or relatively low, relatively rounded or relatively unrounded. All possible combinations occur, so that the system consists of eight vowels that can conveniently be diagrammed as a cube with a vowel at each corner:

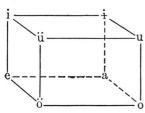

This arrangement can be arrived at from a consideration of the articulation, or even more clearly from the morphophonemic relationships. Thus /i ü ɨ u/ are alike in being relatively high, but in addition every suffix which contains one of these has allomorphs containing each of the four. Such affixes are accordingly conveniently described as containing high vowels. The allomorphs of such suffixes are conditioned by the vowel of the preceding syllable: /i e/ condition /i/; /ü ö/ condition /ü/; /ɨ a/ condition /ɨ/; and /u o/ condition /u/. This marks off four groups of vowels: front unrounded, front rounded, back unrounded, and back rounded. A second group of suffixes contains either /e/ or /a/, both low unrounded vowels. /e/ occurs following any front vowel /i ü e ö/, /a/ after any back vowel /ɨ u a o/. Thus the arrangement of the Turkish vowels in a cubic diagram reflects both structural relationships and phonetic character. The Turkish vowels are very evidently units in a system, the interrelationships of which are of fundamental significance in the language.

The phonemes of a language are more than individual units to be individually identified and described. A third definition of a phoneme may therefore be stated as follows: a **phoneme** is one element in the sound system of a language having a characteristic set of interrelationships with each of the other elements in that system. These interrelationships are of various kinds. They may be reflected in morphophonemic interchanges, in sequences of phonemes possible within morphemes, or in the functions of the units within stretches of speech. The system may be very sharply defined, or more diffuse and indefinite, but such relationships are always evident in some degree.

16.15 These three definitions (in terms of contrasts between phonemes, non-contrasting classes of sounds, and systematic relationships) are complementary. No one of them gives a full picture of the nature or significance of the phoneme. Together they provide an adequate base for either the depth of understanding which can be sought in an elementary course or, with only slight modifications of detail, for the most technical discussions. However, all three imply some further basic considerations which cannot longer be allowed to remain tacitly assumed, but must be discussed if these definitions are not to be badly misinterpreted.

16.16 All our discussion of the phoneme has been on the assumption that the stream of speech is divided into **segments,** each of which can be assigned to some phoneme. There are various ways in which that division can be conceived. Most commonly the consonants and vowels of English are assumed to follow each other in a sequence, each beginning at the end of the preceding one. The stresses occur more or less simultaneously with the vowels, and the pitches simultaneously with all the others. This model will be sufficient for the present, but another possibility will be suggested in Chapter 22.

Thus, overlooking for the present discussion all stresses, pitches, and related phonemes, an English word like *bit* was assumed to consist of a sequence of three sounds. Probably most observers would have little difficulty in agreeing with this analysis. But in a word like *key* the practical problem is quite different. Some might hear it as a sequence of three items, as the phonemic transcription /kiy/ indicates. Others will hear it as only two [ki], still others might hear it as four [khiy]. All three of our definitions of the phoneme have by-passed or overlooked the problem of how many phonemes there are in any stretch of speech, though it is obviously basic to each of them. How an utterance is heard and divided (**segmented**) depends in part on the phonemic background of the observer. Different languages divide similar phonetic material into different numbers of segments or divide at different places. The pattern of segmentation is one of the linguistic patterns of the language, and segmentation in accord with those patterns is implied in each of the three descriptions of the phoneme.

16.17 None of the three definitions makes a clear statement on another matter. Speech is a process that involves activity of the human brain, articulatory system, and sensory organs, and as such can be legitimately and productively studied by psychologists. The phoneme is not, however, a psychological concept; it cannot be defined in psychological terms. Our description of the process of learning of a phonemic distinction in this chapter was not intended as any sort of definition of a phoneme, but only as a subsidiary, or even parenthetical, remark. Obviously, psychological processes are involved in the production and recognition of phonemes, but no adequate psychological definition of the phoneme has yet been produced.

Speech also involves certain acoustical phenomena. Somehow, these carry the phonemes; but phonemes are not, however, any sort of physical reality discernible by instrumental techniques or direct observation. The phoneme cannot, therefore, be acoustically defined.

The phoneme is instead a feature of language structure. That is, it is an abstraction from the psychological and acoustical patterns which enables a linguist to describe the observed repetitions of things that seem to function within the system as identical in spite of obvious differences. The phoneme is, in short, a linguistic feature only. It is not a feature of a single utterance, but a statement of similarities in numerous utterances. An utterance is not properly a sequence of phonemes, but a sequence of concrete examples of allophones of phonemes. Phonemes are not events but classes of events. As such they do not have the same sort of reality as a specific part of a specific utterance. In a certain sense they are the intellectual creation of the linguist who examines those specific parts of specific utterances. But though they are the creatures of the observing linguist, he is not free to create as he will. The phonemes of a language are a set of abstractions which will more adequately describe certain features of the utterances of that language, past, present, and future, than any other set. They are a sort of model of the utterance. The linguist's task is to find that model which most adequately fits the observed facts. The language imposes real limitations and often quite narrowly circumscribes the freedom of the linguist to set up his model. The reality of the phoneme lies in these limitations.

17

Phonemic Analysis

17.1 A professional linguist approaching the scientific analysis of a hitherto unrecorded language and a layman attempting to attain a speaking knowledge of a second tongue face the same fundamental problem. Nothing more than crude preliminary work can be done until some grasp of the phonemic system is obtained. Without this the material is inaccurately perceived, and reproduced in terms of the phonemic patterns of the mother tongue, or heard and recorded as an unmanageable complex of intergrading and unorganized sounds. The layman, if he is "gifted at languages," may in time acquire a working control of the phonemic system by trial and error. Unfortunately, many never get beyond the barest minimum necessary for elementary communication. The linguist seeks control of the phonemic system as a conscious goal and proceeds toward it by deliberate steps. Some parts of his procedure can be of value to anyone who is learning a new language, either as assistance in avoiding common difficulties of learners, as a means of speeding his progress, or as a method of helping him to understand what he is doing and the reason for certain "peculiarities" of the language he is studying. In this chapter we will describe some elementary aspects of an analytic method which might be used.

17.2 The first process in analyzing the phonemic system of a language other than one's mother tongue is to make a transcription of a sample. A number of utterances are transcribed from the speech of a native informant. Great care is taken to insure that the transcription is as nearly consistent as possible — that is, that every sound is recorded by the same symbol throughout. An attempt is made to record every discernible feature of the speech in as great detail as is possible with accuracy. An investigator thoroughly trained in phonetics will record a very large number of slightly different sounds, using symbols from one of the established transcription systems. A person of less preparation for the task will record fewer distinctions, and may perhaps need to make up *ad hoc* symbols for many of them. In either case it will be pure coincidence if the transcription correctly indicates more than a few of the phonemes. The recording will be influenced in some degree by the phonemic system of the investigator's language. A competent linguist can suppress this somewhat by reason of his wide experience with languages and his training in phonetics; his transcription is made not in terms of the phonemic system of his mother tongue, but in terms of the cumulative experience of many linguists with a large number of languages, and reflects all of the distinctions which this polyglot background has taught him to recognize.

Any such preliminary transcription may be expected to depart from a purely phonemic representation in various combinations of the following:

(1) It may be **over-differentiated.** That is, separate symbols have been used for two or more variants of a single phoneme, or non-linguistic differences may have been recorded. This would be the case with an Arab making an analysis of English and writing [k] and [q] for /k/.

(2) It may be **under-differentiated.** That is, the same symbol may have been used for two or more different phonemes, or for a combination of allophones belonging to two different phonemes; or some linguistically significant feature may not have been recorded at all. This might be the case with an American attempting to analyze Arabic and writing [k] for both /k/ and /q/.

(3) It may be wrongly segmented. That is, a single symbol may have been used for a sequence of phonemes, or a sequence of symbols for a single phoneme. This would be the case if an Amer-

ican attempting to analyze German were to record [č] for /tš/, or a German were to record [tš] for English /č/.

(4) There may be gross personal errors of various kinds.

The process of analysis consists of discovering the instances of each kind of deviation and applying the necessary correction. By this means, the transcription is brought, by successive stages, nearer to being an adequate phonemic representation of the language. The process may involve a very large number of successive approximations.

17.3 Over-differentiation can be discovered and corrected from the record alone by rigorous procedures (provided under-differentiation and gross errors do not seriously obscure the evidence!). It is for this reason that a linguist attempts to make the most meticulous transcription feasible. This minimizes but does not eliminate the incidence of under-differentiation. The record of a good phonetician can frequently be analyzed with some ease and directness. The process is largely one of sorting out of the record that information which is significant and disregarding the rest. The records of persons not experienced in phonetic transcription generally present much greater difficulties, since under-differentiation will very probably occur. No process of sorting relevant from irrelevant information can be adequate in such a case, since some significant distinctions are wholly omitted from the data. Under-differentiation and gross errors can be found and removed only by renewed reference to the speech of the informant, though not infrequently strong suspicions of their existence and nature can be raised from the record. Some of the problems involved will be discussed in Chapter 21. Incorrect segmentation can also frequently be detected from a good record, particularly such a transcription as an experienced field linguist is likely to make. Being aware of the dangers, he may take extra care to record adequate data at critical points.

17.4 For the present we will overlook the possibilities of under-differentiation and gross errors and assume that we have a phonetic transcription which deviates from phonemic only in over-differentiation, and later in the chapter also in incorrect segmentation. Of course, such an assumption can be made for purposes of presentation of method only. As with morphologic analysis, discussed in Chapters 6 and 7, all the various processes must be carried out more or less simultaneously. Indeed, it is usually convenient and necessary to conduct grammatical and phonologic analysis together. This is done only as a matter of practical procedure; the two are not to be confused.

Before the analysis of a language is completed the analyst must assure himself that the phonologic results are independent of the grammar. That is, he must be able to describe the phonemic system and support his analysis without any appeal to any morphologic results beyond the bare assertion that pairs of utterances are actually different. The converse is emphatically not true; an adequate grammatical description must presume an adequate and complete phonologic description. The morphology must be stated in terms of morphemes, which in turn are stated in terms of the phonemic system of the language. No other basis is wholly adequate or satisfactory for anything beyond preliminary statements. The most frequent limitation on further progress in understanding the grammar of a language is an inadequate phonemic analysis, commonly one which has made an adequate analysis only of the consonants and vowels.

17.5 In the last chapter we discussed three complementary definitions of a phoneme. Each of the three has implications for phonemic analysis. The method advanced in Chapters 2, 3, and 4 was based on one of these definitions alone, and was in that measure inadequate. For the present purpose, the most important of the three is that presented in 16.7, but both the others contribute in important ways. A phoneme was defined as a class of sounds and two criteria were set up for the assignment of any two sounds to a single phoneme. The first of these was phonetic similarity. This imposes the requirement that the analyst take care not merely in transcribing the sounds of the language so that each symbol in his preliminary notes will always represent the same sound, but also that he record with care the phonetic nature of each sound. This can be done by using symbols from a conventionally established set in which each symbol carries a phonetic definition, or by carefully describing the phonetic character of each sound represented by an *ad hoc* symbol or by an unorthodox use of a familiar symbol. In this chapter and the accompanying problems we will use symbols in values defined in Chapter 15.

The second requirement of our definition of a phoneme is certain patterns of distribution: complementary distribution or free variation. The demonstration of either of these can be made step by step, but the procedures are somewhat different. We will first describe a method by which phonemic groupings based on complementary distribution can be detected. This consists of three steps: finding suspicious pairs, framing a hypothesis, and testing.

17.6 First, TABULATE ALL THE SOUNDS found in the sample, using suitable phonetic classifications. List **suspicious pairs,** that is, pairs of sounds which seem to be phonetically similar, and hence possibly allophones of the same phoneme. One sound may be included in several such pairs. Disregard pairs of sounds which are so different that they cannot be allophones of the same phoneme. For example, if the data shows [m k kʰ], you may assume that [m] and [k] will be assigned to separate phonemes, but [k] and [kʰ] MAY be allophones of one phoneme. The latter, therefore, are to be considered as a suspicious pair.

The following are commonly allophones of the same phoneme, and hence should be suggestive of sounds which should be listed as suspicious pairs. Examples are given in [ ].

Corresponding voiced and voiceless sounds [k g] [s z]
Corresponding stops and fricatives [k x]
Bilabial and labiodental stops, fricatives, nasals, or stops and
    fricatives [b ḅ] [ʋ v] [m m̩] [p f]
Dental, alveolar, and retroflex stops, fricatives, laterals, or
    stops and fricatives [t ṭ] [t ţ] [d l] [t θ]
Alveolar and alveopalatal fricatives [s š]
Palatal and velar stops or fricatives [k ḵ] [k ḳ] [x x̣]
Corresponding aspirate and unaspirate stops [tʰ t]
All nasals, except that [m] is usually distinct [n ŋ] [n ñ]
All varieties of [r]-like sounds and many [l]-like [r ř] [r̃ ʀ] [ř̃ l]
Dental and alveolar flaps and stops [d ř] [t ř]
Uvular [ʀ] with velar or uvular fricatives [ɣ ʀ]
[h] and all unvoiced velar or palatal fricatives [h x]
All pairs of adjacent vowels [i ü] [ɨ i] [æ a] [o ɔ]
Semivowels and labial, palatal, or velar fricatives [w ʋ]

Such a list cannot be exhaustive. There are other combinations of sounds that occasionally will be found to be allophones of the same phoneme.

17.7 Examine the distribution of each member of each suspicious pair. Attempt to FRAME A HYPOTHESIS which will account for their distribution. This hypothesis should be based either on observed peculiarities, or on parallelism with the situation already found in similar pairs. For example, if you have established that [p] and [b] are in complementary distribution and are now considering [t] and [d], it is reasonable to try a hypothesis similar to that found to fit in the case of [p] and [b]. There is no assurance that they will show close parallels, but since phonemes are elements in more or less integrated systems, there is an appreciable probability that they will do so.

The distribution of allophones may be conditioned by any phonologic feature in the language. Among the commoner are the following:

Immediately preceding or following phonemes.

Preceding or following phonemes at a somewhat greater distance, though the probability decreases with distance. Vowels of successive syllables not infrequently affect each other.

Position in syllable, word, clause, etc., provided these can be phonologically defined.

Relationship to stress, pitch, or other similar features.

Combinations of two or more of these factors.

The conditioning operating in complementary distribution often parallels assimilation or other well-known morphophonemic changes. Italian /n/ has allophones [n] and [ŋ], the latter occurring for example in /biánko/ 'white' [biáŋko]. This distribution parallels the English assimilation of /n/ to /ŋ/ before /k g/. There is, however, this basic difference: In English two different phonemes are involved, since /n/ and /ŋ/ contrast elsewhere as in *sun* /sə́n/ : *sung* /sə́ŋ/. In Italian very similar sounds are two allophones since [n] never contrasts with [ŋ]. Many such cases can be cited. The types of sequences which arise as the result of morphophonemic changes should be looked for in framing a hypothesis concerning any suspicious pair of sounds. Incidentally, if the hypothesis does not prove correct it may suggest something about morphophonemic relationships which should be followed up in a different place in the analysis.

In some cases the conditioning may seem to be "inexplicable."

Actually, it does not matter whether an "explanation" can be made or not, for any such "explanation" is nothing more than another description of an observed distribution. Many types of correlations occur for which it has never been felt necessary to coin a label. This lack of a special term does not, of course, affect their validity in any way.

17.8 After a hypothesis has been framed, TEST IT BY TABU-LATING THE DISTRIBUTION of each sound in relationship to the suggested conditioning factor or factors. Be sure in doing so to tabulate ALL the relevant data. It is at this point that care must be taken to ensure the statistical validity of the result. The hypothesis must account for every occurrence of each member of the suspicious pair. If the tabulation shows a correlation between the distribution of the sounds under test and the hypothetical conditioning factor, accept the hypothesis as a working basis. Consider the conclusion as very tentative unless the number of instances included in the tabulation is appreciable. Obviously, if the sample includes only one occurrence of each of two sounds, the two can almost always be shown to be in complementary distribution unless the examples are a minimal pair. The more complex the hypothesis, the more extensive the data required to support it.

If the hypothesis does not work out, it must be either rejected or modified. When a tabulation shows quite close correlation but a few exceptions, the exceptions should be carefully examined. They may seem to have some common factor which may be taken into account in a modification of the original hypothesis. With a new hypothesis, a new tabulation must be made. When there seems to be no further reasonable hypothesis available, consider that the two sounds are members of separate phonemes. However, in such a case bear in mind that there may be complementary distribution, with a conditioning factor that has not yet been noticed. Your conclusions are all tentative until the analysis is completed and they have been checked one against the other.

17.9 We may illustrate the method by a partial analysis of the following Spanish words. The amount of data, here as in most of the workbook problems, is very close to the minimum. In field work many times thirty words would be considered essential. Moreover, these words were selected to illustrate certain parts of the system only. Several phonemes are not represented at all.

[aʋana]	Havana	[duřař]	to endure	[peřo]	but
[bala]	ball	[ganař]	to earn	[peřo]	dog
[baɣa]	rope	[gato]	cat	[pipa]	pipe
[beso]	kiss	[gola]	throat	[pondeřoso]	heavy
[boða]	wedding	[gosař]	to enjoy	[poŋgo]	I put
[buřo]	burro	[kasa]	house	[siɣařo]	cigar
[damos]	we give	[kuʋa]	Cuba	[teŋgo]	I have
[dios]	God	[laɣo]	lake	[toðo]	all
[deʋeř]	to owe	[naða]	nothing	[taʋako]	tobacco
[donde]	where	[nuðo]	knot	[uʋa]	grape

The first step is to tabulate the sounds recorded and to identify the suspicious pairs. The latter have been indicated by loops.

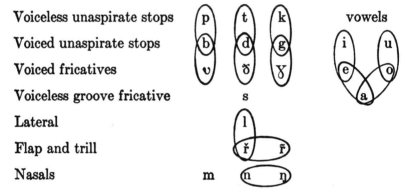

Voiceless unaspirate stops

Voiced unaspirate stops

Voiced fricatives

Voiceless groove fricative

Lateral

Flap and trill

Nasals

The first pair to examine is [p] and [b]. Both occur initially, so no hypothesis based on position in the word is feasible. It could be a matter of the following phonemes, so we make the following tabulation:

	Before [i]	Before [e]	Before [a]	Before [o]	Before [u]
[p]	/	//	/	//	
[b]		/	//	/	/

This table certainly shows no evidence of complementary distribution. We might set up the hypothesis that [p] and [b] are conditioned by the next consonant. If we tabulate this we get the following result:

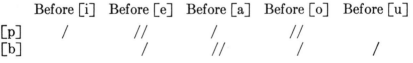

Before	l	ɣ	s	ð	r̃	ř	p	n	ŋ	–
[b]	/	/	/	/	/					
[p]						/	/	/	/	/

Both occur before [r̃], so this hypothesis is unworkable. Even if we did not have [per̃o] and [bur̃o], the tabulation would hardly prove anything, since, with so many different positions being tabulated, the data is insufficient. We must conclude that [p] and [b] are not in complementary distribution, or that our present data is insufficient to indicate the pattern.

The second pair to be examined is [b] and [ʋ]. It is immediately noticeable from the word list that [ʋ] does not occur initially. We therefore set up the hypothesis that [b] is found only initially in words, [ʋ] only medially. We then check this hypothesis by the following tabulation:

	Initial	Medial
[b]	/////	
[ʋ]		/////

The hypothesis is sustained, and we conclude that [b] and [ʋ] are allophones of one phoneme, which we will write /b/. We may now replace the transcription [aʋana] by [abana]. This is still written in [ ] rather than / / because we have not yet established the status of the other sounds.

On the assumption that [d] and [ð] parallel [b] and [ʋ] we next turn to these two and test the equivalent hypothesis by the following tabulation:

	Initial	Medial
[d]	/////	//
[ð]		////

This hypothesis is not sustained. Nevertheless, it seems significant that [ð] is found only in medial position, so we examine the instances of medial [d]. These suggest a modification of the hypothesis — that [d] occurs initially and after [n]. We therefore make a new tabulation:

	Initial	After [n]	After vowels
[d]	/////	//	
[ð]			////

This hypothesis is sustained. The two are allophones of one phoneme which we will write /d/. [naða] may be rewritten [nada].

This should raise the question as to why a similar distribution was not found for /b/. The reason was simply lack of data. More extensive lists would certainly include some such word as [bomba] 'pump.'

The pair [g] and [ɣ] might be expected to show the same relationship. Make the necessary tabulation to test this and the remaining untested pairs.

17.10   While examining the data to detect cases of complementary distribution which will establish two sounds as allophones of a single phoneme, notice should be taken of any evidence which will prove the converse. The most valuable is, of course, minimal pairs. You must take care to insure that the pairs are indeed minimal, rather than differing by some feature which has not been adequately recorded. However, minimal pairs may be very hard to find, particularly in the small corpus of material that is likely to be available at the early stages of an investigation. You know from experience with English, in which you can draw from a very large vocabulary, that minimal pairs are sometimes quite difficult to find. Actually, English seems to have more minimal pairs than many languages. In some they are exceedingly infrequent. Minimal pairs are useful when found, but not necessarily to be expected, and not essential to the work of analysis.

In 2.23 another method was suggested. It involves the use of **sub-minimal pairs,** that is, items that differ in only two, or perhaps three, respects. These are of value because they restrict severely the hypotheses that can be suggested as conditioning any possible complementary distribution. When the number of possible hypotheses is small, it is possible to examine each of them. If all can be ruled out, then it may be taken as proved that the two sounds are not allophones of one phoneme. Minimal pairs are merely the limiting case, where there is no possible hypothesis of conditioning.

17.11   Free variation presents somewhat different problems. When two sounds are in free variation, they can obviously be found in similar environments — and, if the data is adequate, in identical environments. That is, they will occur in what might at first sight be taken for minimal pairs. These pairs are the same morpheme or sequence of morphemes occurring sometimes with one variant and at other times with another variant of the phoneme under consideration. They are not properly minimal pairs, because by definition minimal pairs must differ in both content and expression.

To put it in another way, given two utterances which are alike except in one feature, this may constitute evidence that the two sounds are phonemically distinct, or that they are variants of one phoneme. Which conclusion is to be drawn depends on whether or not the two utterances differ in content, and if they do, whether or not the difference of content is consistently correlated with the difference in expression. If there is no correlation of differences in content and expression, then we have free variation.

This, however, is not enough. For many Americans both [wiθ] and [wið] occur with no discernible conditioning. This is therefore a case of free variation. However, very many words always have [θ], and many others always have [ð]. Indeed, minimal pairs can be found to show that [θ] and [ð] are phonemically distinct. The case of [wiθ] and [wið] is an example of free variation between two allomorphs of a single morpheme and is not phonologically relevant. To establish that two sounds are members of a single phoneme, free variation must be observed throughout a phonologically defined range of occurrences, not merely in certain morphemes. This means that to use this criterion in phonemic analysis it is necessary to have a large number of items, each of which is recorded several times. It is not likely that such evidence will be obtained in a preliminary transcription. It is usually necessary to return to the informant to elicit additional material to either support or refute any hypothesis of free variation.

17.12 The examination of each suspicious pair and a decision in each case either for or against the hypothesis that they belong to the same phoneme is not enough. Phonemes are not isolated entities. Our third characterization of the phoneme in 16.14 was as an element in a more or less integrated sound system. It is, therefore, essential that the individual conclusions be weighed against the background of the total phonemic system as it emerges in the course of the work.

Moreover, piecemeal analysis may easily lead to inconsistencies. In English [p⁼] and [pʰ] can be shown to meet the requirements for inclusion in one phoneme. The same technique will produce the same result with [p⁼] and [b]. This might seem to indicate that [p⁼], [pʰ], and [b] should all be classed together. However, [pʰ] and [b] are easily proved to belong to separate phonemes. [p⁼] must be assigned either to /p/ or to /b/; it cannot belong to both. Nor can [p⁼] be set up as a third separate labial stop phoneme, since it does not contrast with either of the other two. A choice must be made as to which of the two it will be assigned to.

Traditionally, [p⁼] is assigned to /p/. There is some evidence to support this, but it is complex and somewhat tenuous. Any analysis not based on full and detailed information about the distribution — information far beyond what would be found in a first investigation — will provide no basis for a decision. The assignment of [p⁼] would then have to be arbitrary. Decisions which are wholly or very largely arbitrary are frequently required.

If arbitrary decisions are to be made, they frequently must be made in several places within one phonemic analysis. For example, the assignment of [t⁼] to /t/ or /d/ and of [k⁼] to /k/ or /g/ rests on indecisive evidence parallel to that bearing on [p⁼]. To make the systematic relationships within the phonemic system evident, all three of these decisions should be made the same way. Thus if [p⁼] is assigned to /p/, then [t⁼] should be assigned to /t/ and [k⁼] to /k/.

17.13   So far we have assumed that our preliminary record is correctly segmented. This is not necessarily the case and cannot be taken for granted. However, there is no need of raising a question about every segmentation point; certain types of sounds and sound sequences are particularly likely to be differently treated in different languages. These should be considered as suspicious and checked in the analysis.

The following are most likely to be recorded as sequences while requiring analysis as single segments:

Stop + aspiration (aspirate stop)	[th] [kh] [ph], etc.
Stop + homorganic fricative (affricate)	[ts] [tθ] [kx]
Alveolar or dental stop + lateral (lateral affricate)	[tɫ] [dl]
Homorganic nasal + stop	[mb] [nt] [ŋk]
Glottal stop + stop (glottalized stop)	[ʔk] [kʔ]
Consonant + semivowel	[kw] [ny] [ly]
Stressed vowel + vowel glide or semivowel	[ow] [iy] [eᵊ]
Semivowel or vowel glide + stressed vowel	[ye] [ⁱu] [wu]

17.14   Such sequences may be interpreted as single segments if they are limited in number and:

(1) If they are in complementary distribution or free variation with single sounds. For example, in Kikuyu (Kenya) [mb] and [b] are not phonemically different. There are two options; either [mb] is an allophone of /b/ (a unit phoneme), or [b] is a variant of some such sequence of phonemes as /mb/. In Kikuyu the preferred interpretation is that [b] and [mb] are allophones of a phoneme /b/, and that hence a segmentation between [m] and [b] is incorrect.

(2) If the sequences are such that treatment as unit phonemes will result in an overall simplification of distributional statements. For example, in Bannock (Idaho) the following simple consonants are found to be phonemic: /p t k b d g m n ŋ w s h ʔ/. In addition there are the following phonetic clusters: [ts tš kw dz dž gw]. These are all of suspicious types, so that it would be quite feasible to interpret them as unit·phonemes: /c č kʷ ǰ ǰ gʷ/. This has the advantage of eliminating all clusters and thus simplifying a description of phoneme sequences.

(3) If the clusters seem to occupy a place in the total phonemic system of the language comparable to that of undisputed unit phonemes. For example, in Hindi, [č čh ǰ ǰh] parallel the four series of stops in many respects and fill out the phonemic system to a high degree of symmetry.

Naturally, any such criteria must be used with caution, but not infrequently it will be found that two or all three of them reinforce each other and point very clearly to treatment of certain sequences as unit phonemes.

17.15   Conversely, what the investigator perceives as single segments may be better treated as sequences under the following conditions:

(1) If apparent single sounds are in complementary distribution, or otherwise not phonemically distinct, from sequences of sounds. This is the exact converse of the case cited above. For example, in English a word like *bottle* is pronounced either as [bátl̩] with a syllabic [l̩] or as [bátɪl] with a short but distinct vowel. These are in free variation in all comparable environments, and so not phonemically distinct. We have considered /bátɪl/ as the better

interpretation, making the single segment [ļ] a variant of the sequence of phonemes /il/.

(2) If what is recorded as a single sound occurs in a distribution which is typically occupied by a sequence of phonemes. For example, in Egyptian Arabic, vowels are phonemically either long or short, as may be seen in the contrast /ba·rid/ 'cold' : /bari·d/ 'mail.' Single short consonants occur after either long or short vowels. Clusters of two consonants occur commonly only after short vowels. There are no clusters of three or more consonants. Long consonants occur commonly only after short vowels. There are no clusters of a long consonant and any other consonant. That is, long consonants have the same restrictions on occurrence as do clusters of two consonants. They may, therefore, be interpreted as clusters of two identical consonants: [bar·ad] 'cool' is interpreted as /barrad/, in contrast with /barad/ 'file.' This brings the pattern into line with such words as /zikrin/ 'mention' or /kursi/ 'chair.'

(3) If such an interpretation will fill out gaps in a list of clusters. For example, in Swahili there is an extensive series of clusters of the type /Cw/, but no [bw]. There is, however, a single segment [ʋ] which can be interpreted as /bw/.

The following types of sounds are often best interpreted as sequences of phonemes:

Long vowels	[a·] = /aa/
Long consonants	[m·] = /mm/
Syllabic consonants	[ṇ] = /Vn/ ~ /nV/
Nasal vowels	[ã] = /an/ ~ /aŋ/
Affricates and other types mentioned in 17.13	[č] = /tš/

17.16 In some languages the pitch phonemes are distributed in a way that correlates with vowel length. For example, in Loma a short vowel has either a low pitch /`/ or a high pitch /´/. Long vowels and diphthongs have low, high, rising, or falling pitch. The most useful way of interpreting this is to assume that the long vowels and diphthongs are sequences of two short vowels, each of which has an associated pitch phoneme. Thus [a·] with high pitch is /áá/, with falling /áà/, and with rising /àá/. This is a very special instance of cogent evidence for resegmenting. Similar patterns do not occur in all languages. Some have only a single pitch phoneme with any vowel, long or short. Others have one, two, or even three pitches associated with a single vowel irrespective of length.

17.17 Throughout the preceding discussion we have seemed to be inordinately concerned with transcription. The process of phonemic analysis has been presented as a matter of starting from a non-phonemic transcription, juggling symbols, and gradually approximating a phonemic spelling. This is the easiest way to describe the process, and actually it is very nearly what is done by a practicing linguist. However, the linguist's concern is not with the symbols as such, but with the classes of sounds behind the symbols. His task is to start with a raw impressionistic interpretation of sounds heard and gradually discern interrelationships between the sounds, until he is finally able to make simple and general statements about the sound system of the language. His objective is the most general and the simplest description which is adequate to describe the totality of linguistically significant features. Through the process more is done than merely to juggle the symbols, which are merely labels for sounds or classes of sounds; the basic nature of the symbolization is altered. At the start, the symbols stand for occurrences of sounds which are impressionistically identical, having the same acoustic effect as far as the observer can judge. At the end, the relationship between the symbols and the sounds is much less direct. For a direct relation between sound and symbol has been substituted a direct relation between structure and symbol. A phonemic symbol such as /b/ does not stand directly for any phonetic entity, but for a structure point in English phonology. That this structure point is generally associated with an acoustic event which may be described as a voiced bilabial stop is important, of course, but it is not the primary significance of /b/. The manipulation of the transcription is merely the outward expression of an analytic process which seeks to penetrate behind the acoustic or phonetic facts to the linguistic structure.

18

Phonemic Field Work

18.1 In the last chapter one possible procedure in phonemic analysis was described. In it, a detailed phonetic transcription is first made. Then this record is studied to find instances of complementary distribution. These point to the merging of two or more phonetic entities of the record into one new unit. As changes of this sort are made, the transcription is approximated to phonemic. The changing transcription points out to the linguist the phonemic features of the language.

Such a technique is comparatively easy to describe in print, because most of the operations deal with written symbols. It is also quite appropriate for use with workbook problems, since in them the data must be presented in written form. It is, however, less directly useful in field work. It depends for its success on the ability of the linguist not only to make detailed phonetic observations, but especially to do this with a very high degree of consistency. Only a little variation in the transcription can very seriously obscure the complementary distribution for which he is looking. There are many possible sources of such variation, ranging from mere inconsistency with symbols to alterations in his hearing. Indeed, the very sharpening of his ear as he continues to work with the language, necessary as it is to good field work, may produce changes in transcription which are disastrous. Few linguists can, prior to any phonemic analysis, produce a sizable corpus of sufficiently detailed and consistent transcription. Even for the few who can, it is probably seldom very efficient to do so. Phonetic recording is always a great deal easier when done against a background of understanding of the phonemic system. For these reasons, actual field work is very seldom done precisely as described in Chapter 17.

This is not to say that Chapter 17 is entirely beside the point. On the contrary, the procedure there described can be modified to meet the conditions of field work. The description of the procedure in its pure form serves as an excellent point of departure for understanding the modifications. All the questions suggested in that chapter must be raised in field work. All the techniques described are applicable in some way in the field situation. Some linguists operate largely on the basis of these techniques, making phonetic transcriptions and searching through their transcribed data for evidence of complementary distribution. But few, if any, first transcribe all the necessary data and then phonemicize. Rather, they alternate between gathering data and analyzing it. A procedure of this kind will be described in the next section.

18.2   The field linguist usually begins by eliciting what he hopes will be very short utterances. These are needed because long ones can be extremely difficult to hear correctly, to imitate, or to transcribe, and because the structure of short utterances is commonly simpler than that of very long ones. Ideally, one-word utterances are best, but they are not always easy to obtain. People speak in sentences, not words. It is very difficult for many people to isolate individual words from sentences. In some languages one-word sentences may be very rare and difficult to find. But in most languages comparatively short utterances can be elicited if one asks for the names of familiar concrete objects — that is, the equivalents of certain English nouns. Equivalents of adjectives or verbs may be much more difficult to get by themselves, and should not ordinarily be attempted at the early stages. A list of ordinary (in the informant's culture!) tangible objects is generally the best material to use in starting the elicitation.

These items are asked for, one at a time. The informant is requested to repeat his answers three or four times. The linguist both listens and watches, using every means at his disposal for precise and accurate observation. Each item is transcribed in the greatest feasible detail. Whenever either the informant or the linguist becomes tired, the work is discontinued for a while. After a few sessions of this sort, a few pages of notes have accumulated. Most items have been re-elicited and checked at more than one session.

For the next step of the work the informant is not needed. The data are thoroughly tabulated. Suspicious pairs are listed and examined for complementary distribution, in much the way that was described in Chapter 17. However, the results of this examination are used with caution. If two sounds are found to be in complementation, no conclusion is drawn until all the items concerned can be carefully rechecked. If the number of occurrences of the sounds thought to be in complementary distribution is small, a decision will be postponed until additional material can be gathered. Often two sounds will be found to be almost in complementation. These also are checked carefully; sometimes the apparent exceptions will be found to be mere errors in transcription. The first round of tabulation does not produce an analysis, however partial, but only suggests a number of crucial points for checking.

After the first set of tabulations, there will follow rechecking with the informant and collection of additional material. When enough has accumulated to make it worth while, a second round of thorough tabulation will ensue. By this time the corpus may be sufficient that some uniting of allophones can be done with fair confidence. A new system of transcription is thereafter adopted. This ignores those differences which are now assumed to be nonphonemic. Of course the linguist does not merely neglect these distinctions; he remains alert to any evidence that might controvert his conclusion. But he no longer writes into his transcriptions distinctions which he is confident will not be needed.

Since his field notes will contain material transcribed in two or more different ways, it is important that all recordings be dated from the beginning. Likewise, all changes in transcription practice must be recorded and dated. Successful field work requires careful bookkeeping.

With a new, and presumably better, transcription, more data are gathered. Perhaps the old word lists are gone over again and re-recorded. The linguist also begins, slowly, to broaden the range of material which he elicits. Sentences of more than one or two words, though still short, are asked for. These may, of course, bring new features into the problem. (Note how the presentation of English phonemes in Chapters 2 and 3 was simplified by restricting attention to monosyllables.) When a sizable amount of material has been collected, new tabulations are made. From these, again, note is made of all interesting cases of complementary distribution and near complementary distribution. These are, as before, rechecked with the informant. After rechecking, some additional conclusions about the phonemic system may be made, and the transcription is modified as needed.

The process is one of alternating between transcribing and analyzing, starting each cycle from a new vantage point. Each effort at tabulation and analysis is only partial and tentative, but each successive effort becomes more definitive. How many such cycles may be required before a fairly satisfactory analysis and transcription emerge is a matter of the skill and working habits of the linguist. Each such partial analysis differs from that described in the last chapter largely in the degree of confidence which is placed in the transcription. It is carried only so far as the transcription is felt to warrant, or so far as can easily be checked. After every tentative conclusion, the data on which it was based are rechecked with the informant.

18.3 This seemingly very mechanical process of transcribing and tabulating may be the most easily observed aspect of the linguist's work. But it is only the external part. Internally he is receiving a great deal of ear training of the same sort that one must undergo to learn a language. A large part of his progress in phonemicizing is as much the result of change in hearing as it is of the formal analysis which he is evolving. The two, of course, go hand in hand. As his ear adjusts to the patterns of the language, his transcription improves, and his formal analysis becomes better based. As his understanding of the system emerges, it provides guidance for his ear training. It is doubtful whether any good analytic work can be done without acquiring at least some minimum amount of "feel" for the language. Appearances to the contrary, no linguist ever works on a language wholly from outside it.

Most successful field linguists go beyond this minimum. Usually they make at least some effort to learn to pronounce the language well and fluently. This helps their ear training and accelerates their getting the needed "feel" for the sound system. Often they attempt to build up a real speaking and hearing command of the language. For analysis of the gross features of the phonology (and equally of the grammar) an extensive fluency is not necessary, though often very helpful. In rapid reconnaissance work it may not be possible. But for working deeply into the details of structure it is essential.

This might suggest that the best analyst would be a trained native speaker. Of course, for most languages no such is available nor likely soon to be. But even for the favored languages, this is not necessarily true. There are matters in which the native-speaker linguist has a decided advantage. But there are also instances where his familiarity with his mother tongue will hide patterns or put them out of perspective. At some points the trained and experienced foreigner coming into the language through concurrent learning and analysis is more perceptive. Language learning is valuable to the analyst not only because it brings him to a "feel" for the language, but also because the struggles of learning unfamiliar patterns are, in themselves, revealing.

It follows, then, that the best possible team for a really comprehensive attack on a language would include both a linguistically trained native speaker and a competent non-native linguist. If such cooperation is not possible, either the linguist must acquire a very good speaking knowledge of the language, or the native analyst must obtain good linguistic training including some extensive experience with languages other than his own. Without broad language experience and real command, only gross preliminary work can be done.

18.4 Certain facts about language point to difficulties with a procedure like that of 18.2, and suggest an alternative. The number of sounds in any given environment is always less than the total in the language. This is true because, if complementary distribution occurs, then some sounds are missing in any given environment. It seems that complementary distribution does indeed occur within at least some of the phonemes in every language. Moreover, the sounds that contrast in any given environment are likely to be more sharply different, phonetically, than are the numerous allophones which might be observed if all the environments were taken together. In any attempt to make a precise phonetic transcription of whole utterances, however short, a very large part of the effort is expended in making just those distinctions which are going to prove non-significant. This is obviously wasteful. It might be easier, then, to restrict one's attention to one environment at a time. Within each environment a careful comparison might be made to ascertain what contrasts occur there. This can be done without any concern whether these same sounds occur anywhere else, and without any effort to make the fine phonetic distinctions which might distinguish the sounds in one environment from very similar sounds in another.

These observations provide the basis for another approach to phonemic analysis. This is much less easily described in print, since it concentrates on the hearing of contrasts rather than on the manipulation of transcription. The crucial items must be heard rather than seen. In the following discussion some English examples will be used. These will enable the reader to imagine what is heard and worked with. But it must be borne in mind that what is described is some foreign linguist's initial approach to English. He will not hear English sounds as the English speaker hears them, and hence not exactly as the reader reconstructs his impressions.

18.5 The investigator would begin as in any other approach by eliciting what he hopes will be short utterances. During one part of his work he will concern himself only with initial consonants, at another with final vowels, and so forth. For example, he might be working on English initial consonants. He would hear some which would seem clearly to be clusters, and might leave these aside to concentrate on those which seemed to be single or probably analyzable as single. Among others he would hear [pʰ tʰ kʰ b d g], and being stops rather than fricatives or resonants like the other consonants, these might be singled out for attention as a group. There would, of course, be observable variation in all of these, but the six would stand out as being reasonably distinct from one another. That is, their several ranges of variation would not overlap, and might not even approach one another closely.

Attention is focused not so much on the sounds as such, but more on the contrasts which exist between them and the system of sounds which these contrasts delineate. For example, within the stops there is a contrast between three that are unvoiced, aspirate, and fortis, and three that are voiced, unaspirate, and lenis. There is a contrast between a pair with labial articulation, a pair with apical, and a pair with dorsal. He would write such symbols as [b] in his notes, but primarily to indicate something which contrasts with other possibilities in being stop rather than continuant, voiced rather than voiceless, and labial rather than apical or dorsal. He would find that these contrasts define, within a broader system of consonants, a system of stops which may be diagramed thus:

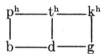

At another time, he might examine consonantal sounds occurring between two vowels. Here again (in some dialects) he would find six stop units. If examined closely they would be found to be different from the six units found in initial position, though not always sharply different. For example, the voiceless ones are more strongly aspirated in initial position than in medial, where they range from unaspirated to moderately aspirated. The voiced stops tend to be voiced throughout in medial position, but to start unvoiced in initial position, though the difference might be very hard to hear consistently. If all these stops were taken together, making a close and consistent transcription would be very difficult. If a single position is taken at a time, the most difficult discriminations may be by-passed. Furthermore, if attention is focused, not on the units but on the contrasts, the problem may be further simplified. Again there is found to be a contrast between one set less voiced, more aspirate, and more fortis, and another set more voiced, less aspirate, and more lenis. The same three-way contrast in point of articulation is observed. The system of stops in medial position may be diagramed thus:

The diagrams of the two systems of stops are the same in shape, and similar points in the two can be matched up. The process can be visualized in terms of laying one map of the units and their relationships on top of the other, then stretching or shortening a bit here and there until they fit one over the other. The stretching and shortening would represent the elimination of minor phonetic differences of no phonemic consequence.

18.6   The process of analysis can never be quite as simple as that just described. The most serious difficulty is that it is never possible to know in advance exactly what will be the pertinent environments. If the environment is defined too broadly, the effect may be to jumble together two quite different sets of allophones, thus losing a great deal of the advantage of this approach. If the environment is defined too narrowly, there may be great difficulty in getting enough material. The art of phonemic analysis on these lines is in the selection of a useful set of positions for examination. It may not be at all obvious to the outsider what these should be. The linguist must be constantly on the watch for any little indication of a better delimitation.

An almost over-simple English example will show the difficulty. The linguist approaching English in this way might very well not find a six-member set of initial stops. What he will find will depend on what items appear in his rather haphazardly drawn sample of words. In some cases there might be eight rather clearly marked stops: [pʰ tʰ b d], [ḵʰ] in *key*, [kʰ] in *coat*, [g] in *geese*, and [g] in *goat*. This possibility is, of course, a reflection of the fact that mere initial position is not enough to define the readily hearable allophonic variation in English velars.

Two things might be done. One would be to examine the various stops in initial position for complementary distribution within this environment, following much the same method described in the last chapter. Thus, [ḵʰ kʰ] might be considered as a suspicious pair. If an adequate sample can be gathered — that is, a sample of items with these two in initial position — the hypothesis of complementary distribution could be examined. It would be found that these two are in fact distributed in a way that correlates with the articulation of the following vowel. Thus it would be possible to reduce the eight initial stops to a system of six. Of course, at the same time it would be desirable to check pairs of voiced and voiceless stops sharing the same point of articulation. In this case they would turn out to contrast, and with luck, good minimal pairs (like *coat* : *goat*) might be found to prove it.

The second possibility would be to delimit the environment more closely. That is, attention might be restricted not merely to the position before vowels, but more specifically to that before front vowels. If this were done, there would be found a system of six stops. Before back vowels there would be found a different, but obviously equivalent, system of six stops. These would match up easily with each other and with other systems of six stops which might be found in other positions. This answer to the difficulty seems simple and straightforward, but this is deceptive. In the first place, the problem of determining what is the significant environment remains. There is no way to know in advance that it is defined in terms of the frontness of the following vowel. In the second place, every time environments are refined the amount of data available is cut. It takes a good number of items to establish the system of contrasts in a given position, just as it does to establish the fact of complementary distribution. Moreover, while frontness and backness of the vowel is pertinent in relationship to velar stops, it is not with apicals and labials. Splitting the environment on this basis helps at one point, but only complicates matters at others. It will be feasible to seek phoneme systems only in a rather small number of selected environments. Any allophonic variation which obtrudes within these environments must be handled by looking for complementary distribution.

18.7   In matching up the sound systems found in various environments, it will not always be found that they have the same number of units and the same patterns of interrelationships. English presents a very simple instance. In some dialects the contrast between /t/ and /d/ has been lost between vowels. (These are the speakers who do not distinguish between *latter* and *ladder*.) This type of English will be found to have a system of six stops in some positions, but only five in others. Two of the systems that must be matched can be diagramed as follows:

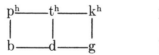

This can be resolved by equating [T] with one of the two alveolar stops of the other system, or by maintaining it as in some way different from either [tʰ] or [d]. (That is, are *latter* and *ladder*

both /lǽdər/, both /lǽtər/ or both /lǽTər/? And if the latter, what is the status of /T/ in the system?) American linguists generally have preferred to match wherever possible; some Europeans, to maintain units like /T/ in which the voiced : voiceless contrast is said to be **neutralized.** If the match is to be made, there must be an appeal to phonetics and a careful study of the ranges of variation of the stops under discussion. In some such instances the phonetic characteristics of the sounds involved will render the decision quite obvious. In other instances it may be a very delicate decision. In occasional instances the choice can only be made arbitrarily. Of course, the difficult decisions will also have to be faced, in a different guise perhaps, in any other approach.

Often enough, holes will occur in one or more of the systems simply because of limitations in the data. For example, in many positions, there is a system of English fricatives as follows:

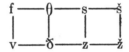

This occurs both in final and in medial positions. However, in final position [ž] is quite rare. *Garage* is probably the commonest example, but this does not have [ž] with all speakers. With the small corpus of data typically used in phonemic analysis, particularly in preliminary field work, rare phonemes like this are easily missed. An occasional gap in a system may cause no great difficulty in matching the several systems to get the comprehending phonemic system of the language as a whole. But if such gaps are numerous, the true picture of relationships may be very obscure. When it is remembered that [ð] is also rare in many positions, and hence likely to be missed, and further that [ž] is actually missing from the system in initial position, the possibilities of grave matching problems increase.

18.8 The two approaches to phonemic analysis (18.2 and 18.5–7) are not incompatible, in spite of considerable and basic differences. Field work cannot proceed mechanically along a course meticulously laid out in advance. The techniques described are aids, devices to assist in testing guesses that the linguist makes, and ways of ordering the data to suggest fruitful hypotheses. Indeed, this is one reason that some "feel" for the language is so vital: the experience of learning and attempting to communicate through the language is one of the best sources of hypotheses which can profitably be tested. One essential to good field work is alertness to any clue of whatever kind that will suggest a hypothesis and ability to frame it in such a way that it can be tested. The other essential is suitable techniques of systematic and reliable testing. Without such, searching for hypotheses becomes mere speculation. Without hypotheses, the techniques become meaningless and uncontrolled manipulations. The process of analysis, as a whole, is not one single operation which must proceed along one line of development, but a sequence of hypothesis makings and testings. There is no need for uniformity of method, and, indeed, different hypotheses are often best tested in different ways.

It follows, therefore, that linguists vary widely in their field-work procedures. These range through a spectrum from something very close to the technique described in 18.2 to something very much like that described in 18.5. Various little tricks may also be used. Some of these are highly personal; others are widely known and used. There can, therefore, be no typical field-work program. There will be given in the next sections a narrative account of an actual first informant session. This represents my own way of working, though of course I do not always proceed in exactly the same way. Field work is a little like chess: I might plan my opening move long in advance; the close of the game will be dictated by the situation I find myself in. The language in this investigation is Ewe, spoken in Ghana and Togo, West Africa. From general knowledge of African languages, I had some idea as to what sort of things to expect but very little specific knowledge of Ewe.

18.9   When I came to the session I had in mind a list of "nouns" which I planned to elicit. I went through this list rather quickly. Some responses were transcribed after only a single hearing, others after one or two repetitions. The list was slightly altered in the course of elicitation. After asking for 'fire' (42), I asked for 'fireplace.' The informant told me that there were two words, one referring to the general area and one to the specific spot. I put down both, adding the gloss 'kitchen' for the general area. After I had asked for 'goat' (22) the informant volunteered a word for 'sheep.' I added this, though I had not planned on eliciting it. Again, when I asked for 'stirring stick' (46), he volunteered 'ladle.' Note

that the food plants asked for are ones that I knew were grown
in West Africa. The transcription on page 298 reproduces my
notes as they stood after about an hour's work. They are changed
in no essential respect, though they have been typed for legibility,
and a few symbols were changed to conform to those of Chapter
15. The original notes were spread over four pages, leaving ample
space for corrections and comments. By the end of the second hour
many items had been changed or annotated. Pitch was recorded
by lines through the transcription but at the stage of my notes
which are reproduced here I had not yet been able to identify the
tones on five words — even tentatively. In three words I had not
been able to settle on a vowel quality and so wrote [ke/ε kpe/ε
ze/ε] to indicate my hesitation between [e] and [ε].

Even before the whole list had been recorded, I had started
checking and comparing. For example, item 13 sounded enough
like one I had heard earlier that I glanced up the list, found that
the item was 'hair,' (5) and asked for the two together for comparison. When heard together, they gave a strong impression of
being a minimal pair. The difference was heard to be in the articulation of the consonant: labiodental in [fu] 'hair,' and bilabial in [ɸu] 'bone,' (The tone markings which cannot easily be
printed will be omitted in citing forms in the discussion.) The
contrast ın the two [f]-like sounds was marked by adding a diacritic to the fronted one. 'Foot' (12) was compared. The consonant was thought to match that of [ɸu] 'bone' rather than [fu]
'hair' and so was also marked as fronted. (This was later found to
be an error.) The very next word seemed to fit into the same pattern: [ʋu] 'blood' has a clearly bilabial consonant. As other labial
fricatives appeared these were compared with this one. The next
one to be heard was in [devi] 'child' (18) and seemed to be clearly
labiodental. A contrast of [v : ʋ] would be consistent with the
contrast of [f : ɸ], but unfortunately no wholly satisfactory evidence was found in this first session. All cases of [v] (18, 24, 32, 55)
were medial and all of [ʋ] (14, 29) were initial. Had the data been
more copious, this would have been considered an instance of
complementary distribution, but in this small corpus it might be
just an accident. Note was made that in future sessions a watch
should be maintained for initial [v] and medial [ʋ].

In the second word elicited, [asibide] 'finger,' it was noticed that there was a very markedly dental [d̪], and a diacritic was added at the time to note that fact. The next [d]-like sound to be heard was in [aḍu] 'tooth' (9). This was not dental, nor was that in [aḍe] 'tongue' (10). These three words were compared and the

1	hand	aɓĭ	19	tree	atĭ	37	stone	kpe/ɛ
2	finger	asĭbĭḍe	20	leaf	aŋogbā	38	hoe	agbleɲu
3	arm	aɓɔ	21	root	ke/ɛ	39	jar	goɓ
4	head	ta	22	goat	gbɔ̃	40	fire	dzo
5	hair	fū	23	sheep	alɛ̃	41	fireplace	mlegbwĭ
6	eye	ŋˑku	24	dog	aṽu	42	kitchen	dzoɖoƒe
7	nose	ŋotĭ	25	elephant	tĭgliñĭ	43	pot	ze/ɛ
8	mouth	nuŭ	26	snake	da	44	stirring stick	
9	tooth	aḍu	27	water	tsi			agbletsitsĭ
10	tongue	aḍe	28	house	xɔ	45	ladle	tsĭtsĭ
11	ear	to	29	door	ʋɔ	46	mortar	tou
12	foot	aƒɔ	30	roof	xɔta	47	pestle	tatĭ
13	bone	fū	31	river	toƒsĭ	48	yam	te
14	blood	ʋu	32	forest	aʋe	49	cocoyam	makaɲĭ
15	person	ame	33	path	mɔ	50	banana	akoḍu
16	man	ŋotsu	34	village	koƒe	51	rice	molĭ
17	woman	ñonu	35	field	agble	52	meat	lã
18	child	deʋĭ	36	ground	aŋ̆lgba	53	cloth	aʋɔ

Transcript of Ewe field notes

contrast was confirmed. I tried imitating 'tooth' and 'tongue' using the type of retroflex [ḍ] familiar to me from Hindi, and this was accepted by the informant. Imitation with a dental [d̪] was emphatically rejected. I marked [aḍu] and [aḍe] as retroflex. Thereafter, I made a point to observe every [d]-like sound to be sure which articulation occurred. Each could be assigned to either [d̪] or [ḍ].

In this procedure the transcription was chiefly useful as an index. For example, at item 13 the informant's response sounded very much like something I remembered hearing before. Glancing up my list, I found [fu] at item 5. This told me that I should ask for 'hair' if I wished to compare. I did not refer back to see what I had RECORDED and then compare it with the RECORDING of the later word. Rather, I made the comparison between the

1	hand	àsí	19	tree	àtí	37	stone	kpé
2	finger	àsìbìdě	20	leaf	ǎŋūgbǎ	38	hoe	àgblènú
3	arm	àbɔ̌	21	root	kě	39	jar	gɔ̌
4	head	tǎ	22	goat	gbɔ̌	40	fire	dzɔ̀
5	hair	fú	23	sheep	ālé	41	fireplace	mlékpúí
6	eye	ŋkú	24	dog	àvǔ	42	kitchen	dsɔ̀dófé
7	nose	ŋɔ̌tí	25	elephant	tíglínyĭ	43	pot	zě
8	mouth	nǔ	26	snake	dà	44	stirring	
9	tooth	àdǔ	27	water	tsì		stick	àkplédǎtsítsí
10	tongue	àdě	28	house	xɔ̀	45	ladle	tsítsí
11	ear	tó	29	door	ʋɔ̀	46	mortar	tɔ̌
12	foot	àfɔ̀	30	roof	xɔ̌tǎ	47	pestle	tātí
13	bone	fú	31	river	tɔ̌sísí	48	yam	tè
14	blood	ʋù	32	forest	àvě	49	cocoyam	mākāní
15	person	àmè	33	path	mɔ́	50	banana	àkɔ̌dú
16	man	ŋútsù	34	village	kɔ́fé	51	rice	mɔ́lĭ
17	woman	nyɔ́nù	35	field	àgblè	52	meat	là
18	child	ɖèví	36	ground	ānyígbá	53	cloth	àvɔ̌

Words elicited in first session phonemically transcribed

actual PRONUNCIATIONS as I elicited them together from the informant. It was only because I intended using my record for nothing more than a reminder of the proper glosses that I was content with the very rapid initial recording. In the first run-through I was mainly trying to get a line-up on suitable items for future comparison.

Two words, [asibiɖe] 'finger' (2) and [agbletsitsi] 'stirring stick' (44), seemed to have four syllables. Eight others seemed to have three. These were left aside for this session since they are more difficult to work with than the shorter one- and two-syllable words which seemed to be available in abundance. At some later time these would have to be examined, and they might then prove very useful. For example, [asibiɖe] 'finger' looks very much as if it includes a morpheme meaning 'hand,' and may accordingly have some grammatical interest. Mental note was made of this, but it might be many sessions later before this clue would be followed up.

When all the words shown on page 298 had been accumulated, I went over the corpus, assembled words of any given type of initial, and compared them with one another and with other groups. For example, [ta] 'head' (4), [to] 'ear' (11), [tɔsisi] 'river' (31), [tou] 'mortar' (46), [tati] 'pestle' (47), and [te] 'yam' (48) are all recorded with initial [t]. This merely means that they are all worth comparing. They were checked to confirm that they do in fact all have the same initial. Then they were compared with [ɖa] 'snake' (26). In making such comparison, I was guided by the notion of suspicious pairs as in 17.6. So likewise [ɖa] 'snake' was compared with [ḍevi] 'child' (18) to be sure that the dental : retroflex contrast is pertinent and that each item was correctly recorded. Had there been more than one item with initial [ɖ] or [ḍ], each group would first have been listened to for consistency, then the whole group would have been compared with words having phonetically similar initials. In this way all of the contrasts in initial position were examined and a list (at first not complete) was made of the sounds in this position. After this the position between two vowels in CVCV words should be studied, and the list of contrasting sounds in this place worked up. This was left for a future session. The vowels should be given similar treatment.

18.10   To native speakers of European languages, most of which have nothing quite like tone, this feature has traditionally presented special difficulties. It has commonly been assumed that these are insurmountable, that Westerners simply cannot learn tone languages, and even that tone is not amenable to systematic analysis. In actual fact, in some languages tone is very easy to analyze, and should not be at all difficult to learn. In others it can be very complicated, as indeed can any other part of the phonemic or grammatical system. On the whole, tone should be expected to present no more difficulty, and commonly much less, than any other part of the sound system — provided that it is approached systematically and with an appropriate methodology.

With tone, a systematic approach is much more crucial than with the consonants and vowels. With the latter, a workable approximation may be produced by an impressionistic approach. This may be nothing more than simple imitation and recording in terms of the sound systems of European languages with only slight modifications. A good field technique will get results that are better, occasionally much better, and get them much more rapidly. With tone, however, an uncontrolled approach usually gets nothing at all, and very seldom achieves results that are of any practical value. Because of the difficulties that Europeans (including many linguists) have had with tone, they often seriously underrate its importance. In field work with tone languages, it is commonly advisable to put the first systematic analytic efforts on the tone system.

The techniques for the analysis of tone are essentially the same as those for consonants and vowels. If there is any basic difference, it rests in the fact that most people are able to make a better phonetic transcription of consonants and vowels than of tone. Therefore, the technique described in Chapter 17 is less often applicable. There are a few special tricks which are of particular value in tone analysis, though some of them are also useful with consonants and vowels.

18.11 One of these tricks is the isolation of tone by humming or whistling. Many people have great difficulty in identifying tone patterns. This is true even of some who are excellent musicians; tone is functionally so different from melody that they cannot easily adjust to it. Often it is relatively easy to tell that two syllables are tonally alike or tonally different, but difficult to tell what they are or how they differ. It may be much easier with a whistled tune. For many people, it is much easier to equate a tone pattern on a spoken utterance with a whistled tune than it is to identify the tones directly. Whistling or humming is, then, a useful intermediate between an elicited utterance and a transcription.

When the linguist whistles or hums tunes to match the informant's utterances, the informant sometimes learns the technique. It is then possible to isolate a tone pattern and ask the informant if it is correct. After a bit of practice, very reliable responses may be obtained to this type of question. With some informants, unfortunately, the isolation of tone from the rest of the utterance is so unnatural that they are never able to hear the connection, and so may not even understand what the linguist is doing when he whistles or hums to himself. Informants who do hear the relation may sometimes learn to isolate the tones themselves. In that case, they can be asked, in difficult cases, to whistle or hum a tone pattern after speaking an utterance.

It should be borne in mind that any division of utterances into component parts must be learned. An ordinary speaking knowledge of a language is only the ability to produce normal utterances in their entirety. An untrained informant cannot isolate vowels from words; indeed, he may not be able to isolate words from sentences. The process is easier for literate informants, but more risky. They are too prone to be influenced by the spelling, which may not reflect the pronunciation accurately, and may utterly distort pronunciations when required to dissect them. The process is always more difficult to teach to an illiterate informant, but the results are commonly more reliable. Many even highly educated people are illiterate with regard to tone, however, since in many languages tone is omitted from the standard writing system. In a few cultures, the technique of isolating tones is already widely known. In Mazatec (Mexico) messages are conveyed by whistling the tone patterns of sentences. In some languages of Africa messages are transmitted by beating out the tones on drums tuned to two or three pitches. That such things should be possible, incidentally, indicates how important tone can be in a language.

18.12   Another technique useful with tone is what can be called the **monotony test.** This was the first special technique I used in the Ewe work to attack tone, and it can best be made clear by resuming the narration of that session.

In the corpus were a considerable number of monosyllabic words. These were drawn off and sorted according to the tone as it had been recorded. Since three tones had been marked, there resulted three lists:

High tone			Mid tone			Low tone		
5	hair	fu	4	head	ta	14	blood	ʋu
13	bone	ƒu	11	ear	to	28	house	xɔ
33	path	mɔ	26	snake	ɖa	29	door	ʋɔ
37	stone	kpe/ɛ	40	fire	dzo	48	yam	te
			43	pot	ze/ɛ			
			52	meat	lã			

The informant was asked to pronounce each of these groups as lists. The first and third, [fu ʃu mɔ kpe/ɛ] and [ʋu xɔ ʋɔ te], each gave a monotonous, singsong effect, indicating that each group was tonally uniform within itself. To be certain, the experiment was tried several times with the items in different orders; the results always were the same. The group tentatively marked as having mid tone did not give the same monotonous effect. It was found to be quite mixed. The items that stood out as different were removed, until finally only [ḍa dzo lã] 'snake fire meat' were left. Once this had been done, these three remaining words gave the same even, monotonous sound, and could be assumed to be uniform in tone.

Such a test does not, of course, prove that these lists are correctly labeled as having high, mid, and low tones, respectively, but only that they are each internally uniform. Nor does it prove that the three lists are all different. As a next step, one item from the high-tone list was inserted into the mid-tone list. The informant was asked to recite 'snake bone fire meat.' The inserted item, [ʃu] 'bone,' stood out as prominently different from the rest, and as clearly higher. Then he was asked for 'hair bone path snake stone' (the high-tone list plus one from the mid-tone list). In this, [ḍa] 'snake' stood out as definitely lower than the rest of the list. The tentative mid-tone list was found, as had been expected, to be lower than the high-tone list. The same result was obtained in comparing the high- and low-tone lists. But when the mid- and low-tone lists were compared, the result was different: the mixed lists had the same even, monotonous sound that indicates uniformity. What had been transcribed at first in two ways and then sorted into two lists, labeled mid tone and low tone, turned out to be alike. Therefore these two lists were combined.

The three monosyllabic words originally assigned to the mid-tone list but later removed were now tested by inserting them, one by one, into the two tonally uniform lists. One, [to] 'ear,' was found to fit with the high-tone group. The others, [ta] 'head' and [ze/ɛ] 'pot,' did not fit in either; whatever they are, they are neither simply high tone nor low. In the same way, the several monosyllabic words not tone marked in the original record were tested and assigned, when possible, to the proper list. Of these, [tsi] 'water' (27), was found to fit the list starting with [ʋu], that is, to be low-toned. The remainder were put aside to be reexamined later when more of their kind had accumulated. It might be expected that a few additional lists of tonally uniform words neither simply high nor low might then be sorted out.

Much the same procedure was used with the two-syllable words. There were a large number of these which were recorded as having the second syllable higher than the first. These were sorted out, checked by the monotony test, and finally found to fall into two groups: [ŋku ŋɔti alẽ tati] 'eye nose sheep pestle' (6, 7, 23, 47), with the tone sequences mid-high; and [asi ḍevi ati] 'hand child tree' (1, 18, 19), with the tone sequence low-high. Another group, [kɔfe mlegbwi tsitsi] 'village fireplace ladle' (34, 41, 45), was found to have the tone sequence high-high. Each list was found to be internally consistent and clearly different tonally from the other two.

There is one very necessary caution in using this technique. It can easily be understood from an English example: Compare the pitch on *three* in *One, two, three.* with that in *One, two, three, four.* The difference, of course, is not one of tone but of intonation. The last word in a list has a different contour from that of all the rest. Tone languages commonly have intonation superimposed in various ways on the tone. Not infrequently there can be something quite comparable to English list intonation, functioning to set off the last member of a list from all the others. It is, therefore, important to avoid comparing list ends with other words. This is best accomplished by varying the order of the lists as was done in checking the assignment of words to tone groups.

Much the same rule should be applied in comparing any two items: always ask for the two in both orders. This can be just as important in comparison of consonants or vowels as in comparing tones. For example, to be sure of the bilabial : labiodental contrast the words 'bone hair' (13, 15) [ɸu fu] were elicited and compared and then 'hair bone' (15, 13) [fu ɸu]. There may be allophonic differences, or equally important, the position in a series may affect the linguist's hearing in subtle ways.

18.13   Another technique especially useful with tone, but also frequently of value with other types of phonemes, is that of **frames.** Frequently a suitable frame is provided by the numerals. This was the only one for which there was time in the informant session being reported here. After a number of nouns had been sorted into tone groups by the monotony test, the first six numerals were elicited. Then the informant was asked for 'one house, two houses,...' picking suitable nouns from both the group with low tone and the group with high tone. A representative from each group is shown below:

one	ḍekā	one house	xɔ ḍekā	one bone	ɟu\ḍekā
two	eve	two houses	xɔ eve	two bones	ɟu\eve
three	etɔ̄	three houses	xɔ etɔ̄	three bones	ɟu\etɔ̄
four	ene	four houses	xɔ ene	four bones	ɟu\ene
five	aṭɔ̄	five houses	xɔ aṭɔ̄	five bones	ɟu\aṭɔ̄
six	aḍē	six houses	xɔ aḍē	six bones	ɟu\aḍē

It is easy to compare the tone on [xɔ] and [ɟu] with those on the numeral when they are adjacent in the same utterance. The first five numerals seemed to start on low tone, and the tone of [xɔ] was found to match. This is in line with my decision from the monotony test that [xɔ] has low tone. As I expected, there is always a sharp drop in tone from [ɟu] to the first syllable of the numeral. In 'one bone' and 'five bones' the tone on [ɟu] is matched by that on the final syllable. In [ɟu atɔ̄] the drop on the second syllable is clearly more than in [ɟu aḍe]. This confirmed my impression that [aḍe] 'six' is tonally mid-high, rather than low-high like [atɔ̄] 'five.' The one puzzling result was [xɔ aḍe] 'six houses.' I expected a tone sequence low-mid-high, but instead heard the first two syllables alike. This phrase was carefully compared with the others, and I concluded that the [xɔ] was in this context raised to mid tone rather than that the first syllable of [aḍe] had been dropped to low.

The best frames are ones which do not themselves change under any circumstances and which cause no change in any element inserted into them. The Ewe numerals are not, therefore, a wholly satisfactory set of frames for tone analysis. But even so, they are of great help. The fact that changes occur merely requires that more care be taken in using them. It may well be that some better frames can be found, but probably the best frames cannot be recognized until after the tone changes are comparatively well understood and the analysis is already rather far along. In using frames, one must always check carefully and be on the lookout for tone changes which are automatic when certain tone sequences occur, as well as for tone changes which are part of the grammar of the language.

18.14   By the use of monotony tests and frames, the general outline of the tone system of Ewe soon began to appear. It was found that there were three level tones, phonetically roughly do, re, mi. (Some other three-tone languages have tones much closer together and in others they are more widely separated.) These may be written in a phonemic transcription /ˋ ˉ ˊ/. There are also gliding tones. These account for some of the words that could not at first be assigned to tone groups. The gliding tones seem best analyzed as sequences of tones.

It is one matter to establish the tone contrasts that exist in the language and another to mark correctly the tones in all individual words. When tone glides occur, hearing is very much more difficult. Some vowel sequences make tones more difficult to hear (for an English speaker; the Ewe man has no trouble!). Some consonants mask tone distinctions, and in many languages the tones show allophonic variations conditioned by adjacent phonemes. All this means that some words will be easy to mark, and some will present great difficulties. It may be some time after the general system is established before all the details can be delineated.

18.15   The consonant system of Ewe was much slower in emerging. It is a larger and more complex system, and there are many more contrasts, all of which must be checked out carefully. In only one respect is it easier than tone: the English speaker feels more at home in a consonant system, however complex, because English has one roughly parallel in form and function. The English pitch system is functionally very different from the Ewe, so the inexperienced person feels ill at ease with the Ewe tone system, in spite of the fact that it is actually simpler than the intonation system of English.

The consonant system being so extensive, it is hardly surprising that not all the members were found in the small sample gathered in this first session. Four, /w y h ɣ/, were later found to have been missed. Moreover, there are some puzzling holes in the system itself. There is a contrast of /ɖ/ with /d̪/. But there is only one voiceless apical stop, the dental /t/. A great deal of searching will be needed before a linguist would be satisfied that there is no */ʈ/ in the language. It would require several times as much work before the consonant and vowel systems would emerge as clearly as had the tone system at the end of one informant session.

The phonemic system turns out to be as follows:

Consonants:	Stops			t		ts	k	kp
		b		d	ɖ	dz	g	gb
	Fricatives	ʃ	f			s	x	
		ʋ	v			z	h	
	Resonants	m		n		ny	ŋ	
		w		l		y	ɣ	

Vowels:	i	e	ɛ	a	ɔ	o	u	Nasalization:
Tones:	ˋ	ˉ	ˊ					

The symbols used are generally those of the standard Ewe orthography, and hence differ in some details from those used in the description of the informant session above, and also from those of Chapter 15. Two of them are used in quite unusual ways: /ɣ/ is used for a voiced velar fricative with very light friction that patterns as a resonant, and /h/, not needed in its usual value, is used for a voiced velar fricative with much heavier friction. /dz ts ny gb kp/ are all digraphs representing single consonants. This can cause no difficulty, either in orthography or in phonemic transcription, since the only consonant clusters that occur in Ewe have /l/ as the second member.

The vocabulary elicited in the first session is given on page 299 in phonemic transcription using these symbols. This can be compared with the rough transcription in the preliminary field notes. There were three errors in the consonants, and nine in the vowels (plus three words where the vowel was not decided at first). But there were only fifteen words correctly marked for tone. Many of these errors were comparatively minor: low-high for the sequence mid-high, or mid-low for low-low. A few were very badly wrong, as high-mid for low-low to high in item 3. It will be noted that the very bad errors were more common at the beginning of the list, and that there were only five correct tone markings in the first half of the list as compared with ten in the second half. As the session progressed, my hearing of Ewe tone was starting to improve. Before the first session had been completed many of the original errors had been partially or wholly corrected. The remaining difficulties were largely with the gliding tones.

It is of interest to note that the standard orthography is in most respects parallel with the phonemic transcription. There are three important differences: (1) Tone is not marked. This occasionally causes some trouble. Note that 'ear' (11) and 'mortar' (46) are spelled alike, *to*, as is another word with low tone, meaning 'buffalo.' There are many other such pairs or sets of words distinguished only by tone. Only the context will distinguish them. But even the best reader must, occasionally, stop and reread a sentence or two before he gets a meaning that seems appropriate. The lack of indication of tone may be considered as a serious defect in the orthography. (2) The phoneme /l/ has both [l]-like and [r]-like allophones. The Europeans who introduced the writing of Ewe wrote these differently. The spelling *r* is used after dental and prepalatal consonants, *l* elsewhere. Thus /tló/ 'turn' is spelled *tro*, /nylà/ 'be vexed' *nyra*, but /blá/ 'tie' *bla*, and /klá/ 'bid farewell' *kla*. (3) Capitalization and punctuation follow much the same rules as in English. The following are the capital forms for the letters not used in English:

ɖ Ɖ,   ƒ Ƒ,   ʋ Ʋ,   ŋ Ŋ,   ɣ Ɣ,   ɛ Ɛ,   ɔ Ɔ

18.16 Only a few years ago, a field linguist's equipment was very simple: notebooks, paper, pencils, and, as was commonly said, some old shoe boxes to house his files. Much of his work was the tedious task of carefully transcribing page after page of material dictated by the informant. This was often even more tiring for the informant than for the linguist, and it was sometimes a triumph of human relations to keep him at his task and producing useful material. After this followed long hours of copying out suitable portions of the corpus onto small paper slips and filing. In this way the material that could profitably be compared was assembled and made accessible. Notebooks and files were the pride and despair of the linguist. Large amounts of valuable data were amassed, but no one ever devised a filing system quite adequate to the linguist's demands. Clerical procedures varied from one linguist to another as much as did elicitation and analytic techniques.

The development of the tape recorder has been hailed as changing all this. Great quantities of text can be easily and rapidly recorded. Even more important, the unnatural slowness and interruptions of dictation can be eliminated. Much of the drudgery is taken out of the informant's work. The inexperienced linguist has little faith in his transcriptions, but trusts the machine, since it records with "high fidelity." He can now approach his field work with a new confidence. Few linguists go into the field today without a tape recorder. Too many go with far too much reliance on their machine.

The basic operations remain much the same as before. The recorder cannot do phonemic analysis. Text material on tape is of very little use until it is transcribed onto paper. The tape recorder does not materially decrease the tedium of transcription, but it does provide an excellent alibi for procrastination. Indeed, it is often far more difficult to transcribe from a tape than from an informant, and from any but a technically excellent recording, it may be effectively impossible. Phonemic analysis can be done from a tape, but it is always more difficult than directly from speech. For analytic use, however, the tape must be very carefully planned, and very well recorded. The most important instrument in phonemics remains the trained human ear. Other instruments are seldom any more than aids to listening, or means of preserving the evidence for another ear to hear.

There are ways in which a tape recorder, properly used, can be of real assistance. Always there must be careful planning. And there must be correlation with a program of old-fashioned field work: integrated eliciting and analysis as described in this chapter, transcribing, and filing. The place of recording instruments in phonemic field work is always ancillary.

Tape-recording equipment for field use must be selected with care. "Home" recorders are seldom sufficiently well built either mechanically or electronically to give dependable service for any appreciable length of time under field conditions. Some professional machines are better, though often bulky, heavy, and expensive. All types are designed to meet requirements other than those of field linguistics. Ruggedness, ease of service and repair, and recording quality are the chief desiderata. Recording quality said to be "good enough for speech" is not generally useful for phonemic field work, and nothing less than what is considered "adequate for music" will do.

Microphones are often the weakest link. Those provided with machines are almost never satisfactory, and crystal types should never be relied on. Medium-priced dynamic microphones are usually the best choice, both for ruggedness and tone quality. With both machines and microphones, specifications should be studied closely before a selection is made. Advice should be sought from persons who are acquainted with the special problems of recording under adverse conditions.

Machines should be serviced regularly, heads cleaned and demagnetized. Recording quality should be checked occasionally. A linguist who plans to be on the field in a remote area for any length of time must be prepared to do this servicing himself, as well as make some types of repairs. He should be equipped with necessary tools, certain replacement parts, and a service manual. And he must have at least a rudimentary understanding of tape-recorder operation.

The most difficult problem in the field is maintaining correct speed. Elaborate accessory equipment can accomplish this, but is seldom feasible. Instead, it is better to record at whatever speed comes out, but make a record of the speed actually used. The best way to do this is to blow a 440-A pitch pipe before and after every recording. Later it will be possible to adjust playback speed to match the tone on the tape to another 440-A pitch pipe, and so obtain correct playing speed and a relatively distortion-free reproduction.

Tapes, particularly those already recorded, must be handled with care. Heat, vibration, excessive humidity or dryness, and particularly proximity to electrical equipment may severely damage them. Low-grade tapes should never be used, and ultra-thin tapes avoided. Tapes must be evenly wound. Valuable tapes should never be put on a machine which is not known to be in good running condition.

All of these suggestions — and a lot more could be made — indicate that field tape recording is not the easy, foolproof procedure that some people think it is. A linguist using a machine needs to understand a good bit of its theory and operation if he is to get good results. He must understand what it can and cannot do, that is, the way in which it fits into the total process of language recording and analysis. Used within its limitations as a part of a well-planned program, it can be of great value. Seen as a short cut around all of the drudgery of eliciting and transcribing, it can be worse than useless.

19

Interpretations of English Phonemics

19.1   The literature dealing with English pronunciation is extensive and diverse. Most of it makes no claim to be scientific, so that it requires no discussion here. But even within the smaller body of works that purport to describe English phonology on a scientific basis, there are considerable and often perplexing differences. It seems almost as though no two authors can agree, and that few even approach agreement. As a practical matter it is important to understand these differences, since otherwise a large mass of important literature is inaccessible.

There is another reason for close attention to this diversity. The scientific competence of descriptive linguistics to handle the data of human speech can best be judged by comparing such divergent analyses. Unless the results are reproducible and the work of different linguists more or less reconcilable, no great validity can be claimed for the methods. English is a good subject for such a comparison, because a large number of investigators, representing various points of view within descriptive linguistics, have made and published analyses of this language.

19.2   The problem is perhaps best presented by giving a summary in advance and then discussing the details against this framework. The following five general heads subsume the more important of the differences which can be observed between phonemic analyses and the resultant transcriptions.

(1) Differences in SYMBOLS. The selection of a symbol is dictated by tradition, expediency, the purposes of the work, and the arbitrary whim of the analyst. None of these factors is significant in judging linguistic science, but any variation in symbols can be the source of practical confusion.

(2) Differences in the MATERIAL TREATED. English is spoken in a number of dialects, each with its own phonologic system. An analysis can be based on any one of these, and may accordingly differ from an analysis based on another dialect. But these systems are not wholly different, so that it is possible to base an analysis on a group of dialects, or on all the dialects taken together. Such an analysis must have fundamental differences from one based on any single dialect.

(3) Differences in INTERPRETATION OF THE DATA. There are in English, as in most languages, a few points in the structure where the data does not point unambiguously to one single interpretation. When the evidence approaches an even balance, it may be expected that both solutions will find supporters. Disagreements arising from this source are less significant in judging linguistic science than is the fact that the differences can themselves be predicted. A linguist examining the phonology of a language can identify the points at which divergences of interpretation can be expected.

(4) Differences in the CONCEPT OF THE PHONEME. Linguistics, fortunately, has not had any one generally accepted orthodoxy, though within restricted circles minor systems have been rather rigidly promulgated. The result has been a free give-and-take and exploration of various methods and theoretical formulations. This has contributed both to immediate confusion and to ultimate progress.

(5) Differences in the STATE OF LINGUISTIC RESEARCH. Descriptive linguistics is a relatively young and very rapidly advancing science. (The years 1924 and 1933 are among the leading candidates for the birth date of American linguistics.) Certain features of English phonology have only recently been understood, and several still lie on the farther side of the frontier. Each later analysis has

had important data available which the framers of earlier statements could not have known.

19.3   The transcriptions of consonants used in ten books [1] and the present introduction are tabulated below. Those consonants which are omitted from the table are written essentially alike by all.

This Book Trager & Smith Fries	Pike Nida	Bloom- field	Bloch & Trager	Jones Kenyon	Thomas	Ward
ð	đ	ð	ð	ð	ð	ð
š	š	š	š	ʃ	ʃ	ʃ
ž	ž	ž	ž	ʒ	ʒ	ʒ
č	č	č	tš	tʃ	tʃ	tʃ
ǰ	ǰ	ǰ	dž	dʒ	dʒ	dʒ
y	y	j	j	j	j	j
hw	hw	hw	hw	hw	ʍ	ʍ
hy	hy	hj	hj	hj	ç	hj

19.4   Perhaps the most minor, but by no means the least troublesome, of the differences shown in the table is in the matter of symbols. From a purely scientific point of view this problem is trivial. Symbols can be assigned arbitrarily. Some linguists have certainly exploited this liberty too freely. But on the whole, most linguists have attempted to be as consistent with past precedents as was practical. The difficulty has been that the precedents have not always been consistent, and the practical exigencies have sometimes been severe.

British phoneticians (among whom are Jones and Ward, with

---

[1] Bloch, Bernard and George L. Trager. 1942. *Outline of Linguistic Analysis.*
Bloomfield, Leonard. 1933. *Language.*
Fries, Charles Carpenter. 1948. *Teaching and Learning English as a Foreign Language.*
Jones, Daniel. 1950. *The Pronunciation of English.* 3rd ed.
Kenyon, John Samuel. 1940. *American Pronunciation.* 8th ed.
Nida, Eugene Albert. 1949. *Morphology.* 2nd ed.
Pike, Kenneth Lee. 1947. *Phonemics.*
Trager, George L. and Henry Lee Smith, Jr., 1951. *Outline of English Structure.*
Thomas, Charles Kenneth. 1947. *An Introduction to the Phonetics of American English.*
Ward, Ida C. 1945. *The Phonetics of English.* 4th ed.

the Americans Kenyon and Thomas following them) have generally adhered rather closely to the conventions of the **International Phonetic Alphabet,** usually known as **IPA.** This is the result of a long process of development starting in 1888 with the formation of L'Association Phonétique Internationale. One of the original objectives of this organization was the creation of an alphabet which would have a distinctive symbol for every sound in human speech, and which would supplant the chaos of notations, then in use, by one internationally recognized standard. This was, of course, long before the development of the phoneme theory in anything approaching its modern form, and before European linguists had had much experience with "exotic" languages. As phonetic knowledge increased, the alphabet was expanded. This was not done haphazardly; each proposed symbol was given careful consideration by the membership and adopted or rejected by vote of the council. Even today, almost every issue of *Le Maître Phonétique,* the journal of the Association, carries a discussion of some proposal or the announcement of a decision on some symbol.

The IPA has one great merit. The principles which were set up to guide the development rejected the use of **diacritics** (marks added to letters to modify their values) in favor of entirely new letters which would be so designed as to harmonize with each other. In time, diacritics had to be taken up again, simply because the number of sounds for which symbols had to be supplied was overtaxing the ingenuity of the Association members. Nevertheless, IPA has provided a basic repertoire of symbols that are simple and of pleasing design. (Of course, not all the IPA proposals are equally felicitous in either regard!) The symbols used by Jones, Kenyon, Thomas, and Ward all follow closely the recommendations of IPA. The rules state, "Affricates are normally represented by groups of two consonants (ts, tʃ, dʒ, etc.), but, when necessary, ligatures are used (ʦ, ʧ, ʤ, etc.)." Jones and Kenyon elect the first alternative, Ward the second. Thomas writes /č ǰ/ the same as Jones and Kenyon, but for a different reason.

19.5   In the meantime, interest in American Indian languages (Amerind) was growing among American anthropologists. They worked out a notation for recording their materials, but were less concerned with discussing the principles of the notation and the design of symbols than with practical field work. Their material had to be printed, and they tended to select such symbols as would be at hand in a reasonably well-equipped print shop. Small caps, italics, raised letters, punctuation marks, Greek letters, and the diacritics commonly stocked were all exploited. The result was far from esthetic in appearance, but it served its purpose.

In time the influence of the IPA began to make itself felt among American linguists. The Americanist practice accommodated itself more and more to IPA usages. Certain of the older conventions have almost wholly disappeared, but American linguists have maintained a certain independence from the IPA. This has been reinforced by their primary interest in phonemics rather than phonetics.

Recently the typewriter has begun to exert an influence on the selection of symbols. (The books of Fries, Nida, Pike, and Trager and Smith are all reproduced from typed copy.) This is the primary reason for the use of đ ² by Pike and Nida for /ð/. Use of the typewriter has also contributed to the American preference for š ž č ǰ as against the IPA ʃ ʒ tʃ dʒ.

One of the most troublesome of the differences between transcriptions is in the use of y and j for /y/. The IPA uses j, following the orthographic conventions of German and Scandinavian languages as well as the modern spelling of classical Latin. The Americanists use y, following the precedent of English orthography. It is largely to minimize this confusion that the palatal affricate is usually written ǰ instead of the simpler j. (IPA used y for a different purpose, the high front rounded vowel [ü].)

19.6   Aside from these differences of symbolization, there is practical unanimity in the analysis of the English consonant system with the following exceptions:

The majority treat /č ǰ/ as two unit phonemes. A few, including Bloch and Trager and Thomas, treat these as clusters. (Jones and Kenyon transcribe with two letters, but list tʃ and dʒ with the other consonants, and apparently consider them as having the status of units.) There is no simple and conclusive evidence for either analysis. *Why choose?* : *white shoes* has been advanced as a

---

² Throughout this discussion / / will be used to mark phonemic equivalents in the system of Chapters 2, 3, and 4 of this book. The symbols under discussion will be written without bracketing. This does not imply, of course, that they are not phonemic, but merely that we are discussing symbols and phonemic analyses rather than phonemes as such.

minimal pair, but in most pronunciations open transitions confuse the picture. But there does seem to be a growing body of rather involved reasoning, which, while not conclusive, does generally favor the unit-phoneme hypothesis. In any case, the difference in interpretation does not indicate a sharp difference between linguists, because each recognizes this problem as a relatively indecisive case, whatever may be his judgment of the total weight of the evidence.

Phonetically /hw/ is sometimes a cluster [hw] and sometimes a single sound [ʍ]. It can be interpreted phonemically either as a unit or a cluster, but linguists are almost unanimous in preferring hw. Any reasoning which would seem to support the interpretation of /hw/ as ʍ would seem to require a similar interpretation of /hy/ as ç. That Ward is not consistent is perhaps partially explained by the fact that both are rather unusual in the type of English with which she is concerned.

The suggestion is occasionally met with that /š ž č ǰ/ be interpreted as sy zy ty dy. This has never been worked out in detail, and will work, if at all, only under severe restrictions as to dialect and type of data. For many, *suit* : *shoot* is something like /syúwt/ : /šúwt/, and contrasts of /č/ : /ty/ and /ǰ/ : /dy/ can be found in many dialects, e.g., *June* : *dune* /ǰúwn/ : /dyúwn/.

19.7 If these same systems are compared with regard to the syllable nuclei, it will be seen that they fall into two traditions which differ most obviously in their treatment of the so-called "long vowels." The basis of the difference can be seen most clearly through a detailed examination of one instance; for this purpose we will select the nuclei of *bit* and *beet*. There are at least four features in which the common pronunciations differ:

	NUCLEUS OF *bit*	NUCLEUS OF *beet*
Tongue position:	lower and backer	higher and fronter
Tenseness:	laxer	tenser
Duration:	shorter	somewhat longer
Glide:	not appreciable, if present at all, downward and backward	generally appreciable, very short, upward and forward

These fall into two groups. The first and second are differences in vowel quality. If they are considered as controlling, the two nuclei should be transcribed by two unit symbols, commonly ɪ and i. The third and fourth indicate a contrast between a short simple vowel and the same vowel plus an additional element; if these are controlling, the two nuclei should be written as i and iy or the like. In either case the other set of contrasts becomes an incidental phonetic feature. Following one analysis, tense vowels are followed by non-significant glides. Following the other, there is a tenser allophone of /i/ (and other vowels) before /y/. A transcription of the type of ɪ and iy is an eat-your-cake-and-have-it-too proposition which cannot seriously be suggested as a phonemic analysis, though it may be useful as a phonetic transcription.

19.8   The six transcriptions in the simple vowel tradition are as follows. The equivalents in the system of chapter three are in some cases only approximate because of variability in application of the symbols.

Jones	Ward	Kenyon	Thomas	Fries	Pike		Jones	Ward	Kenyon	Thomas	Fries	Pike	
i:	i	i	i	i	i	/iy/	ɑ:	ɑ	ɑ	ɑ	a	a	/aH/
i	ɪ	ɪ	ɪ	ɪ	ɩ	/i/	ʌ	ʌ	ɑ	ɑ	a	a	/a/
ei	eɪ	e	e	e	e	/ey/	–	–	ʌ	ʌ	ə	ə	/ə́/
ɛ	ɛ	ɛ	ɛ	ɛ	ɛ	/e/	ə	ə	ə	ə	ə	ə	/ə/
a	æ	æ	æ	æ	æ	/æ/	ə:	ɜ	ɜ	ɜ	–	–	/ə́H/
–	–	a	–	–	–	/æH/	–	–	ɝ̣	ɝ	ər	r	/ə́r/
u:	u	u	u	u	u	/uw/	–	–	ɚ	ɚ	ər	r	/ər/
u	ʊ	ʊ	ʊ	ʊ	ʊ	/u/	ɑi	aɪ	aɪ	aɪ	aɪ	aⁱ	/ay/
ou	oʊ	o	o	o	o	/ow/	ɑu	aʊ	aʊ	aʊ	aʊ	aᵘ	/aw/
ɔ:	ɔ	ɔ	ɔ	ɔ	ɔ	/ɔH/	ɔi	ɔɪ	ɔɪ	ɔɪ	ɔɪ	oⁱ	/ɔy/
ɔ	ɒ	ɒ	–	–	–	/ɔ/							

19.9   The first two transcriptions to be considered are based on a type of southern British speech called "Received Pronunciation" or "RP." Both are done by British phoneticians of very similar viewpoint, and in fact represent identical analyses. That given by Ward is a so-called "narrow transcription," that is, one which records a relatively large amount of phonetic detail. That given by Jones is more nearly a "broad transcription." (A purely "broad transcription" would use e a o for Jones' ɛ ɑ ɔ.) This school of phoneticians (they do not consider themselves as phonemicists or as linguists) is relatively little concerned with the concept of the phoneme. Jones' book relegates the phoneme to the last chapter, a bare two pages, and in Ward's book the subject is treated only little less incidentally. The nearest approach to the descriptive linguist's concept of the phoneme is their "broad transcription." This is viewed, however, not as a more adequate statement of patterning, but as a device by which the facts can be stated with a minimum of notation, though at a sacrifice of precision as compared with a "narrow transcription." The viewpoint is thoroughly phonetic. When variations of pronunciation are discussed (and they are generally contrasted with RP as a norm), it is never certain whether they should be construed as phonemic or allophonic (neither term is used). The greatest difference between these systems and those to be discussed below is, therefore, not so much in details of interpretation as in basic theoretical framework.

One peculiarity of RP must be mentioned. The mid central vowel /ə/ occurs only without stress. When stressed it is always replaced by /əн/ (Jones' ə:, Ward's ɜ). In words like *cup, dull, mother*, the stressed vowel, written ʌ by Jones, is a rather high variety of /a/. The British systems, then, accurately reflect the phonetic facts by distinguishing between ə:, ə, and ʌ.

19.10   Kenyon's transcription — and Thomas' differs only in minor details — is essentially an adaptation of the Jones and Ward system to one kind of Mid-Western American English, though three special symbols are added to facilitate remarks comparing other dialects. The theoretic basis is essentially the same, and the outlook is primarily phonetic. One peculiarity of the system arises from a too slavish following of the British precedent. Kenyon uses ə, as do Jones and Ward, to represent unstressed mid central vowels. A vowel of identical quality does occur under stress in America, but following British precedent Kenyon uses ʌ for stressed ə. Thus both Jones and Kenyon write *cup* kʌp. However, the RP and American rendition of this word are quite different, both phonetically and phonemically. The British vowel is somewhat lower than the American and is in fact usually a high variety of /a/, while the American is a variety, often rather low, of /ə/. Thus Jones' kʌp represents /káp/, Kenyon's kʌp, /kə́p/. One result of this transfer of values is to provide the phoneme /ə/ with two symbols. One, ə, is used only when unstressed; the other, ʌ, only when stressed. The two are in complementary distribution, but the obvious phonemic conclusion is not drawn; the orientation is too strongly phonetic. Kenyon's discussion of the phoneme is limited to less than one page.

Jones makes a clear distinction between /a/ ʌ and /aн/ ɑ:. The transfer just described leaves only one symbol for the two, and Kenyon writes ɑ for both /a/ and /aн/. In many Mid-Western dialects the contrast between the two is not very clear, and little damage is done; both *father* fɑðɚ and *bother* bɑðɚ are written with the same vowel. But in some dialects the two are quite different /fáнðər/ and /báðər/. This is one instance of a significant distinction which the use of this type of transcription frequently conceals.

Kenyon also treats /ər/ as a unit. This is justifiable in much the same way as is treatment of /ey/ as a unit e. But for this he provides two symbols, ɝ and ɝ, paralleling ə and ʌ, and with as little justification.

19.11   Fries and Pike follow Kenyon in all essentials. Their much closer contact with descriptive linguistics and phonemic theory, however, causes them to drop the superfluous symbols, and to free themselves from the typographic trivialities common to this line of development.

One problem which these two transcriptions raise, and which Pike has discussed at length elsewhere, is the justification for treating /ay aw ɔy/ as diphthongs, and /iy ey uw ow/ as unit phonemes. This is primarily another question of interpretation of somewhat ambiguous data. With /ay/ the evidence points more clearly to a diphthongal interpretation than with /iy/. Pike feels that this justifies treating one set as diphthongs and the other as simple vowels. Most linguists consider that the difference is far from sufficient to allow a difference of treatment, but that either all long vowels should be treated as diphthongs (as in the next group of analyses), or all should be treated as unit phonemes. The latter treatment has been followed by some, but in most cases these linguists have continued to write /ay/ as ai, or something of the kind, as a digraph symbol for a unit phoneme, much as Kenyon treats tʃ.

19.12   One of the early analyses in the diphthong tradition is that of Bloomfield (1933). His analysis was based on his own speech, which was described as more or less representative of the

Chicago area. Naturally, many of the 36 possible nuclei are not provided for, as they could not readily be found in this dialect. Aside from some symbol differences (j for /y/ and ɛ for /æ/), the following points need comment. Bloomfield knew only one contrast of the type /V : Vн/, /a : aн/ in *bomb : balm*. He did not recognize the diphthongal nature of the second one, and so wrote these as ɑ and a. This is quite understandable, since the analysis is not clear unless a series of such contrasts are available. Moreover, since he did not detect /o/ (which he probably used, though rarely), he used o for /ə/ when stressed. Unstressed /ə/ was written sometimes as e and sometimes as o. This left a diphthong of the type /oн/ or /ɔн/ without a contrasting simple vowel, and he accordingly wrote it as a unit ɔ. Bloomfield's full list, together with his own key words, is as follows:

i	*bit*	ij	*see*		
e	*bet*	ej	*say*		
ɛ	*bat /æ/*				
ɑ	*sod /a/*				
a	*balm /aн/*	aj	*sigh*	aw	*now*
u	*put*			uw	*do*
o	*son, sun /ə/*			ow	*go*
ɔ	*saw /ɔн/*	ɔj	*boy*		

19.13 The next important analysis in this tradition was that of Bloch and Trager (1942). The chief advance was the recognition of a series of /н/-diphthongs. The lengthening element in these was considered phonetically similar to pre-vocalic /h/, with which it is, of course, in complementary distribution, and was written h. It is notable that the material on which the analysis was based included an Eastern dialect in which /н/-diphthongs are common and the contrasts more conspicuous than in the Chicago dialect. The discovery of the diphthongal nature of Bloomfield's a and ɔ eliminated the need of two of his symbols. The addition of ə eliminated a very unsatisfactory feature of the earlier analysis. Since /o/ was still not clearly recognized, o was used for Bloomfield's ɑ (/a/), thus freeing a to replace Bloomfield's ɛ (/æ/). Note that several of these changes are only matters of symbols, but the addition of h and ə were significant advances, while o continued its peregrinations. The following nuclei are listed:

i	*pit*	ij	*beat*			ih	*beer*
e	*pet*	ej	*bait*			eh	*bear yeah*
a	*pat* /æ/	aj	*bite*	aw	*bout*	ah	*bar calm*
o	*pot* /a/	oj	*boil*	ow	*boat*	oh	*bore law*
ə	*cut*					əh	*burr*
u	*put*			uw	*boot*	uh	*boor*

19.14   Trager and Bloch,[3] in a fuller treatment the preceding year, had pointed out that all of the combinations which were omitted from their table (əj, uj, iw, etc.) occur in other American dialects. This paper included a footnote as follows:

> We do not claim that the compartments of this table will accommodate all the syllabic phonemes of all dialects of English, though we believe that the exceptions will be very few and in each dialect statistically unimportant. Thus, BB [Bloch] pronounces *gonna* (*I'm not gonna do it*) with a short vowel in the first syllable which is phonetically very close to the vowel of German *Sonne*. Though it occurs nowhere else in his pronunciation of English, it must perhaps be reckoned as independent phoneme parallel to the six short vowels. . . .

Through the next decade, two hints in this statement were followed up in a series of advances which were finally summarized in the important publication of Trager and Smith (1951). The system proposed by these authors needs no detailed discussion because it is the basis of that presented in Chapter 3, except that they continued the use of h for what we have chosen to symbolize ʜ.

19.15   The first of these trends was to follow up leads such as Bloch's /o/ in *gonna*. The result was the disentangling of /o/, /a/, and /æ/, which were somewhat confused in Bloch and Trager; the addition of /ə/; and most importantly the addition of /ɨ/, thus producing a system of nine vowels.

The addition of /ɨ/ calls for further comment. This phoneme is notably absent from all systems described here except that of Trager and Smith. Yet it is exceedingly common. It runs as high as 17 percent of all nuclei in my speech, provided the sample has a moderately high average word length. (/ɨ/ is commonest in unstressed syllables.) It is probably reasonably common in every

---

[3] Trager, George L., and Bernard Bloch, "The Syllabic Phonemes of English," *Language* 17 : 223–246, 1941. (The footnote quoted is on page 243.)

dialect. Yet it has not been recognized until recently. Two groups of facts, one about the language and one about linguists, explain this remarkable occurrence.

Though /ɨ/ is exceedingly common, the distinctions /ɨ : ə/ and /ɨ : i/ carry a very low **functional load.** This means that minimal pairs are relatively infrequent, or more precisely that the contrast is seldom called upon to signal differences between utterances. A functional load of zero would imply that the distinction was non-phonemic. The functional load of these two contrasts, while certainly not zero, is one of the lowest in the English phonologic system. Moreover, such minimal pairs as do occur mostly involve syllables that are commonly pronounced differently when re-stressed forms are given in isolation. Thus, most Americans will say /jɨst/ in *He just came.*, but when asked *How do you pronounce "just"?* will answer /jə́st/. I find that something like ten percent will pronounce *children* /čɨ́ldrɨn/ in isolation, but about half will use the /ɨ/ in a context. The result has been a general confusion of /ɨ/ with /i/, /ə/, and even /e/.

Phoneticians have made much of the tendency, which is real enough, for unstressed vowels to lose the quality which they might be expected to have under stress and become more mid and more central. This tendency led to the quite unwarranted theory that all unstressed vowels become ə — a theory that is sometimes modified to permit a limited number of other vowel qualities under weak stress. This theory is patently untrue. Any English nucleus whatever may occur unstressed, though admittedly some are quite rare (many are rare enough stressed!). The theory was salvaged by the complementary theory that ə (generally distinguished from ʌ) is exceedingly variable. This became more or less a fixed idea with many, and contributed to deafening them to the occurrence of /ɨ/. Such a theory is possible because of the low functional load of all vowels in unstressed syllables. It is not, however, low enough to justify any such sweeping generalizations. The discovery of the phonemic contrast between /ɨ/ and /ə/ has been associated with a complete rethinking of the nature of unstressed vowels.

19.16 The second trend in development of phonemic analysis of English syllable nuclei has been a broadening of the base. Bloomfield's transcription was based on his interpretation of his own dialect alone. Bloch and Trager worked, jointly, in developing a transcription to cover the speech of both, though they represented different dialect areas. Other workers brought into the stream additional data from various areas. Trager and Smith were able to base their treatment on an exceedingly wide range of experience with American dialects. The result has been a gradual shift in the nature and objective of the statements. The 36 nuclei currently recognized do not represent the phonemic structure of any one existing form of English. What Trager and Smith have produced is an overall analysis of English dialects, collectively. This is a very different thing from a phonemic analysis of a single dialect.

In a phonemic analysis we expect each element to contrast with each other element. In an overall pattern analysis, this happens in a special way: each pair can be found to contrast in some dialect, but may not contrast at all in some other dialect. For example, some dialects use /aw/ but not /æw/; others /æw/ but not /aw/; still others use both /aw/ and /æw/, but in complementary distribution. In each of these cases no contrast can be established between /aw/ and /æw/. But there are dialects in which these two do contrast; in one dialect, for example, *lost* is /láwst/ and *loused* is /lǽwst/. If the overall analysis is to cover this dialect, as it must to describe American English as a whole, it must provide separate representation for /aw/ and /æw/, even if most dialects do not show a contrast. /ow/ and /əw/ are commonly without contrast. In some dialects the word *road* is pronounced /rówd/, in others /rə́wd/. Most Americans have learned to overlook the difference to the extent of recognizing another's /rə́wd/ as equivalent to their own /rówd/ or vice versa. In my own speech I use both, more or less in free variation. However, in some dialects there is a contrast, so that the two must be distinguished in any discussion of the overall pattern. Moreover, if my own speech is to be seen in its proper place among American dialects, it is important that this variability between /rówd/ and /rə́wd/ (a matter in which many others are quite consistent) needs to be noted. An overall pattern type of analysis will be much more useful in comparing dialects than will be an analysis based only on the contrasts actually used in any one dialect.

19.17   For certain practical purposes, a transcription of the Trager and Smith type can conveniently be modified, as was done for the textbooks prepared for the English-for-Foreigners Program of the American Council of Learned Societies. This method promises to be of sufficient importance to warrant a brief description.

Some phonemes cause no trouble, even when the printed materials are used by teachers from a wide variety of dialectal backgrounds. For example, /i/ is pronounced in very nearly the same list of words in all dialects. A writing such as pít will therefore serve equally well for any of them. *Dowɳ* is transcribed dáwn. Many teachers will pronounce it /dáwn/, but many others will say /dǽwn/. But since the teacher who says /dǽwn/ is likely also to say /æw/ in every word which is transcribed aw, this will not mislead the student. He can learn to associate his teacher's /æw/ pronunciation with the aw transcriptions in his textbook. If he learns to speak /æw/, he will speak an acceptable form of English, even if slightly different from that other students will learn from other teachers. Some Americans distinguish *have* from *halve* by using a diphthong in the second. These are written hǽv and hǽhv. This transcription will serve the needs of the teacher who makes a distinction, no matter what may be the exact nature of the distinction he makes. Others can merely overlook the graphic difference between æ and æh. Again, the student will learn an acceptable form of English in either case, provided he follows the usage of his teacher.

The most complex situation is with a group of words, *log, watch,* etc. whose pronunciation is quite variable from dialect to dialect. In some dialects these words are pronounced with the same vowel as *cot*, which is written a. In others the vowel in these words is the same as that in *caught* etc., which in these textbooks is transcribed ɔh. To write *log, watch,* etc., with either a or ɔh would cause trouble to a large number of possible teachers; they are therefore written by a special symbol ɔ. The students of one teacher must learn that a and ɔ are pronounced alike; those of another that ɔh and ɔ are pronounced alike. Again, either type of pronunciation will yield an acceptable variety of American English.

19.18   The transcription used in the textbooks of the English-for-Foreigners Program is therefore basically a compromise. Compromise is necessary, only because the transcription is required to do something which a phonemic transcription cannot do — that is, give a usable indication (an approximation) of the pronunciation of any dialect which a teacher is likely to speak. The teachers in the program will be drawn from a variety of American dialect areas. That this can be done without serious violence to the facts arises from two factors. One is the low functional load of many of the contrasts. Indeed, any foreigner who hopes to understand spoken American English must learn to equate /aw/ and /æw/ and other similar pairs. Without this ability, he will be able to understand only the dialect which he has learned from his teacher. The second factor is a careful selection of pronunciations which are current over the widest areas in America. If certain local peculiarities had not been avoided, the result would have been much less useful.

19.19   There is another type of modification in the transcription used in some books in the series. For example, in the edition for use by Turks, /č ǰ š ž/ are written ç c ş j. The latter are the symbols in the regular Turkish orthography for phonemes rather similar to the English /č ǰ š ž/. This change makes the transcription much easier for the Turkish student to use. In textbooks of this kind transcription is a device to facilitate teaching. As such there is no need for indicating all the niceties of every detail of the phonemic system, and even less for subservience to irrelevant habits of writing. Nevertheless, behind all the modifications, the transcriptions are ultimately based on a detailed and thorough analysis of English structure. This is quite different from any haphazard rule-of-thumb "phonetic respelling."

19.20   One more transcription system needs to be noted. This is the one used by Nida (1949). It is in the diphthong tradition. Since it was used merely to transcribe his own pronunciation of a limited corpus, there was no need for representing a large number of nuclei. Since he has only one /н/-diphthong, /ɔн/ in *bought*, and does not list the corresponding simple vowel, it is more convenient to write this as a unit, o, than to introduce an otherwise unneeded symbol for the glide. The major inadequacy is the use of the symbol ə to represent both /ə/ and /ɨ/. The transcription can be conceived as that of Trager and Smith (which, however, it antedates), modified to the needs of a single dialect. As such it would seem to be reasonably satisfactory, and may be taken as an example of a type of transcription which can be expected to become fairly common. The list of nuclei given is as follows:

i	*fill*	iy	*feel*		
e	*pen*	ey	*pain*		
æ	*pan*				
a	*pot*	ay	*bite*	aw	*about*
o	*bought*	oy	*coy*	ow	*boat*
u	*put*			uw	*boot*
ə	*but*				

19.21   Space allows only passing mention of transcriptions of stress and pitch. The IPA tradition generally indicates primary stress /´/ by ´ and "secondary" (here called tertiary) /`/ by ˌ placed before the initial consonant of the syllable. Thus in Kenyon's transcription, ˈʃuˌmekɚ appears for /šúwmèykər/.

The failure to recognize secondary stress, in the sense discussed in Chapter 4, arises from considering the word as the largest unit to be examined. Words in isolation rather seldom have /^/, and clear contrasts with /`/ are even rarer. This limitation on the data is another peculiarity of the British school of phoneticians headed by Daniel Jones, and is incorporated in his definition of the phoneme.

19.22   Most systems of transcription give no indication of pitch. This is in large part a historical matter, since the phonemic analysis of English intonation is a comparatively recent achievement. Fries and Pike describe four phonemic levels of pitch (which they number downward; see 4.14). Their system does not indicate the clause terminals; the analysis and classification of these terminals is still more recent, and appears in Trager and Smith only. Earlier. attempts to record intonation were necessarily impressionistic. Some authors, notably Jones, used a series of dots and lines written above the transcription of consonants and vowels in a manner reminiscent of musical notation.

The failure of early attempts to analyze intonation led to a conviction that its structure was somehow basically different from that of the consonants and vowels. This is reflected in the refusal of some linguists to use "phoneme" in this connection, even now that contrastive units can be isolated. In turn this had the effect of stultifying research. Intonation was cast out as a portion of language structure not susceptible to exact analysis. As so often happens in science, progress was made only when the dogmas were questioned and methods elaborated in one connection (consonants and vowels) were applied in a very different connection (intonation). That these developments should take time is hardly surprising. Descriptive linguistics is still a young science, and we do not yet know fully the limits of applicability of its methods.

The phonemic analysis of English intonation may well be one of the major turning points in linguistics. The phonemic analysis of a system of consonants was first accomplished several millennia ago by the unknown inventors of the Semitic alphabet. The extension of the achievement to a vowel system is nearly as old. The analysis of the intonation system is the most original extension of this age-old method accomplished by modern linguistic science. The phonemic analysis of English pitches has already proved fruitful in stimulating important advances in our knowledge of other languages, and so has an importance far beyond its direct contribution to our understanding of our own language.

chapter

20

Phonemic Systems

20.1 English was described in Chapters 2, 3 and 4 as having a total of 46 phonemes. It is quite natural to ask whether this is more or less than the average number. A search through the literature will reveal that languages have been reported with totals varying from only a bit above a dozen (for certain Polynesian dialects) to nearly a hundred (for certain languages of the Caucasus). Some reflection will, however, raise considerable doubt as to the validity of any such comparisons; indeed, in many languages only the consonants and vowels have been adequately described, and there is reason to believe that every language has significant contrasts in stress, pitch, transitions, or terminals, and usually in several of these categories. Many language descriptions overlook these completely, even in what purports to be exhaustive listing of the phonemes, often as the result of earlier and inadequate understanding of phonologic principles and methods. The reported minimums are therefore certainly too low.

Moreover, the number of phonemes found depends in part on the methods pursued in the analysis. Not infrequently there are situations in which two or more interpretations are possible. These usually involve problems of segmentation where there is as yet no universally agreed-upon rigorous method. As a result, linguists may disagree as to the number of phonemes in a given language — in some cases with about equally good justification for either conclusion. In the languages which have been reported to have very high numbers of phonemes, there are always some phonemes which might alternatively be interpreted as sequences of phonemes, thus reducing the total appreciably. Unless identical procedures have been used in the analysis, there is little validity in comparing counts of phonemes.

20.2 If comparisons of total numbers cannot be made, there may still be the possibility of comparing languages on the basis of the presence or absence of certain phonemes or types of phonemes. This has commonly been done. It has long been customary to distinguish "tone languages," meaning those in which pitch is significant, in contrast with those languages, like English, in which pitch was assumed to be insignificant. Closer investigation of English has completely demolished the usefulness of this distinction. Indeed, at the present time there is no natural language in which phonemic distinctions of pitch have been proved to be absent. It would be extremely rash to say that pitch is significant in all languages, because careful examination of this facet of phonology has been made for only a few languages. As we shall see below, the real basis for the distinction of "tone languages" from others is a structurally significant pattern in the use of pitch distinctions.

20.3 There is another objection to comparing languages on the basis of the presence or absence of certain phonemes. What precisely is meant if one says that English, Loma, Luganda, and Kiowa are alike in having a /b/ phoneme? Very little, unless one can maintain that the /b/ of the four languages is in some respects the same thing. But, as we have seen, phonemes can be defined only in reference to a given speech form. Each of these languages has its own set of phonemes and of contrasts between phonemes. It happens that, for certain reasons, partly non-linguistic, the symbol /b/ has been selected to represent one member in each system. This fortuitous circumstance is, in the case of these four languages, the only link, and the comparison just quoted is linguistically meaningless. The English /b/ is a voiced labial stop, the only such phoneme in the language. The Loma /b/ is one of four voiced labial stops in its system, each contrasting with the others in some additional feature. The Luganda /b/ contains a voiced labial stop allophone, but also a voiced fricative allophone, and the latter is approximately as common as the former. The Kiowa /b/ is used to represent a voiced labial fricative, there being no voiced stop to require the use of this symbol. Our statement is comparable to saying, "This hat, this dress, and this pair of shoes are all the same size, since they are all sevens."

20.4 What we have just said is another expression of the non-congruence of phonemic systems which inevitably plagues us in any work involving two languages. It is necessarily involved in any possible kind of comparison. Nevertheless, there is still some value in comparing phonologic systems, provided care is taken to minimize the tendency to superficiality which common symbols and common terminology produce. The results of comparison may have little or no scientific validity but great practical value in giving a background which will contribute to an understanding of language. One great advantage the experienced linguist has is that he has some feeling for the range of possibilities in languages. Though even he may occasionally meet with a system far different from anything he might have expected, his feeling for the possibilities is helpful in guiding his investigations and suggesting interpretations. Statements of comparisons are, in some measure, a short cut to this background.

20.5 Our criticism of a type of crude comparison in 20.3 suggests a somewhat more fruitful approach: the examination of the types of contrasts which exist within a language and which set its phonemes apart. For simplicity, let us restrict our attention for the present to phonemes which are either stops or include stops as important allophones, or pattern in some way as stops.

English has two series of stops, traditionally labeled "voiced" and "voiceless." These labels are largely conventional, as the actual contrasts are much more complex. The two series differ in one or more of three contrasts. The first series is typically voiced, unaspirated, and lenis; the second voiceless, aspirated, and fortis. However, the voice is often quite weak in /b d g/, and there are more or less voiced allophones of /p t k/. Unaspirated allophones of the voiceless series occur, and in many positions the degree of aspiration is quite variable. The fortis : lenis distinction may be very tenuous. Though the contrast is quite complex, it is well maintained in most (not all!) of the positions in which stops can occur.

Phonemic systems with two series of stops are quite common.

The contrast between the two may, however, be quite different. For example, in French the contrast is very largely one of voice. Both series are unaspirate. Both are, by English standards at least, quite fortis. The French voiced stops are generally more strongly voiced than are the English, and typically voiced throughout, in marked contrast to the gradual onset of voicing in English initial stops and the gradual decrease in voicing in English final stops. The use of the same symbols /p t k b d g/ and the labels "voiced" and "voiceless" tends to obscure the basic differences between the two systems.

Another possibility is that the contrast may rest entirely or largely in a difference of aspiration. This seems to be the case in many Chinese dialects. Such systems show some resemblances to English, where aspiration is one of several distinguishing features of stops, but none at all to French, in which aspiration is not significant.

20.6   There is, of course, no necessity that there be two series of stops. In Kutenai (Idaho and British Columbia) there is only one series /p t k q/. These are normally voiceless, but may rarely be slightly voiced. Ojibwa (Great Lakes Region) has only one series of stops. These have both voiced and voiceless allophones. They are usually transcribed /p t c k/, using the traditionally voiceless symbols, but this selection is arbitrary. As the usual English spelling of the name indicates, the stops may be heard as more nearly comparable to English /b d ǰ g/.

20.7   Three series of stops are not uncommon. One common type, represented for example by Sotho (South Africa) has a voiced series, a voiceless aspirate series, and a voiceless unaspirate series. In Kiowa (North America) the three series are all voiceless, and distinguished as simple, aspirate, and glottalized. Korean has been analyzed as having three series. One is simple, with both voiced and voiceless allophones. One is aspirate and voiceless. Linguists have not been able to reach any agreement on the description of the third. It has been described as very fortis, as glottalized, or as merely doubled. If merely doubled, it can conveniently be represented by a cluster of identical stops, e.g., /pp/, in which case there are only two series. Or the third series can be interpreted as clusters of a phoneme arbitrarily symbolized by /q/ and a stop, e.g., /pq/.

Hindi and many other languages of India are generally said to have four series of stops: voiceless unaspirate, voiceless aspirate, voiced unaspirate, and voiced aspirate. Of course, it is obviously possible to reduce these to two series, each of which can occur in clusters with a following /h/. Linguists have disagreed as to which analysis is preferable. Apparently, the situation is not the same in all Indian languages.

Of course, if the number of phonemes is reduced by treating some as clusters, the differences which exist between languages are not removed. They are merely transformed from differences in the inventory of phonemes into differences in the inventory of clusters. There is little practical difference between saying that Hindi contrasts with English in having four rather than two series of stops and saying that Hindi differs from English in having clusters of stops plus /h/. Different phonemic analyses are merely different ways of describing the structure which actually exists in the language.

Finally, Sindhi (Pakistan) has been reported as having five series. Four are comparable to those just listed for Hindi. In addition there is a series of voiced glottalized or voiced implosive stops. These may be represented as /p pʰ b bʰ ɓ/, etc.

20.8   We may find similar divergencies if we examine the contrastive points of articulation which occur in various languages. We shall continue to restrict our attention to those in which stops occur. Probably the most frequent situation is one rather like English, in which there are three groups of stops, one labial, one apical, and one dorsal /p b   t d   k g/. French has a system which is the same in broad outline, and for which the identical symbols are traditionally used. There are, however, very significant differences in detail. In articulation, the French apicals are typically dental; in English they are typically alveolar, with rare dental allophones. Superficial similarities must not be allowed to mislead and obscure differences of detail.

Two contrastive apical articulations are not infrequent. In most of the languages of India, for example, there are phonemic contrasts between dental and alveolar, or dental and retroflex, at least in the stops. The extreme is reached in Malayalam in the south where there are three apical articulations, dental, alveolar, and retroflex, all contrasting in voiceless stops.

Two contrastive dorsal articulations occur in many languages.

The Kutenai example mentioned above includes such a contrast. Mam (Guatemala) also uses such a contrast, which, together with a contrast between a glottalized and non-glottalized series of stops, produces a system quite different from English.

Rather more rarely are there additional contrasts in the labial region. The commonest of these is a contrast between bilabials and labiovelars. The latter have double articulation, simultaneous in both labial and dorsal regions. This contrast is found in many languages of Africa, and is often reinforced by some other difference, commonly more fortis articulation in the labiovelars. An extreme case is found in Loma (Liberia) where there is a contrast between three labial articulations, bilabial with /p b ɓ/, labiovelar with /kp gb/, and labiodental with /v/ (the latter is a stop, and contrasts with a voiced labiodental fricative).

Conversely, one or the other of the more common articulations may be lacking. This is the case in Tlingit (Alaska), which has no labials except /w/, and this in spite of a rather large number of consonant phonemes. Some languages have limitations of a different sort. Yoruba (Nigeria) has four groups of stops in two series /b kp gb t d k g/. The pattern is unsymmetrical in lacking a labial in the voiceless series. Many African languages have a partial series of implosive stops. In Zulu, for example, the following stops are found /p' pʰ b ɓ t' tʰ d k' kʰ g/. The labial implosive occupies a non-symmetrical position in the system in contrast with the glottalized, aspirated, and voiced series which extend through each of the three articulations.

20.9 Similar observations can be carried through other portions of phonemic systems, and the greatest possible divergencies can be found between languages. There is no need to detail them. It will suffice to remark that every possible phonetic contrast must be considered as at least potentially the base for a phonemic contrast in some language. In some instances, the distinctions seem to an American to be most minute and impossible of accurate discrimination; but in making such a judgment we merely reveal our own bias, arising out of our English background. We should remember that some English contrasts seem hopelessly difficult to foreigners, notably that between /t/ and /d/ in common pronunciations of *latter* and *ladder*, or that between /n/ and /nt/ in a common pronunciation of *can* and *can't*.

20.10 The discussion of systems of stops in the last several paragraphs was couched in terms of articulatory phonetics. Our interest at the moment is, however, rather in phonemics than phonetics. Our chief excuse for using phonetic terminology is that it is the convenient and traditional apparatus for labeling sounds and classes of sounds. Still, there is a deeper justification in that frequently the phonemic interrelationships parallel the phonetic, as may be seen in English. There is no need of resorting to articulations to identify or define the various categories of English phonemes. For example, /p t k f θ s š č/ can be set off from all the other phonemes of English by the fact that they condition the allomorph /–s/ of {–Z₁}, or the allomorph /–t/ of {–D₁}, or both. Having been so defined, they may conveniently be labeled as "voiceless" consonants. Similarly, /s z š ž č ǰ/ can be identified as those sounds which condition the allomorph /–iz/ of {–Z₁}. The group defined by this structural pattern is identical with the phonetic group of groove fricatives plus affricates. Numerous other pecularities of distribution or morphophonemic alternations can be found to define each class of English phonemes. The terminology of articulatory phonetics serves as a convenient source of labels for many of the classes so found.

20.11 Similar types of relationships will be found to operate in other languages. The phonemic structures which they reveal seldom flatly contradict phonetic facts, but frequently do impose definite interpretations on the phonetic facts. In English, there are numerous differences in distribution between stops and affricates. This is not true for Hindi. The two phonetic sound types pattern alike in many respects. It is, therefore, useful to consider affricates not as a class apart, but only as a phonetically different type of stop. This is phonetically justifiable. The result is a symmetrical pattern of twenty stop phonemes:

/p	t	ṭ	č	k
ph	th	ṭh	čh	kh
b	d	ḍ	ǰ	g
bh	dh	ḍh	ǰh	gh/

20.12 A very clear instance of distribution paralleling phonetic classification may be seen in Kutenai. The phonemes /p t k q s ł x ¢/ can occur as first members of initial clusters;

/ˀ h l m n w y/ can occur as the second member of a CC– cluster, as the second or third member of CCC– clusters, or as the third or third and fourth members of CCCC– clusters. There are other comparable restrictions in clusters occurring elsewhere. /p t k q s ł x ¢/ are all voiceless; /ˀ h m n w y/ all either are voiced or involve some other activity of the vocal cords. The distribution in clusters, therefore, parallels a fundamental phonetic distinction.

20.13   As the last example suggests, one interesting facet of the phonologic structure of a language is the patterns of sequences of phonemes. The consonant clusters of English constitute an excellent example. It is relatively simple to make a complete list of those found at the beginning of utterances in a formal pronunciation, but in very informal pronunciations the problem becomes very much more complex. Excluding those found only in proper names, I have a total of 34 of the form CC– and 8 of the form CCC–. Other Americans (for example, those who say /tyúwn/ *tune*) have a slightly different list. A bare enumeration does not reveal much, however. More significant is an analysis of the formation of these clusters. One possible way to make such an analysis is to classify the consonant phonemes of English on the basis of their occurrence in utterance initial:

Never in word initial	/ŋ ž/
Only alone in word initial	/v ð z č ǰ/
Either alone or in clusters in word initial	
Only as first member of the cluster	/b d g s š h θ/
Only as the last member of the cluster	/y w r l m n/
As first, middle, or last member	/p t k f/

Such a classification might be carried much further, and will reveal that there is hardly a pair of English phonemes which can be used in identical lists of contexts. For example, /pr– tr– kr– pl– kl–/ occur, but not /*tl–/. This peculiarity is shared by /t/ and /d/ : /br– dr– kr– bl–   gl–/ occur but not /*dl–/. Phonetic similarities between /t/ and /d/ are paralleled by phonologic characteristics. It is notable how often, even in the brief tabulation above, similar parallels can be found.

20.14   The clustering patterns of other languages may be quite different from that of English. At one extreme is a number of languages, including most of the Polynesian group, in which no consonant clusters occur. At the other extreme are some languages which use sequences of consonants which seem utterly impossible to speakers of English. In Cœur d'Alene (Idaho) 81 CC– initial clusters were reported, 41 CCC–, and 2 CCCC–. Final clusters are even more numerous: 192 –CC, 74 –CCC, 13 –CCCC, and /–¢'x̣stxʷ/ were found. In Bella Coola (British Columbia) numerous whole words without vowels are reported: /tmk'mɫp/ 'jack pine tree,' /sk'lxlxc/ 'I'm getting cold,' /ɫkʷ'tx̣ʷ/ 'make it big!' These indicate a fundamentally different phonologic structure from the one familiar to English speakers.

20.15 Not only do languages differ in the number and size of clusters, but they also differ in the details. For example, the phonemic system of English and that of Serbo-Croatian have some sounds which can be very broadly interpreted as the same. Each also has certain sounds which cannot be identified at all with phonemes in the other. In comparing the two it seems desirable to give the English /y/ and the Serbian /y/ special treatment, as there are some complications in each instance. The results of a comparison of initial clusters is as follows:

	English clusters	Serbo-Croatian clusters
Common to both: pr– pl– sp– br– bl– tr– st– dr– kr– kl– sk– gr– gl– fr– sf– sl– sm– šm– sn– spr– spl– str– skr– skl–	24	24
English only: fl– šr–	2	
Serbo-Croatian only: pt– tk– bd– gd– šp– št– šk– žb– žd– žg– zb– zd– zg– tm– km– pn– kn– dm– gm– dn– gn– mr– ml– mn– ps– pš– pč– tv– kv– gv– čv– čl– čm– jb– sv– sh– sr– šč– šv– šl– tl– dl– zv– zr– hm– zl– žv– žl– žm– žn– vr– vl– zm– zn– ht– hv– hr– hl– svr– smr– štr– škr– zdr– zgr– ždr– stv– skv– zdv– svl– žgl–		70
/y/ clusters excluded	8	14
Serbo-Croatian clusters containing phonemes without English counterparts		30
English clusters containing phonemes without Serbo-Croatian counterparts	8	
	42	138

There is, of course, no reason why English should have /fl–/ but not /vl–/, any more than that Serbo-Croatian should have /vl–/ and not /fl–/. These matters are just features of the structure of the two languages.

If a similar examination of the final clusters is made, the results are very different. Only /–st –št –zd –žd/ are common in Serbo-Croatian. In addition /–nt –nd –rȼ –ys –ps –lm/ occur in some partially assimilated loan words. This is in very sharp contrast to English, where final clusters are both numerous and various.

20.16   So far we have been discussing the structural relationships within consonantal systems. The same thing can be done for vowels, in English and in most of the other languages of the world. Some hints of the possibilities were given in 16.14. The interrelationship of the consonants and vowels, however, presents a different set of problems. The presentations in Chapters 2 and 3 of these two portions of the English phonemic system were almost completely independent of each other. No attempt was made there, nor since, to prove that there is a phonemic contrast between any individual consonant and any individual vowel. It is very doubtful that this can be done in English, and certainly it cannot be done by any method such as that used in Chapters 2 and 3. The nearest we can come to minimal pairs is contrasting words such as *stone* /stówn/ : *atone* /ətówn/. These are, however, not strictly minimal pairs, because the /ə/ is associated here and in every similar word with /ˇ/ or some other stress, whereas /s/ never is. This means that /s/ and /ə/ are in complementary distribution. There are two reasons for not classing them as allophones of a single phoneme: first, there is no phonetic similarity; second, almost any consonant can be shown to be in complementary distribution with any vowel.

Consonants and vowels do not contrast individually because they occupy fundamentally different places in the total structure of English utterances. This basic difference of function is enough to justify treating each consonant as phonemically distinct from each vowel, and also for treating vowels and consonants as two different divisions of the phonemic system. Any other course, while it might reduce the inventory of phonemes, would greatly complicate our statements concerning the composition of utterances. Perhaps the most obvious of these structural differences between vowels and consonants is that every vowel is accompanied by a stress, and conversely, every stress is accompanied by a vowel. Another is that English vowels rarely occur in clusters, and with the exception of /ə/ rarely or never at the ends of utterances.

20.17　The problem of the complementary distribution of /s/ and /ə/ seems trivial. There is no phonetic similarity, and every speaker of the language feels strongly that there is no close relationship, a feeling which represents the speaker's recognition of the structural cleavage between vowels and consonants just mentioned. But there are other pairs where the problem is quite different. /y/ shows a real phonetic similarity to /i/. Here, then, is a pair of sounds which are both phonetically similar and in complementary distribution, yet they are listed as two phonemes. This is necessary because of phonemic patterning within the language. There is a group of [ᵻ]- or [y]-like sounds which contrasts with consonants: *yell* [yél] : *tell* [tél], or *lay* [léy] : *let* [lét]. Because of this they must constitute a member of the consonantal system of English. There is another group of [i]- or [y]-like sounds which contrast with vowels: *bit* [bít] : *bet* [bét]. Because of this they must constitute a member of the vocalic system of English. We have two alternatives. The English phonemic system may be set up:

Consonants /t y . . ./　OR　Consonants /t . . ./
Vowels　　　/e i . . ./　　　　Vowels　　　/e . . ./
　　　　　　　　　　　　　　　Ambivalent /i . . ./

The second alternative does reduce the inventory (/i/ stands in place of both /i/ and /y/), but at the expense of additional complexity of statement, both in the phonology and the morphophonemics. Moreover, though not a conclusive test by any means, the fact that the "average American" is not easily convinced of any identity of /y/ and /i/, even in spite of the common confusion of the two in traditional spelling, suggests that the first alternative is more nearly in accord with the structure of the language. The same problem arises with /w/ and /u/ and with /н/ and /ə/.

20.18　The problems of the last paragraph may give the impression of being trivial, but this is far from the case. In many languages there is no contrast between consonantal [y] and a vocalic [i] or the like. The overall phonologic structure of other languages may not require such clear distinction between consonantal and vocalic systems as does English. The American working with such a language is easily led into wrong conclusions, as is the speaker of such a language who is working with English. The status of [i]- or [y]-like sounds — that is, the classification as consonant or vowel, or ambiguously as either, or perhaps as belonging to a third category in the language — is one of the questions which must be faced in making a thorough phonemic analysis of a language. Procedural techniques for making such a judgment cannot be presented here, but must obviously be based on attempting to discover whether there is any such cleavage as that existing in English between consonants and vowels, what is the nature of that cleavage, and how each phoneme fits into the system. There seem to be languages in which the vowel-consonant dichotomy is much less significant than in English, perhaps even lacking.

20.19   This suggests that the distinction between vowel and consonant is not phonetic, but phonemic. This is indeed true. The /r/ of many American dialects is phonetically more similar to the vowels than to the other consonants. However, /r/ patterns as a consonant. To avoid difficulty at this point, the terms **vowel** and **consonant** should properly be reserved for use in phonemics, and the terms **vocoid** ("vowel-like") and **non-vocoid** should be used in phonetics. That serious damage is not done by the indiscriminate use of "vowel" and "consonant" is merely another instance of how closely phonetic and phonemic structural categories often parallel each other. Nevertheless, it is not essential that they do so, and not infrequently there is a lack of conformity in detail between the two. In these instances it is important to use care in the application of terms.

20.20   The dichotomy between consonants and vowels is a basic one in English, but there is a still more fundamental division — that between vowels and consonants as a group, the four stresses and /+/ as a second, and the four pitches and three terminals as a third. Between these three sub-systems there is the same lack, or rather impossibility, of direct contrast as between consonants and vowels. Each of the three groups has such peculiarities of distribution —.within the phonologic structure of English utterances — as to clearly set it off from each of the others. In addition, this division within the phonemic system is paralleled by a division within the morphemic system which cuts the morpheme inventory into three groups. That is, some morphemes consist of (or are statable in terms of) consonants and vowels. These morphemes never contain phonemes of any other sub-system. Another set of morphemes is composed of stresses and /+/, and only of these elements. A third set consists of pitches and terminals, and only these. The three groups occupy quite different places in the grammatical structure of English. Of course, there is no complete independence between the three sets of phonemes, nor between the three sets of morphemes, but the division is deep and basic.

20.21   This division is, of course, a characteristic feature of English structure, as are all the lesser subdivisions. It is shared in all its essential outlines by some related languages, and by chance some others more remote may have something quite similar. But it is by no means a universal pattern. There is a very large number of languages in which the structure is quite different. Unfortunately, we as yet understand the full phonemic structure of so few languages that it is not possible to exhibit complete systems in contrast with the English system. However, some parts of the pattern are well established for many languages. In many, root morphemes consist of combinations of consonants, vowels, and pitches, and these parts of the phonemic system presumably are more closely related than comparable phonemes in English. We have reason to believe that in many such languages ("tone languages") there is another sub-system including phonemes comparable to English terminals and associated with a grammatic sub-system comparable to English intonation. There are hints of other types of phonemic organization equally different from that of English in other ways.

Whether a combination of three major phonemic sub-systems (as in English) occurs frequently in other languages or not, we do not yet know. I suspect that all languages will prove to have at least two, but I am very certain that the place of phonetically comparable elements in these sub-systems will vary widely from language to language. Forms of speech differ not merely in the inventory of the phonemes they contain, but even more fundamentally in the ways in which they organize them into systems.

Phonemic Problems
in Language Learning

21.1 No one ever has a command of more than a fraction —
usually a very small fraction — of the vocabulary of a language.
A normal individual learns new words daily, and at certain periods
of his life makes vocabulary additions in great numbers. For an
American student these include the latest slang, new words occasioned by technological advances, special terminology of the
subjects he is studying, and miscellaneous words of all kinds
learned as his contacts broaden. At the same time, words continually pass out of his active vocabulary. Few people can recall
the slang of a decade ago; and the forgetting of technical terms is
the lament of students and professors alike. Vocabulary is a
transient feature of any person's command of a language, coming
and going with comparative ease and rapidity.

Any speaker of a language necessarily has a much more complete control of the grammar than of the vocabulary. To be sure,
there may be syntactic constructions which he never uses, and
some of these may not be completely clear when he hears or reads
them. Many derivational patterns he may not recognize as such,
even though he is quite familiar with words containing them. Some
few features of the inflectional system may be relatively unfamiliar

or completely strange to him. In short, few approach very closely to an absolute command of the morphology, but morphology is never as partially known or as transient as vocabulary.

With the phonology, the demands are higher. A person who lisps — that is, who uses an incorrect allophone of a single phoneme, /s/ — is immediately spotted by a native speaker of English as deviant. Incorrect pronunciation of even a very rare phoneme or cluster can render speech conspicuously strange or even objectionable. It can interpose a serious social barrier between the speaker and the members of the speech community. Of course, some deviations from the general usage are tolerated much more readily than others. While it is often possible to avoid the use of troublesome words or constructions, there is seldom any possibility of manipulating the conversation so as to avoid certain phonemes or phonemic combinations.

A speaking knowledge of a language, therefore, requires very close to a one hundred percent control of the phonology and control of from fifty to ninety percent of the grammar, while one can frequently do a great deal with one percent or even less of the vocabulary.

21.2 Command of the phonology is evidently a central problem in learning to speak a language. It is, moreover, the point at which adult language learning is likely to be most unsatisfactory. Occasional persons do learn to speak a second language fluently and well without special procedures, but they are exceptional. Many immigrants living in America for decades still are unmistakably foreign in their speech. Command of phonology shows little correlation with education; college professors and unskilled laborers have the same difficulties. Some even lose command of the mother tongue through long disuse without mastering their new language. If many years of hearing and speaking do not lead to an adequate command, it is evident that an adult must give some special attention to the phonology in his study of a second language.

Children seem to learn new languages comparatively rapidly and satisfactorily. One incidental reason is that they are less obsessed than adults with piling up a large vocabulary. Thus they tend to concentrate more on the patterns of phonology and morphology. The most important factor is that they approach the new language with less deeply fixed habits of speech. At some time early in adolescence a point is reached where phonologic patterns become set; thereafter a new set of habits cannot easily be acquired without a sort of forced conformity to the old. No such point seems to be reached with regard to vocabulary, nor is there as great a degree of rigidity attained in morphology. The special problems of the adult in language learning are primarily phonologic.

21.3 This chapter is entitled "Phonemic Problems in Language Learning," and it is perhaps necessary to justify this title. We are assuming that the objective is to learn to speak the language, not primarily to draw up a phonemic description. The two tasks are quite different. Of the billions of people who speak some language fluently and acceptably, only a few thousand have ever given any thought to the phonology of their language. Of those who have, many have entirely erroneous ideas on the subject. An understanding of the phonemic system is certainly no prerequisite to a speaking command of any language.

What is needed is the ability to operate the vocal apparatus without conscious effort so as to produce sound patterns characteristic of the language being learned. This is a matter of muscular habits, of recurring patterns of movement. The phonemic system of the linguists is basically a description of these patterns. If the mastering of a new phonology is to be attacked deliberately and systematically, there must be some descriptive statement as a basis for planning. This a phonemic analysis can provide. It is not, of course, all that is needed, since an adequate program must also be based on a sound theory of learning.

For an adult to learn a language, it is not essential that he be a competent phonemicist. If his work is in charge of a teacher who has a thorough understanding of the problems, the necessary direction can be provided from outside. Even in this case, however, some clear idea of the general nature of the problem is very helpful and may contribute both to the effectiveness and rapidity of his learning. If such a teacher is not available — which is the more usual situation for many languages — then the student himself must provide the direction. Without this his efforts may be largely pointless, or, what is worse, they may be effective in establishing incorrect speech habits. As a very minimum, the student must understand the general nature of the problem, and be alert to every possible indication of inadequate pronunciation. Some specific information on the special problems of the learning of the specific language with his specific background is a most desirable addition. An elementary understanding of linguistics may make the difference between success and failure.

21.4   There are always two primary factors which must be taken into account. The first is that phonemic systems (or, more particularly, the phonological patterns which they describe) are incommensurable. No one can be effectively stated in terms of another. Pronunciation of an utterance in conformity with the habits of a different language will almost inevitably produce an unsatisfactory result. Hearing an utterance in terms of the patterns of another language may frequently result in failure to understand. The second factor is that the patterns of the mother tongue are typically so deeply ingrained as to control the adult's hearing of all sound, irrespective of the foreignness of its patterns. In learning a second language, the problems stem about equally from two sources, the new language and the old.

While our concern here is with phonology, it may be pointed out in passing that the learning problems in connection with the morphology and syntax are much the same. Learning new patterns is only part of the process. Freeing oneself from old patterns is equally important, and sometimes more difficult. Information on the grammar both of English and of the new language is of help — though, of course, one must learn to speak from habitual patterns without any reference to such systematic formulations.

21.5   Knowledge of the phonemic system of the second language is not enough. Textbooks of Hindi always give some description of the pronunciation, though few are couched in phonemic terminology. /p/ and /ph/ are often described as differing in that the latter has a "puff of breath" added, or something of the kind. This is true enough, and it is essential information. But taken by itself it can be exceedingly misleading. A student immediately perceives the problem as that of adding aspiration to an already familiar sound. Hindi /p/ is accordingly pronounced as English /p/, that is, usually as [ph]. To pronounce Hindi /ph/, an effort is made to add further aspiration. The results are quite various and almost universally unsatisfactory. Not infrequently something approaching [phǝh] is heard.

A more careful writer may state that Hindi /p/ is more or less similar to English *p* in *spin*, whereas /ph/ is like *p* in *pin*. This is of no help to the average American because: (1) He does not under-stand the distinction intended, since he hears /p/ in *spin* and *pin* to be alike, as English phonemic patterns require. (2) He is unable to say the *p* of *spin* in such a context as Hindi /pəl/ 'moment' since his patterns are invariably to use [ph] in such an environment. He therefore confuses /pəl/ with /phəl/ 'fruit.' (3) The statement is illustrative — in a minor and comparatively innocent way — of a common confusion of sound and symbol, or of speech and writing, a confusion which is quite natural for him and which will continue to give him trouble unless it is actively combatted.

21.6 Note that the instance mentioned in the last section is a PHONEMIC, not a PHONETIC, problem. No new sound is involved. Both [p] and [ph] are quite familiar, as indeed are a number of other closely similar sounds. It is merely the usage that is new. In the one language, /p/ and /ph/ are allophones of a single phoneme; in the other, they are two contrasting phonemes.

The phonologic problems in learning a second language are largely those of learning new uses for old sounds rather than learning new sounds. Even in a language with clicks, popularly considered the epitome of strangeness, there is little that is new. Every American knows several of these clicks and uses them in driving horses, in participating in a gossip session, or in amusing a baby. It is the use — that is, their place in the linguistic patterns, describable as their phonemic status — which is new and which creates a major difficulty. New sounds can cause difficulty, but they are never so large a part of the problem as the average student fears.

21.7 One desideratum, therefore, is a knowledge of English phonemics. That is one reason why four chapters are devoted to this topic in this book. These should give some understanding of the over-all patterns of English phonology. This, however, is not enough. To make effective use of this knowledge a student must know accurately how it applies to his own speech. He must know which of the thirty-six syllabic nuclei of English he habitually uses, and where. He must be able to identify them, and it is helpful if he can produce any of them at will. He must understand not only the inventory of phonemes, but also a good bit about the allophones. As we have pointed out, comparison of two phonemic systems by contrasting the lists of phonemes can be quite misleading. The point of contact between any two systems is phonetic. The problem may be stated as that of disassembling the student's speech patterns into the allophones, and of reassembling the allophones into new units, perhaps adding a few in the process.

21.8   The second desideratum is a knowledge of the phonemic system of the language to be learned. This may be more difficult. There are four situations which need to be mentioned:

1. *There may be a relatively good analysis.* Unfortunately, few languages have as yet had such analyses published. Some are presented in a way that is particularly convenient for a learner; others are published primarily for the use of linguistic specialists and are presented in a very technical manner. In any case, if an analysis is available, the student who must plan his own work, or the teacher directing the study of others, has a relatively simple task. He can compare the statement directly with the known facts about the student's native speech and his attempts at speaking the new language. This should suggest the points that will require special practice and the places where careful watch must be maintained to detect likely errors.

We have seen that there is considerable variety in the analyses which have been proposed for the vowel system of English. Any one of them would be useful for a student learning English as a second language. (Some of them would be helpful only if he were learning that dialect to which the description applies.) This does not mean that they are all equally useful. Most of them fail to distinguish /i/ from /ə/, /i/, or /e/, and a native-like command of English phonology must include proper use of /i/. However, errors at this point are less serious than those involving most other phonemes. Indeed, the fact that /i/ could so long be overlooked is largely explained by the fact that, while it is certainly phonemic, it is set off from other phonemes by contrasts which are few in number and relatively unimportant in function.

For most foreigners learning English, there is a pedagogic value in those analyses which emphasize the diphthongal nature of English "long vowels." This is one of the most characteristic features of the English phonemic system. A common error of many foreigners in learning English is to fail to make many of these diphthongal, using instead the pure vowels to which past experience has habituated them. Conversely, a common feature of an "English accent" in many languages is the use of these diphthongal nuclei in place of pure long vowels. Since this is so, there is a slight but real advantage in making the contrast clear by an obviously diphthongal notation for English.

In many other languages such divergent analyses are possible. Any type of analysis is usable to the extent that it actually states the facts of the language. When there is a choice in the interpretation of the data, that analysis is to be preferred which most clearly exhibits the differences between the language to be learned and the learner's mother tongue.

21.9   2. *There may be a good but incomplete analysis.* One of the common faults of descriptions, from the point of view of their usefulness in planning a language-learning program, lies in their failure to describe pitch, stress, and rhythm, and particularly transitions and terminals. In many languages, adequate descriptions exist of consonants and vowels, and nothing whatever of other parts of the system. The danger is that such analyses, actually useful as far as they go, may be worse than useless, by reinforcing the tendency of students and teachers alike to neglect these other facets of phonology.

In general, patterns of intonation and rhythm are the sources of the greatest difficulties to the average American, though many of them never realize it. They must receive considerable intense direct attention. This must come early in the program, before speech habits involving English-like intonation are entrenched. First priority should be given to these aspects before every other feature of the language. If the available sources do not describe them in a useful way, the student or his teacher must work them out.

Another type of incompleteness that reduces the usefulness of an otherwise excellent phonemic description is the omission of adequate phonetic descriptions of the allophones. A mere list of the phonemes will, of course, provide a useful warning against various errors that a student can make. But it is not enough to guide a student in his work. It will not make clear the relationships between the two phonemic systems with which he must deal. They can be compared only on the phonetic level. If an adequate statement is not given, it must be more or less supplied by identifying the phonemes in the speech of the native informant and observing their phonetic character.

21.10 3. *There may be a poor analysis.* The wise course is to reject it entirely and proceed as if there were none. The problem is to recognize it as poor. The only final recourse is to check the statement against the speech of a native informant. The best linguist may produce a statement of phonology which is for the learner's purpose seriously incorrect. It may be based on a different dialect. It may even have been based on observation of an informant with a speech impediment (This has happened!). Even if these are remote possibilities, they cannot be wholly discounted. The speech of the native informant is always the final authority.

There is usually some internal evidence of poor analysis of phonology. The following, particularly several of them together, may be considered as presumptive evidence of untrustworthiness:

(a) Some state pronunciations in terms of English equivalents with little or no qualification. Even when competently done (a rare case!) this can be misleading. "*Bata* . . . does sound very much like *barter*." This is not very bad (nor good enough) if you pronounce the latter /báнtə/, as presumably the author does, but very bad if you say /bártər/ or /báнrtər/ as most Americans do. The facile statement that "vowels are as in Italian" is more commonly made by people who speak no Italian than by those who do: it is almost always meaningless.

(b) Some direct students to overlook features. "Some consonants are aspirated, and should then be written with a *h* following: e.g., *dhunhu* 'a small hill.' As, however, the aspirate is not always distinguished by Europeans, we have decided to disregard it, except where its omission might cause confusion."

(c) Some pessimistically state that a proper pronunciation is impossible to acquire. Presumably the author himself failed, and may have failed likewise at other points. "TL — wholly indescribable, almost unattainable, and very seldom used."

(d) Some make free use of impressionistic and largely meaningless terms. "Make the vowel as full and rich as you like."

(e) Some express linguistic features as the result of racial or other irrelevant attributes. "His flighty and pleasure-loving disposition is the most noticeable of his characteristics, and shows itself particularly in his language."

(f) Some seem particularly concerned with sounds that are *not* in the language being described. "The consonants *f, q, v, x, z,* do not exist."

(g) Some descriptions utterly confuse spelling with pronunciation. "This restricted orthography accounts for some of the multiple and confusing letter sounds which appear in the following table."

(h) Some seem confused by the native speaker's seeming perversity: ". . . it seems impossible for a native, even in spelling, to give *g* the simple hard sound of *g* in *go* — it always has the nasal preceding."

(i) Some confuse phonemics and phonetics. "Many phoneticians claim that *ch* and *j* are compound sounds. They were probably led to this error because the sounds are not heard in French or German, and they were led to analyze them as compounds of *tsh* and *dzh* in order to explain them. All nations that have them have heard them as simple sounds. . . ." The last statement might be paraphrased "In all languages where they occur as phonemes they are phonemes."

(j) Some state the pronunciation of the present day language in terms of deviations from a known or reconstructed parent language. "This letter is pronounced by . . . as *a* in most languages, or as *ah* or the *a* in *father* in English. It has never been doubted that this was the original sound. . . ."

(k) Some are patently contradictory. ". . . there are no diphthongs. . . . The following five English words give pretty nearly the sounds of the five . . . vowels, a, e, i, o, u, far   fail   feel   foal   fool."

(l) Some suggest ridiculous gymnastics. ". . . it is best described as an attempt to pronounce *feed* with the front part of the mouth and *food* with the back part of the mouth."

Note however: Statements that do not include the terms "phoneme," "allophone," etc., or statements not in the usual format employed by descriptive linguists, are not necessarily to be rejected. Some excellent descriptions have been produced by writers with little technical training, or with training received prior to the present development of phonemic terminology. Some others have been written by phoneme-conscious linguists in deliberately non-technical language. Conversely, some authors have used technical terminology with no adequate understanding of their meanings.

21.11 4. *There may be no analysis whatever.* In this case the student or the teacher must make one. This does not mean that he must draw it up in the finished form in which a professional linguist would publish it, though this might be highly desirable for other reasons. But he must be constantly on the lookout for any significant contrast or lack of contrast, and be prepared to draw as much as he can from any hints in his informant's speech, his own errors, his informant's corrections, and the reactions of others. His analysis may be inchoate, but it must be adequate to direct his attention to the trouble spots. It will be helpful if the student can produce a phonemic script in which he can keep his notes and prepare his drill materials.

The remainder of this chapter will be devoted to some hints on this matter supplemental to the techniques described in Chapter 17. They will be stated primarily from the point of view of the needs of a language student, but much of what is said will apply also to a technical linguistic analysis.

21.12 In 17.2, four types of errors were listed as commonly occurring in preliminary transcriptions made for phonemic analysis. They are also characteristic of the student's first gropings after a new phonemic system. Not all are equally serious. In general, a moderate amount of over-differentiation is not disastrous. It will add some unnecessary complications to the morphology and increase the load that the student must master. Excessive over-differentiation may leave the student hopelessly enmeshed in details that might have been avoided by correct classing of the allophones into more manageable units.

Under-differentiation is much more serious. It may render speech unintelligible. Unfortunately for the student, it does so only in certain instances. He can usually get away with poor pronunciation long enough to become thoroughly established in habits which will lead to trouble later. Even when misunderstandings do not arise, the result can be quite obnoxious to native speakers. Consider, for example, your own reactions to the common failure of certain foreigners to distinguish /θ/ from /s/ or /t/, and /ð/ from /z/ or /d/. The occasional total misunderstanding is minor compared with the constant irritation that such a pronunciation occasions.

No systematic procedure will discover and correct under-differentiation. But there are certain situations which should cause suspicion and lead to careful re-examination of the data. As in so many instances, the only definite answer must come from careful rechecking with a cooperative native informant.

21.13   One indication of possible under-differentiation is excessive numbers of apparent **homophones,** that is, words which appear to be the same in pronunciation. Every pair of homophones should be checked with the informant to determine whether he considers them as actually alike. If he reports them as different, or especially if a second informant is able to identify correctly the words which the first informant is asked to pronounce, there is under-differentiation. The task is then to discover what is the feature that has been overlooked or confused with another.

There is an accessory value in this. Many of the pairs will prove to be minimal. These constitute exceptionally valuable drill material, since errors cannot be so easily overlooked. Moreover, if they were not distinguished at first, they will be minimal pairs for precisely those contrasts on which drill is most needed.

21.14   Another means of discovering under-differentiation is to make careful note of utterances which are misunderstood. If certain items keep reappearing, it is indicative of some trouble in the pronunciation of these particular words. If many of these contain the same "sound," it may well be that the trouble is in that place. A careful check should be made, taking note of the words or "sounds" that seem to be misunderstood. Errors are important data in correcting pronunciation as well as in extending analysis. They should be noted with both uses in mind.

21.15   In some cases, apparent irregularities in morphophonemic changes may suggest places where the phonology is suspect. In Loma (Liberia) word initial phonemes are changed in certain contexts which cannot be defined here:

[péle] becomes [véle] and so all		[p] become [v] before [i e ɛ a]	
[pótè]	[wótè]	[p]	[w] before [u o ɔ]
[dódo]	[lódo]	[d]	[l]
[tíli]	[líli]	[t]	[l]
[séi]	[zéi]	[s]	[z]
[bíli] becomes [víli], and so many		[b] become [v] before [i e ɛ a]	

[bú]   [wú]   [b]   [w] before [u o ɔ]
[báfà] remains [báfà] and so many [b] remain [b] in any context.

The system is quite regular. (The tabulation is fragmentary; the
regularity would be more evident if all the possible initial consonants were considered.) It is therefore suspicious that [b] should
show two contrasting patterns, one like [p] (as [d] is like [t]), and
one of no change. Investigation will show that the transcription
[báfà] is incorrect. It should be [ɓáfà], with a phonemically different initial, an implosive voiced bilabial stop contrasting with the
simple voiced bilabial stop of the other examples. With this correction, the transcription is now phonemic; [ ] can properly be
replaced by / /. The patterns of initial consonant change are found
to be quite regular. Of course some languages have morphophonemic patterns that are much less symmetrical, so that apparent irregularities are not necessarily evidence for such a
conclusion.

21.16 Whatever consideration calls attention to a possible
under-differentiation, the next step is to make new recordings.
Then these must be carefully checked to be sure that the distinctions now recorded are actually phonemic. It is very easy to
imagine you hear a difference when you strongly suspect that there
should be one. You must be sure that the contrast you hear is real
and that it is significant.

21.17 At the first approach to a new phonemic system, students are occasionally troubled by apparent random variability
in the pronunciation of certain words. Sometimes this is due to a
vacillation between two alternative pronunciations of one morpheme, similar to that between /rúf/ and /rúwf/ for some Americans. This is not a phonemic problem, as is evident from such
pairs as *look* /lúk/ : *Luke* /lúwk/, in which no such variation is
observed. Other instances are quite obviously of a different type.

One element in learning to understand a spoken language is to
learn to hear every sound as an instance of one of the phonemes
of the language. There is, of course, a certain amount of random
variation within each allophone, as was pointed out in 16.8. Most
instances of a given allophone are more or less similar to a mean
value for all instances, and also rather more distant from the mean

values of any other phonemes. In other words, each allophone has a characteristic range of variation.

Let us consider a large population of instances of each of two phonemes, /X/ and /Y/, in some simple environment in which they contrast. The distribution in regard to some single measurable factor might be something as follows:

MEAN VALUE OF /X/   MEAN VALUE OF /Y/

This large population is perhaps the sum of past experience which has set the phonemic pattern of the individual hearer. This will lead him to interpret any sound near the mean value of /X/ as an instance of /X/, and any sound near the mean value of /Y/ as an instance of /Y/. A sound halfway between the mean values will be interpreted more or less randomly as either /X/ or /Y/. Only if the distance from both mean values is great will it be heard as a "strange sound." Of course, such intermediate sounds are very rare in the language from which the past experience was drawn. That fact is represented in the diagram by the dip in the frequency curve between the two humps.

Suppose this hearer starts to study a language in which there is no phoneme comparable to either /X/ or /Y/, but one, /Z/ whose mean value is intermediate between those of /X/ and /Y/. The diagram below represents all three of these. Until the learner

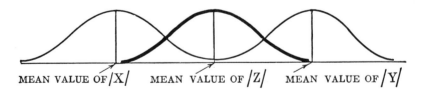

MEAN VALUE OF /X/   MEAN VALUE OF /Z/   MEAN VALUE OF /Y/

assimilates the new pattern and establishes a new set of norms by which to classify the sounds he hears, each instance of /Z/ will sound to him as either /X/ or /Y/. Which reaction occurs will be partly the result of randomness of his responses (particularly when an instance of /Z/ is near its mean value), and partly of the randomness of the pronunciation of /Z/ (particularly when the instance of /Z/ is less close to its mean value). Successive repetitions of the same word may sound quite different (one with /X/ and one with /Y/) to the student, but quite alike (both with /Z/) to the native speaker. The one hears them as more different than they actually are, the other as less different.

21.18   By this time some such experiment as the following has undoubtedly been used in your class. Some non-English sound, say [ṭ], is pronounced and the class is asked to identify it. Some will call it [t] and some [k]. Very few will report it as wholly strange, though a few will call it a "strange [t]" or a "peculiar [k]" or something of the kind. Most Americans will assign [ṭ] to one or the other of their English phonemes, until they have been trained to recognize it as a distinct entity. Some will be reasonably consistent in calling it [t], others more or less consistent in identifying it as [k]. Some will hear it sometimes one way, sometimes the other. The proportions will depend in part on the precise degree of retroflexion used. The difference between different students in their reactions is the result of difference in past experiences.

Vacillation in hearing what the informant insists is identical should suggest this type of explanation. The lack of agreement between observers, if two or more are present, should raise the same possibility. Sometimes such confusion can be cleared up by tabulation. Sometimes it may cause considerable difficulty in the distributional patterns of other phonemes. Usually the problems are most easily eliminated by closer attention to phonetics and by rechecking with the informant.

21.19   What has been said here must not be taken to imply that phonemic analysis, however thorough and competent it may be, can either assure — or, even with good fortune, produce — an adequate command of the phonology of a language. It cannot. It can only provide a basis for planning the work and illuminating the problems which arise. This is, however, an essential service. Together with training in phonetics, close attention to phonemics may enable a student to make an excellent first approximation quickly and easily. Two problems remain: to achieve a pronunciation which is acceptable in the last detail, and to make it all automatic. The ultimate polishing can only be had by close attention to the speech of an informant, to mimicry of every detectable mannerism, and to constant drill. These things are the real essentials. But without direction they can become quite as profitless as they are tedious. There is no easy road to language learning. However, an intelligent approach may both expedite progress and insure a better result.

||||||||||||||||||||||||||||||||||||||||||||||||||||||||||||||||||||||||||||||||||||||||||||||||||||||||||p
◇◇◇◇◇◇◇◇◇◇◇◇◇◇◇◇◇◇◇◇◇◇◇◇

22

Acoustic Phonetics

22.1   The theoretic basis of music has been understood for a very long time. It has long been believed that somehow speech must be subject to much the same basic principles, but until recently no one has been able to show the relationship clearly. In very recent years new instruments have been developed which make it possible to record and measure various features of sound waves in such a way that the significant features of quality can be correlated with known facts about the physical basis of music. Both can now be brought within one comprehending physical theory. Of course, such a theory is no more able to explain speech than it is to explain music. It can merely describe the physical features of sound which are used in speech and music and demonstrate that they are basically similar. How they are used is a matter for study by the special methods of musicology and linguistics.

These new developments obviously hold great theoretical importance to linguistics, particularly for phonology. The revolution in thinking which they seem to be stimulating promises to be profound. But they have much more than just theoretic interest, since they have provided many new and powerful tools for the analysis of certain phonetic features of great importance in language. Some knowledge of the basic principles of acoustic phonetics is becoming essential for an understanding of modern linguistics.

22.2 An understanding of the elementary physical principles behind music is essential for any understanding of the nature of these new developments. While many of the students who use this book have some acquaintance with them, it is necessary first to present some very elementary principles for those whose background does not include either acoustics or music theory.

The physically simplest sound is one such as that approximated closely by a high-grade tuning fork and known as a **pure tone**. A properly designed fork will vibrate with great accuracy at a constant frequency. This frequency can best be stated in **cycles per second**, abbreviated **cps**. One **cycle** is the complete movement from some fixed point to one side, thence back through the starting point to the other side, and thence back to the starting point. Such movement is continued with gradually diminishing strength until the energy imparted by striking has been expended. The count of the cycles completed in one second is the measure of the frequency. The frequency is one convenient measure of the pitch of the sound which is produced. Or, as a tuning fork can produce only one tone, it is sometimes stated as the pitch of the fork itself. Cycles per second is the measure of pitch preferred by physicists.

Another convenient and familiar measure is in terms of the musical scale. The pitches used in conventional Western music are designated by the letters A to G, or by letters with sharps or flats added. The piano keyboard contains eight notes designated A. Under one system of tuning, these have the following frequencies:

First note on Keyboard	27.5 cps.
	55
	110
A below Middle C	220
A above Middle C	440
	880
	1760
	3520

Each of these notes differs from those above and below it by an **octave**. In frequency each is exactly double that below it. A difference of pitch of two octaves is equal to a multiplying of the frequency by 4 or $\frac{1}{4}$, three octaves to multiplication by 8 or $\frac{1}{8}$, etc.

All notes designated by the same letter differ by an integral number of octaves.

22.3   If A (220) and A (440) are sounded together the combination is said to be **harmonious**. This is the acoustic impression whenever there is a simple mathematical relationship between the frequencies. In this case the ratio is 1 : 2. If A (440) and E (659.2) are struck together the resulting sound is also harmonious. In this case the ratio closely approximates 2 : 3. That this is only approximate is the result of compromises which are made in order to enable a piano to be played in more than one key. If on the other hand A (440) and A flat (415.3) are played together the sound is unharmonious. There is no simple mathematical ratio between the two frequencies.

All notes having frequencies which are exact multiples of a given frequency are said to be **harmonics** of it. The basic note in such a series of harmonics is called the **fundamental**. There are various ways of designating harmonics. We shall use numerals representing the multiplier. For example, A (440) is the 2nd harmonic of A (220).

22.4   While a tuning fork produces a very nearly pure tone, few other instruments do. Typically a musical instrument produces a fundamental frequency and a whole series of harmonics. The relative strength of these harmonics determines the sound quality of the instrument. This may be demonstrated by an electric organ. This instrument can produce a close approximation to a pure tone. It also produces a series of harmonics. The organist can produce various effects by mixing the fundamental and various harmonics in different proportions. In this way various instruments can be imitated and other new and strange sound effects produced. Criticisms of the tone quality of the electronic organ arise in part from the fact that only a relatively short series of harmonics is so used. Actually tone quality is affected in some way by every audible harmonic.

This can be a very large number. Consider a bass voice pitched at A (110). The following frequencies will be produced:

Note sung	A	110 cps.	Fundamental
1 octave higher	A	220 cps.	2nd harmonic
	E	330 cps.	3rd harmonic

2 octaves higher	A	440 cps.	4th harmonic
	C sharp	550 cps.	5th harmonic
	E	660 cps.	6th harmonic
	about G	770 cps.	7th harmonic
3 octaves higher	A	880 cps.	8th harmonic
		990–1650	9th, 10th, 11th, 12th, 13th, 14th, 15th
4 octaves higher	A	1760 cps.	16th harmonic
		1870–3410	17th–31st harmonics (15 in all)
5 octaves higher	A	3520 cps.	32nd harmonic
		3630–6930	33rd–63rd harmonics (31 in all)
6 octaves higher	A	7040 cps.	64th harmonic
		7150–13970	65th–127th harmonics (63 in all)
7 octaves higher	A	14080 cps.	128th harmonic

Somewhere in the next octave (20,000–25,000 cps.), the limit of human hearing is reached. In this example it might be at about the 200th harmonic. The actual limit varies from individual to individual. The higher audible frequencies are of little importance in speech. Home tape recorders are generally designed to record up to about 8000 cps., dictating machines perhaps 4000 cps. The latter record speech intelligibly, but hardly naturally, and do occasionally interfere in small ways with understanding.

22.5   The second feature which must be stated to describe the vibration of a tuning fork is the amount of movement which there is in each cycle. The most familiar measure of this is the **amplitude.** We will not attempt an exact definition, as to do so would lead us further than necessary into physics. However, amplitude is related in a loose way to loudness. After a tuning fork is struck the note gradually fades away into silence. This drop in loudness is the psychologic response to a decrease in amplitude.

If two tones are sounding at once the frequency and amplitude of each can be stated. The quality of the sound heard will depend on the two frequencies and the relative amplitude, the loudness of the sound on the absolute amplitudes. As linguists we are interested primarily in sound quality. Our only direct interest in loudness is in relative loudnesses (an approximation to stress) of successive sounds. We, therefore, have little interest in amplitude as such, but are much concerned about relative amplitude.

The physicist would add one more variable, **phase,** by which he would specify any complex sound. Like absolute amplitude, this has no linguistic significance, though it does have importance in some non-linguistic aspects of human hearing. We mention the matter only for the benefit of those who have studied physics, and we need not attempt a definition.

These two variables, frequency and relative amplitudes, are adequate to describe the quality of any steady continuing sound. Such sounds are not characteristic of speech, where the sound quality seems to be continuously varying. It is therefore necessary to state the changes of frequencies and relative amplitudes with time. The time dimension is fundamental in all linguistic work.

22.6 All that is linguistically significant (and a lot more!) about a given sound (say an approximately steady portion selected from an utterance) can be stated by listing the frequencies which enter into its composition and the relative amplitudes of each. Such an analysis of sound is generally best presented graphically, in which case it is called a **spectrogram.** Sound spectrograms can be produced by an electronic device known as a **sound spectrograph.** This is the instrument which is basic to the new advances in acoustic phonetics, though many other instruments have also made important contributions.

Actually, it is physically impossible for a spectrograph to produce anything more than an approximation to a true spectrogram. It is not possible to make an exact measurement of the amplitude at an exact frequency. Instead it is necessary to measure the amplitude of any and all frequencies which fall within a **band** of frequencies. In one setting of a familiar type of spectrograph the width of the band is 45 cps. Very roughly one band extends from 0 to 45 cps., the next from 45 to 90 cps., and so forth through the range of frequencies of interest in speech analysis. In the diagram on page 210 a crude schematic spectrogram is presented. The sound represented is approximately [e] said at the pitch of A (220 cps.). The strongest harmonic is the third, and the amplitude at that frequency has been listed as 1.0. The amplitudes of

SCHEMATIC SPECTROGRAM

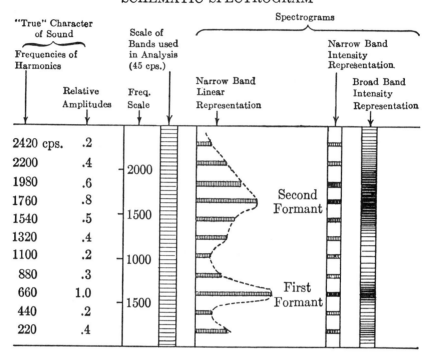

the other harmonics as far as the eleventh are given in terms of fractions of the amplitude of the third harmonic.

Since the lowest pitch involved is 220 cps. (the fundamental), there is no amplitude recorded in the first band (0–45 cps.), nor the second (45–90 cps.), third (90–135 cps.), nor fourth (135–180 cps.). The fifth band (180–225 cps.) includes the fundamental, and so some amplitude is recorded by a short line. Then there are several bands with zero amplitude until the band 405–450 cps. is reached. This contains the second harmonic, and so another short line is recorded — and so forth to the highest frequency in the diagram, 2500 cps. The result is one type of spectrogram. As may be seen it is only an approximation. (And in actual operation some factors not mentioned would enter to produce other small differences from the "true" picture.) It is, however, a representation which, in spite of all its shortcoming, reveals a great deal about the sound being analyzed.

22.7   The chief limitation of such a spectrogram is that it can be used only on samples of sound which are reasonably uniform. To study the change of sound quality we need to make such spectrograms of numerous samples, spaced a few centiseconds apart. These are, however, awkward to compare. Some of these limitations can be removed by another setting of the machine. In this the amplitude in each band is shown by the darkness of coloration. Each harmonic appears as a gray spot; the spaces between remain white. The strongest harmonics are nearly black, the weakest very faint. Such a spectrogram is said to have **intensity representation,** in contrast with the **linear representation** spectrogram just described. The diagram gives a schematic example of such a spectrogram of the same sound sample.

The limitation of an intensity representation is clearly seen in the diagram. It is not possible to read off the differences in color with any exactness. In fact, if the machine is adjusted one way, all that are weak are missed entirely, though the strong and moderate ones are clearly differentiated. It can be adjusted to bring out the weaker bands, but then the moderate ones are as black as the machine will register, and hence not distinguishable from the strongest. This lack of precision and versatility in registering amplitude is the chief drawback of this type of spectrogram.

The advantage of intensity representation is that the whole spectrogram of a single short sample of sound is narrow. It is therefore possible, in effect, to record a number of such spectra, representing successive sound fractions, in a series. This introduces the time element and makes it possible for the spectrogram to record not only the sound quality of a sample, but also the changes which take place in speech.

In practice the spectrograph does not make analyses of successive portions independently. Instead the amplitude within any one of the bands is measured through one playing of a recording. A stylus marks the result as it moves across the paper. The stylus then moves up slightly and records again as the amplitude is measured in the next band. Thus a continuous spectrogram of a sample up to 2.4 seconds in length is obtained. The usual type of spectrogram used in phonetic investigations is of this type. Frequency is represented, as in the schematic diagram on page 362, by the vertical dimension on the paper. Time is represented by the horizontal dimension, and amplitude at any given frequency at any given time by the blackness of the image at that point. This complicated representation can be made by a spectrograph in only a few minutes after the sample is recorded magnetically on its drum. The operation is largely automatic.

22.8 A variety of facts can be read off such a spectrogram. In the first place, the frequency of each harmonic is easily discernible. On our schematic spectrogram eleven harmonics are visible. (An actual spectrogram would usually extend to a higher frequency and hence show several more.) The lowest of these is in the band 180–225 cps. (On an actual spectrogram the bands are not so sharply demarcated, but the principle is the same.) We therefore know that the fundamental frequency is somewhere in this range. This is not very precise, somewhere between a bit above F and a quarter tone above A. Such a measurement would be utterly inadequate for musical work! But if we examine the tenth harmonic we find that it falls in a band 2160–2205 cps. The frequency of the fundamental must be one tenth of this, that is it must lie between 216 and 220.5. This is close enough for speech work, and perhaps of some value in music. Measurement of a higher harmonic would allow yet greater precision.

But measuring the pitch at a single point is by no means all. Even without measuring, the risings and fallings of the higher harmonics give a graphic picture of the intonation or other pitch phenomena of speech. Not only the phonetic expression of the pitch phonemes, but also some aspects of the terminals can often be clearly seen, and if necessary measured.

22.9 When a spectrogram such as that in the schematic diagram, or an actual product of the spectrograph, is examined, it will be found that at most points on the time scale certain harmonics or groups of adjacent harmonics are strong, while others are weak. If the pitch is rising or falling rapidly, it will be seen that this strength is not a property of specific harmonics as much as of regions in the spectrum. If a given vowel is said with a rising inflection, the spectrogram will show a number of regions in which the harmonics are strong. Each harmonic will rise with the rise in pitch. As it enters one of these regions it will become stronger. As it passes out above it will become weaker again. Such a region in a spectrum is called a **formant**. There may be only one harmonic within a formant, or there may be a number. Harmonics can enter or leave a formant either through pitch change, or through changes in the position of the formant. Diagrammatic representations of these possibilities are given below.

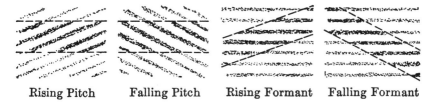

Rising Pitch   Falling Pitch   Rising Formant   Falling Formant

22.10 The positions of the formants, particularly the first and second, are correlated with the qualities of vowels. Any two points in a spectrogram in which the formants are in the same positions will be found to have the same vowel quality. Any two points in which the formants occupy different positions will be found to have phonetically different vowel qualities. The gross character of vowels can be specified by stating the positions of the first two formants. This is usually done by measuring the centers of highest intensity. Thus a formant may be stated to be located at 600 cps. There may or may not be a harmonic just at this point. If the speaker's voice is pitched at 120 cps. (roughly B flat), there will be. If it is at 110 cps. (A), there will not be. However, a formant has appreciable width. Harmonics within a short distance on either side of this center frequency will be strengthened. The formant will therefore be evident no matter what the fundamental pitch of the voice.

22.11 In order to make the formants more clearly visible, the sound spectrograph can be set with a band width of 300 cps. instead of 45 cps. The spacing of the bands is not altered, so that there is a considerable amount of overlapping of the bands. The result is that the amplitude is averaged out. It is obvious that this will have the effect of making individual harmonics unrecordable unless the fundamental pitch is above 300 cps., and not clearly visible even then. However, the formants will show distinctly as prominent dark bands on the spectrograms. Such **broad band spectrograms** are much easier to read directly, but less suitable for exact measurement. An indication of the relationship of a broad band spectrogram to a narrow band spectrogram, and to a linear representation, is given in the schematic diagram on page 362.

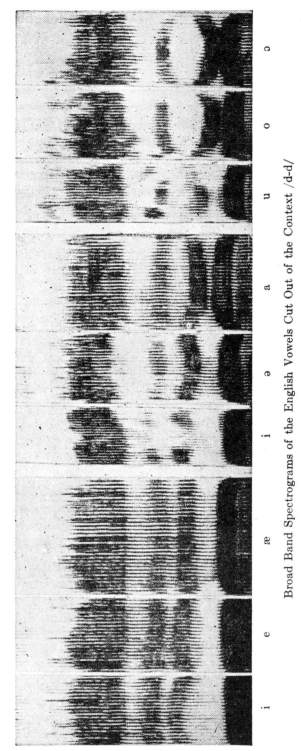

Broad Band Spectrograms of the English Vowels Cut Out of the Context /d-d/

Broad-band spectrograms are more commonly seen in the published literature than are narrow-band spectrograms.

22.12   The positions of the first two formants seem to be closely correlated with some of the more significant phonetic features of vowel quality. This can be seen by examining labeled spectrograms such as those on page 366. The following table gives approximate positions characteristic of English vowels said in isolation. Bear in mind that these figures do not represent anything of the range of allophonic variation.

[i]	400, 2100	[ɨ]	300, 1500	[u]	450, 1000
[e]	500, 1800	[ə]	600, 1300	[o]	550, 900
[æ]	650, 1700	[a]	700, 1100	[ɔ]	650, 800

You will notice that, in general, the position of the first formant is correlated with the height of the vowel, and that of the second formant with the frontness of the vowel.

22.13   In order to explain the significance of formants, recourse must be had to another basic concept of acoustics. This is **resonance.** If two tuning forks of the same frequency are placed near together and one is struck, the second will start vibrating. The sound waves from the first have excited the second. A similar effect can be had by striking a tuning fork near an empty vessel of the proper size. The air column (physicists refer to any mass of air which vibrates as a unit as an **air column**) within the vessel will vibrate, reinforcing the sound of the fork. This is resonance. If the size of the air column is changed, the frequency at which it will resonate will be changed. This is easily demonstrated by adding or removing water. Changes of shape can also effect the frequency at which an air column will resonate, though this is harder to demonstrate simply.

Another characteristic of resonating air columns can be demonstrated by an experiment based on a tuning fork and a resonator tuned to the same frequency. These can be set up so that strong resonance is produced. If the exciting frequency (that produced by the tuning fork) or the resonating frequency of the air column is changed slightly so that they are no longer exactly in tune, resonation does not cease abruptly, but becomes somewhat weaker. As the difference in frequency increases, the resonance becomes progressively weaker until it becomes imperceptible. Any air column resonates most efficiently at some single frequency, and with diminishing efficiency at adjacent frequencies. There is thus a band of resonance, the width of which (that is, how fast the resonance falls off with changes of exciting pitch) depends on many factors, including the shape of the air column and the nature of the vessel that encloses it.

Now consider an experiment in which some sound source produces a complex sound consisting of a fundamental and many harmonics. Near this is placed a vessel enclosing an air column which has been so adjusted as to resonate over a rather wide band. All the harmonics which fall within this band will be strengthened. Those near the center of the band will be strengthened most, those a little to either side somewhat less. The spectrogram of the resulting sound would show a formant in the band at which the air column resonates.

22.14   The spectrogram of a vowel shows a series of formants. On the analogy of the experiment just described, we may assume that each of these formants represents the band of resonance of some air column somewhere in the vocal tract. Since the frequency of each formant is correlated in some way with the position of the tongue, it follows that the resonating air columns must be in some way controlled by tongue position. In a vowel like [i] the high point of the tongue divides the mouth into two cavities, only partly set off from each other to be sure. Various experiments have suggested that the two halves of the mouth are associated with the two lower formants. The first formant is apparently produced by resonance in the throat and back of the mouth; the second by resonance in the front of the mouth. This is of course an oversimplification, since the shapes of these cavities are very complex and the resonance patterns must also be complex.

That this has some measure of truth may be seen by graphing the vowel positions in terms of the two formant frequencies. Since the high vowels have a low first formant, we will set up a scale with the position of the first formant reading from top to bottom. Since back vowels generally have lower second formants, we will set up a scale for the positions of the second formant reading from right to left. Each vowel can then be indicated on the chart at the intersection of the proper two measures. The result is remarkably like the familiar arrangement of vowels based originally on tongue position. In the accompanying chart, the nine English vowels are so indicated. In some instances two or more allophones have been taken into account, hence the larger areas assigned to certain vowels.

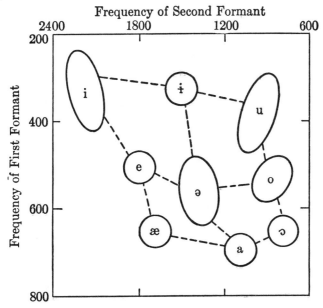

22.15   The interpretation of various consonant sounds presents more complications, but the same principles will be found to explain many of the observed phenomena. Consider a sequence like [kæk], said without aspiration. The stops will appear on a spectrogram as periods of time without any noticeable amplitude at any frequency, that is, as blank sections representing silence. In the middle of the syllable the formants will be at the characteristic [æ] position. As [k] is said, the tongue is in contact with the roof of the mouth. To reach the [æ] position, it falls rapidly, passing through the positions of various vowels. We may therefore expect that between the first [k] and the [æ] the formants will curve rapidly through positions characteristic of certain high vowels. Just before the second period of silence representing the second [k], the formants should again shift rapidly as the tongue moves toward a velar closure. The observable effect will be characteristic of all velar sounds. The actual stop portion (silence) will be identical for [p t k]. These three sounds are distinguishable on the spectrograms, and presumably in hearing, only by their effect on the formants of adjacent vowels, or other features of the transition from consonant to vowel or vowel to consonant. We cannot here describe the effects, but they can be observed on any good spectrogram and are described in detail in the literature.

22.16   What has just been said of stops is also true of other consonants. The acoustic features observable in the brief moment when the consonant is actually articulated are seldom adequate to unambiguously identify the consonant. They can be read with surety only by using the effects which the consonant has on the following or preceding vowels. From a phonetic point of view it is not wholly satisfactory to consider phonemes as following one another in a neat sequence, one being finished before the next begins. Instead, the end of one overlaps the beginning of the next. Each moment in a sample of speech may be considered as a group of **cues,** each one of which serves in some way to identify some sound. Some of the cues at one moment may belong to a sound which has already been clearly marked by cues in preceding moments. That is, they are the last members of the sequence of cues that identifies a sound. Others may be the first members of a sequence that will identify a succeeding sound. That this is so may be demonstrated without a spectrograph by cutting a tape recording in two and playing each piece separately. If it is cut in the right place, it will be found that there are two or three sounds that can be clearly heard on either part of the tape. The cues which together make up one of these sounds have been divided between the two pieces, leaving enough of each in each tape to permit identification, though obviously the total effect is necessarily very abnormal.

22.17   Turning aside for a moment to phonemic theory, the question may be asked, if sounds overlap in this way, why do we hear them as in a lineal sequence, as we do in the case of consonants and vowels? It is not enough that the centers of the series of cues follow one another — maybe they do, but we cannot be sure. Our own psycho-physical limitations would prevent our hearing them individually anyway. Even if the sounds did not overlap, the ear would smear them so that in our perception they would seem to overlap.

The answer is simply that we hear the whole complex of features together, but distinguish differences of order by differences of total impression. We learn to do this by much the same process as we learn to distinguish individual phonemes. We can only do it because there are contrasts for different orders of phonemes. A minimal pair like *cat* /kæt/ : *act* /ækt/ is an example.

That the order of phonemes is based on contrasts may be shown by considering stresses. It probably would never occur to the average American to ask, even in the most vague form, the question, which comes first, the /æ/ or the /'/ in such a word as *cat?* The question is meaningless, not because the /æ/ and /'/ are simultaneous (we cannot know for certain that they are!); nor even because they obviously overlap, since the /k/ and /æ/ do also; but simply because there is no evidence by which the question can be answered. That is, we do not have contrasts of the type of /*k'æt/ : /*kæ't/. If we did, the question would become important, and the answer would become accessible. In fact, the answer would probably be quite obvious to the average American, just as it is obvious that *cat* is not /*ktæ/.

There has been considerable debate in recent years about the relationship of "segmental" phonemes (consonants and vowels) to "suprasegmental" phonemes (stresses and pitches). The traditional distinction is that "segmental" items form a linear sequence of segments, in contrast to "suprasegmental" items which do not, but rather overlap the segments. This is not true at all, since phonetically both groups are alike in overlapping. The distinction is a phonemic one. Each group (and the "suprasegmental" must be divided into two groups in English) — consonants and vowels, /′ ^ ` ˇ +/, and /1 2 3 4 ↘ ↗ →/ — forms a sequence. There is a contrast between /′`/ and /`′/, or between /2 3/ and /3 2/. The three sequences of phonemes cannot be condensed into one because we lack contrasts like /′ æ/ : /æ ′/, /3 ′/ : /′ 3/, or /3 æ/ : /æ 3/. The English phoneme /+/ is exceptional in that there are contrasts between /t +/ and /+ t/, *night-rate* : *pie trade*, as well as /+ ′/ : /′ +/. /+/ is also a classic instance of overlapping of phonemes, since it is not ordinarily possible to identify any segment of the stream of speech as /+/, as it is with, say, /t/. /+/ is marked only by certain cues which accompany adjacent segments.

22.18 One other feature of spectrograms must be briefly described. On a narrow-band representation, there will be some areas in which the regular striations representing harmonics will not be visible. Instead there is a mottled appearance. On broad-band spectrograms these areas will be filled with a general gray color. This represents sounds in which amplitude is measurable at all frequencies, or randomly distributed, instead of being organized into harmonics with appreciable amplitude and intervening frequencies with none. This is known to physicists as **white noise.** It is characteristic of fricatives, and is the type of sound known to articulatory phoneticians as **friction.**

A voiceless fricative shows only such white noise. The various fricatives differ in the portions of the spectrum in which the white noise is concentrated, as well as in transitional effects on adjacent sounds. In [s] it is mostly at a high frequency, in [θ] mostly rather low. Voiced fricatives show the same random patterns superimposed on the harmonics.

Whispered vowels show the same formants as spoken vowels, but they are formed by the reinforcement by resonance of fricative noise produced at the larynx.

22.19   As we have briefly sketched, the various features which are heard by the ear can generally be identified on the spectrograms. That some cannot, as yet, may be due only to the present imperfection of our machines, or more likely, to our lack of familiarity with the interpretation of the results. The observed patterns can be correlated closely with our previous notions of articulatory phonetics. The sound spectrograph shows how it is that the human ear can relate what is heard to the methods of producing the sounds. We are beginning to understand not only how sounds are produced, but what each method of production does to the sound, and hence are moving toward an understanding of how a person can reproduce what he hears. The latter is a basic problem of language, though just outside the domain of linguistics.

23

The Process
of Communication

23.1 Language, as we have been examining it, is a complex of structures of various kinds. The analysis of a language must proceed by separating out the various parts, but a full understanding of language cannot be gotten if they are left as detached details unrelated to one another. The various elements are of significance and interest primarily because they fit together into one integrated system which people use in communication. This function of language provides a framework within which language can be looked at more or less as a whole.

Such an approach to language can be fruitful because communication is a much broader process than language. It includes a number of phenomena which, though showing basic similarities to language, are very much simpler. Starting from some of the most elementary forms of communication it is possible to develop certain principles which will be applicable to language. In recent years a whole new branch of science, **communication theory,** has arisen in this way. Though the full implications for linguistics are just beginning to emerge, it is already quite evident that some powerful new insights are likely.

23.2   There are certain elements which can be listed as essential to any communication process, including language. The following are of some interest to us:

1. A **code,** an arbitrary, prearranged set of signals. A language is merely one special variety of code; and the science of linguistics deals, in its strictest delimitation, only with this aspect of communication.

2. A **channel,** some medium by which the signals of the code are conveyed. This may be audible sound in the range from about 100 cps. to perhaps 7000 cps. (as in the case of speech), a band of radio frequencies (compare the now familiar use of the term "channel" with reference to television), light, electrical impulses carried on a wire, or mechanical devices of various kinds.

3. The process of **encoding,** by which certain signals in the code are selected and put into the channel. The selection is typically done in response to some outside condition — that is, one communicates what is observed. The way in which this is to be done is the meaning of the code, and is prearranged.

4. An **encoder,** the person or device which performs the process of encoding.

5. The process of **decoding,** by which the signals are identified and a course of action is affected by them.

6. A **decoder,** the person or device by which the process of decoding is performed, and whose course of action is thereby affected.

It is worth pointing out that either the encoder or the decoder or both can be either persons or machines. A traffic light is part of a communication system; it does not matter whether the signals are selected by a policeman or a mechanical device. An automatic temperature control system is a communication system in which the encoder is a device in the living room and the decoder another device in the basement. The human factor may be essential in language, but not in communication generally.

23.3   The significance of these elements can be seen in a very simple and familiar case — the case of Longfellow's account of a central event in his poem "Paul Revere's Ride." The code was an extremely simple one: "One, if by land; and two, if by sea." This was arranged in advance between the two principles: the encoder, the friend who remained in Boston, and the decoder, Paul Revere, who crossed the river to Charlestown. The process of encoding was the selection of the proper signal (two lanterns) and hanging them in the belfry of Old North Church. When Paul Revere saw them, he mounted his horse and rode off to Lexington: the process of decoding was not merely the identification of the signal; it determined which of two previously planned courses of action he was to follow.

In a code such as this there are certain very evident limitations. It could transmit only a very limited amount of information. No hint could be given about the size of the force, the time of departure, details of the route, or any other facts, no matter how important, which the friend might have picked up in his wanderings through Boston. The two men could, of course, have agreed in advance on a code which would have permitted them to transmit as much detail as they cared. But it would have been wasteful to agree on a very elaborate code unless they had foreseen some real value in further details. Presumably they believed that this simple code would be adequate for their purposes, without involving them in any unnecessary complexity or danger. A code can be designed to transmit any amount of intelligence that may be desired, but there are always certain limitations on what any given code can convey.

23.4   The notion of the capacity of a code, and the closely related one of the actual amount of information transmitted, have proved to be very useful, once proper definitions are set up to allow of precise measurement. A measure of the amount of information which a code can convey is obviously related to the number of alternative signals. Paul Revere's code is at the minimum, with two signals. The amount of information increases as the number of alternatives increases. — These statements are not so much obvious facts about codes as they are the beginning of a technical definition of **information.** By this definition information is by no means the same as in any popular definition of the term.

Information is measured in units called **binits.** ("Binit" is preferred by many linguists; communication engineers usually use "bit.") By definition, a code with two alternative signals, both equally likely, has a capacity of one **binit** per use. A code with four alternatives is defined as having a capacity of two binits per use; one with eight alternatives, a capacity of three binits. That is, the capacity in binits of a code of this type is the logarithm to the base two of the number of alternative signals in the code. This mode of definition is made desirable by certain mathematical considerations which are beyond the scope of this present discussion, as are likewise most of the direct mathematical consequences of the definition.

23.5   For the benefit of those students not conversant with the mathematics involved, the following rough interpretation of **logarithm to the base two** may be given:

If we start with 1 and multiply by 2 repeatedly until we reach the number of signals, the number of times we multiply will be the Log_2 of the number of signals:

1	$= 1$	$\text{Log}_2\,1$	$= 0$
1×2	$= 2$	$\text{Log}_2\,2$	$= 1$
$1 \times 2 \times 2$	$= 4$	$\text{Log}_2\,4$	$= 2$
$1 \times 2 \times 2 \times 2$	$= 8$	$\text{Log}_2\,8$	$= 3$
$1 \times 2 \times 2 \times 2 \times 2$	$= 16$	$\text{Log}_2\,16$	$= 4$
$1 \times 2 \times 2 \times 2 \times 2 \times 2 \times 2 \times 2 = 128$		$\text{Log}_2\,128 = 7$	

Such a definition is not adequate for our purposes, since we may need to consider a code with some other number of signals, say 3. We might expect that $\text{Log}_2\,3$ would be somewhere between $\text{Log}_2\,2 = 1$ and $\text{Log}_2\,4 = 2$. We cannot easily imagine multiplying by 2 one and a fraction times, nor can we readily see what the fraction would be. The value is a little below 1.585. (Most logarithms will not come out even, no matter how many decimal places are calculated.) Just to give some idea of what such logarithms are like, we give here the following short table:

$\text{Log}_2\,1$	0.000	$\text{Log}_2\,9$	3.170
2	1.000	10	3.322
3	1.585	11	3.459
4	2.000	12	3.585
5	2.322	13	3.700
6	2.585	14	3.807
7	2.807	15	3.907
8	3.000	16	4.000

23.6   One crucial aspect of this definition of information can be made clear by another very simple communication system. Consider a store with a burglar alarm. This is a part of a communication system in which the encoder is a mechanical or electrical device, and the code includes only two signals: silence or alarm. Now consider the policeman whose beat passes the store, and whose responsibilities include acting as the decoder in this system. Night after night he goes by, decodes the signal of silence, and responds by continuing on his beat hardly conscious of the store or of the communication system in which he is functioning. But finally, one night the alarm rings; his usual nightly routine is suddenly and drastically changed.

Since we have defined the decoding process in terms of determination of a course of action, we are forced to the conclusion that the communication process is markedly different when the alarm rings from when it does not. Reflection will show that the difference rests in the unexpectedness of one signal, compared with the frequent and expected occurrence of the other. We express this by saying that more information is conveyed by the alarm than by the silence.

23.7 We have defined the capacity of a code of two signals as equal to one binit. This was predicated on the signals being equally likely. In a system such as we have just described, the amount of information in the alarm is much greater than one binit; that in the silence much less. An exact mathematical definition is possible: The amount of information in any signal is the logarithm to the base two of the reciprocal of the probability of that signal. That is: $I = \text{Log}_2 1/p$.

This formula may require some explanation for some students. The probability of a signal may be considered as the proportion of all the signals which are instances of the signal concerned. For example, suppose that in a given code there are two signals. We observe a large number of messages and find that on the average signal A occurs once to every fifteen occurrences of signal B. We therefore estimate the probability of signal A as 1/16 or .0625, and that of signal B as 15/16 or .9475. Probabilities will always be less than 1, and the sum of the probabilities of all the signals in any code will always be exactly 1. The reciprocal is merely a fraction turned upside-down. The reciprocals of the probabilities of the two signals are therefore 16/1 or 16.0 for A and 16/15 or 1.067 for B. The amount of information I for signal A is therefore $\text{Log}_2 1/(1/16)$ or 4.00 binits. For signal B it is 0.093 binits. Signal B is 15 times as frequent as A, but carries only 1/43 as much information.

From the amount of information in each signal we may calculate the average amount of information per signal. Using the same example —

    1 occurrence of A, each carrying 4.00 binits = 4.00
    15 occurrences of B, each carrying .09 binits = 1.39
    16 occurrences carrying a total of   5.39
        Divide by 16 to get an average of   .34 binits

The details of this calculation are much less important than the following principle which it illustrates: The full capacity of a code is realized over a period of time only if all the signals have equal probabilities of occurring. In this instance, the unequal frequencies of the two signals reduce the efficiency of the code to about one third, since if they were equally likely, the capacity of the code would be 1.00 binit.

23.8   Suppose we set up a code in which there are two signals A and B, both equally probable, which can be sent at the rate of one signal per second. By our definition this code has a capacity of one binit of information per second. Suppose we send for four seconds. Any of the following messages might occur, all with equal probabilities:

AAAA AAAB AABA AABB ABAA ABAB ABBA ABBB
BAAA BAAB BABA BABB BBAA BBAB BBBA BBBB

Sixteen signals of equal probabilities represent a capacity of 4 binits. Since each such message requires four seconds for transmission, this works out to a capacity of one binit per second. This figure checks with our first calculation. (Incidentally, to make this sort of check possible is one reason that information is measured in terms of logarithms in the way we have described.)

Now suppose it is agreed that each signal will be repeated exactly twice. If no other change is made in the system, any of the following messages can be sent in four seconds:

AAAA   AABB   BBAA   BBBB

Our decision to repeat has reduced the capacity of the code to only 2 binits in four seconds, or to half a binit per second. That is, it has reduced the efficiency of the code by one half.

The unused capacity is the result of our decision to repeat, and so may be labeled as **redundancy.** Here again, this term is not necessarily used in any sense in which it is popularly used, as we shall see. It is a technical term in information theory, and requires a technical definition in terms that will fit with the definition of information. We define **redundancy** as the difference between the theoretical capacity of any code and the average amount of information conveyed; it is expressed as a percentage of the total capacity. Thus, our decision to repeat each signal twice introduces a redundancy of 50 percent.

Redundancy is not synonymous with repetition, nor is it necessarily the result of repetition. In the last section we calculated the average amount of information in a signal for which the probabilities are 1/16 and 15/16 to be .34 binit. Since the average amount of information would be 1 binit if the probabilities were equal (1/2 and 1/2), the disparity in the probabilities introduces an average redundancy of 66 percent.

23.9 In the example of the last section we calculated the redundancy by listing all the possible messages (16) and all the messages (4) which could be used under the special restriction imposed, and computed the amount of information in each case. This is quite feasible in such an example, but under some conditions would be very unwieldy or even totally impossible. There are, for example, 205,962,976 theoretically possible combinations of five phonemes, taken from the English stock of 46 phonemes, if no special restrictions are imposed. It is easy enough to compute the total information which might be carried. Log_2 46 equals 5.52; there are therefore 5.52 binits of information in each occurrence of one phoneme, and 27.62 binits for a sequence of five phonemes. But to list all the sequences of five phonemes which are actually used in English would be exceedingly laborious, and would not yield a very accurate picture because of the unequal probabilities of the various combinations. Fortunately there is another way of approaching the problem.

Consider again the example of the last section. The first signal can be either A or B, and the probabilities are equal. This first signal, therefore, carries one binit of information. Suppose it turns out to be A; consider the probabilities for the second signal. Here it is no longer equally likely that it will be either A or B, since we had agreed that we would repeat each signal twice. It is therefore a practical certainty that it will be A. The amount of information carried by this signal is therefore zero binits. The third signal can be either A or B, so this signal carries one binit of information. Since the fourth signal is also a repetition of the third, it is known in advance, and so no information is conveyed. We may in this manner compute the total information in each signal separately, and add these figures to get the total amount of information in the message as a whole. The results of the two methods, provided each calculation is done thoroughly, are the same. If the complexities are such that it is not possible to do the calculations thoroughly, it may nevertheless be possible to do them with sufficient completeness to provide a usable approximation to the correct figure.

23.10   Using this method, let us examine the redundancy in some language materials. Just for convenience, we shall use written English for our first example; spoken language could be examined in much the same way.

An English sentence can begin with any letter whatever. However, there are wide variations in the frequencies of various letters. Sentences like *Xerxes was a Greek general.* are quite possible, but very rare. Sentences beginning with *T* are very common; seven of them occur in section 23.9, in which the total number of sentences is only nineteen. A count of a moderate sample of sentences gave the following frequencies of initial letters:

T	.23	B	.06	P	.02	D	.01	V	.00
I	.13	M	.04	L	.02	E	.00	Q	.00
A	.10	F	.04	R	.02	G	.00	K	.00
H	.08	N	.03	C	.01	J	.00	X	.00
S	.08	O	.02	Y	.01	U	.00	Z	.00
W	.07								

If all twenty-six letters had equal frequency, that frequency would be .038. Nine of the letters exceed this average. *T* is 6.1 times as frequent as the average. On the other hand, seventeen letters are less frequent than the average, most of them very much less frequent. With such disparity, we would expect appreciable redundancy. The average amount of information in the first letter of an English sentence is about 3.10 binits. If all twenty-six letters were equally probable, the total information would be 4.70 binits. The average redundancy, considering only the first letter in a message, is therefore about 34 percent.

Suppose now that we examine the second letter in each sentence. Let us take the commonest case, that where the sentence begins with *T*. There is very little freedom of occurrence. As the second letter, *x* and *l* do not occur at all, or perhaps very rarely in sentences starting with non-English words, as *Tlalocan is a Mexican anthropological journal*. Overwhelmingly the commonest is *h*, having a frequency of about 88 percent. Next most probable is *o*, with a frequency in the neighborhood of 6 percent, while *a*, *e*, *i*, *u*, *w*, *r* are occasional and make up most of the remaining 6 percent, and a few others, though rare, are not wholly unexpected. (*Tschaikowsky was a musician*. etc.) The redundancy figures to about 83 percent.

But this is by no means the extreme. Consider the sentences which begin with *Q*. Almost every one of them has *u* as the second letter. Exceptions would include only such rare sentences as *Qaraqalpaq is a Turkic language*. The redundancy here approaches very closely to 100 percent.

The process can be continued as far as we desire. After *Th*, *e* has a frequency of about 83 percent, *i* about 8 percent, *a* about 3 percent, and so on. Several of the letters will not be found at all. The redundancy figures to about 77 percent. One more step: If the sentence begins with *The*, the next character is likely to be space (53 percent), *y* (18 percent), *n* (14 percent), *r* (12 percent). Clearly, this is because *the*, *they*, *then*, and *there* are not only very common words in English, but more likely to occur at the beginnings of sentences than elsewhere.

23.11   We have here our first indication of a source of the high redundancy of written English. In addition to variations in the frequencies of letters as such, and to certain restrictions on sequences of letters as such (*q* is generally followed by *u*), there are considerable restrictions imposed by the fact that letters are used to spell words, and that words as such have widely differing frequencies and places of occurrence.

In any code comparable to written English, there are various levels of organization. Each of these imposes on messages certain restrictions which are reflected in the redundancy of the language as a code. These restrictions arise simply because such codes have structure. Structure is merely a set of limitations on freedom of occurrence and hence inevitably produces redundancy.

23.12 Before we go on, it would be well to get away from written language, with its special problems yet to be discussed (see Chapters 25, 26, and 27), even though it does afford convenient material for analysis and presentation. The situation is not vastly different with spoken English. We would find for example that /ð/ is a relatively common phoneme at the beginning of English sentences (about 18 percent); /ŋ/ does not occur at all in this position. After /ð/, /ə/ would be found to be very common, with a frequency in the neighborhood of 50 percent. After /ðə/, /+/ would be very common. This would be merely a reflection of the fact that the morpheme /ðə/ *the* is very common in this position in English sentences. The method of procedure is not different from that which might be used with written language, except that the material for analysis would have to be transcribed first, and it would be more necessary to specify what dialect is represented in the data.

23.13 We may list the following as particularly interesting sources of redundancy in spoken English. The list is not exhaustive:

1. VARIATION IN FREQUENCY OF PHONEMES. It is characteristic of language that all elements vary widely in frequency. The kind of distribution illustrated above for English initial letters, or for French verb classes graphed in Chapter 9, may be expected with any other kind of data. For example, in my own speech /ɨ i ə e/ are comparatively common; /ɔ/ is quite rare. Among the consonants, /t n s/ are much commoner than /θ ž/. /4/ is much less frequent than the other pitches.

2. RESTRICTIONS ON SEQUENCES OF PHONEMES AS SUCH. In my speech /ɨ/ is very frequent, but the sequence /ɨw/ is very rare, and /ɨy/ or /ɨн/ are not used at all. By contrast /ow/ is much more common than /o/ without a glide. /iŋ/ is comparatively common, but /iyŋ/ does not occur. /nk/ is rare, but /ŋk/ is common. With every vowel there occurs one and only one stress. All such limitations — and a very large number can be listed — increase redundancy by making individual phonemes more probable in certain statable environments and less probable in others.

3. NON-USE OF POSSIBLE MORPHEMES. Such sequences as /θæt/ or /siyg/ are quite possible under the restrictions imposed by

English phonologic patterns and could easily be used as morphemes. The fact is, however, that, for largely fortuitous reasons, they are not. Considerably more than half of the English morpheme shapes of this order of size are not used. Such complete non-use of certain signal patterns must contribute to redundancy. But it is worth noting that this reserve of possible morphemes is of vital importance if the language is to alter its vocabulary to meet new needs, as every language must.

4. VARIATION IN FREQUENCY OF MORPHEMES. The striking illustration of this is found in the English /ð/. This probably occurs in fewer morphemes than any other English consonant (except possibly /ž/). However, many of them, noticeably /ðə/, /ðey/, /ðæt/, /ðət/, /ðen/ are among the commonest morphemes in the language. Largely as a result of this, /ð/ is a relatively common phoneme. Moreover, it is noticeably more common at the beginnings of words than elsewhere, in spite of the fact that it occurs at the beginning in only a few frequently occurring words. The same circumstance, of course, explains the very high frequency of /ə/ after /ð/.

5. RESTRICTIONS ON THE SEQUENCES OF MORPHEMES. Every such restriction necessarily increases redundancy. But restrictions on distribution are essential if the language is to have structure. A language in which morphemes could be placed in any order at will would be completely inoperative. Such a language would be unable to express any relationships between morphemes, and hence an utterance would be nothing more than a list of vocabulary items, about as illuminating as a random sample from a dictionary.

6. SEMANTIC RESTRICTIONS ON WHAT IS LIKELY TO BE SAID. While such a sentence as *The green absolute signals the ineffable hypotenuse.* is grammatically quite acceptable (i.e., it follows a common syntactic pattern), it is quite unlikely to be said, since no context is imaginable. But again, it is essential to the flexibility of language that utterances which cannot be foreseen in advance to be useful are possible. What would have been thought a century ago of a sentence like *Light is both particle and wave.*? All the vocabulary was available then. So was the syntactic pattern. But the sentences would probably have been about as intelligible as that cited just before it. If English could not have allowed an utterance like this, the growth of modern physics would have been

severely hampered when the need to make such a statement did arise.

In every language, factors comparable to these six, though differing widely in detail, are found. Redundancy is not an imperfection in language, but an essential feature, without which language would be inoperative.

23.14   Communication theory has been developed primarily by engineers interested in the design of telephone and telegraph circuits. Their problem is to produce equipment with the maximum efficiency in the use of channels. This necessitates some method for measuring theoretical channel capacity as well as the amount of that capacity used in the transmission of any given code. The usefulness for this kind of problem of calculations of the type just described is now established beyond question. The method has been elaborated to a very high degree and is being extensively used.

As linguists have become acquainted with the results, two types of questions have arisen: What are the implications of this body of knowledge for linguistic theory? Do these methods have anything to contribute to practical problems of linguistic analysis?

As regards the first question, there seems little doubt that the implications are considerable. They are, however, as yet only vaguely perceived. This is partly because few linguists have as yet more than a very superficial knowledge of communication theory. It is also partly because the two approaches are so fundamentally different that it will take considerable labor to establish in detail the relationships between the two bodies of theory. But in spite of this lack of definite evidence, the indications are that communication theory will make important contributions to linguistic theory.

Linguistic theory, particularly as developed by American linguists, has been intimately based on analytic method. The first question is, therefore, not really separable from the second. The crucial question is whether the methods of information theory can be brought to bear on specific linguistic problems. That is, are there questions about language structure which can be answered by the methods of communication theory, and if so, can they be handled as well or better than by traditional methods of descriptive linguistics? Work in this field is just getting under way, but there is some possibility that linguists will find methods of applying the new techniques to their own characteristic problems in a fruitful way. If this occurs, the implications for linguistic theory will follow inevitably.

23.15 In 9.8 a brief mention was made of the Turkish system of vowel harmony, which results in a special type of restriction on the freedom of occurrence of vowels in successive syllables. For example, a number of suffixes have allomorphs containing the vowel /ü/ which occur if and only if the preceding syllable contains either /ü/ or /ö/. The effect is to produce a very striking kind of redundancy. It would seem that this might be a fruitful problem on which to test the usefulness of techniques based on communications theory in the analysis of a structural phenomenon.

As an exploratory experiment a sample of 1,000 five-syllable words was taken and the vowel sequences in each tabulated. The sequences /e i e i i/ and /e i e i e/ were each found to occur 28 times. 307 other sequences were also found, nearly half of them only once each. If we assume that this sample is adequate, the total information carried by the vowels in such words is about 7.62 binits. The theoretical average capacity of the vowels in such words would be 15.00 binits. (There are eight vowel phonemes in Turkish. If these were equally probable, the eight possible signals in any given syllable would carry 3.00 binits of information, and five syllables would carry 15.00.) The redundancy is therefore just under 50 percent. This does not seem extreme, though we have insufficient data to make comparison with other languages, and so do not really know whether such a figure is high or low.

Suppose that vowel harmony were followed rigorously throughout the word. The maximum total information carried by the vowels of five-syllable words would be 7.00 binits. (The first syllable might have any one of eight vowels. Equal probabilities would give the maximum capacity of 3.00. Each successive vowel must be either the proper one of /i ü ɨ u/ or the proper one of /e a/. Thus each successive syllable will carry only 1.00 binit maximum.) If this calculated capacity is compared with the observed capacity, it will be found that the two are rather similar. This suggests one of the following: (1) If vowel harmony even approaches the effectiveness on which we based our calculation, redundancy of other sources must be either lacking or very small. Or, (2) if other sources of redundancy make any appreciable contribution, vowel harmony must be that much less effective. The most fruitful use of the whole investigation would seem to be the possibility that more detailed examination will enable us to determine with some precision the actual source of the observed redundancy, and so to see the functional significance of vowel harmony within the total system. This would seem to be indicative of the general usefulness of the method. Probably there are few if any structural problems which can be directly analyzed by this method, but there would seem to be many instances where it will reveal the functional significance of some structural detail in the whole system of the language.

23.16   We may proceed to such a detailed analysis by calculating the redundancy in individual vowel positions, or even individual dimensions of contrast, or in various sequences of vowels. The amount of detail that must be tabulated is quite large, and its full presentation here is not feasible. The following samples may however indicate something of the possibilities:

If we examine the vowel of the first syllable only we find the following observed frequencies:

/i/	129	/ü/	61	/ɨ/	38	/u/	96	
/e/	267	/ö/	46	/a/	294	/o/	69	I = 2.63

The redundancy occasioned by disparate frequencies of the eight vowels in this position is only 12 percent, which would seem rather low. But we need not stop with that. We may note that of the vowels, 503 are front vowels and 497 are back. The redundancy here is very nearly .00. High vowels total 324, and low vowels 676, giving a redundancy of 10 percent. Unrounded vowels total 728, rounded 272, producing a redundancy of 16 percent. The largest part of the total redundancy observed in the vowels of the first syllable is therefore due to the less efficient use of the contrast rounded : unrounded, and not at all to the contrast front : back, which is used with high efficiency.

Or we may examine the vowels of each successive pair of two syllables. For example, taking the vowels of the next to the last and the last syllables we find that the total information is 3.42 binits, as against a maximum capacity of 6.00. The redundancy is 43 percent. However, 2.31 binits of information is ascribable to the fourth syllable (redundancy, 23 percent), leaving only 1.11 carried by the fifth vowel (redundancy, 63 percent). The greater part of the difference in redundancy is the effect of vowel harmony.

Numerous other calculations can be presented which would further identify the various factors which contribute to the redundancy of successive Turkish vowels. There is one difficulty common to them all: we do not have enough data from other languages to provide a basis for interpretation. Nevertheless, the calculations do seem to indicate that the method can, with further experience, provide a useful technique for interpreting linguistic structure.

23.17 In 23.13 we listed some of the sources of redundancy in a language. It is quite evident from a consideration of these that redundancy is an essential feature of a language. That is, if redundancy were eliminated, it would be at the cost of eliminating all structure, leaving an utterly unworkable code. Redundancy is a consequence of structure, and it is perhaps in this regard that linguists are most interested in it. There is, however, another rôle, quite important in some instances.

There is always a possibility that something will go wrong in the complicated process of communication. Difficulties can arise in the process of encoding or decoding. Signals can be lost in the channel, or stray signals can get into the channel and be confused with elements of the code. The latter is quite familiar in everyday spoken language. It is noise, extraneous sounds that are heard with the speech and which we cannot wholly separate from the speech. The ultimate effect of all the sources of error is the same, and communication theorists have given a technical definition to **noise** to cover them all. (This is merely another case comparable to the redefinition of information and redundancy.) **Noise** is any unpredictable interference with a communication system. "Unpredictable" is the essential item in the definition, since if noise could be known in advance, it could be eliminated.

Noise is potentially present in every communication system. Naturally, some systems have more noise than others. The amount of noise can sometimes be predicted from the characteristics of the encoder, the decoder, or the channel, and noise can be measured in a statistical way.

23.18 Noise, of course, detracts from the efficiency of a communication system. Any perfect code (one that uses the full capacity of the channel) is unusable in the presence of noise, since any noise will alter the message. The obvious way to avoid trouble is to introduce redundancy. We commonly do this by repetition, but any other method would have the same effect. An effective code must have sufficient redundancy to compensate for any noise in the system. Since a language typically has an appreciable amount of redundancy inherent in its structure, it is always possible to use it in the presence of a moderate amount of noise.

When the amount of noise is greater, more redundancy may be needed. This is a common experience. When hearing conditions are bad we commonly find it necessary to spell out proper names. (Proper names seem to have less redundancy than the average in English.) We may use the familiar names of the letters /éy bíy síy . . ./. But since these names do not have as much distinctiveness as might be wished, we may use such locutions as /bíy⁻→ æ̀zin⁺ bɔ́ʜstin/, or we may use a special set of letter names with higher redundancy /éybɨl béykər čárliy . . ./. These are merely devices to increase redundancy when the noise level is high.

23.19   Though the redundancy in language is of direct benefit to the users, it is something of a nuisance to the linguist in his analysis and description. A straightforward description of any utterance would completely bog down in attempting to state a lot of detail which, because of high redundancy, is of no significance. The basic technique of the science of linguistics is actually one of sorting out redundant and nonredundant features, so that each type can be given the treatment which is most efficient descriptively. This sorting is performed on a number of different levels and gives rise to the "allo– and –eme" principle which is so fundamental in linguistics.

We may illustrate by considering allophones and phonemes. The differences between allophones of any given phoneme are features of speech which are redundant, once both the phoneme and the environment are known. By first making certain general statements about allophones, we may thereafter eliminate this redundancy from further consideration by the device of mentioning only the phonemes.

Phonemes are not redundant at this level. They may, however, be so at some higher level, so we may again repeat the process of separating redundant from nonredundant features. For example, in Turkish vowel harmony, there is a contrast between /i ü ɨ u/ and /e a/, but none within these groups. (There is a phonemic contrast because not all vowels are subject to vowel harmony.) If we consider each group of phonemes as morphophonemically the same, perhaps setting up some special symbols such as H (high vowel) and L (low vowel), we can rewrite such a word as /göstermektedir/ 'for example' as /göstLrmLktLdHr/. Such a technique will eliminate from our transcription all the redundancy due to vowel harmony, reducing the average redundancy of vowel sequences in such words by a very considerable amount.

23.20   It is at the level of phonemicizing that the greatest amount of redundancy is removed. Complementary distribution is only a special case of redundancy. In effect we ask the question: In any given environment, which will occur, A or B? If this proves to be predictable in every environment, the redundancy of the contrast is 100 percent, and we say they are in complementary distribution. But this process of classing allophones into phonemes is only one aspect of the process. Long before this, a great deal of redundancy has been eliminated. Our first phonetic transcription groups an immense variety of sounds into relatively few groups, each of which we transcribe by a single symbol.

23.21   What is the redundancy of speech at this level? Various physical considerations suggest that the total capacity of the channel used (all frequencies of sound which the human vocal apparatus can produce and the ear hear) is of the order of magnitude of 50,000 binits per second. Considering the phonemes as the messages to be transmitted, speech uses something of the order of 50 binits per second (less if we take account of redundancy in the use of the phonemes). That is, the redundancy of speech at this level is in the neighborhood of 99.9 percent.

This would seem highly inefficient, but when we consider the noise that must be overcome it is not unreasonable. In the first place, the vocal apparatus imposes some severe limitations on the combinations of signals which can be produced. For example, there is a characteristic pitch range for every voice. To control the full 50,000 binits per second, the encoder would have to be able to use every distinguishable frequency, whether within his normal range or not, and to produce any combination of these pitches, whether they bear harmonic relationships to each other or not. In the second place, speech must operate under a wide variety of conditions. Reverberation, resonances in the environment, and numerous other factors all contribute to modify speech sounds. That is, even in what we call "quiet," there are considerable possibilities of what the engineer calls "noise." To convey the full 50,000 binits per second, all these environmental factors would have to be controlled. In the third place, speech must be possible for all members of the community. The smaller and differently shaped vocal tract of a child cannot produce exactly the same sounds as those of an adult. We must learn to switch codes and to identify as /i/ or /s/, or whatever, the vastly different sounds produced by a small child, an adult, a person with laryngitis, or one out of breath from exertion. Moreover, we must be able to do this in a quiet room, in a noisy room, in the open spaces, or wherever we meet others. The miracle is that we can do this at all. Only the very high redundancy of speech at the sub-phonemic level makes this possible.

Variation in Speech

24.1   One of the most evident facts about speech is its variability. If a large body of utterances in a given language is examined, it will be found that no two of them are identical — certainly not if sufficiently refined methods of measurement are used in observing them. Before any description of speech can be made it is necessary to bring some sort of order into the data. This can be done only by concentrating attention on some particular type of variation to the exclusion of all others. Since there are many different aspects which may be selected for study, there are several different methods of approach to a systematic description of language. Each of these is supplemental to all the others; no one can be completely understood without some acquaintance with the others.

24.2   Faced with a large body of utterances in a given language, the descriptive linguist starts by selecting a sample of the data for special study. This he does in a characteristic way, which necessarily predetermines the type of results he will obtain. He may attempt to eliminate certain types of variation of minor interest to him by restricting his attention as far as possible to utterances produced by one speaker under a single set of circumstances. Within this narrowed corpus he seeks out expressions which differ minimally in content and expression. By comparing these he determines the minimal differences in the expression which are associated in any constant way with differences in the content.

By this means he discovers two sets of elements out of which the expression structure of the language is elaborated, the phonemes and the morphemes. When, either through necessity or choice, he does enlarge his data by examining utterances of other speakers or other circumstances, he does so in such a way as to divert his attention as little as possible from these minimal contrastive elements and their combinations.

24.3   Another quite valid, but basically very different, approach would be to sort out from the total mass all those sets of utterances which are alike in content. This will eliminate one of the variables with which the descriptive linguist is concerned. Within each set, these utterances can then be compared and the variation studied. This may be done by seeking correlations with non-linguistic factors, commonly the speaker and the circumstances. Obviously, the results are predestined to be fundamentally different from those which the descriptive linguist will attain, since the variation under examination is precisely that which the descriptivist will attempt to eliminate.

For example, suppose we were to sort out a large number of English utterances which we identify in some manner as being *I'm going home*. These will vary among themselves in the general level of pitch, in the speed of utterance, in the degree of nasality, and in a number of other features which the descriptivist would disregard, since he does not find them to be phonemic. They will also differ in certain phonemic features. Some samples will include /hówm/, others /hóm/, still others /háwm/. Both /gôwiŋ/ and /gôwin/ and several other variants will be found. Other parts of the utterance will show other comparable contrasts. The problem is to reduce these variations, both phonemic and sub-phonemic, to order. The objective is an empirical description of the range and significance of variation in English utterances that are in some way equivalent. Beyond that, we would like to make some generalizations about linguistic variation as a characteristic feature of language. Here is the basis for a second type of linguistic science. Since most workers have restricted their attention to single aspects of the problem, we lack a general term for the discipline as a whole.

24.4   Variation can best be systematized by correlation. One possibility would be to determine, for example, whether there is any correlation in our sample of utterances between /gôwin/

(rather than /gôwiŋ/) and /hɔ́wm/ (rather than /hówm/). I do not know what the answer would prove to be, nor has this approach been attractive to workers in the field. Another possibility would be to seek correlations with known facts outside language.

Experience has shown that there are certain categories of such facts which are particularly useful in the study of speech: the social context of the specific utterance, the social position of the speaker, the geographical origin of the speaker, and the age of the speaker. Each of these provides a useful body of generalizations. Moreover, each of these correlations is of sufficient general interest that a body of prescientific folklore has arisen. In addition, there is variation which correlates with the individual identity of the speaker, a fact which is also well known and socially significant. Specific scientific study has, however, not been generally profitable, except in regard to "speech defects" (individual peculiarities of a type which are a social handicap). Beyond this there is a residue of variation which seems entirely random (not correlated with any known factor). This is the fraction of the data which is of no interest in the present problem, as linguistically unconditioned subphonemic variation is of no interest to the descriptivist. It may, of course, be of interest in some other approach; for example, it could well be that some of this variation is correlatable with atmospheric conditions — pressure, humidity, temperature, etc. — in which case it might well be of great interest to an acoustic physicist.

24.5 It is characteristic of descriptive linguistics that the data is handled in a specific way. Typically, a given segment either is or is not a given phoneme. When, as in the case of English /č/, there is a delicate balance of evidence for the interpretation either as /č/ or as */tš/, we do not make a statistical statement. Instead, descriptive linguists unequivocally treat it either as a unit phoneme or as a cluster. Descriptive linguistics is an either-or proposition, and its methods are applied only where the data can be so quantified.

By contrast, the study of other types of variation in speech is thoroughly statistical in its requirements. Much of the data is observed in terms of continuous variation, as when we make observations on the degree of aspiration in stops, on the pitch of the voice or the duration of an utterance, or the like. This must be correlated with non-linguistic facts which are also subject to continuous variation. There are in many cultures no sharp delimitations of social classes, but gradations of classes. There is no discrete territorial organization into dialect areas, but a geographical continuum. The vast majority of the data is subject to continuous variation and can be prepared for analysis only by statistical procedures.

The method of correlation which we must employ is statistical in nature. Moreover, the statistical methods which are needed are often complex. With a large number of factors to be considered, all of which operate on the same material, speech, it is not surprising that the isolation of individual factors and the assessment of their effects is no simple procedure.

It is this difference in basic method, more than anything else, which makes publications from this division of linguistics seem so utterly different from those in descriptive linguistics. The difference is not superficial or incidental; it is the result of fundamental differences in the data under examination.

24.6   Basic to all the problems of language variation is the complex process of linguistic change. This is no single entity, but the cumulative effect of a number of quite different processes operating more or less independently. We will discuss only four of them: phonetic change, phonemic change, analogic change, and borrowing.

24.7   Phonetic change may perhaps best be described in the form of a specific and more or less artificial example. Consider a language in which there are two phonemes: /t/ which is fortis, and /d/ which is lenis. A lenis stop is one in which the contact of the lower articulator (here the tongue) against the upper articulator is RELATIVELY weak. If the strength of articulation of a long series of apical stops is measured, we may expect to obtain a frequency distribution something like the following:

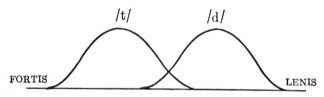

(It is not unusual for the distribution curves to overlap. Redundancy, operating at various levels, will preserve the workability of the system, provided the overlap does not get too large.)

A given speaker maintains this distribution by **monitoring** his own speech. That is, he compares the sounds he hears himself produce against a set of norms. This is actually his own crude intuitive statistical summary of his past experiences with the sounds of the language. Now suppose some unknown factor (or at least one outside our range of study) causes some of the speakers in this community to average slightly more lenis in their pronunciation of /d/. These more lenis pronunciations will figure in the total experience from which the norm is determined. The normal range of variation of /d/ will shift slightly in the direction of more lenis pronunciation. If this continues, /d/ may become so lenis that it is frequently incompletely closed, that is, a fricative [ð] instead of a stop [d]. The shift may continue until [ð] is much the commoner pronunciation.

What we have just described is a phonetic, not a phonemic, change. /d/ still continues to contrast with /t/, just as before. Phonetically it has shifted from a stop to a fricative, but unless something else has also happened to change the patterns of contrast, there is no change in the phonemic status.

24.8 There are two important characteristics of such a change that require comment. In the first place, what is shifting is not the pronunciation of a specific sound in a specific place, say a certain word. If it were, we might expect the same sound to change in a different way in some other place. Instead, the shift affects the statistical norm based on all occurrences of the given phoneme in a given environment — that is, on all occurrences of a certain allophone. In turn this norm controls the pronunciation of this allophone whenever it occurs. Phonetic change, therefore, affects allophones as wholes. Within the understanding that the effect is statistical, phonetic change affects any given allophone consistently. This is commonly expressed by saying that PHONETIC CHANGE IS REGULAR. This means that any phonetic change will affect all instances of the sound concerned in the positions in which it is operative. The same phonetic change may affect all the allophones of a given phoneme, or only a single allophone.

The second significant characteristic is that PHONETIC CHANGE IS A SOCIAL PHENOMENON. The statistical norm which controls the pronunciation of each allophone is not based on one person's pronunciation, but to some extent on the speech of every individual whom the speaker hears. Not all of them will have an equal effect on the norm. In general, speakers of higher prestige will exert more influence than those of lower. The frequency of contact will also be very important. Thus, phonetic changes within the speech of any intimate group are very likely to be shared. When contact is less intimate, greater differences in the rate or even the direction of change can be expected.

24.9 To continue the example of 24.7: Suppose that the shift from stop to fricative pronunciation of /d/ affected only /d/ between vowels. At the end of the process described, we will have three phonetic ranges:

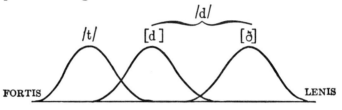

There are, however, still only two phonemes, since [d] and [ð] are allophones in complementary distribution. Now suppose that through some other process, which has been going on concurrently, some of the vowels disappear. The result might be:

/VdVCV/ [VðVCV] becomes [VðCV]
/VdCV/ [VdCV] becomes [VdCV]

[d] and [ð] are now in contrast, hence separate phonemes /d/ and /ð/. Phonetic change has led to **phonemic change.** In this instance, as is the most common case, phonemic change is not produced by a phonetic change affecting the changing phoneme, but by the change of some factor which conditions allophones. With this change, new patterns of contrast arise, and the allophones become phonemes.

We may give an example from English. At one time English had a phoneme /n/ with allophones [ŋ] before /k/ or /g/ and [n] elsewhere. Thus *sing* was something like /síng/ [síŋg]. Then under certain conditions final /g/ dropped. [síŋg] thus changed to [síŋ], and so came to contrast with *sin* [sín]. This raised [ŋ] to the status of a phoneme /ŋ/, but also left /ŋ/ with a rather peculiar distribution; mainly it occurs in those places where /g/ dropped, or where it is followed by /k/, or in a few places where it has appeared by other changes.

Since phonemic change is generally the cumulative result of a series of phonetic changes, it is also regular. That is, whenever the proper conditions obtain, PHONEMIC CHANGE OCCURS WITHOUT EXCEPTION.

24.10 Analogic change is very different in its mechanism and effect. The process is a familiar one. Let us take an example. Suppose that a speaker does not recall the plural of *mouse*, and following the prevailing pattern in English says /máwsiz/. The chances are that this will not be copied, and hence will not contribute to a permanent change in the language. But if various factors combine in the right way, the outcome might be different and /máwsiz/ might establish itself as the regular plural of *mouse*.

The noticeable fact about this kind of change is that each individual change stands or falls on its own merits. There is no reason to expect that, if this change should establish itself, *louse* would follow the same analogy. The plural might continue to be /láys/, or change to /láwziz/ on the analogy of *houses*, or some more obscure analogy might become the pattern. ANALOGIC CHANGE IS NOT REGULAR. It may, and frequently does, produce an increase in irregularity, but it may equally exert a regularizing effect.

24.11 Borrowing is just what its name implies — the copying of a linguistic item from speakers of another speech form. The most evident instances are those in which the two forms of speech are quite different. The loan words sometimes preserve characteristics by which their foreign origin can be readily discerned, as in the case of *bwana*, a recent introduction to American English whose Swahili origin is marked by the peculiar initial cluster /bw/. In other cases loan words are made to conform more closely to the phonologic or morphologic patterns of the language, but such cases can usually be easily identified by tracing their etymology. The commonest case, however, is that of loan words in one dialect taken from another closely related dialect. These instances may be very difficult to identify, often appearing as minor exceptions to otherwise regular phonemic changes. Just as with analogic changes, borrowing is a more or less random and unsystematic process. Individual items are involved, seldom definable groups of words.

24.12   With these four types of linguistic change in mind, we can now examine briefly some of the features of linguistic variation. The most spectacular and best known is that between geographical forms of speech. When the differences are small, these are known as **dialects.** When larger, they are known as **languages.** However, no exact definition of these two terms is feasible. They have for so long been used in widely varying meanings that it is nearly hopeless to impose any uniformity on their usage, even if some suitable criterion could be found.

The process of dialect formation can best be understood if we hypothecate a socially homogeneous population with only local mobility and speaking at the start a more or less uniform language. (Needless to say, such a situation is a highly hypothetical one!) Now consider what will happen if some conspicuous phonetic change gets underway at some one spot in the territory. As we have noticed, phonetic change is a social affair. It will be shared with any speaker with whom intimate contacts are maintained, and there is considerable probability of its being shared to some extent by speakers with whom contacts are more casual. Either the innovation will spread into areas surrounding the center of origin, or the influence of the speech of the surrounding areas will lead to its suppression. If it is successful in spreading, we should expect the change to have proceeded farthest in the center of origin. Away from the center the change should become less and less conspicuous. There would, however, be a gradual lessening of its influence, rather than any abrupt ending. We can make an analogy as follows: Consider a flexible membrane, perhaps of rubber, stretched across a frame. Then consider a body pushing against the membrane at some point. The membrane is not torn, but it is displaced from its original position by an amount that decreases as you move away from the center of disturbance. In the figure on page 399 we give diagrams indicating the situations at two successive stages of this process. We can map the effect by noting the points at which a certain degree of change has been attained. A line indicating the limit of some stated degree of linguistic change is known as an **isogloss.** As the process of change continues, the isogloss would seem to move outward, away from

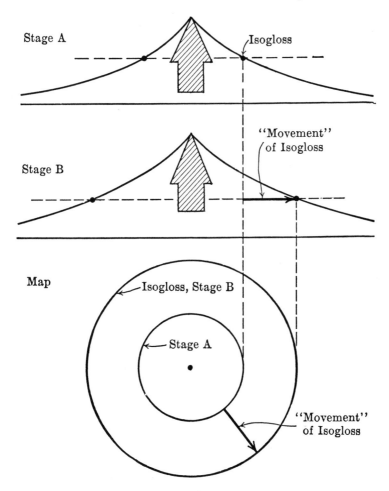

the center of innovation. On the diagram, we have indicated the position of the isogloss at each of the two stages, together with its apparent movement.

24.13 A linguistic change in a more or less homogeneous population can be most easily described in terms of the appearance and movement of isoglosses across a map. These isoglosses are, of course, statistical abstractions which cannot be directly observed. The precision of our analogy, or of the diagrams accompanying it, is never found. When such a line is drawn, it merely indicates the compiler's conclusion from the data at hand that within the line one pronunciation is commoner, and outside, another. As a change spreads, there are always some speakers who maintain the old form longer than their neighbors. There may be individuals outside the area which we limit by an isogloss who have adopted the new feature ahead of their neighbors.

An isogloss is a representation of statistical probabilities. As such it is a convenient means of description, but may be misleading if the apparent sharpness of distinction between the areas is not carefully discounted. The drawing of isoglosses is one of many places where it is easy to be over-precise. The reading of them is even more dangerous, since the reader has not seen the intricate mass of data upon which they are based.

24.14 We can add one bit of realism to the picture just drawn by suggesting that the **density of communication** is not everywhere the same. Suppose for example that the language area is bisected by a barrier of some sort — perhaps a large river, a mountain range, or a major political boundary. As a result, there is less communication between people across the barrier than on either side. Barriers are seldom absolute, however, so that there is typically some communication. Now consider some innovation spreading from person to person as they communicate with each other. The effect may be pictured in terms of an isogloss moving across the territory. When this isogloss reaches the region of low density of communication (the barrier), its progress will be retarded. We may expect it to take considerably longer for the isogloss to cross the barrier than to traverse an equal distance elsewhere.

If instead of one isogloss there are a number of them moving across the area at the same time, we may expect that they will all tend to be retarded at the barrier and hence pile up. The result is what is sometimes referred to as a **bundle** or **fascicle** of isoglosses. The history of the individual isoglosses in such a bundle may be quite different. Some may have been arrested in approximately their present position for a long time; others may have just arrived. Some may even be in process of comparatively rapid transition across the barrier. Some may be moving in one direction, and some in the other. Often it is impossible to trace all the factors which account for the particular assortment of isoglosses observed at one place. Nevertheless, any geographical area of low density of communication is likely to be marked by such a bundle of isoglosses.

24.15 Since the presence of an isogloss is a graphic way of portraying a transition in speech characteristics from one area to another, a bundle of isoglosses may be interpreted as marking a zone of relatively great transition in speech. We may, therefore, think of it as indicating a **dialect boundary.** Such a boundary is rarely, if ever, sharply abrupt. In the first place, the individual isoglosses represent transitions that are seldom other than gradual; commonly there are quite clear exceptions on either or both sides of the line. In the second place, the various isoglosses in any bundle seldom coincide exactly. As you pass from one dialect area to another, you will commonly observe the appearance of one new feature after another. There is almost never any one place at which one dialect gives way suddenly to another, and which would show on a map as the coincidence of a number of isoglosses of major importance.

Not infrequently a bundle of isoglosses will run along rather close together for a distance and then fan out. The classic case is that of a bundle of isoglosses running across Germany separating the "northern" dialects from the "High German" dialects. For most of the distance the boundary is quite sharp. That is, the isoglosses by which the dialectal differences can be described run rather close together, though they do cross and recross each other in an intricate tangle. But as they approach the Rhine Valley, the various lines separate. Some continue about the same trend, others turn southward, and still others northward. That is to say, in the Rhine Valley the boundary is much less sharp than it is to the East.

24.16   A typical instance of a dialect boundary of the sort that we might expect from the description above runs across Virginia along the Blue Ridge Mountains. From the Potomac to the Roanoke, the Blue Ridge is a relatively narrow and sharply defined range rising up suddenly from the Piedmont on one side and the Shenandoah Valley on the other. Crossings are relatively few, and none are particularly easy. The higher ridges are unoccupied, and are now largely national park. Particularly prior to the development of modern transportation, the two halves of the state lived rather separately from one another. It is, therefore, not surprising that a major dialect boundary should lie here, separating the Midland group of dialects from the Southern group.

However, the physical boundary is not the whole basis for distinction, as there are other physical boundaries which are just as effective in restricting communication but are of less linguistic significance. The Appalachian Ridges to the west of the Shenandoah Valley are a case in point. Moreover, some major dialect boundaries have no obvious physical basis. An example of the latter type is the boundary running east and west across the middle of Ohio, Indiana, and Illinois, and which may be conveniently

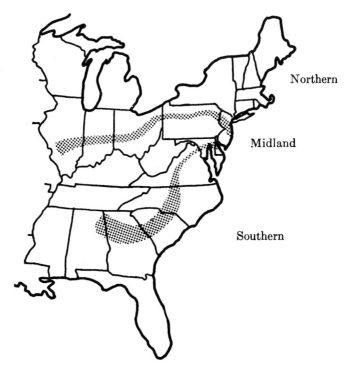

Northern

Midland

Southern

Major Dialect Areas in the Eastern United States

(The westward extent of these areas is not yet known.)

described as approximately following U.S. Highway 40. While not as sharp as the boundary along the Blue Ridge, it is quite evident, and the speech difference between the northern and southern parts of these states is quite marked. The basis for this boundary is of quite a different sort, since there is no important physical barrier.

There are three major dialect areas in the eastern United States. They developed out of the three major centers of settlement on the Eastern seaboard. The westward expansion carried New Eng-

landers across the northern Middle West. Pennsylvanians crossed
the mountains into the southern Middle West and followed the
valleys southwestward into the Appalachian Highlands. The
Southern Coastal settlements spread inland to the mountains and
southward along the Piedmont into the Gulf States. The result is
the three major dialect areas approximately delineated on the
map on page 402. While this is greatly oversimplified (for example, Southern elements are quite as prominent as Pennsylvanian
in much of the Midland), it does serve to indicate that historical
factors are often of major importance. In the United States, one of
the chief means of movement of isoglosses has been the movement
of the people themselves.

24.17 Because of the complexities of topography, settlement
history, interregional communication, and prestige of regional
centers, dialect boundaries are often vague, complex, and difficult
to delimit. Dialects are seldom subject to the neat classification
which we might desire, and which the layman sometimes imposes
upon them. For example, American folk-linguistics recognizes two
major dialect areas, "Southern" and "Northern." But there is no
discernible linguistic division at or near the Mason-Dixon line.
"Southern" dialects are exceedingly diverse. The sharpest dialect
boundary in the United States runs directly through the South
roughly along the Blue Ridge mountains. A "Northern dialect"
is as much a fiction as a "Southern dialect." There are greater
similarities of speech between southern Indiana and the Blue Ridge
of Virginia than between the former and northern Indiana or the
latter and eastern Virginia.

It would be nearly as fallacious to speak of three dialects,
Northern, Midland, and Southern, unless it is understood that each
of these is more properly a group of dialects, and that the boundaries between the major areas vary from rather sharp in a few
localities (such as the Virginia Blue Ridge) to very indistinct and
gradual.

24.18 If we examine the difference between any two dialects,
preferably separated by quite a distance, we find that they are of
two kinds. Some are quite regular in the sense that they are repeated over and over and may be observed almost universally in
all words of a certain kind. These are largely phonetic and phonemic differences. For example, those words pronounced with /aw/

in New England and upper Middle Western dialects are mostly pronounced with /æw/ in certain dialects of the coastal South. The same items are pronounced either with /əw/ or /aw/ in eastern Canada. The latter variation is not capricious; /əw/ occurs generally before voiceless sounds, /aw/ before voiced.

An example of a phonetic difference is the pronunciation of /ð/ used by some speakers in the Metropolitan New York area. This is a dental stop, rather than a dental fricative. Because it is dental rather than alveolar it contrasts with /d/, so there is no phonemic difference at this point between this form of speech and that found elsewhere. Non-New Yorkers, however, commonly misinterpret such a /ð/ as a /d/, since the phonetic basis of the contrast is quite different in their speech.

24.19 Since analogic changes are independent of each other, dialectal differences of this origin cannot be expected to show any great regularity. For example, the past tense *holp* /hówp/ for the verb *help* is now widespread only in the South and the southern Midland. It represents the older form; *helped* /hélpt/ has replaced it by analogic change in most other dialects. By contrast, the analogic formation *knowed* /nówd/ is much more common in the South, though found sporadically throughout the East. Another new analogic formation, *drinked*, is found rather commonly in northern New England, in the Chesapeake Bay region, in the Carolinas, and occasionally through the remainder of the East.

It is, thus, not possible to make such generalizations as can be made with phonetic and phonemic differences. A familiar notion of American folk-linguistics is that the Southern highlanders speak "pure Elizabethan English." This is manifestly untrue. They do have a number of conservative traits of language, as for example *holp* (which they share with many lowland Southerners), but these are counterbalanced by many innovations not found outside the area, as well as by innovations that they share with other regions. "Pure Elizabethan English" became extinct with the Elizabethans, but its elements persist, mixed with various innovations, in ALL English dialects. There is no reason to expect a significantly different proportion of such survivals in the Southern highlands than would be found elsewhere, but the assortment of features which have persisted may be expected to be rather different from one area to the next.

24.20 Another complication in any neat picture of geographic dialects arises from the fact that the people in one community do not all speak alike. In a culture such as ours, in which there is a measure of class distinction, the most obvious difference is likely to be that between classes. Not infrequently there is more difference between upper- or middle-class speakers in one community and the lower-class speakers of the same community, than there is between the upper- or middle-class speakers of two rather distant communities. For example, *holp* /hówp/, though quite widespread throughout the South, is seldom used by the educated, urbanized middle class. They say *helped* /hélpt/, much as would a New Englander of the same class, and they tend to look on /hówp/ as rustic or ungrammatical. It is therefore not possible to speak of /hówp/ as a Southern expression without some qualification.

In any given area, it is possible to recognize and describe a system of **social dialects.** These cannot be expected to be clearly distinct from one another, but the concept is in general a useful one. As a general scheme, three such are commonly listed: cultivated speech, common speech, and folk speech. **Cultivated speech** is characteristic of educated, urbanized, and generally middle- or upper-class people. It is that which is taught, with various degrees of success, in the schools; it is used on the radio and generally carries high prestige. **Folk speech** is characteristic of isolated rural people and is fast disappearing in many areas. **Common speech** is merely a convenient label for the greater part of the range of intergradation between the other two.

In general, geographical dialectal differences are most pronounced in folk speech, and least pronounced in cultivated speech. Nevertheless, there are regional variations even in the latter. In the Southern mountains, certain Midland locutions which are not greatly different from cultivated speech farther north are condemned because they do not conform to a cultivated speech standard largely based on lowland Southern patterns. Certain characteristics of this Southern cultivated speech would be similarly condemned in other regions. While cultivated speech is more uniform than folk speech, the standards that prevail in various parts of the United States are different and occasionally contradictory.

24.21 Possibly as a result of differences of social dialect, there are also differences in **levels of speech.** By this we mean that a single speaker, without departing from the conventions usual in his area, speaks differently in different social situations. Different vocabulary, constructions, and even pronunciations are used in formal address and in familiar conversation. Such differences are found in the speech of all Americans. Probably they are somewhat less conspicuous with speakers of folk speech than with those who use cultivated speech (with the exception of a few of the latter who use a formal style in all circumstances and thereby appear affected).

In general, formal speech tends to approach cultivated speech more closely; informal speech tends to conform more to folk usages. Particularly in the case of educated and urbanized speakers, the most conspicuous difference may be greater conformity to written usage in the case of formal style.

24.22 No discussion of dialectal differences, however brief, should omit some mention of **eye dialects** and special dramatic dialects. By the former we designate certain quite conventional spellings which are used in written literature to indicate that the speaker is using folk speech. These include such items as *hoss* for *horse, massa* for *master, sez* for *says, wuz* for *was,* etc. Some of these represent, not always very well, actual differences in pronunciation between folk speech and cultivated speech, or between different geographical dialects. A surprising number of them, including *sez* and *wuz,* have no such basis at all. /sez/ and /wəz/ are the common pronunciations of both words in all American speech, folk and cultivated. The use of these spellings to indicate folk speech is therefore purely conventional. Eye dialect is not, therefore, to be considered as an actual portrayal of folk or regional speech so much as a stylized literary device to signal that folk speech is intended. It may also be interpreted as evidence on the linguistic folklore of Americans, and it indicates how unrealistic, and often prejudiced, our linguistic notions generally are.

Much the same can be said about dramatic renditions of dialects. While some actors are excellent mimics and know some dialects thoroughly, most use an artificial and conventional stage dialect; no Irishman speaks like the typical stage or radio "Irishman." Increased public sensitivity has cut down some of the crudities of representation of certain ethnic and national minorities. But the characterizations of "country rubes" are in general a most marvelous garbling of discordant elements from various folk dialects and from no identifiable source.

Both these phenomena are evidence of a tremendous popular interest in speech variation. Probably no other aspect of linguistics has so great a popular appeal in this country. It is unfortunate that the general public should be misinformed on most aspects. What is needed is a more intelligent and appreciative attitude toward dialect, speech levels, and individual speech characteristics.

25

Writing Systems

25.1 Written communication must be sharply distinguished from spoken. The common tendency to use "language" to refer to either indiscriminately has so frequently given rise to serious confusion, not merely among lay people, but also among professional linguists, that many are reluctant to use it of any written code at all, even with explicit qualification. Many linguists consider all forms of writing entirely outside the domain of linguistics and would restrict the discipline to the consideration of spoken language only.

Nevertheless, the relationships between speech and writing are close and intimate. Many of the same methods of study can be used in dealing with both, and the structures revealed are in many respects similar. But if both are to be treated within the framework of a single discipline, it is essential that they be clearly distinguished at all times. The term **language,** when used in any linguistic context without qualification, should be reserved exclusively for vocal language, that is, for communication by means of speech. The qualified term, **written language,** will be used here, in default of any other unambiguous term, for a total system of communication based on writing.

25.2 A written language includes as one level of its structure a **writing system.** This term will refer to a system of conventions in the use of certain symbols as the basic signals in a code known as a **written language.** For example, the conventions of English spelling, conceived as patterns of uses of the familiar letters of the alphabet, are a part of the English writing system. In the same way, the somewhat different conventions of Dutch spelling constitute another writing system, though the alphabet used in both is the same. The difference in writing systems is apparent in the evident non-English appearance of such words as *zijn, haar, nieuwe*, etc. They contain sequences of letters which are unusual or quite strange to the English writing system.

25.3 Not only does a writing system have its own structure which can be studied, but there is also a set of conventions of relationship between the writing system and certain structures (commonly phonologic) in an associated spoken language. These also require discussion, but it is essential to avoid confusing these relationships with the conventions internal to either code. We refer to these relationships between structures in written languages and structures in spoken languages as **fit.** This chapter will be concerned with writing systems and the fit between them and the spoken languages.

25.4 A writing system consists of a set of **graphemes** plus certain characteristic features of their use. Each grapheme may have one or more **allographs.** The graphemes and allographs have a place in the writing system comparable to that of the phonemes and allophones in the phonology, and the relationship of graphemes to allographs is comparable to that between phonemes and allophones.

A convenient example may be drawn from the familiar form of written Greek. As used in modern printed books there are two forms of the letter sigma. At the ends of words it is written **s** elsewhere σ. These two symbols are in complementary distribution and have a similar reference to the phonology of spoken Greek. They are therefore considered as allographs of a single grapheme, $\langle \sigma \rangle$. (Graphemes may be indicated by a notation included in $\langle \; \rangle$. This is comparable to the notation / / and { } for other fundamental structural units.) A series of minimal and subminimal pairs will easily establish the graphemic contrast between σ and most other symbols in the system. The process is basically the same as that by which the phonemes of a spoken language are established, and most of the same problems arise.

For example, only $\varsigma\nu\rho\kappa\chi\xi\psi\iota\epsilon\eta\alpha\omega\upsilon$ occur at the ends of words. (That is, before space; in a discussion of writing systems, **word** has the quite specific meaning of a portion of text marked off by space or comparable markers, and does not give rise to the difficulties which are seen in spoken languages.) s is therefore in complementary distribution not only with σ, but equally with ten other symbols, $\beta\gamma\delta\zeta\theta\lambda\mu\pi\tau\varphi$. An analyst must, therefore, make the decision with which of these to class s. This is obvious to anyone who knows the Greek alphabet, but largely because his first introduction to σ and s was as alternative forms of a single letter with a single name, sigma. An independent decision would have to be based on the fit of written to spoken Greek, internal structure of the graphemic system, and changes of graphemes in combination — in much the same way that comparable phonemic problems might be solved in the light of phonetics, phonemic structuring, and morphophonemics.

The Greek writing system also makes use of the symbol Σ. This shows special relationships to σ, exactly comparable to those existing between A : a, B : β, ... It will be found best to treat Σ as consisting of two graphemes $\langle\sigma\rangle$ and $\langle\equiv\rangle$ (capitalization) and all the others in the same way. This is analogous to the way to which pitch and vowel quality are commonly separated in a phonemic analysis of a spoken language. That is, capitalization is in many ways comparable to a "suprasegmental" phoneme.

25.5   Typically (and as a first approximation for our discussion), each grapheme represents some portion of the structure of the associated or underlying spoken language. The latter is the **reference** of the grapheme. Since the spoken language expression consists of two major structural systems, there are two major types of graphemes from the point of view of their references.

The most familiar type of grapheme is that with a **phonemic reference**. The three letters in *box* represent English graphemes of various subtypes of this type. The reference of b here and of $\langle b\rangle$ generally is /b/. There is some, but relatively little, variation. The reference of x here is /ks/, a sequence of phonemes. A phonemic reference need not be a single phoneme, but can be any phonologically definable structure. The reference of o in this instance is /a/ (in some dialects /ɔ/), but the grapheme $\langle o\rangle$ has a very considerable number of references, including commonly /ow/, /a/, /ə/, /ɔ/, etc. The reference of a grapheme may be single-valued or multi-valued. These complexities are merely instances of the intricate fit which exists between the English writing system and English phonology. Yet in spite of the complexities, the references of most of the graphemes are basically phonemic. In Swahili the spelling *ng* refers to /ŋg/, whereas *ng'* refers to /ŋ/. ⟨'⟩ has a phonemic reference, though of a peculiar sort, since it marks the absence, not the presence, of a phoneme /g/.

25.6   A second type of grapheme has a **morphemic reference.** This is the case with English *&*. The reference is typically to the morpheme {and}; not, it is important to note, a sequence of phonemes /ænd/. Two lines of evidence present themselves. First, *&* may be read /ænd/ /ən/, /iŋ/, or as any other of the numerous allomorphs of {and}, and in no other way (if we overlook the infrequent case where it is read /et/ — another morpheme — in the special context *&c.*) Second, if *&* represented a sequence of phonemes, then spellings such as **s&* for *sand*, **h&* for *hand* and **&rew* for *Andrew* would be possible. But no such spellings occur. (Note: The argument is not that **s&* would occur, but that spellings of this sort could occur. English spelling is sufficiently arbitrary that we cannot base anything on the non-occurrence of any specific possible spelling.)

Another somewhat different instance of an English grapheme with morphemic reference is English ' in *boys'*. The apostrophe here indicates the presence of a morpheme which consists of a phonemic Ø. In *boy's*, ' also has a morphemic reference since it serves to mark the morpheme {-Z₂}, here spelled –'s, as distinct from {-Z₁}, which would be spelled –s in this context. *Boys, boy's,* and *boys'* are phonemically identical, but morphemically distinct. Therefore, any graphic difference must be considered as having a morphemic reference.

25.7   Graphemes with morphemic reference are commonly called **ideograms.** These are defined as representing an IDEA, and this definition is often interpreted as implying that they have no direct connection with spoken expression. A possible more precise use of the term ideogram would be to label graphemes with markedly multi-valued morphemic reference in distinction from those with more nearly single-valued reference. + may be taken as an example approximating this in English, since it can be read *plus, and, more,* etc. All these are phonemically and morphemically quite different, but have some contact on the content plane. The reference of + might be taken to be the common content in *plus, and, more,* etc. But to do so is probably unnecessary. Instead, + differs from & only in having a greater variety of MORPHEMIC references; that is, + has a multi-valued morphemic reference; that of & is nearly single-valued.

25.8 Chinese is the typical example of a writing system which is alleged to be ideographic. If this implies any lack of precision in the reference of the characters, it is not ideographic. The majority of the graphemes (of which there are necessarily a very large number) have unambiguous morphemic references. In any given dialect of Chinese, any given symbol will be consistently read in the same way — that is, morphemically the same: there may be allomorphic variations.

The Chinese writing system is generally assumed to have developed from pictorial representations. Some of the signs probably went through a stage of rather loosely defined reference to content rather than expression before each became tied to some specific morpheme. Nevertheless, the Chinese writing system seems to have had basically morphemic reference since its beginning as a SYSTEM. (A rebus is not a writing system, but a puzzle. As long as the Chinese characters were merely rather vaguely defined pictorial representations, they were not a writing system, but something more nearly comparable to a rebus.) In expanding the stock of characters to the present stage where there is a grapheme for almost every morpheme, recourse was had to ideographic and phonologic devices. Popular discussions of Chinese writing systems for Westerners commonly dwell upon these. They do make an interesting presentation. But the ultimate result was a system of graphemes, each of which (with unimportant exceptions) has a specific morpheme as its reference. That some of the graphemes are compound in origin is evident, but more of historic interest than of structural significance. (For that matter, *w*, called /dớbilyùw/, is obviously compound in origin, but that does not have appreciable effect on its structural significance in the English writing system.)

25.9 The peculiar nature of the Chinese writing system has so affected thinking about the language as to deserve a somewhat parenthetical digression. Many Chinese morphemes consist of a single syllable. Since they are represented in writing by a single grapheme, it early came to be the convention to consider each character as representing a syllable, and vice versa. As a result, two-syllable morphemes were written by two-character graphemes, and these were in turn interpreted as representing two separate vocabulary items. Since, moreover, each character in a text is written separate from all others, and no groups of closely associated characters are set off by spaces from other such groups, it became traditional to equate the characters with those portions of the text which are written separately in European languages. As a result each Chinese character is commonly said to represent a "word." Hence there has arisen the legend that Chinese is "monosyllabic," that is, that each word consists of a single syllable. Nothing is farther from the truth. There are numerous instances of so-called "words" which never occur except with some other specific "word." For example 珊 occurs only with 瑚, and vice versa. The combination 珊瑚 means 'coral' and is read *shanhu*. If neither occurs without the other, there can be no basis for separating them in any analysis of either the spoken or the written language, except of course on the a priori assumption: character = syllable = word. The two individual syllables are neither words nor morphemes, and the two characters are not separately graphemes. Instead there is one grapheme, traditionally written as two characters, and its reference is one two-syllable morpheme. The confusion, and this is merely the beginning of it, arises largely from a failure to keep spoken and written Chinese clearly apart as distinct, though related, codes.

25.10   Writing systems such as that of Chinese, where the majority of the graphemes have morphemic references, are comparatively few in number. More often the graphemes typically have references within the phonologic system of the spoken language. Individual graphemes can stand for individual phonemes, or for sequences of phonemes. When the former is the case predominantly, the system is called **alphabetic writing.** In the latter case the references are usually definable types of sequences which may be called syllables, and the system is a type of **syllabic writing.** The total list of such graphemes is called a **syllabary,** this term taking the place of the familiar "alphabet."

In speaking of syllabic writing systems, the term **syllable** is used

in a specific technical sense as that portion of the stream of phonemes in speech to which a grapheme has reference. It is usually
definable for any given language and writing system. Most commonly each syllable consists of one vowel and all preceding consonants. The division into syllables for the purpose of the writing
system may be largely independent of any division which might be
suggested by any direct examination of the spoken language. That
is, from the point of view of the phonology, it may be wholly or
largely an arbitrary division.

25.11   One of the best examples of a syllabic writing system is
that used for some time in writing the Cherokee language. It was
invented in 1821 by Sequoya, for whom quite deservedly the giant
trees of the Pacific coast were named. It proved to be of great usefulness to the Cherokee people for many years. The table gives
the signs used together with a conventional romanization. The

D	a	R	e	T	i	ᐁ	o	O	u	i	ʌ
f	ga	Ꮭ	ge	Y	gi	A	go	J	gu	E	gʌ
OᏏ	ha	ᒎ	he	A	hi	F	ho	Γ	hu	Ꮮ	hʌ
W	la	Ꭶ	le	P	li	G	lo	M	lu	Ꮀ	lʌ
Ꮤ	ma	OI	me	H	mi	3	mo	Ꭹ	mu		
θ	na	Ꮎ	ne	Ꮒ	ni	Z	no	Ꭸ	nu	Oᕀ	nʌ
I	gwa	Ꮂ	gwe	Ꮁ	gwi	ᏍᎵ	gwo	Ꭻ	gwu	Ɛ	gwʌ
ᕼ	sa	4	se	b	si	Φ	so	Ꭷ	su	R	sʌ
Ꮭ	da	Ꮛ	de	Ꮧ	di	Λ	do	S	du	Oᑐ	dʌ
Ꭽ	dla	L	dle	G	dli	Ꮾ	dlo	Ꮫ	dlu	P	dlʌ
Ᏻ	dza	V	dze	Ꭿ	dzi	K	dzo	Ꭹ	dzu	Cᵙ	dzʌ
G	wa	Ꮗ	we	Ꮎ	wi	Ꮻ	wo	Ꮒ	wu	Ꮽ	wʌ
Ꮙ	ya	ᏸ	ye	ᏸ	yi	᏶	yo	Gᵙ	yu	B	yʌ

ᵓ	ka
ᵗ	hna
G	nah
ᵊ	s
W	ta
ᵑ	ti
Ꮢ	tla
ᵬ	

The Cherokee Syllabary

latter is not to be taken as a phonemic representation, but rather as a possible writing system of an alphabetic type. Each symbol represents a vowel and a preceding consonant. There is nearly one-to-one correspondence between the pronunciation and the writing. Some departures, as provision of a symbol for *ka* beside a symbol for *ga* must be taken as evidence of influence from English where the voiced : voiceless contrast is phonemic, as it is not in Cherokee.

25.12 True syllabic writing systems are not common. A few ancient, and mostly poorly understood, systems are thought to have been syllabic. The recently deciphered Minoan B was syllabic. In recent times several other preliterate peoples have developed syllabaries, in much the same way as did the Cherokee, getting the idea of writing by symbols representing sounds from some written language associated with Western civilization. In a few cases, notably Cree (Canada) and Miao (southwestern China), missionaries have designed syllabaries as a means of reducing languages to writing. None of these, however, have been of more than local importance, and many have been abandoned in favor of alphabetic writing systems.

The one exception to this generalization is the Japanese syllabary. Since Japanese is a large and important language spoken by a highly literate people, its writing system is of major importance. The development of the syllabary antedates, and is independent of, contacts with Western culture. It is derived ultimately from the adaptation of the Chinese characters to the Japanese language. It is, therefore, necessary to return to the consideration of the former and examine the way in which they can be adapted for use with a language other than that with which they originated.

25.13 China is today, and has long been, a country in which a number of languages (by local convention usually called "dialects," though they differ as widely as the languages of Europe) are spoken. Many of them do, however, have certain basic similarities, which are produced in part by common origin and in part by common civilization. The result is that the morpheme inventories can be more or less matched up. On this basis, with exceptions of minor significance, any morpheme in any Chinese language can be written by using a character which a neighboring language would use for a morpheme of the same meaning. Thus the grapheme 人 is used in each language for some specific morpheme having the meaning 'man.' The morphemic reference will of course be pronounced quite differently in some of the languages: in Peking Mandarin [ˊrən], in Canton [ˎjɑp], in Hakka [–ɲin], in Suchow [√nɛn], in Fuchow [ˋnəŋ], in Amoy [√laŋ], and in T'ang Min [√tʃin]. The character 火 'fire' has reference in each of the same languages pronounced [ˏxwo ˊfɔ ˋfɔ ˋhɒu –hui ˏhɛ ˏhɔ]. This produces the peculiar result that documents written in different language areas can be read in any part of China, though the spoken languages are completely unintelligible to persons from another area who are not bilingual.

Much the same thing is true in Europe of those graphemes which are morphemic in reference. Thus $2 + 3 = 5$ may be read in English *two plus three is five*, in German *zwei und drei ist fünf*, in Italian *due e tre fanno cinque*, and in each other language in accordance with the vocabulary and grammar of that language.

25.14   Such adaptation does impose some special requirements on the writing system. It is not possible to match up the morpheme stock of all the various Chinese languages completely. Each of the languages other than Mandarin will require some changes. The grapheme 冇 is needed in Cantonese to write the meaning 'have not,' but is not used in Mandarin. Some characters are used differently in different languages. For example Mandarin writes 香蕉 to represent its two-syllable morpheme for 'banana,' while Cantonese, having a one-syllable morpheme for the same meaning writes only 蕉. There are also differences of order and of style, so that the written language is not entirely uniform over all of China.

25.15   With the spread of Chinese learning, this same method of writing has been carried outside of China into areas in which the language structures are quite different. In every case the same common factor of Chinese cultural influences has operated to reduce certain of the difficulties. Annamese, Korean, and Japanese have all been written in the same way, by using Chinese characters for those morphemes which have translation equivalence to the original reference of the character, or for Chinese loan words. The difficulties of adaptation are, of course, much greater when the grammatical structure of the language is radically different from that of Mandarin Chinese.

In particular, Japanese is a highly inflected language with

numerous and often complex affixes. By contrast, most Chinese morphemes are roots, though a few affixes do occur. This means that no Chinese equivalents can be found for many commonly occurring morphemes. Various makeshifts were tried before a satisfactory method was elaborated. There are, in general, two alternatives: Additional morphemic signs could have been invented to represent the affixes as such, in much the same way as new characters have been developed to represent morphemes needed in colloquial Chinese languages. Or, signs of phonemic reference could have been added to the system. The latter course was taken, and a syllabary was developed out of patterns found within the Chinese system.

The Japanese syllabary has developed in two forms, *katakana* and *hiragana*. These are practically merely alternative written shapes of the same system. The basic graphemes are given in the following table. There are several additional features of the system that need not be described here.

ア あ a	イ い i	ウ う u	エ え e	オ お o
カ か ka	キ き ki	ク く ku	ケ け ke	コ こ ko
サ さ sa	シ し si	ス す su	セ せ se	ソ そ so
タ た ta	チ ち ti	ツ つ tu	テ て te	ト と to
ナ な na	ニ に ni	ヌ ぬ nu	ネ ね ne	ノ の no
ハ は ha	ヒ ひ hi	フ ふ hu	ヘ へ he	ホ ほ ho
マ ま ma	ミ み mi	ム む mu	メ め me	モ も mo
ヤ や ya		ユ ゆ yu		ヨ よ yo
ラ ら ra	リ り ri	ル る ru	レ れ re	ロ ろ ro
ワ わ wa	ヰ ゐ wi		エ ゑ we	ヲ を wo	・ン ん ‑n

Katakana and Hiragana

25.16 The Japanese syllabary was developed primarily as an adjunct to the Chinese characters, and is generally so used today.

The roots are typically written in Chinese characters (known in Japanese as *kanji*), and the affixes in *hiragana* or *katakana*. Frequently the pronunciation of the *kanji* is indicated by writing small *hiragana* symbols beside it. Alternatively, Japanese can be written wholly in one of the syllabic scripts. The difficulty with this is that the written style has numerous homophones, so that ambiguity may result. But if a colloquial style is adhered to, no such trouble should arise. That is to say, *hiragana* or *katakana* is reasonably adequate to represent spoken Japanese, but not satisfactory for the highly specialized literary written language.

25.17   Alphabetic writing systems are those in which the graphemes typically have reference to single phonemes. We must say "typically" because greater or lesser departures are almost universal. Ideally, an alphabetic system should have a one-to-one correspondence between phonemes and graphemes. That is, each grapheme would represent one phoneme, and each phoneme would be represented by one grapheme. This condition is approximated (in some cases extremely closely) in the phonemic transcriptions of linguists, but in practical alphabets only to a limited extent. There are almost always other non-linguistic factors which must be taken into account when a new alphabetic writing system is to be designed. Older systems may not have been phonemic to begin with, but commonly become less so as linguistic change operates on the spoken language. The one-to-one relationship is chiefly useful as a point of departure in discussing the fit of writing systems to spoken languages.

The discussion in the remainder of this chapter will concern itself with some of the problems of fit of alphabetic systems to their spoken languages. Much of what is said applies in much the same way to other types of writing systems.

25.18   English has been shown to have a phonemic system in which a number of sub-systems can be distinguished. Every other language probably has some similar phonemic sub-systems, though we cannot expect that the divisions will parallel those of English in detail. Alphabetic writing systems apparently are always restricted to the representation of selected sub-systems of the phonology.

For example, the apparent ancestor of most of the alphabetic writing is that developed for the Phoenician language. This consisted of 22 graphemes. At the time there were apparently 22 consonant phonemes constituting a relatively well marked sub-system within Phoenician phonology. Within the limitation that only this one sub-system was represented at all, the Phoenician writing system was as close to being phonemic as any writing system ever is. There was no notation whatever for vowels or any other sub-system of the phonology.

The oldest form of the Greek alphabet gave essentially phonemic representation of the vowels and consonants. It did not, however, give any indication of the pitch system, which we know to have been phonologically important. A system of diacritics to represent the pitch system was developed much later, and is customarily included in the modern conventions for the writing of ancient Greek.

25.19 The Phoenician alphabet has been denied the status of a true alphabet because of its failure to write vowels. By the same token, the classical form of written Greek would have to be denied alphabetic status because of failure to indicate pitch contrasts. Greek pitches and Phoenician vowels are alike in constituting separate phonologic sub-systems from those represented in the writing system. Even the modern conventions of spelling ancient Greek would fall short, since there is every reason to believe that the phonemic system included more items than have been recorded. In particular, vowel length is known to have been phonemic, though it is only partially recorded by the accident that the vowels /æ/η and /ɔ/ω occurred only long.

No alphabetic writing system is known which represents every sub-system in the phonology of the spoken language on which it is based. Such a system would unambiguously represent anything which could be said understandably. As we shall see this is not a good statement of the function of a writing system, which is rather to record a written language. The latter is different in certain ways from a spoken language. Moreover, it is doubtful that an alphabet which did accurately record speech would be practical. However, since almost no experimental work has been done on the design of writing systems, one cannot make any such statement categorically.

25.20 The problem of alphabet design, as far as our present empirical notions take us, would seem to include determining what is the phonemic system of the language, what are the sub-systems into which it is organized, and which of these are advantageously represented in the orthography. This latter question is most frequently raised in connection with pitch systems of so-called "tone languages" (in which the pitch phonemes are components of the commonest type of morpheme). In these, pitches usually constitute a sub-system, but one far less distantly removed from the consonants and vowels than is the case in a language like English. In some such languages, orthographies both with and without markings for pitch have been tried. Results, as far as they are available, are contradictory. In some languages, pitch marking seems to contribute greatly to the usefulness of the orthography. In others, it seems to have little practical value, and native users tend to omit the pitch marks in writing, apparently largely disregarding them in reading. We can only guess at the controlling factors.

The question is seldom raised as to whether other parts of the phonology need to be written. This is undoubtedly due to the dominance of the traditional pattern of European orthographies, in which consonants and vowels are written, with the addition of partial indication of stress in some cases. Were more native speakers of Semitic languages engaged in setting up orthographies, the question of writing vowels might be raised more frequently than it is, with results that no one can predict. Many languages have been written in orthographies patterned on Arabic, and generally they have had rather loose indication of vowels. It is hard to say what part of the reported inadequacies of these writing systems is due to prejudices of European observers, to other shortcomings of the Arabic script, or to the lack of thorough indication of vowels. Certainly, the question would be worth raising as to whether indications of consonants and vowels; or consonants, vowels, and pitches; or consonants, vowels, and stresses are the only types of alphabetic writing systems that are useful.

25.21 A second type of departure from one-to-one relationship between the phonology and the writing system is due to conformity to other writing systems. This arises in several ways. Most commonly it is the result of borrowing not merely a set of symbols, but also more or less of the rules of fit; and also it results from a conscious or unconscious disinclination to take sufficient liberties with the system. A very early example is the adaptation of the Phoenician writing system to the kindred dialect of Hebrew. In spite of close relationship, Hebrew had more consonant phonemes than Phoenician. We do not know exactly how many, since certain of them were disappearing at about this time. One that is thoroughly attested can be written as /*ś/, though we do not know its exact phonetic value. This was written with the same character as that used for Phoenician and Hebrew /*š/. Presumably, this was the "nearest equivalent" in some rough sort of way. In any case the Hebrew writing system lost the one-to-one character which the Phoenician prototype had, with consequences that will be discussed in 25.25.

25.22 English orthography fails in many respects. These go back to many origins, but among them is a too slavish following of the Latin writing system. The Latin alphabet, rather close to a one-to-one representation of the consonant and vowel phonemes, consisted at one time of 21 letters. Within the period when Latin was still a living language, two more, *y* and *z*, were added to provide for new phonemes introduced into the language in Greek loan words. Three others, *j*, *v*, and *w* are medieval or modern additions. *J* and *v* have been read back into the classical texts, whence we read *Veni, vidi, vici* for an earlier UENI UIDI UICI. (The contrast of capitals : lower case is modern.) English-reading people have stubbornly resisted any further additions. This is in spite of the fact that an older writing system for English (written Old English or "Anglo-Saxon") used a few other letters, including ð and þ (θ). The retention of these and the addition of several others would have provided a much better base for a practical English orthography. Some other European nations have been a bit less conservative than English. Norwegian has added æ ø å; Spanish added ñ and considers *ll* and *rr* as single alphabetic units; and similar small departures have been made in other languages. But most European writing systems include all 26 of the "Latin Alphabet," whether they are all used or not. In general, the alphabet has been considered something not easily tampered with. This attitude has been carried out of Europe in recent years by some missionaries. (The vast majority of new writing systems have been and are being designed by missionaries.) One even claimed as the chief virtue of the orthography he had created, that it employed all twenty-six of the letters and no others!

25.23 In recent years, and as one of the important products of newer understanding of linguistics, there has been a tendency toward freer use of the Latin Alphabet. This includes a greater willingness both to discard unneeded symbols and to add others as required. The conspicuous example is the development of the "Africa Orthography," a series of flexible recommendations for the design of new writing systems for African languages. The result, when well applied, has been increased simplicity, readability, and, frequently, improvement in appearance.

25.24 Conformity to some other writing system, even at the expense of a one-to-one relationship, may sometimes be desirable, especially in areas where bilingualism is common. Thus it has frequently been judged necessary or desirable to make orthographies conform to that of the dominant or governmental language in the area. This does not always sacrifice the one-to-one relationship, even though at first sight it would seem to do so. For example, in some Spanish areas a phoneme /k/ may have to be written *c* before *a o u* and *qu* before *i e*, following a similar convention in Spanish. But since *c* and *qu* are in complementary distribution, they may be considered as allographs of one grapheme, and hence the one-to-one relationship is preserved at the grapheme level, though not at the allograph level.

25.25 Purely orthographic troubles, as well as deeper problems to be mentioned in the next chapter, are sometimes the result of historical change in the phonology of the language. Consider again the Hebrew writing system mentioned in 25.21. At the time of the establishment of the writing system there were three phonemes /*s/, /*ś/, and /*š/ with which our example is concerned. The first was written ⟨s⟩. The second and third were both written as ⟨š⟩. In the course of time the contrast between /*s/ and /*ś/ was lost. There were now two phonemes /s/ and /š/. The difficulty is that now one phoneme /s/ is written two ways, ⟨s⟩ and ⟨š⟩, and one grapheme ⟨š⟩ has two phonemes as reference, /s/ and /š/. The situation was not satisfactory at the start of the development, but it was worse at the end.

The results of change are not always so undesirable. There is some reason to believe that the grapheme ⟨ꜥ⟩ was used to represent two phonemes, /*ꜥ/ and /*ɣ/. But the historical development (probably completely independent of the writing system) was for these two to fall together into one phoneme /ʕ/. The result was that what had been a failure of the one-to-one relationship was remedied by the fortuitous course of phonologic change.

Nor is it necessary that there be a confusion such as that between /*ś/ and /*š/ to begin with. The oldest form of Hebrew apparently had a phoneme /*b/ which was written ⟨b⟩. At a somewhat later date this had developed two quite distinct allophones [b] and [v], but as they were in complementary distribution and hence still allophones of one phoneme, the relationship with ⟨b⟩ was still one-to-one. In modern Hebrew, however, they are no longer in complementary distribution. The old /*b/ has been replaced by two phonemes /b/ and /v/, but the writing system still contains (in one form) only one grapheme ⟨b⟩, and the relationship has become two-to-one.

25.26   If a writing system does not represent the whole phonemic system, as we have seen none do, then it follows that written representation of spoken material may be less clear than the speech it records. This is of course true in English, as we pointed out in 11.16. Written language usually compensates for this by various devices, most of which fall within the topic of the next chapter, but some are part of the orthography or writing system. The most familiar of these is word division, a sort of crude morphemic signal. Its effectiveness may be realized by trying to read material in what is sometimes called a "phonemic transcription," but without indication of stress, pitch, transitions, or terminals. With word divisions given, such material can be read with no great difficulty; without word divisions it can be exceedingly obscure.

Another device is arbitrary spelling distinctions. This device may separate words brought into homonymy by omission of part of the phonemic system from the base of the orthography. Latinxua, an alphabetic writing system for Chinese, does not indicate the pitches. It is believed by the designers of the system that only a few pairs of words can be confused because of this. These pairs have been distinguished by artificial, arbitrary spelling devices which are not used generally in the system. Thus *liz* 'chestnut,' *mai* 'sell,' *yanz* 'courtyard,' and *Shansi* 'Shansi' are given the spellings which the rules would suggest, whereas *liiz* 'plum,' *maai* 'buy,' *yaanz* 'garden,' and *Shaansi* 'Shensi' have spellings arbitrarily set up to be distinctive. Incidentally, it is to be noted that the last two, the provinces Shansi and Shensi, are accidentally distinguished by a similar device in English spelling, the usual Western pronunciation being derived from the spelling.

Though not so purposefully planned, numerous pairs of words in English are distinguished by arbitrary spelling differences. *hole* : *whole*, *lead* /léd/ : *led*, *boy* : *buoy*, etc. The virtues of such distinction are sometimes overlooked by advocates of spelling reform. It may well be that, short of a sufficiently drastic change, "correction" of a few of the most glaring cases on a haphazard basis may actually make for greater difficulties in the use of the English writing system. The design of an orthography (spelling reform is merely a small-scale attempt) is a difficult and intricate matter about which we as yet know all too little.

26

Written Languages

26.1   A written language is basically a representation of a spoken language. It is, however, very seldom an exact reflection. Mention was made in the last chapter of some of the ways that a writing system might fail to represent the phonology fully and accurately. These are, however, only special instances out of many other differences — often much deeper differences — between a written and a spoken language. These differences are found at all levels of structure — phonology, morphology, syntax, vocabulary, and style.

26.2   Dialectal variation in spoken languages is a very familiar phenomenon. Dialectal variations are also found in written languages, but they are generally minor and not at all obvious. In English a few are well known: *colour* : *color, gaol* : *jail, corn* : *grain, the government are . . .* : *the government is . . .*, etc. Differences between the spoken English of Britain and the United States are considerably more numerous and often much greater.

This situation is very nearly universal. Dialectal variation in a written language is almost always much slighter than in the associated spoken language. Sometimes speech differences may be so extreme that there is no mutual intelligibility, whereas the written language in the two areas is identical.

26.3   An illustrative case is that of German. Over most of Germany and Austria, in a large part of Switzerland, and in small portions of other European countries, the people consider their language to be German. They are, of course, aware that not all spoken German is alike, and they may be conscious of considerable differences between their own and other speech also called German. But even when these differences are extreme, they consider the difference as merely dialectal. Many of these "dialects" are completely unintelligible to speakers of other dialects of German. The differences are far greater than can be found in the United States or among the more familiar dialects of Britain. Some are more distinct than the different Scandinavian languages, Swedish, Danish, and Norwegian.

Yet over all this region with its tremendous speech diversity, there is one universal written language with only very minor dialectal variations. As a result, any literate person can communicate with any other in writing, or by a spoken rendition of written German, which is a very important special dialect of quite different status from the local colloquials. It is often known as "Schriftdeutsch." Every school child is taught to read, write, and speak this common literary language. For many of them the task is little different from that of learning a second language. If American children were taught to write and speak Schriftdeutsch and to consider their spoken English as merely a German dialect, their situation would be only a little more extreme than that of some German and Swiss children.

Obviously for many people in the German area there may be very great differences between their speech and the written language they most commonly use. In some parts of Switzerland, for example, the colloquial uses /ksiy/ 'been.' In a more formal situation, as in school or church, Schriftdeutsch would be spoken, and /ɡəveHzən/ would be used for 'been.' In writing, *gewesen* would be used, not only in all formal situations, but in most informal as well. That is, *gewesen* would commonly be written where one might say /ksiy/.

In English we have something of the same thing, but it is very much less extreme. For example, I commonly use /yúwɔHl/ as a plural pronoun contrasting with the singular /yúw/. This is restricted to colloquial situations. When speaking formally I use only /yúw/ for either singular or plural. In writing I use standard English *you* almost exclusively, just as a Swiss would use standard

German. Not infrequently when reading aloud I say /yúwɔʜl/ when the context demands it, though *you* is written. The difference is that such cases are comparatively rare in English, but very common in some dialects of German.

26.4 Written German had a long and gradual development. It was originally based on a Middle German dialect. By historical accident its use spread over most of the Middle and High German dialect areas and over a large part of the Low German dialects. It successfully displaced most of the other written languages which had started developing in the area. Thus there came about a remarkable degree of uniformity in written language over a large area.

Two other written languages were, however, successful in resisting this spread. This was largely the result of differences in their political situation. Each spread throughout the Germanic area of the political unit in which it arose. Thus we have today Dutch in the Netherlands and Flemish in Belgium. It is not surprising that this should have happened, since common written language is an important factor in integrating a political nation, and since the unity within encourages the spread of any culture pattern throughout a major political unit. The unique element in the German situation is that the common written language could have spread beyond one national state, and that it should have produced as little irredentism as it has.

The spoken bases of Dutch and Flemish were very similar. The two written languages were accordingly very similar, and the trend in each has been toward conformity with the other. As a result these two have become almost identical, differing little more than British and American written English.

The spoken dialects of the Netherlands and adjacent parts of Germany were practically identical. The written languages used in the two areas are, however, quite different. The geographic and social limits of written languages are not necessarily correlated with those of spoken languages. This is only one case of many of similar discrepancies which can be cited both in Europe and elsewhere.

26.5 In some instances the origin of the written language is quite clear. In many others it is very obscure or involved. Let us, however, assume the simplest case: A new written language is developed based on one single dialect, A. After it has been reasonably well established its use spreads to adjoining areas using related spoken dialects. As its area of use widens it comes in contact with ever more divergent dialects, and ultimately with dialect B, which differs markedly from dialect A. Speakers of B will learn to write this written language, and so to use some of the vocabulary and grammatical patterns of dialect A, many of which are unnatural to them. It is almost inevitable that they will introduce into their writing some vocabulary and perhaps some grammatical usages of their own speech. What speakers of B write is not, therefore, identical with the original written language. Instead it is modified somewhat in the direction of B. Dialect differences, perhaps only very minor, have appeared in the written language.

Some of these new usages will be taken up by writers from other dialect areas, thereby reducing the distinctiveness of the written dialect in the area of B. Items originating in dialect B may, thus, spread throughout the written language. Often they will become alternatives existing alongside usages originating in dialect A or similarly introduced from other dialects. One effect is to enrich the vocabulary and grammatical repertoire of the written language. This is a common source of the synonyms which are so abundant in some written languages.

A second and ultimately more important effect is to produce a new literary language which is not merely a reflection of any single dialect, but a composite of many. If this process is continued, the point may be reached where there are appreciable differences between written and spoken language for all dialects.

26.6   Modern literary Italian is an excellent example of this process. This can be traced rather definitely to an origin based on the speech of Tuscany. Dante's *Divina Commedia* was the first significant publication in Italian. It had an immediate and deep influence on the development of the written language, and that influence has continued. Dante based his work on the speech of his native Tuscany. A large proportion of the other early writers of importance were also Tuscans, and the region was for some time the cultural center of the Peninsula.

This written language was gradually adopted throughout the area which later became Italy. It came to be associated with dialects which were markedly different from that on which it had been based. Some authors from remote areas succeeded in writing in very accurate imitation of their Tuscan models; others introduced numerous elements from other Italian dialects. Some of these were in turn imitated in Tuscany and elsewhere. With the rising importance of Rome as an Italian cultural center, it was inevitable that many usages from that area should be introduced and spread. But no dialect area failed to make its contribution. Modern written Italian is not provincial, but the common language of the whole country. In many respects it is a sort of average of all the local dialects.

26.7 A common written language such as German or Italian is a powerful unifying force in a national or cultural area. It is also a necessity if a flourishing literature is to be developed, since it is not economically feasible to develop a separate written literature for every minor local dialect. In many parts of the world today, adequate written languages are badly needed in order that the peoples concerned may take their rightful places in the modern world. No nation can afford the long, slow process of development by which the written languages of Europe mostly came into their present situations. It is desirable to short-cut this slow growth by some quicker way to an adequate written language usable by a sufficiently large population to support a vigorous literature. One device has been the deliberate design of so-called "union" languages.

The Shona group of dialects occupies a large part of Rhodesia and adjacent Portuguese East Africa. There are six reasonably clearly marked groups of dialects, each showing appreciable local variation. Five of these were reduced to writing by missionaries, and in four of them the whole New Testament was translated. An appreciable amount of publication was done in each. However, all the Shona dialects together are spoken by only a little over a million people. This is hardly enough to support an adequate output of printed materials in five different written languages. Accordingly, in 1929 a committee began work on a survey of the language problems in the area. As a result of their work, a new written language known as Union Shona was designed. It has since largely replaced the older written forms and is now quite generally used throughout five of the six dialect groups. The committee decided that it was impractical, for reasons as much social and geographical as linguistic, to bring the Kalanga dialects into the scheme. A unified grammar was set up, based largely on the Karanga and Zezuru dialects. The vocabulary was drawn largely from four of the dialects, and it was agreed to discourage the introduction of new words from others. A new and improved spelling system was introduced. For example, *c* is now written instead of the older *ch*, and five new letters were proposed to write phonemic distinctions previously overlooked.

Since that time Union Shona has become well established. There has, of course, been opposition, both in general and to specific features, but it has not been serious. Numerous publications have appeared, including the entire Bible. The scheme is proving its value in many ways. Not only has the course of development been greatly speeded, but a natural group of dialects has been selected for inclusion. In time the artificiality of the design will become less obtrusive and a highly satisfactory written language may be expected to develop.

26.8   Such union languages are not always equally successful. Union Ibo for a large and linguistically very diverse area in southern Nigeria had a very different outcome, and has been largely abandoned. The failure seemed to be due to poor selection of the features to be included, and to inadequate attention to the social and political differences in the area. That is to say, there was inadequate field investigation both in linguistics and anthropology on which to base the proposal.

This and other experience has shown that the successful design of a written language requires thorough knowledge of the linguistic, social, political, and practical aspects of the problem. Hence it requires cooperative work by linguists, anthropologists, administrators, educators, missionaries, and native leadership. It is one of the very practical problems to which descriptive linguists and dialect geographers can make important contributions.

26.9   Written languages not only are influenced by the spoken languages with which they are used; they are also influenced by other written languages. This is most evident in their early development. Generally the first authors in any newly written language are bilingual. Often they are only secondarily speakers of the language being "reduced to writing." In the worst case their command of the language may be poor. But even when the author is a native speaker, his literary education has usually been wholly through the medium of another language. His understanding of the nature and possibilities of written language is based on the writing system and literary grammar employed elsewhere. It is almost inevitable that certain conventions of the pattern system will be carried over, irrespective of their suitability.

Foreign influence does not cease after the literary conventions of the new language are firmly established. Authors are much more likely to be bilingual than are the general public. They sometimes make a conscious effort to imitate models from other literatures. Still more frequently they are unconsciously influenced by literary patterns in other languages. Translations also play an important part in this process. It is rarely possible to translate without some conformity, often considerable and fundamental, to the language structure of the original. The patterns so introduced may be copied and in time be thoroughly assimilated into the written language. In many languages the Bible is among the first publications; this has been an important fact in bringing a certain measure of common usages into many written languages.

26.10   The English writing system includes a number of features other than the alphabet. One prominent element is the punctuation system. For example, consider the marks of sentence ends, ⟨.⟩ ⟨?⟩, etc. In the first place, a "sentence" is regarded as "expressing a complete thought," or something of the kind. The writing system requires that it must have a terminal mark and begin with a capital letter. In the second place, "sentences" are classified on the basis of whether they "state a fact," "ask a question," etc. These differences determine which of the several terminal marks will be used. Somewhat comparable structures are marked in spoken English by the use of the intonation contours. The two systems are, however, quite independent. Sentences which would be written with ⟨?⟩ are clearly divided in speech into two groups with sharply contrasting intonations. One of these uses patterns which are also commonly used with sentences which would be written with ⟨.⟩. (Cf. 4.18.) There is, therefore, only more or less incidental correlation between the punctuation marks and the different intonation contours. Indeed, intonation contours commonly end at places where punctuation marks are prohibited, as between certain subjects and the following predicates.

There is a fundamental difference in attitude toward the two parts of the writing system. The alphabet is assumed to represent sounds. Everyone expects, therefore, that there will be differences of spelling from language to language. The punctuation marks, however, are not conceived of as representing features of speech. Instead, they mark logical units of connected writing like "sentences," "statements," "questions," "dependent clauses," and the like. Since these are phrased in terms of logic, they are generally assumed to be universal. People do not expect to find differences of punctuation from language to language. Indeed, they are often irritated by the very minor differences which they do find between English and, say, French or German. Because the punctuation system of all European languages has grown up through mutual interaction and on the basis of a common "logical" grammar, all are basically similar. Certainly, they are far more similar than the intonation systems in the corresponding spoken languages.

26.11   In recent years a very large number of languages of Asia, Africa, and America have been "reduced to writing," usually by Europeans and Americans. Generally an attempt has been made to adapt the alphabet to the sounds of the language. But punctuation and capitalization have in most cases been carried over with little or no change. For example, proper names are usually capitalized, whether this has any functional value in the language or not. First words of sentences are capitalized, though this is strictly redundant, even in English, since sentence ends are also marked. Questions are carefully distinguished by $\langle ? \rangle$ though in many languages all questions are clearly marked by special words.

The significant thing is not so much that these conventions are carried over, as that no questions are commonly raised about them. This is, of course, almost inevitable if they are conceived in terms of logical categories which are more or less universal.

No one knows what would be the outcome if thoroughgoing study were applied to problems of this kind. There may well be far better methods of indicating syntactic relationships in written language than any which have been developed hitherto. No appreciable amount of research has ever been devoted to this question, though a much larger amount of attention has been given to the problem of selecting alphabets and spelling conventions for new written languages. Indeed, there is available very little descriptive data on how the English, or any other, punctuation system is actually used. The large volume of published material which is available is predominantly normative and almost wholly based on "logical" categories.

26.12 We must not consider the question of punctuation for a new written language as a trivial problem. Punctuation marks syntax. It is predicated on a certain type of syntactic structure. The patterns used in the spoken language may be very different. If European punctuation is introduced, there must be pressure in the direction of European syntax. At the minimum this may do nothing more serious than to favor certain perfectly natural constructions at the expense of others. In some cases it has, however, introduced previously unknown patterns. Of course, the question is much more extensive than we have framed it. Punctuation, capitalization, and word division are only the most obvious features of a much larger set of patterns. Various elements of syntax are carried over from one language to the next, often with the result that the written language departs in significant respects from the spoken language on which it was based.

26.13 A third factor influencing the fit of written and spoken languages is linguistic change. The picture presented up to this point has been largely static. Actually, the spoken dialects are relatively rapidly moving entities. Change is taking place continually in every aspect of every dialect, though, of course, not all of these changes are independent of those in other dialects. Moreover, written languages are also subject to change beyond the broadening of the base which has just been described. The problem then can be stated in terms of the comparative rates and directions of change in the written language and the spoken dialects.

The most obvious instance is the changes in phonology and the relatively much slower change in orthography. Almost inevitably, the fit of orthography to pronunciation deteriorates. This is, of course, a major source of spelling difficulties in English. But though orthography is notoriously conservative, it must not be assumed that it is immutable. A letter-by-letter transcript of the first edition of the King James Version (1611) will show the actual extent of change.

As printed in 1611:	*As in modern printings:*
And hee said, A certaine man had two sonnes: And the yonger of them said to his father, Father giue me the portion of goods that falleth to me. And he diuideth vnto them his liuing.	And he said, a certain man had two sons: and the younger of them said to his father, Father, give me the portion of thy substance that falleth to me. And he divided unto them his living.

26.14 Spelling reform in many languages has been, as in English, largely a private matter. Certain individuals have flouted public opinion and made changes in their own spellings. Whether such innovations prevail depends on public reaction, and this is a wholly unpredictable matter. Some have been accepted by increasing numbers of people until the new spelling has come to dominate. Thus, in America *jail* has replaced *gaol*, though the latter remains in Britain. Many others have failed of general acceptance. A number of proposals are currently competing with older spellings, often generating appreciable controversy, as in the case of *nite* : *night*. With such a haphazard process it may be expected that there will be no consistency in the directions of change. Most of the changes are probably to be considered as in the direction of simplicity and better fit, but this is not always the case, as when *rhyme* supplanted an older *rime*.

In some other areas, notably Scandinavia, the initiative is largely official. For example, the Ministry of Education in Denmark recently decreed that all old spellings in *aa* would be replaced with *å*. No Dane is compelled to make the change, but the schools will now teach the new form. Swedish orthography has had a reasonably thorough revision about once each generation. This has not, however, insured that spelling will accord with pronunciation, since a number of phonemic distinctions are still unrecorded, and unpronounced letters, though diminishing in number, persist.

26.15 The effects of phonologic change on the fit of a writing system are various. Of course, a phonetic change without accompanying phonemic change has no effect. Phonemic changes may merely produce an alternative but unambiguous orthographic device. For example, *light* was at one time pronounced /líxt/; *gh* was the usual spelling for /x/. Through a series of changes /líxt/ became /láyt/. But since exactly parallel changes affected a large number of other words, the result was primarily to add *igh* to the list of possible spellings for /áy/. Thus there can be little confusion in reading; *light* can only spell /láyt/. The converse is not true; one must learn to spell *light* and not **lite*. The patterns of phonemic change in English since about 1400 have been so complex and have so often been further influenced by analogic changes that the consequences are not always as simple as this.

Some aberrant spellings have another function within the structure of written English. Consider the pair *sight* and *site*. It is quite clear and correct to write *The sight is pleasing.* or *The site is pleasing.* That these two words are homophonous does not affect their usability within the written language. But neither of these sentences is used in normal speech. Instead, something like *It's a nice view.* or *I like the location.* are much more likely. The ultimate effect of these spellings is to provide a semi-morphemic writing system for the language. Within the limits of the alternative spellings possible, one is selected to act as a marker of the specific morpheme meant. The difference in spelling between *sight* and *light* has a phonemic reference; that between *sight*, *site*, and *cite* has a morphemic reference. The English writing system is, therefore, only partially phonologic in its basis.

26.16 Written and spoken languages differ in their vocabularies. The first impression is always that the long-established written language has a much larger vocabulary than any spoken dialect. In part, this is illusory. The general public, and even professional linguists, have notoriously underestimated the vocabularies of spoken languages. Colloquial words can easily be missed, as some are under verbal taboos which prevent their use in writing entirely and in public speech partially. They may, nevertheless, be widely current in the community. Others apply only in situations where written communication is unlikely, as, for example, technical terms in daily activities. (Few languages other than English have the vast literature on cooking which pours out each month from American publishing houses.) Others are unrecorded because more literary forms are preferred in speaking in the presence of strangers.

There are, however, two characteristics of literary vocabularies which seem to be sufficiently general to require comment. These are the relative abundance of homonyms and of synonyms.

26.17   Many written languages have large numbers of **homo-nyms**. This is not strictly an accurate way of stating the matter, since many of them are amply distinct in spelling, though they would be pronounced alike. Some of them owe the difference in spelling to the conservatism of orthography which we have just mentioned. English is only modestly equipped with such pairs. Literary Chinese, however, has very many more. It is quite readily possible to construct long passages which are quite intelligible to the eye, but utterly incomprehensible to the ear.

Occasionally homonyms are artificially distinguished by some orthographic device. A somewhat unusual case in point is the English word *calorie*. Several definitions have been proposed, two of the common ones giving values differing by a factor of 1,000. An arbitrary convention was established of writing one *Calorie* and the other *calorie*. This is now little used, but does persist in the abbreviations *Cal.* and *cal.* A somewhat similar instance is the word *species* /spíyšìys/, of which the singular and plural are alike both in spelling and pronunciation. Abbreviated, however, there is a distinction, *sp.* : *spp.* (The doubling of the final letter is a common written allomorph of {$-Z_1$}.) Occasionally these abbreviations are used in contexts where no other words would be abbreviated, simply because they are less ambiguous than full forms. Moreover, they are occasionally used as glosses in written English *species* (*sp.*) : *species* (*spp.*).

26.18   The second peculiarity of written vocabularies is the abundance of **synonyms** or near synonyms. Often these are words originating in different dialects. Or one or more may be loan words from some other language. In any case, once a word enters a literary language it tends to persist, since there is a certain per-manence to written records lacking in any spoken utterance. Moreover, in some literary traditions the repetition of a word is considered poor style except when a special effect is desired. This puts a special value upon synonyms. However, this feature of style is not universal. In some languages exactly the opposite effect is sought; repetition, especially following certain established pat-terns, is considered desirable.

A third force favoring extensive groups of synonyms in some languages is the lack of indication of intonation and other qualities of voice associated with emotion. As a substitute, words of similar denotation but diverse connotation can be employed. For example, a purely colloquial reporting of an extended dialogue will take the the form: ". . . So he said . . . So he said . . ." The intervening utterances will carry intonations approximating those in the original, and so conveying the emotional tone. In a literary report *said* will be replaced throughout by verbs selected from a list including *asked, exclaimed, shouted, snapped, growled,* etc. Each of these, in effect, can be analyzed as carrying two functions: One (the denotation) is to replace *said,* the other (the connotation) is to portray the emotional tone of the utterance reported.

26.19 All these forces may interact to produce very complex relationships between speech and writing — how complex may best be seen in a situation where there are two competing written languages associated with the same spoken dialects. One such case is in northern India. One written language, known as Urdu, was developed in a Muslim cultural environment and uses the Persian form of the Arabic alphabet. The other, Hindi, was developed in a non-Muslim environment and uses the Nagari script which was borrowed from Sanskrit. These are more than merely two forms of writing for the same language. If Urdu is transcribed into Nagari, it is still recognizably Urdu. There are many other differences, and the two must be considered as more or less independent written languages, each with its own characteristic structure and vocabulary. The two differ in part because they were originally based on somewhat different spoken dialects. Each has spread over a very large and linguistically diverse territory. There are, however, areas in which Urdu is rarely used, even by Muslims, but where Hindi is the prevailing written language. There are also areas where Urdu is used but not Hindi. Since they have not been used in identical territories, they have been subject to different influences from spoken dialects. The external influences have also been different. Urdu has been subject to influence from Persian, and this has affected every level of structure, not only vocabulary. In Hindi the Persianizing forces have been much weaker, but there has been a strong pressure for conformity to Sanskrit patterns. Probably most important of all, however, is the fact that each has developed more or less independently of the other. The historical changes which are inevitable in any language, spoken or written, have been different. As a result, Hindi and Urdu show important and quite evident differences, and both are quite different from the spoken dialects of the area.

26.20   Thus far, the discussion has centered around the structure of written languages and their dependence upon spoken languages. This is only part of the picture. The interaction is in many respects mutual. As dialects contribute to a standard written language, the latter exerts forces on the dialect, producing convergence from that side too. The relationship is rather more complex than in the opposite direction for two reasons. The first is that usually only a small number of the speakers of the dialect are literate, and hence subject to direct influence, whereas almost all of the writers also speak some dialect. Moreover, the spoken language is likely to have a complex structure of levels of speech. The written language, will, of course, also have a set of literary levels, but these are probably less significant.

One effect of a well established standard written language is the creation of a speech form which approximates an oral rendition of the literary language. This is familiar enough in English, where a certain type of oratory, now less popular than formerly, was scarcely anything else than a spoken written English, with a special kind of intonation substituted for the punctuation. From that, all intergrades can be heard with decreasing use of literary vocabulary and sentence structure, until a purely colloquial speech is reached. Actually, few educated Americans are able to speak without some evident traces of the literary language.

26.21   The general influences of literary language on speech are probably much more significant than any of the more obvious details. But the latter are easier to point out, and collectively indicate a large group of changes. Among the more obvious are **spelling pronunciations.** For example, I usually read *awry* as /ɔ́ʜriy/, though I know, when I reflect, that /əráy/ is etymologically better. *Solder* is heard increasingly frequently with an /l/. Not all spelling pronunciations are substandard; some are very widely accepted. For example, use of /l/ in *soldier* is a recent development of this kind, as the word was earlier /sówjər/. A very large percentage of the rarer literary words, when pronounced at all, are pronounced as the spelling would indicate, irrespective of what oral phonologic tradition might have indicated. The same is true of more common colloquial words than is commonly realized.

Then there are such evident intrusions of written forms into speech as /yùwnéskow/ for *UNESCO* and /ɔ́nràʜ/ for *UNRRA*. Most of our plural formations of Latin and Greek origin (see 8.10.6) are preserved in speech, or enter speech in the first place, through the influence of written forms. The occasional American who consistently says /ày⁺ šæl . . ./, and even those who only occasionally use such forms, reveal the influence of writing, since this usage originated in written English.

Language Classification

27.1 Descriptive linguistics is concerned with two very different but intimately related tasks. The first is to describe individual languages or dialects in terms of their own characteristic structure. For each of the numerous speech forms this is a separate task; the structure of no other language is directly relevant. Linguists and all who make use of their results are naturally interested in knowing how this work is progressing and how much remains to be done. This raises the question as to how many languages there are.

The second task of descriptive linguistics is to develop a general theory of language structure — that is, to set up a conceptual framework within which an investigator can work as he seeks to understand a specific language. This theory must be sufficiently general and flexible to provide for any type of language structure that may be encountered, but also sufficiently precise and systematic to give real help. This second task can only be accomplished by comparing numerous languages and language descriptions, and abstracting from them those patterns which seem of interest and significance.

Since languages are so numerous, no one can control this large mass of material without some sort of classification. The classification of languages is not within the province of descriptive linguistics, though many descriptive linguists also work on this problem. For descriptive linguistics a language classification is simply a tool provided by another discipline. But it is a tool which cannot well be dispensed with.

This chapter will, accordingly, consider some of the problems involved in the enumeration and classification of languages. The last chapter will give a broad outline of a language classification.

27.2 One basic difficulty is that of defining a language. The word has been so variously used both by laymen and linguists that there is no agreed meaning, except for a general feeling that languages are somehow more distinct than dialects: languages are different kinds of speech; dialects are merely varieties of languages. Nothing as vague as this can be useful as the basis of a scientific enumeration of languages.

It would be quite defensible if linguists would take it upon themselves to redefine the term with sufficient precision that later linguists would be able to understand with some exactness just what is meant. Unfortunately, the problem involves a great deal more than definition of terms. The very nature of language is such that the problem of classification into such categories as language and dialect is intrinsically difficult or impossible. Several criteria can be proposed, no one of which is satisfactory.

27.3 Perhaps the most obvious criterion is that of **mutual intelligibility.** We expect speakers of any given language to be able to understand each other. Conversely, speakers of different languages cannot ordinarily understand each other. We might apply this as a criterion by inverting it: If two people can understand each other, then they speak the same language; if not, then they speak different languages.

Unfortunately, it is not as simple as that. In the first place, intelligibility is a relative matter. Anything from essentially one hundred percent to zero may be found if such a test is applied. How much do two people have to understand of each other's speech to indicate that they speak the same language? Moreover, the matter is much affected by various complicating factors. For example, intelligibility depends on the subject matter. Try the following bit of English: "Stamens dimorphic; anthers oblong to subulate, truncate to attenuate or rostrate at the summit; connective of the larger anthers greatly prolonged and bearing two long basal anterior appendages, that of the smaller anthers much shorter, simple or merely bituberculate." Intelligibility also depends on the intelligence and background of the informant. The person with broader contacts, even if restricted to his own group, may have an appreciably higher comprehension of texts in a related speech form.

27.4   Another criterion which is sometimes a good bit easier to apply is that of enumeration of **common elements**. For example, we may take a list of basic vocabulary and compare two speech forms. Such a list would include the ordinary everyday words for such meanings as: 'father,' 'hand,' 'food,' 'walk,' 'see,' etc. At least a hundred, and preferably more, such words should be used. We may find anywhere from nearly one hundred percent to nearly zero that are common to the two lists. The proportion is then a measure of relatedness. We are left with the same dilemma as before: What percentage of common vocabulary is necessary to indicate that two speech forms are varieties of the same language? In addition there is a new problem: How are we to determine whether two words in two speech forms are the same?

The test of common elements need not be restricted to vocabulary. We can make similar examination of structural elements of any kind. Presumably, every language has a grammar, and that grammar must be shared among all forms of the language. But we know that there are grammatical differences between dialects, so that we cannot set up structural identity as our criterion. What degree of structural similarity is to be expected within a language? What within a dialect?

27.5   Both these criteria have a common failing. Consider an area where a number of small communities, say villages, can be selected for examination. We will choose a number of such villages lying more or less in a line, each a short distance from the next. It could well be that the dialect A of the first village would be mutually intelligible, or have a high percentage of common elements, with B of the second village. Similarly B and C might be indicated as being closely related, and so on through each successive pair until we reach Y and Z. But if we now compare directly the dialects A and Z, spoken some distance apart, we may find a degree of mutual intelligibility approaching zero and a comparatively small percentage of common elements. Obviously, we must conclude that A and Z are to be included in two separate languages. But where are we to draw the line? Each successive pair of dialects examined was found to be closely related. We seem to be in the dilemma of drawing a line between A and Z without drawing it between any two successive dialects.

This is not merely a theoretical consideration. There are many places in the world where just this sort of situation is closely approximated. The vast area of Africa in which Bantu languages are spoken is a case in point. Within this area there are many places where such gradual transitions connect mutually unintelligible speech forms. Not every local vernacular is so joined to all its neighbors, of course, but the phenomenon is sufficiently common to make a satisfactory division of the area into languages essentially impossible. If the several classifications of the Bantu languages which have been attempted are compared, it will be found that there are only a few places in which any measure of agreement is reached. While the inadequacy of the data has contributed to this uncertainty, the major cause of this disagreement among Bantu specialists is the inconclusive nature of the facts, particularly the considerable number of cases of intergradation.

27.6 Another possible method would be to look for conspicuous **bundles of isoglosses,** or if detailed mapping of linguistic features is not available (the more usual situation), to look for the more abrupt transitions. This criterion differs from the last two in that we have shifted our attention from the comparison of speech forms to the boundaries between them. In some cases this can be of great help. If we are faced with a problem such as that sketched in 27.5, we may resolve it this way: Since A and Z are evidently distinct languages, there must be a division between them somewhere. We cannot place this dividing line in such a way as not to separate closely related speech forms, but we can elect to place it at that place between A and Z where there is the most rapid transition. This would be either between those local dialects which, though mutually intelligible, were least so; or, if information is available in this form, in that place where there is the most conspicuous bundle of isoglosses.

27.7 A rather neat refinement of the method of common elements is available. As was pointed out in Chapter 16, it is possible to make a phonemic analysis based on a single dialect of English, or to evolve an **overall pattern** based on a wide range of dialects. In the case of English phonology, such an overall pattern fits the facts of any one of a large number of dialects with quite acceptable precision. We might say, then, that any group of dialects is a single language if it is possible to describe an acceptable overall pattern of some aspect of structure, say the phonology. While this is probably the most satisfactory criterion of all, it is a laborious test to apply, and does not obviate the basic difficulty.

In the first place, how closely must the analysis fit the facts? There is always a certain degree of approximation in any descriptive statement. Any statement of overall pattern will necessarily be a less adequate treatment of any given dialect than a statement based exclusively on that dialect and done with equal care and methodological adequacy. How loosely can an overall pattern fit, and still justify treating the total base as a single language?

For the descriptive linguist, such a criterion is particularly advantageous, since his chief interest in delimiting languages is in defining the systems with which he must be concerned. In effect, this definition of a language would be statable in a rough form as: "A language is any form of speech of which a workable description can be made."

27.8 All of these criteria, and any others which can be proposed, inevitably fail, if it is expected that they can give a conclusive answer to the problem of defining a language or of ranking speech forms as languages, dialects, or other categories. Ultimately, the decision must rest on the judgment of a linguist, though all these methods of measuring relationship can be of immense value in providing the basic data on which the decision must be based.

With written languages, the difficulties are much less acute. These tend to be relatively uniform over wide areas, and the transition from one to another is generally abrupt with little intergradation. The differences between similar written languages may vary from rather minute to quite fundamental ones, so that the ranking problem is not entirely absent. Nevertheless, there are generally a number of discrete units from which to begin in classifying written languages.

In the popular understanding, it is assumed that any language will be written everywhere the same, dialectal differences being restricted to speech. This can be inverted to give a general definition of a language as a form of communication which is written everywhere the same, and of a dialect as a variety of a language which is spoken differently from others. Innumerable difficulties can be seen in such a definition, some of which have been pointed out in Chapter 26. Nevertheless, it is some such idea that the layman commonly has in mind when he asks the linguist, "How many languages are there?"

27.9 If we leave the search for a criterion to distinguish language from dialect and approach the wider problem of classification of languages to show wider relationships, we will find that two of these methods can be sharpened to become rather precise instruments.

The first of these is common vocabulary. Consider two languages, sufficiently different that the question of considering them as a single language does not occur. We have at hand what seem to be reliable vocabularies of each. These we can compare in such a way as to produce an estimate of the proportion of the vocabulary which seems to be similar. By this we need not mean anything very precise at first. If two words look more or less similar in form and have meanings which are suggestive of a relationship, we will count them. From this we will emerge with a percentage figure expressing the common vocabulary.

The question now arises, what, if anything, is the significance of this percentage? We must ask this question, because there is always a possibility that words can be similar by mere chance. We must satisfy ourselves that this does not offer a plausible hypothesis to explain the percentage of common vocabulary which we have found. To do this, we must estimate what percentage it is reasonable to expect by chance. We can do this by selecting pairs of languages which we have every reason to believe are not related in any way, perhaps one American Indian language and one language from Central Africa. Any similarities between such a pair may be considered as due to chance. One investigator found that chance would produce about 4 percent of words "similar" in the degree he was considering. Suppose we have found 20 percent of similarities in our test case. Is this significantly more than 4 percent? Only a statistical measure that takes account of the size of the samples will tell, but if we have examined a few hundred pairs of words, such a measure will show that there is a high probability that the difference is significant.

27.10 The results of this calculation are merely a statement that it is highly probable that the percentage of common words which we found in the two languages A and B is due to something other than chance. The question is what? There are two very likely factors: borrowing (either from each other or from a common source), and/or descent from a common ancestor by the familiar processes of linguistic change. The latter would indicate that the two languages are related in the sense with which linguists are most often concerned. Our statistical investigations have accordingly demonstrated that relationship is a possibility. But they cannot establish it as a fact. To do so, we must demonstrate that some at least of the similar words are actually **cognate,** by which we mean, descended from some common ancestral language.

27.11 Such a demonstration depends on our observation that certain kinds of linguistic change (phonetic and phonemic) are regular. This regularity of change may, under favorable circumstances, make it possible to recognize those items which have been produced by this kind of change. If change is regular in both lines of descent, it follows that there should be regular correspondence between forms in one language and cognate forms in the other. That is, suppose the ancestral language has a phoneme /X/ which by regular change becomes /Y/ in language A, and by a different regular change becomes /Z/ in language B. We might then expect many words with /Y/ in A to correspond with words with /Z/ in language B.

Conversely, suppose we observe that many words in language A containing the phoneme /P/ seem similar to words in language B containing /Q/. We may conclude that this is presumptive evidence that there was in the common ancestor a sound (perhaps a phoneme or perhaps an allophone) which by separate changes became /P/ in A and /Q/ in B. We do not know what that sound was, but we may designate it by an arbitrary symbol, say [*R].

We may find a great number of such **correspondences.** If this is the case, we can postulate a considerable number of allophones for the language, and so reconstruct the parent words for many of our corresponding vocabulary items. From these we can make a phonemic analysis, grouping the postulated allophones into reconstructed phonemes.

27.12 In a sense, what we have just described is the phonemic analysis of a dead and probably unknown language from the evidence preserved in its descendants. But in another, perhaps more accurate sense, it is the discovery and description of an overall pattern of structure covering certain parts of the vocabulary of the two languages. We can make no claim that our analysis is an overall pattern for the two languages as wholes, since it is based on detectable correspondences in selected portions of each language. Those words in which correspondences cannot be found are either assumed to be affected in some way by non-regular linguistic change (analogic change or borrowing, for example), or to exemplify regular phonetic or phonemic changes which we have not yet been able to detect.

27.13 As an example of the method, we may consider the reconstruction of some Proto-Central-Algonquian consonants. This reconstruction is based primarily on the comparison of Fox, Cree, Menomini, and Ojibwa. These four languages are rather closely related, and show quite evident similarities in many sets of words. Consider the following example:

Fox	*Cree*	*Menomini*	*Ojibwa*	
pemātesiwa	pimātisiw	pemātesew	pimātisi	'he lives'
pōsiwa	pōsiw	pōsew	pōsi	'he embarks'
newāpamāwa	niwāpamāw	newāpamaw	niwāpamā	'I look at him'
wāpanwi	wāpan	wāpan	wāpan	'it dawned'
nīyawi	nīyaw	nēyaw	nīyaw	'my body'
kenosiwa	kinosiw	kenōsew	kinosi	'he is long'

The Fox words are generally longer than the others, whereas the Ojibwa are often shorter. We might assume that the development of Fox involved adding final vowels, or conversely, that the others have lost them. The first alternative seems less likely, since it would be necessary to account for the addition of /i/, /wi/, or /a/ in different contexts. It is easier to assume that these are original, and that any final vowel is dropped. There is much additional evidence that the longer forms are older, and our reconstruction will be based on this hypothesis. All the sets of presumed cognates that have /p/ in any one language have /p/ in all. We assume that this is inherited, and so set up a Proto-Central-Algonquian [*p], which we may define as representing the correspondence /p p p p/. Similarly, we may set up [*m], [*t], [*s],

[*w], [*n], [*y], and [*k], representing /m m m m/, etc. (The second /w/ in Fox /wāpanwi/, which has no correspondents in the other languages, is taken care of by our statements about loss of word endings.) The six sets of words may be represented by [*pemātesiwa *pōsiwa *newāpamāwa *wāpanwi *nīyawi *kenosiwa]. These are merely formulae from which we can predict the actual forms in the four languages under discussion. Only secondarily are they guesses as to the actual forms in Proto-Central-Angonquian as the ancestral language of the group.

27.14 A wider sample of the languages will necessitate some modifications of our first conclusions. Consider the following additional sets of words, where attention is directed to the phonemes transcribed in boldface:

anemwa	atim	an**ɛ**m	anim	'dog'
nīnemwa	nītim	nēnem	nīnim	'my sister-in-law'
ineniwa	iyiniw	enēniw	inini	'man'
nēsēwa	yēhyēw	nɛhnew	nēssē	'he breathes'

In these sets we find two new correspondences which can be distinguished from [*n] (/n n n n/) only in Cree: these are /n t n n/ and /n y n n/. These are no chance phenomena, since we can find a number of sets of words for each of them which are quite regular in every other respect. These two must be added to our system of Proto-Central-Algonquian reconstructions, and for this purpose the symbols [*θ] and [*l] are customarily selected. Thus we may reconstruct: [*aθemwa *nīθemwa *elenyiwa *lēhlēwa]. One reason for choosing the symbols [*θ] and [*l] is that Arapaho has these correspondences as /θ/ and /l/, and that many other languages have /l/ for [*l]. *Illinois* is derived through French from the Algonquian word 'man' in one such language. However, we must not assume that we actually know precisely how either of these was pronounced in the ancestral language, nor indeed dare we be dogmatic even about [*p] or [*m].

In all of these reconstructions, and most noticeably the last, we have had to make use of some correspondences which have not been mentioned: those between the vowels, and /s hy hn ss/ which is noted by [*hl]. No single correspondence can be considered as established until enough have been found to enable the worker to reconstruct a number of words or morphemes. The consonant correspondences are of very little value unless we can also account for the vowels. This is another instance of the principle which has been mentioned in other contexts: We cannot establish the phonemes individually without regard to their place in the system as a whole. We cannot consider a morpheme as established unless we can account for the rest of the utterance in which we find it. Languages are integrated systems, and we cannot treat them fragmentarily.

27.15   One more set of words should be commented on:

ōsani   ohtāwiya   ōhnan   ōssan   'his father'

With the exception of the Cree form, this is reconstructed as [*ōhθali]. Actually, the first part of the Cree word fits, since from this reconstruction we would expect a form like /*ohtan/. We can only assume that some sort of analogic change has taken place in this particular word at some point in its history in Cree. No comparative reconstruction can be expected to fit the entire vocabulary in any one of the languages compared. There will be sets in which a partial analogic reformation can be easily detected and a reconstruction made on the basis of the evidence available. There will also be instances in which no reconstruction can be made at all, since there may be no certain evidence to identify any one word as inherited from the ancestral language. Reconstructions never profess to comprehend the entire vocabulary and structure of the languages on which they are based, but only parts which can be proven to be cognate.

The procedure which has just been described is one of the tools of **comparative linguistics.** This discipline is coordinate with **descriptive linguistics** as a second major branch of language science. The methods of the two are basically very similar. They differ largely in the selection of the data with which they are concerned. Rigorous methods of language study were first developed for certain comparative problems. Descriptive linguistics therefore owes many features of its methodology to comparative linguistics. In return, comparative work, to attain the maximum result from its method, must depend on descriptive linguistics for its data. For example, the reconstruction of Proto-Central-Algonquian just mentioned is possible only because adequate analyses had been made of the four languages concerned.

27.16 The methods of comparative linguistics enable us to demonstrate that two languages are related. It remains to determine the bearing of this relationship on the classification.

Total loss of morphemes is an inevitable feature of linguistic change. There is evidence that this loss proceeds at about the same average rate for all languages. A number of calculations have indicated that this rate is about 19 percent per thousand years for the most basic vocabulary. Suppose two languages separate completely so that their subsequent histories are independent, and that in the thousand years subsequent to separation each language loses 19 percent of the morpheme stock they had in common when they were a single language. Each language retains 81 percent of the original stock. Suppose we consider an original sample stock of 200 morphemes. Language A will retain about 162 of them, as will language B. But there is no reason to expect that the two languages will necessarily lose the same items. The most probable outcome is that language B will retain 81 percent of the 162 which language A retains, as well as 81 percent of the 38 which language A losses. This means that A and B can be expected to have about 132, or 66 percent, of this basic stock in common.

Such a calculation can be reversed. If 66 percent of the basic morpheme stock seems to be cognate in two languages, we may assume that they have been separate for 1000 years. If 44 percent is cognate, 2000 years is the most probable period of separation.

This method, known as **glottochronology,** still in the early stages of development, promises to provide a useful basis for interpreting the degree of language relationship. It also provides a means of dating certain events in prehistory. Such dates, like Carbon-14 dates, are statistical. They provide only an estimate of the most probable date, together with some estimate of the probability of any given deviation from such a date.

27.17 The methods of comparative linguistics are laborious and depend on good descriptive materials being available for the languages concerned. They have not as yet been successfully applied to more than a few language groups. The methods of glottochronology, if they are to be rigorously applied, must follow comparative analysis, since they depend on accurate identification of cognates. This is possible only when a systematic analysis of correspondences has been established.

For large areas, languages can therefore be classified only on the basis of direct and uncontrolled comparisons of vocabulary often poorly recorded. This means that our present ideas of language classification must be considered as nothing more than tentative. In general, it may be said that the more refined methods are of greatest need when more remote relationships are concerned. Closely related languages are usually clearly marked by evident similarities, so that intuitive conclusions based on examination of whatever data may be available are often quite reliable. Superficial resemblances between more distantly related languages may be absent, but sufficient evidence of a less apparent kind can often be found by comparative study. However, there is a degree of relationship at which evidence is so scanty that it cannot readily be separated from the chance resemblances which can occur between any two languages. When we say that two languages are not related, we merely mean that the relationship, if any, is so remote that the most powerful methods yet applied to the data cannot detect it. We cannot prove conclusively that any two languages are not related, only that they do not seem to be related at a certain level.

27.18 Africa will serve as a case study for some of the problems of language classification. The Bantu languages are very closely related and show numerous marked common characteristics in grammar and vocabulary. In addition, they occupy a generally compact area from the equator southward, almost to the Cape. Their close relationship was noted at a very early stage in the study of African languages and is universally accepted. Since the group is large, it was assumed to represent a language **family** (the largest taxonomic group usually recognized). Similarly, another group of languages in the northern and northeastern parts of the continent were recognized as related, though there was no agreement on the precise limits of the group. This was designated as the Hamitic family. Between the two lay a large number of languages with no evident relationship to either, nor much with each other. These were designated as Sudanic. Some workers recognized that this was merely a convenient term to cover an assortment of languages whose affinities were not understood (a necessary and useful device at a certain stage of knowledge). But others misinterpreted the Sudanic group as in some way coordinate with the Hamitic and Bantu families. The result has been serious misunderstanding.

These three African language "families" were commonly defined typologically. Thus Bantu languages were described as having a well developed system of noun classes with prefixed class markers and a highly developed system of concord. Hamitic languages were defined as having, among other features, clearly developed gender. Sudanic languages were alleged to be monosyllabic and tonal. Actually, none of these characterize any of these groups. There are Bantu dialects in which noun classes and the concord system are nearly or wholly lacking. Many Sudanic languages (e.g., Bariba, cf. 14.8) have equally complex systems of classes and concord. A typological classification may be useful for certain purposes, but such a classification as this, which was generally interpreted as genetic, though typologically defined, is misleading in the extreme.

27.19   In recent years great advances have been made in our knowledge of African languages. Various elements in a better classification have gradually emerged. First various groups of Sudanic languages were sorted out and shown to be closely related. Then various of these groups were shown to have common descent, and the various resemblances between the largest group of these and Bantu were pointed out. In the meantime, evidence for the falsity of the old typological criteria was accumulating. For example, a close study of the root morphemes of several West African Sudanic languages was published which proved conclusively that some, at least, were far from monosyllabic.

The result was that in 1949 and 1950 a new scheme for the classification of the African languages was advanced and is rapidly winning general acceptance. This unites the largest part of the old Hamitic Family with the Semitic languages (centering in Asia) and one group of the old Sudanic group into the Afro-Asiatic Family. It unites the greater number of the Sudanic languages of West Africa with Bantu languages into the Niger-Congo Family, and it sets up thirteen smaller families to contain the remaining Sudanic languages. These were not claimed to be necessarily independent, but only to be not as yet demonstrated to be related. Since then, four of the thirteen have been united by the discovery of evidence of their common descent and may be known as the

Chari-Nile Family. The new classification cannot be considered as definitive in all details, but it does at least clear the air of the old typological confusions and provide a basis for progress. It would seem to be essentially correct in its main outlines.

27.20 With regard to other parts of the world, our knowledge of linguistic classification is in various of the stages through which African linguistics has passed. In South America no real classification has as yet emerged. In New Guinea languages are classified into two groups: one, Malayo-Polynesian, is like Bantu in being a clearly marked genetic unity; the other, Papuan, is like Sudanic in being only a taxonomic wastebasket out of which we must some day sort groups showing relationship. In some areas our knowledge has passed beyond that now reached in Africa. In Europe, for example, most of the problems of language classification have been met, and a great deal of detailed comparative work has been done.

27.21 The second reason given for our ignorance of the number of languages in the world is the inadequacy of our knowledge. In large areas we have only the most rudimentary information. There has recently appeared a volume purporting to list the languages and dialects of West Africa. The auspices under which it appeared are such as to guarantee high quality and near exhaustiveness within the limits of total scientific knowledge to date. We may therefore take West Africa as a type example to illustrate the problems. There are other areas in which our knowledge is much more complete, e.g., Europe, and some in which it is much less satisfactory, e.g., New Guinea.

Of the considerable number of languages listed, at least a third are entered with some reservations. For many, all that can be said is that some traveler reported a language of that name in a certain region. For many of these, we have no way of judging the actual status. Some may actually be languages. Others are probably poorly marked dialects of some neighboring language listed elsewhere. In a few cases, the reported "language" may actually not designate a speech form at all. Many of these reports are made by people who know very little about linguistics or the languages of the area. Moreover, if some languages are known only from such casual reports, what assurance have we that there are not many others which have not been reported at all?

Sometimes what is reported as a single language is later found to be a group of two or more speech forms, perhaps not even closely related. An extreme case of this sort is the "Mimi" language of French Equatorial Africa. This is known from two brief accounts by travelers. But the two are certainly not based on the same language, and in fact seem to treat two languages of different language families. How many other "languages" are actually similar groups?

27.22 Of course the descriptive work that can be done on any language is enormous. No language can be said to be fully described. It would be utopian to wish for anything approaching complete description for all the languages of the world. To enable us to compile an adequate treatment of the languages of the world in handbook form a minimum objective might be as follows:

For every language and major dialect, there would be needed at least the following: a summary of the phonology and morphology; a vocabulary of, say, several thousand words; a small body of recorded texts together with a translation into some better-known language; a statement of where and by whom the language is spoken, and the name by which it is called by its speakers and the neighboring peoples. With this much information, a definitive listing and classification of languages could be made.

Beyond this, there is frequently need of a much more comprehensive record. The socially more important languages, and a few sample languages from each group, whether socially important or not, should be described much more adequately. Incredibly few languages have, for example, an adequate dictionary, that is, one in which the vocabulary entries run to tens of thousands and in which the definitions are not merely one word translations, but include citations of usages and discussion of the range of meanings. Many more such dictionaries are needed. Still fewer languages have adequate grammars. Too many of the grammars we have are arbitrarily fitted into a mold that is irrelevant or actually contrary to the structure of the language. Serious treatments of syntax are exceedingly rare, and treatments of intonation or similar phenomena are almost non-existent. The basic task of descriptive linguistics, that of describing languages, is very far from adequately discharged.

27.23 If all the world's supply of descriptive linguists could be put on the job of making minimally adequate descriptions of speech forms under a well financed and carefully directed program, it might be that we could meet the first goal within a decade. But apart from the obvious financial limitations, this is not at all feasible. There are other important activities to occupy the time of linguists: perpetuating the profession by training replacements, making their contributions to "liberal" education and the training of specialists in other fields, conducting fundamental research for the advancement of linguistic theory and method, working on the application of their findings to various practical problems like the teaching of languages, and carrying on a program of public relations to acquaint the public with the work which is done and to recruit new personnel for the field. There simply are not enough competent descriptive linguists, nor have they finances and facilities with which to work.

Yet there is a certain urgency in the needs. From a scientific point of view there is an urgency because the data is being lost. Languages are changing or disappearing. Some of them might make important contributions to a basis for a more comprehensive theory. There is also a practical urgency. Almost daily, decisions are being made which should presuppose adequate knowledge of the languages of the peoples concerned. Orthographies are being established and new written languages launched. Vernacular education is being pushed, sometimes with no clear knowledge of the languages concerned or the special problems they present. Efforts are being made to extend government or trade languages at the expense of smaller speech forms; sometimes more information would make possible a transition with less disruption. There is increased need for competence in less known but often widely used languages; often our knowledge of their structure is not adequate for effective teaching.

27.24 All this points to the need of more descriptive linguists. It has recently been estimated that there are only about three hundred in the United States. A decade ago the number was much less, and presumably increase will continue. Nevertheless, there is no prospect that there will be enough professional linguists to do all the field work that needs to be done.

It would seem therefore that there is an excellent opportunity for amateurs in this field. In the past, a great deal of linguistic work was done by such people, missionaries, colonial officials, business men, and others. Their work was not always all that might be desired, but much of it was done before the development of modern methods, that is, at a time when a professional could have done little better. In the present time, one of the most urgent needs of the science is to make its basic concepts and methods known, so that such amateurs can produce results that will be acceptable by modern standards. This should be quite practical, since many of these people have some direct interest in learning the languages concerned, and can directly profit by many of the concepts and techniques in their own language learning.

One of the most monumental undertakings in the field of language study was the *New English Dictionary*. For this, several million quotations from an exceedingly wide range of English literature were assembled by over 1300 readers, most of them volunteers. Although no such organized cooperative effort has ever, to my knowledge, been carried out within the field of descriptive linguistics, and few in the closely allied fields of geographical or social linguistics, it would seem quite possible to do so. The examples of such sciences as astronomy, with a well organized program of comet and meteor observation largely by volunteer hobbyists, and meteorology, with heavy dependence on volunteer weather recorders, would suggest that if such forces could be organized they might prove very valuable. But apart from such large-scale undertakings, there are certainly many ways in which individual workers can assemble important data as a hobby or incidentally to other occupations. For greatest effectiveness, this work would require close cooperation between professionals and amateurs. Given such cooperation, we may expect rapid advance in our knowledge of the languages of the world in years to come.

28

Some Languages and Language Families

28.1   The largest and most important language family, from the point of view of both the social importance of the major languages in the group and their interest to linguists, is the **Indo-European**. The comparative method was very early applied to the study of this family, and more comparative work has been done on Indo-European than on all other groups together. As a result, many features of the family are well known. There is relatively little debate about the limits of the family or the major groups into which it can be divided; but there is still difference of opinion as to the details of interrelationship of the groups. This is largely because the classical methods of comparative linguistics were not adequate to give a decisive answer in this matter. It remains to be seen whether newer methods will succeed. The next several sections will discuss very briefly the major branches of the Indo-European family.

28.2   The **Germanic** languages consist of three groups of important languages: English-Frisian, Dutch-German, and Scandinavian. The first includes only *English*, with more speakers than any other language of the present day, and *Frisian*, spoken by a relatively small population along the coast in the Netherlands and

Germany. On the continent of Europe the Dutch-German language area supports three well-known written languages, *German*, *Dutch*, and *Flemish*. (See 26.10.) The first two, especially, have been carried abroad and are spoken in many parts of the world. *Afrikaans*, one of the two official languages of the Union of South Africa, is a development from Dutch. *Yiddish* is basically a German dialect with a written language using the Hebrew alphabet. Continental Scandinavia supports four written languages: *Danish* in Denmark, *Swedish* in Sweden and Finland, *Bokmål* and *Nynorsk*, two competing writing conventions in Norway. *Icelandic* is also of the Scandinavian group. The oldest extensive documents in any Germanic language are the *Gothic* Scriptures translated by Wulfila in the fourth century, of which, unfortunately, only a part has been preserved. The most ancient Scandinavian records of any length are in *Old Norse* from the twelfth century. The documents from the Dutch-German area before the rise of the modern standard languages represent a number of dialects, of which the most commonly mentioned include *Old Saxon* and *Old High German*. *Old English* is the best designation for the Germanic dialects of Britain before the Norman conquest, though the less suitable *Anglo-Saxon* is often used.

28.3   Of the **Celtic** languages, formerly much more widespread, only four retain any vitality. *Breton* in the extreme northwest of France competes with French and is slowly losing ground. *Welsh*, *Irish*, and *Scots Gaelic* resist submersion in English only by isolation and local nationalism.

28.4   The **Romance** languages contain five very important written languages: *Portuguese* is the language of Portugal and Brazil and the official language of the Portuguese Empire in Africa and Asia. *Spanish* is the language of the larger part of Spain and of most of Latin America other than Brazil. *French* is the official language of France and many former French territories, and one of the official languages in Belgium, Belgian Congo, Switzerland, and Canada. *Italian* is the official language of Italy, and the spoken language of many Italian emigrants. *Roumanian* is the official language of Roumania. In the Romance area, language and political boundaries seldom coincide with any precision. Within Spain the well-marked *Catalan* dialect area is commonly recognized as a separate language, and the *Galician* dialects are more closely related to Portuguese than to Spanish. In the south of France the local dialects are known collectively as *Provençal;* but for the political accident, they might have provided the base for another important written language. *Sardinian* is quite distinct from Italian. In the Alpine regions of northeastern Italy and adjoining Switzerland is a group of closely related dialects known to linguists as *Rhæto-Romanic.* One of these, known as *Romansch,* has developed a written form and become (with German, French, and Italian) one of the official languages of the Swiss Republic. In some areas outside of Europe, local vernaculars derived from Romance languages have developed. Probably the most clearly marked and most important socially is *Haitian Creole.*

Classical *Latin,* as known from its extensive literature, stands very close to the common ancestor of all the modern Romance languages. The latter must, of course, have been a spoken language; this is sometimes referred to as *Vulgar Latin,* but this term is often used in a very inexact way. In ancient times there were a number of other Indo-European languages spoken in Italy. Not all were closely related and many are so poorly documented that no clear evidence of their relationships is available. Those related to Latin are designated as the **Italic** branch. *Oscan, Umbrian,* and *Venetic* belong with Latin in this group. *Etruscan,* the language of one of the most important peoples in ancient Italy, is not Indo-European, and no relationship has been established.

28.5   A large part of Eastern Europe is occupied by speakers of **Slavic** languages. About a half of this population use *Russian,* originally the language of the region centering on Moscow but now spoken across northern Asia, in which area it is supplanting many of the indigenous languages. It is also widely used as a second language in portions of the U.S.S.R. in which other languages are dominant and in countries of the Soviet sphere. This gives it a position as one of the leading languages of the world, probably second only to English in social and political significance. East and south of the Russian area within the Soviet Union are the slightly different *Byelorussian* and *Ukrainian* languages. Three other Slavic languages served as the nuclei around which independent states were organized following World War I. These are *Polish, Czech* and *Slovak* (dialects of one language), and *Serbo-Croatian* (with its two written languages, *Serbian* and *Croatian*).

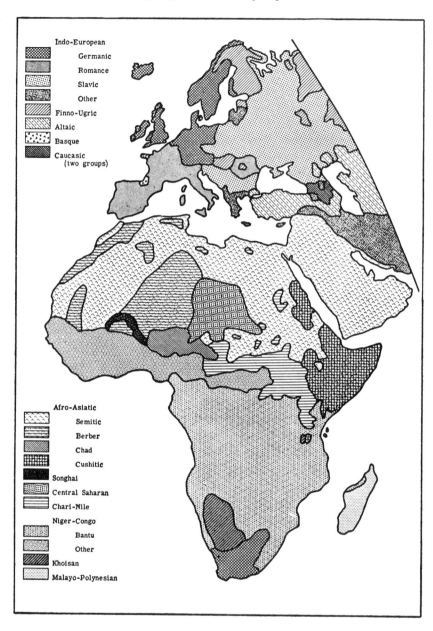

Indo-European
    Germanic
    Romance
    Slavic
    Other
Finno-Ugric
Altaic
Basque
Caucasic
(two groups)

Afro-Asiatic
    Semitic
    Berber
    Chad
    Cushitic
Songhai
Central Saharan
Chari-Nile
Niger-Congo
    Bantu
    Other
Khoisan
Malayo-Polynesian

Chief Language Groups in Europe, the Near East, and Africa

Bulgarian has served in the same way for a somewhat longer time. *Old Church Slavonic* is the first written language of the Slavic group, dating from the ninth century. It is still used as a liturgical language in some of the Orthodox Churches.

28.6 *Lithuanian* and *Latvian* are the only two languages of any social importance in the **Baltic** branch. *Albanian*, with no known close relationship, comprises the **Albanian** branch. *Armenian*, spoken in the southern Caucasus and in scattered communities in the Near East and elsewhere, is generally treated as comprising the **Armenian** branch.

Modern Greek, together with the various older forms of Greek, comprises the **Greek** branch. *Ancient Greek* is a complex of dialects representing successive waves of Indo-European-speaking peoples spreading into the Aegean area. Recent decipherment has extended the known history of Greek to over three millennia. Within such a time-span there must, of course, be considerable change, so that it is important to maintain a careful distinction between the different stages. Unfortunately it is common practice to speak merely of "Greek" without recognizing these differences or indicating the form of Greek which is meant.

28.7 The **Iranian** branch contains four important spoken languages or perhaps groups of closely related languages. In the mountains of eastern Turkey, Iraq, and western Iran is *Kurdish*. A large part of Iran uses *Persian*, and Persian is also an important second language among Muslims in India and Pakistan. Part of Afghanistan and adjacent areas in Pakistan use *Pashto* or *Afghan*. *Balochi* is the main language of Baluchistan in Pakistan. A large number of older Iranian languages have left important literary remains. The oldest is *Old Persian*, known from the sixth to the third century B.C. *Avestan* is the language of the Zoroastrian scriptures. *Pahlavi* was used in the Persian Empire of post-Christian times.

28.8 The **Indic** branch includes most of the languages of northern India and Pakistan. There are a very considerable number of languages in the branch, and several of them are spoken by large populations. A classification based on the spoken dialects does not accord with the usual understanding of the people in India and Pakistan, since *Hindi* and *Urdu* are two literary languages which are used in association with widely divergent spoken forms. Hindi is now the official language of the Republic of India, and Urdu is official in Pakistan. *Bengali, Assamese, Oriya, Marathi, Gujerati, Sindhi, Panjabi, Kashmiri,* and *Nepali* are among the best-known of the group. *Sinhalese,* the chief language of Ceylon, though far removed from the main area, is also Indic.

The Indic branch has a long literary history. A large part of this literature is in *Sanskrit,* still widely used as a literary and liturgical language in India. Sanskrit is of great interest to linguists because of the high development of descriptive linguistic technique culminating in the work of Pāṇini in the fourth century B.C., and because of the stimulus which the introduction of Sanskrit to Western scholarship gave to the development of modern linguistic science. The Vedas, in a language related to classical Sanskrit, are the oldest documents in any Indo-European language, though we have them only in much later copies. The other older Indic languages are known collectively as *Prakrits.*

The Indic and Iranian languages are sometimes classed together as **Indo-Iranian.**

28.9   There are numerous extinct Indo-European languages of which we have some records. These range from rather extensive collections of documents to a few short inscriptions. The better attested ones can be classified with some certainty. The correct place for some of the others is still in question after exhaustive analysis of all the available data. Among the best known are those in the **Tocharian** branch, two languages spoken in Central Asia from the seventh to tenth centuries. These are of interest to comparative Indo-European studies because they add a whole new branch to the data. The other Indo-European languages which cannot clearly be assigned to any of the branches enumerated above are largely known from the Mediterranean area. Among those most commonly mentioned are *Illyrian* and *Phrygian.*

28.10   *Hittite* is known from a large number of inscriptions and tablets beginning about a millennium and a half B.C. Together with a number of other ancient languages also from Asia Minor, Hittite is classed as **Anatolian.** These languages show evident relationship to Indo-European, but the exact nature of this connection is not agreed upon. Some have considered Anatolian as another branch of Indo-European. The majority consider that Anatolian separated from Indo-European before the latter broke up into the present branches, so that Anatolian and Indo-European together constitute a larger group sometimes referred to as **Indo-Hittite.**

28.11   The **Finno-Ugric** family includes three socially important languages of Europe: *Finnish*, *Estonian*, and *Hungarian*. In addition, there are various others scattered over northern Europe and Asia. These include *Lappish*, *Mordvin*, *Cheremiss*, and *Votyak*. The *Samoyed* languages are related.

28.12   The **Altaic** family consists of three branches. The **Turkic** languages include *Turkish; Azerbaijani* spoken in northwest Iran and the Caucasus; and a number of languages or dialects in central Asia, notably *Kirghiz*, *Uzbeg*, *Türkomen*, and *Kazak*. The **Mongol** branch includes several closely related languages usually lumped under the label *Mongolian*. The third branch consists of *Manchu* and *Tungus* spoken to the east of Mongolia.

28.13   The Caucasus is an area of extreme linguistic diversity. In addition to Armenian, Azerbaijani, Iranian languages, Russian, and Ukrainian, which have already been mentioned, there is a large number of languages frequently classed together as **Caucasian.** This is not entirely satisfactory, since there is no demonstrable relationship between some of these, and they should be classed into two families. The **South Caucasian** family includes *Georgian*, with an important and ancient literature, and *Mingrelian*. The **North Caucasian** family contains a very large number of languages, the best known of which are *Abkhasian*, *Avar*, *Chechen*, and *Kabardian*.

28.14   In the western Pyrenees in France and Spain a small population speaks *Basque*. Its affinities are one of the recurrent topics of debate and speculation, and relationship to almost every linguistic family in the Old World has been proposed. None of the proposals seems capable of proof by any acceptable methodology, so that **Basque** remains an independent family.

28.15   The **Afro-Asiatic** family is so-called because it is spoken in northern Africa and southwestern Asia. There are five branches, Semitic, Egyptian, Berber, Cushitic, and Chad. The last four are sometimes known as **Hamitic,** and the whole family as **Hamito-Semitic.** The term is unfortunate, however, because it implies that the four "Hamitic" branches are more closely related to each other than to Semitic, which does not seem to be the case.

28.16   The **Semitic** branch is the best known. Only *Hebrew*, *Arabic*, and some of the languages of Ethiopia are of present importance as spoken languages. Arabic, however, includes a number of very divergent dialects which, but for tradition, might be considered as separate languages. Several ancient Semitic languages are well known and have important literature. *Akkadian* (also called *Assyrian* or *Babylonian*) and *Sumerian*, which is of unknown relationship, but certainly not Afro-Asiatic, are the chief languages of the vast cuneiform literature from Mesopotamia. From these two languages, primarily, we have our oldest historical records. *Aramaic* and *Syriac* are closely related dialects. Anciently, Aramaic languages were dominant as vehicles of government and business in the Near East after the eclipse of Akkadian. One form of Aramaic is of present-day importance as the language of much Rabbinical Jewish literature, while Syriac is a liturgical language in some Eastern churches and the language of much early Christian literature. *Phoenician*, only slightly different from ancient Hebrew, was an important trade language in the Mediterranean and very probably the language in which the alphabet originated. A later form of the same language, known as *Punic*, was the language of the Carthaginian Empire. *Hebrew*, the language of ancient Canaan, is of importance chiefly as the vehicle of the larger part of the Old Testament Scriptures (a small part is in Aramaic). It was supplanted before the time of Christ by Aramaic in spoken usage, but has continued as a liturgical and literary language and is now being revived as a spoken language in Israel. With this long history there were inevitable changes, and Modern Hebrew differs in various important respects from Ancient Hebrew. In the southern part of Arabia the vernaculars known collectively as *South Arabic* are quite different from classical Arabic or the dialects to the north, though classical Arabic is the written language most used in the area. There are three important vernacular Semitic languages in Ethiopia. *Amharic*, spoken in the center of the country, is the official language. *Tigré* and *Tigriña* are spoken in the north. *Ge'ez* (also commonly called *Ethiopic*) is an older language related to these three and is the liturgical language of the Ethiopian Church.

28.17   The second branch of the Afro-Asiatic languages consists of ancient *Egyptian* and its descendant, *Coptic*. The latter remains the liturgical language among the Coptic Christians of Egypt, but has been supplanted by Arabic as a vernacular.

The **Berber** languages are widely scattered over North Africa and the Sahara. In many places they have been supplanted by Arabic, but are still widely used as the home language in many areas. *Kabyle*, *Shilh*, *Zenaga*, and *Tuareg* are among the best known.

The **Cushitic** languages occupy most of the eastern horn of Africa. *Somali*, *Galla*, and *Beja* are spoken by the largest populations and over the widest areas.

The **Chad** languages include an immense number of languages spoken in central and northern Nigeria and around Lake Chad. Most of these are very poorly known, and few are spoken by populations of any size. *Hausa*, however, is one of the most important languages of Africa. It is the first language of a very large number of people, and in addition is a language of commerce over a very wide area in West Africa.

28.18   The Sudan belt of Africa contains a number of small language families, mostly containing only very poorly known languages, as well as several large groups. It is thus an area of considerable linguistic diversity, particularly in certain regions.

The *Songhai* language spoken along the Niger River in the vicinity of the great bend constitutes the most important of these small families, since it is the language of a large population which has had an important part in the history of West Africa.

28.19   Centering generally in the upper Nile Valley, but extending southward to Tanganyika and westward into the Basin of the Chari River almost to Lake Chad, is the **Chari-Nile** family. At the center of the area is the **Nilotic** branch including *Dinka*, *Nuer*, and *Shilluk*. *Acoli* in Uganda, *Masai* and *Nandi* in Kenya and Tanganyika have been erroneously called "Nilo-Hamitic." Actually they have no discoverable relationship to the Afro-Asiatic languages (which include "Hamitic"). In northern Sudan, languages of this group persist as remnants surrounded by Arabic. The best known of these is *Nuba*, spoken along the Nile in the vicinity of the Egypt-Sudan border. The languages to the west are very poorly known but seem to form one branch, the **Central Sudanic**. Probably *Bagirmi* and *Moru* are the most important.

28.20   From Lake Chad northward and eastward is an area occupied by languages of the **Central Saharan** family. Of these, the only one which is well known is *Kanuri*, spoken in northeastern Nigeria and vicinity.

28.21   The most important language family of Africa is the **Niger-Congo**. These languages are spoken in most of West Africa and generally in Africa south of the equator. There are a number of branches, but present knowledge does not provide a definitive classification throughout the group.

The **West Atlantic** and **Mande** branches are quite clearly defined. Both are spoken at the western end of the area. The West Atlantic languages are generally found near the coast from Liberia to Senegal. *Temne* and *Bulom* in Sierra Leone and *Wolof* in Senegal are well known. The most important language of the branch is, however, *Fulani*, spoken by the Fula tribe in widely scattered areas from Senegal to Cameroons. The Mande languages are spoken to the east of the West Atlantic group. The main center is in Liberia and Sierra Leone, where *Kpelle*, *Loma*, and *Mende* are spoken by large populations, and in the areas immediately to the north, where *Malinke* and *Bambara* are the best known.

The coast from Liberia to Cameroons is largely occupied by languages of the **Kwa** branch. A number of these are of great social importance: *Akan* with its dialects *Fanti* and *Twi* in the Gold Coast, *Baoule* in Ivory Coast, *Ewe* in Togoland, *Fon* in Dahomey, *Yoruba*, *Ibo*, and *Nupé* in Nigeria. *Bassa* and *Kru* in Liberia are generally considered as belonging to this branch, but the evidence is not entirely clear. North of the area of these languages a large area is occupied by the **Gur** branch. These are by no means as well known as the Kwa languages, and the branch is not so well established in the classification. *Mossi* is probably the best known and of the greatest social importance.

From the Cameroons eastward across the northern edge of the Congo basin are a number of Niger-Congo languages whose classification is very little understood. They may be all one branch, or divisible into several. *Zande* in Belgian Congo and Sudan is certainly the best known and spoken by the largest population. *Sango*, the lingua franca in much of French Equatorial Africa, also belongs here.

The **Central** branch centers in eastern Nigeria and Cameroons.

It consists of numerous sub-branches, mostly containing languages of which we know relatively little, spoken by small tribes. *Efik* and *Tiv* are exceptions in that each is used by a large population. One group, however, has expanded greatly, spreading southward and eastward over a very large territory. This is the **Bantu** group which, though it covers a larger area than all the other Niger-Congo languages together, is not a branch but only a subdivision of a branch.

There are probably more languages and dialects in the Bantu group than in any other group of comparable rank anywhere. Classification is, therefore, very difficult, and no agreement can be reached at many points. A number of important languages can be listed, however. These are of three kinds: Some are trade or government languages which have recently come to be very widely used far beyond the territory in which they were originally spoken. The most important by far is *Swahili*. This is used throughout East Africa and eastern Belgian Congo, and is occasionally heard in all the adjoining countries. In Congo three other languages have had similar development: *Kongo* in the east, *Luba* in the south, and *Ngala* in the north. These trade languages are used along with the tribal languages, but with a growing tendency to replace some of them. Another group of important languages are the union languages. *Shona*, centering in Southern Rhodesia, was described in 26.7. *Nyanja*, developed on the base of a number of tribal dialects in southern Nyassaland, is another. Finally there are a number of tribal languages which, because of the size or importance of the tribe or other more or less fortuitous circumstances, have become either well known or important. Among these are *Ganda* in Uganda, *Kikuyu* and *Kamba* in Kenya, *Chaga* and *Nyamwesi* in Tanganyika, *Rundi* and *Rwanda* in Ruanda-Urundi, *Bemba* in Northern Rhodesia, *Umbundu* and *Kimbundu* in Angola, *Herero* in Southwest Africa, *Zulu*, *Xhosa*, *Swazi*, *Southern Sotho*, *Northern Sotho*, *Tswana*, and *Venda* in South Africa.

Bantu languages have a system of prefixes indicating gender and number. The names of the languages are sometimes given with these prefixes, and sometimes without. Thus Kongo is sometimes called kiKongo or Kikongo; Ganda is sometimes listed as Luganda, etc. Moreover, the tribes generally have similar names. Thus Luganda is spoken by the Baganda who inhabit Uganda.

28.22   The spread of the Bantu languages and the peoples speaking them is a relatively recent historical development and was still actively in progress at the first European contact. Among the peoples displaced were speakers of the **Khoisan** languages. Two small tribes speaking languages related to this group persist in Tanganyika surrounded by Bantu: *Sandawe* and *Hatsa*. The largest remnant is in South Africa, where the *Bushman* languages and *Hottentot* occupy a large area of sparsely populated desert and scrub.

28.23   *Japanese* and *Ryukyu* form the **Japanese** family. *Korean* comprises the **Korean** family. Both were long considered to be isolated, but it has recently been proved that they are somewhat distantly related to each other.

28.24   The most extensive language family in eastern Asia is the **Sino-Tibetan.** It may be considered as containing two branches, **Tibeto-Burman** and **Chinese.** *Tibetan*, spoken not only in Tibet proper but also in many areas around the borders, and *Burmese*, the language of the dominant people in Burma, are the two largest languages in the Tibeto-Burman branch. The mountainous regions lying between these two language areas in India, Pakistan, and Burma are occupied by peoples speaking a very wide variety of mostly Tibeto-Burman languages. This area is linguistically one of the most diversified in the world, and it is, as yet, very difficult to get a clear picture of the interrelationships of the numerous languages and dialects. *Garo*, *Bodo*, the *Naga* languages, and the *Kuki-Chin* languages belong to this branch. The *Karen* languages of southern Burma are of uncertain affinities, but are usually treated as belonging to the Tibeto-Burma branch.

The **Chinese** languages constitute the second large branch of the **Sino-Tibetan** family. Of these, the most widely used is that known as *Mandarin*. This is the language of roughly the northern half of China. The southeast of China is occupied by a number of languages. Around the mouth of the Yangtse are the *Wu* dialects, of which *Suchow* is the representative most frequently cited. Southward along the coast the linguistic diversity is considerable. These are commonly referred to as the *Fukien* dialects (local custom is to refer to all these languages as "dialects"). Each is known by the name of the city around which it is spoken, e.g., *Amoy*, *Foochow*. Inland there is a large area in which *Hakka* is spoken. South of

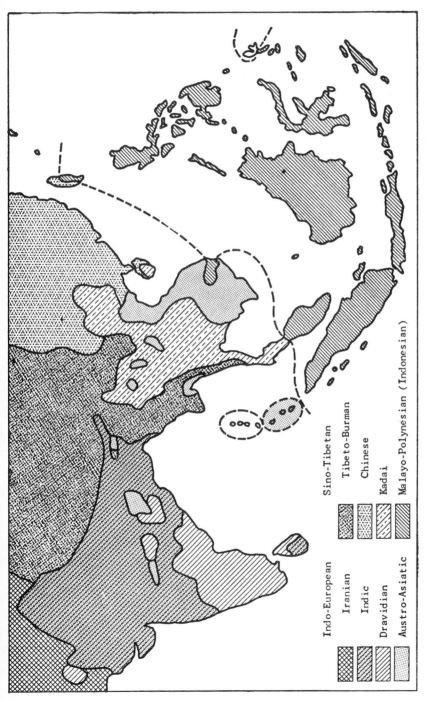

Indo-European

Iranian

Indic

Dravidian

Austro-Asiatic

Sino-Tibetan

Tibeto-Burman

Chinese

Kadai

Malayo-Polynesian (Indonesian)

Major Language Groups, Southeast Asia

Hakka is a large area in which the dialects are collectively known as *Cantonese*. In southwestern China, the local languages are largely non-Chinese, of various relationships, and mostly poorly known to linguists. *Miao* and *Yao* are most frequently mentioned. Mandarin Chinese is extending into the area and displacing some of these languages.

28.25   The **Kadai** family contains a number of small languages of southwestern China and Hainan Island, as well as three large and socially significant languages or language groups. These are *Thai* or *Siamese*, *Laotien* or *Lao* in Indo-China, and the *Shan* languages of Burma. These languages have long been considered as a branch of the Sino-Tibetan family, but it now seems quite evident that the resemblances are largely due to borrowing from Chinese. The wider relationships of the Kadai languages are very much debated.

28.26   The **Malayo-Polynesian** family is, after the Indo-European, geographically the most widespread of all. It extends over most of the Pacific Islands and westward to Madagascar. Two branches may be recognized: **Western** or **Indonesian** includes most of the languages of the populous East Indies. *Malay*, originally the language of the north coast of Sumatra, has become widely extended throughout coastal Sumatra, Malaya, Borneo, and elsewhere. *Indonesian*, the official language of the new republic, is based largely on Malay, but with the admixture of elements from other closely related languages of the area. *Javanese*, *Sundanese*, and *Maduran* are the languages of Java. Of the many languages of Sumatra other than Malay, *Batak* is the best-known. Others include *Balinese* on Bali, *Dayak* in the interior of Borneo, *Makassar* on Celebes. The whole Philippine area uses Indonesian languages: *Tagalog*, *Bisayan*, and *Ilocano* are the best-known. The Indonesian branch extends eastward to Guam (*Chamorro*) and westward to Madagascar (*Malagasy*).

The **Eastern** branch is commonly divided into Micronesian, Polynesian, and Melanesian; however, these divisions are certainly not coordinate. Polynesian is a closely related group of languages spoken over the expanse of the Pacific from Hawaii to New Zealand and Easter Island, as well as on a few islands much farther west. *Hawaiian*, *Tahitian*, *Samoan*, and *Maori* are the best known. Melanesian includes a large number of languages which are related, though commonly only distantly related. The best known is *Fijian*.

28.27 Most of New Guinea and the interior of many adjacent islands is occupied by speakers of languages of unknown affinities. These are arbitrarily classified as **Papuan.** A genetic classification is greatly needed.

28.28 The aborigines of Australia speak numerous languages which are related in a single family, **Australian.** The languages of Tasmania, now extinct, seem to have formed a separate family.

28.29 The **Dravidian** languages are largely restricted to southern India. Four are spoken by very large populations and have highly developed literatures: *Telegu, Tamil, Kannarese,* and *Malayalam. Brahui*, spoken in Baluchistan at a considerable distance from the main center of the family, figures prominently in discussion of the origin of the group. The hills of central India contain many tribes speaking Dravidian languages. The most important are *Gondi, Kurukh,* and *Kui*.

28.30 The **Austro-Asiatic** family consists of a number of languages widely scattered through southeastern Asia and generally surrounded by languages of other families. In the hills of central India are found the *Munda* languages, the best known of which is *Santali. Khasi* is spoken by a large tribe in Assam surrounded by speakers of Tibeto-Burman and Indic languages. *Nicobarese* is used on the Nicobar Islands in the Bay of Bengal. *Palaung* and *Wa* occupy speech islands among the Tibeto-Burman and Kadai languages of upper Burma. *Mon* is spoken in southern Burma where it is dominated by Burmese. Only *Khmer* and *Vietnamese* in Indo-China have any official standing. The latter is spoken by a very considerable population.

28.31 The chief languages of America are Indo-European and have already been mentioned. In order of number of speakers they are *English, Spanish, Portuguese,* and *French*. One Indo-European language which originated in this hemisphere should be mentioned. This is *Haitian Creole*, an offshoot of French, but sufficiently different that treatment as a mere dialect seems extreme. Besides these, other imported European languages, noticeably Italian and German, are spoken by more people in the Americas than any of the aboriginal American languages. Some of the latter do, however, show considerable vitality and continue to be used by large bodies of people. In South America four may be mentioned: *Guaraní* is the home language of most of Paraguay and of many in southwestern Brazil, though most of these are bilingual, using Spanish or Portuguese in public affairs. *Quechua*, the old language of the Inca Empire, is still used by several millions in Peru, Ecuador, and Bolivia, by no means all of whom can also speak Spanish. *Aymará* is the language of many Indians in southern Peru and Bolivia. In Amazonian Brazil a lingua franca based on *Tupi-Guaraní* and called *Lingua Geral* is now being replaced by Portuguese, but has been widely used in the past.

In Middle America there are several Indian languages with appreciable numbers of speakers, though Spanish is making inroads in most areas. In Mexico and Guatemala the following languages are used by a hundred thousand or more: *Nahuatl* (nearly a million), *Quiche, Cakchiquel, Mam, Yucatec, Kekchi, Otomi, Zapotec, Mixtec, Totonac*. North of Mexico *Navaho* is the only language even approaching such a figure. Of the smaller languages, some are rapidly losing ground and are faced with imminent extinction, a fate that has already overtaken a considerable number of languages in the last three centuries. Some of the smaller speech communities are, however, holding their own. Occasional ones show considerable vitality. A few, like Navaho, have increased markedly in number of speakers.

28.32   Listings of American languages are generally based on the situation at first European contact or earliest record. This is by no means contemporaneous over the whole hemisphere, but represents a convenient fiction. In many instances there have been great changes since. Not only have languages disappeared, but because of displacement of populations, many are now spoken in areas remote from their earlier location. The map on page 473 and descriptions are based largely on the distribution at first contact.

A number of language families can be listed for North America, the exact number depending on the author's interpretation where relationships are subject to debate. The classification adopted here is somewhat middle-of-the-road, by no means as conservative as some, but far from as radical as others.

28.33   The eastern coast from Carolina northward to Labrador

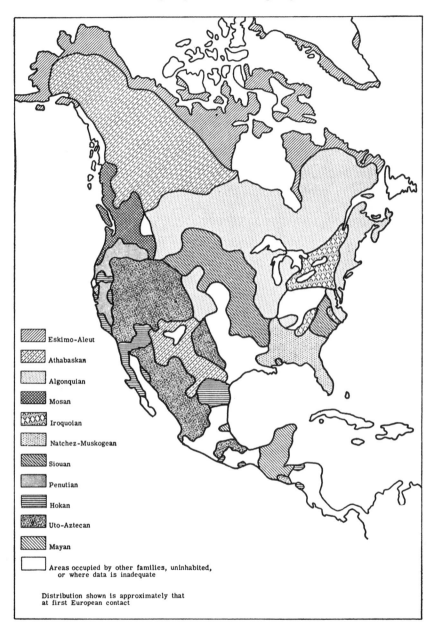

Some Language Groups in North America

was occupied by speakers of **Algonquian** languages. These were, accordingly, the languages with which English and French had their first contacts. A considerable proportion of the Amerind loan words in these two languages are therefore from this source. A large number of place names are of Algonquian origin, even outside the area originally occupied by the languages. For example, the Mississippi was explored from the north, and so bears an Algonquian name: *missi* 'large' plus *sipiy* 'water.'

Massachusetts, though a relatively minor language, is famous for Eliot's Bible, the first modern missionary translation, and the first Bible printed in the United States. *Powhatan, Delaware, Mohegan, Penobscot, Pasamaquoddy,* and *Micmac* were other coastal tribes and languages. These were cut off from the main body of Algonquian languages by the Iroquois on the middle St. Lawrence. But to the north and west of this area Algonquian languages stretch to the Rocky Mountains. Four of these languages, *Fox* (Wisconsin), *Cree* (Hudson Bay and westward), *Menomini* (upper Michigan), and *Ojibwa* (north shore of the Great Lakes) were used by Leonard Bloomfield in one of the first demonstrations of the applicability of comparative methods to languages without literary history (see 27.13). *Potawatomi* (lower Michigan), *Illinois* and *Shawnee* (Tennessee) are related. *Blackfoot, Arapaho,* and *Cheyenne,* spoken on the western plains, represent more distantly related branches of the same family.

28.34 Southeastern United States was an area of somewhat more diversity. The largest family was the **Natchez-Muskogean:** *Creek, Alabama* (including *Koasati* as a dialect), *Chickasaw, Choctaw, Natchez.*

In the mountains was *Cherokee,* still one of the more important Amerind languages of the United States. Cherokee is widely known for its syllabary (see 25.11). This and *Tuscarora* on the Carolina coast were the southern outliers of the **Iroquoian** family, the main body of which occupied the middle St. Lawrence Valley and eastern Pennsylvania: *Huron; Erie; Oneida; Mohawk;* one language spoken by *Seneca, Onondaga,* and *Cayuga;* and *Conestoga* or *Susquehanna.*

In the Southeast also were *Biloxi, Ofo, Tutelo* and *Catawba,* outliers of the **Siouan** stock. This family occupied the greater part of the northern Great Plains: *Dakota, Mandan, Winnebago, Chiwere* (with dialects *Iowa* and *Missouri*), *Dhegiha* (with dialects *Omaha, Ponca, Osage, Kansa, Quapaw* or *Arkansa*), *Hidatsa, Crow.*

To the south of the Siouan area, the main family was **Caddoan,** with *Caddo, Wichita,* and *Pawnee* as important languages. In the lower Mississippi valley, *Tunica, Atakapa,* and *Chitimacha* formed the **Tunican** family. In Tennessee there was *Yuchi,* forming a family of its own.

The Natchez-Muskogean, Iroquoian, Caddoan, Tunican, and Yuchian families are perhaps related, but proof has not yet been advanced. The Hokan languages of the West are usually included, and the proposed phylum is called **Hokan-Siouan.**

28.35 The Arctic and Sub-Arctic coasts from Labrador and Greenland to Alaska are occupied by speakers of the **Eskimo-Aleut** languages. *Aleut* is spoken on the Aleutian Islands. In Alaska there is *Inupik* and from Alaska to Greenland, *Yupik.* These two are commonly called *Eskimo.*

28.36 The Pacific Northwest from the Columbia River Valley to southern Alaska is occupied by a number of languages which share certain superficial peculiarities, noticeably very complex phonology. Many of them have very complicated patterns of clustering (see 20.14). The area is notable for the large proportion of the pioneer work in American linguistics which was done here. Franz Boas worked on a number of languages of the region, and particularly on *Kwakiutl.* Many of his co-workers and students worked on others. Most of the languages fall into three families which are related in one phylum known as **Mosan.** These are **Salishan** with *Bella Coola, Coeur d'Alene, Chehalia, Kalispel;* **Wakashan** with *Nootka, Kwakiutl, Bella Bella;* and **Chimakuan** with *Chimakum* and *Quileute.* There are four languages each of which forms a family of its own: *Haida* and *Tlingit* in Alaska, *Tsimshian* immediately to the south, and *Kutenai* on the eastern edge of the area. Each of these is sometimes assigned to a phylum containing other stocks (see 28.37 and 28.42). Kutenai and Mosan have been claimed to be related to Algonquian, but the only west coast languages of which this has been proved are *Yurok* and *Wiyot* (**Ritwan**) of northern California.

28.37 A large part of Oregon and California is a region of extreme lingusitic diversity. In one recent classification 25 families, nearly one third of the whole number for the continent, were listed as restricted to this area. Except for Ritwan, these seem to be related in two phyla, **Penutian** and **Hokan**. The languages of proved Penutian affinity are all in this area, though there is some basis for believing that *Tsimshian* of British Columbia may be shown to be Penutian. Other, even less certain, affiliations have been proposed between Penutian and various languages or families in Middle America. The following languages, each representing a separate family, may be listed: *Wintun, Maidu, Miwok, Costanoan, Yokuts, Chinook, Kalapuya, Takelma, Siuslaw, Coos.* Chinook provided the base for *Chinook Jargon*, a creolized trade language that was once widely used throughout the polyglot Pacific Northwest.

28.38 The **Hokan** phylum includes a number of California languages, which, like the Penutian, are not very closely related, so that they are often classified in a number of families: *Karok, Shasta, Chimariko, Yana, Pomo, Esselen, Salinan, Chumash. Yana* is widely cited because of a paper of Edward Sapir on the differentiation between men's and women's speech. In Arizona and Lower California is the *Yuman* group, containing a considerable number of languages. The Hokan languages extend far southward. *Tlapanec* and *Subtiaba* are dialects of a single language spoken in southern Mexico and Nicaragua respectively. *Tequistlatec* or *Chontal of Oaxaca* is also spoken in Southern Mexico. *Jicaque* is spoken in Honduras. The languages of northeastern Mexico are assumed to have been either Hokan, or to belong to a **Coahuiltecan** group allied to Hokan. The best preserved, *Comecrudo*, seems to be clearly Hokan, but on most there is so little data that no final answer is possible.

Tonkawa is the only one of several languages of eastern Texas of which we have reliable record. It may be distantly related to Hokan. As we mentioned before, several families of central and eastern United States are sometimes joined with the Hokan to form the **Hokan-Siouan** phylum, but this must be considered as unproven and probably unprovable until a great deal more work has been done on the individual families.

28.39 In Central America the most clearly marked and easily the most important language family is the **Mayan**. This occupies a compact area from the Isthmus of Mexico into Honduras. In the highlands of Guatemala are found *Mam, Kekchi, Quiche, Cak-*

chiquel, Pokomam, Pokonchi, Ixil, and several lesser, languages forming a sub-family. To the west in Mexico are *Tzeltal, Tzotzil, Tojolabal, Chol,* and *Chontal of Tabasco.* With this group belongs *Chorti* in Honduras, though it is the most eastern of the Mayan languages. To the north is *Yucatec.* This area was the center of the pre-conquest Mayan empire, and it is assumed that the language of the empire was close to modern Yucatec. The only Mayan language not in the main area is *Huaxtec,* spoken on the Gulf coast of central Mexico.

28.40   West of the Mayan area in southern Mexico is another region of extreme linguistic complexity. Most of these languages have been very poorly known until recently. The Summer Institute of Linguistics now has active fieldwork underway in most of the languages and dialects, and accurate grammars and word lists are appearing. Comparative work is also getting started, and several small groups of proven relationship have been established. Previously, classification was usually based on general impressions of superficial similarities.

Mixe, Zoque, and *Popoluca of Vera Cruz* form one such group. To the north are *Totonac* in several dialects and *Tepehua* forming another. These two with *Huave* are probably related to Mayan, and the larger group is sometimes referred to as the **Macro-Mayan** phylum.

Zapotec, actually a group of related languages rather than a single language, and *Chatino* form another group where comparative reconstruction is clearly possible, though not yet published.

Mixtec, Cuicatec, Trique, and *Amusgo* form another group in which comparative reconstruction is underway. Trique is becoming well known as the first language to be discovered with a tone system based on five levels.

North of the last group is another composed of *Mazatec, Chocho, Ixcatec,* and *Popoloca of Pueblo.* (Popoloca and Chontal are Nahuatl words meaning 'barbarians' and 'foreigners.' They are applied to many different languages, so that it is always necessary to add some further designation.)

Still farther north are *Otomi* and the related *Mazahua* and *Pame.* To the west is *Tarascan.*

Most of these groups have at one time or another been asserted to be related. **Otomanguean** is a name commonly applied, but differs somewhat in scope from author to author. There is some question as to how much of this collection of languages can ultimately be related to one another. It does seem likely that Otomian, Mazatecan, and Mixtecan are related, and that the relationship may soon be demonstrated. The Zapotecan and Tarascan seem more distant, if related at all.

28.41 The most recent arrival in the area is *Nahuatl*, the language of the Aztec empire at the time of the conquest. The Nahuas established colonies throughout Middle America, at least as far as Nicaragua. Their language is still spoken in many areas scattered throughout the region. Nahuatl was one of the few Amerind languages to develop a writing system before European contact. Most of these documents have been lost, but there are many writings from the period immediately after the conquest in what is known as *Classical Nahuatl*. This language is the largest single source of the Amerind loan words in European languages.

Nahuatl is the most southerly member of the **Uto-Aztecan** family. The center seems to be in the Great Basin and the Colorado Valley: *Shoshone, Paiute, Tubatulabal,* and *Hopi.* From southern Arizona into northwestern Mexico is a second large area with *Papago, Pima, Tarahumara, Cora,* and *Huichol. Comanche* was spoken in the southern Great Plains.

28.42 The main area of the Uto-Aztecan family is interrupted by languages of the **Athabaskan** family. These are evidently an intrusion from the north; the main body of the family is in the far northwest of Canada and central Alaska. Here the best known are *Sarsi* and *Chipewyan.* That this is the center of diffusion is indicated by the fact that *Haida* and *Tlingit,* apparently related to the Athabaskan family, with which they form the **Na-Dené** phylum, are immediately adjacent. Moreover, the southern languages form a compact group of closely related languages known collectively as *Apachean.* The most important of these is *Navaho,* the most extensively studied of all American Indian languages. There is also a small group of Athabaskan languages in northern California: *Hupa, Chasta Costa,* and *Mattole.*

28.43 The southern Athabaskan languages are spoken by nomadic peoples surrounding the sedentary pueblo peoples. The latter speak a variety of languages, many of them restricted to a single village. These fall into three families: **Tanoan, Keresan,** and

Zuni. The first certainly, and the last possibly, are related to the Uto-Aztecan family and form the **Aztec-Tanoan** phylum.

28.44 Just as the smaller groups are frequently related to form larger groups, we may expect that some of the largest groups are related to each other at a still deeper level. Many suggestions have been made, none of them supported by conclusive evidence. For example, the Finno-Ugric and Altaic families are commonly united into a **Ural-Altaic** family, and this is sometimes extended to include Japanese, Korean, and even Eskimo. Others have seen the relationships of Finno-Ugric with Indo-European, or with Dravidian, or with Austro-Asiatic. Another favorite hypothesis has been the relationship of Indo-European to Semitic. Of all such proposals, the best that can be said is that none are as yet proven. By the nature of the case it is impossible to disprove any such theory. We may expect that continued work will result in more comprehensive categories. However, in many of these proposals, the relationships postulated are at such a deep level that they are probably not demonstrable by direct comparison of present-day languages. Instead, they must await more thorough knowledge of the reconstructed ancestral forms of the various language families. It may be that when we have a clear picture of the older stages of some of the families we will be able to achieve important results by comparisons of these reconstructed languages. In the meantime, a cautious attitude must be maintained with regard to broader groupings of language families.

Selected Bibliography

Allen, Harold Boughton (ed.). *Readings in Applied English Linguistics.* New York: Appleton-Century-Crofts, 1958. 428 pp.

Atwood, Elmer Bagby. *A Survey of Verb Forms in the Eastern United States.* Ann Arbor, Mich.: University of Michigan Press, 1953. 53 pp. + maps.

Baugh, Albert Croll. *A History of the English Language,* 2d ed. New York: Appleton-Century-Crofts, 1957. 506 pp.

Bloch, Bernard, and George L. Trager. *Outline of Linguistic Analysis.* Baltimore: Linguistic Society of America, 1942. 82 pp.

Bloomfield, Leonard. *Language.* New York: Holt, Rinehart and Winston, 1933. 564 pp.

———. *Outline Guide for the Practical Study of Foreign Languages.* Baltimore: Linguistic Society of America, 1942. 16 pp.

Boas, Franz (ed.). *Handbook of American Indian Languages.* Bureau of American Ethnology, Bull. 40. Washington, D.C.: Government Printing Office, 1911, I, 1–83.

———. *Race, Language, and Culture.* New York: The Macmillan Co., 1940, pp. 119–242.

Brown, Roger William. *Words and Things.* Glencoe, Ill.: The Free Press, 1958. 398 pp.

Carroll, John Bissell. *The Study of Language: A Survey of Linguistics and Related Disciplines in America.* Cambridge, Mass.: Harvard University Press, 1953. 289 pp.

Chomsky, Noam. *Syntactic Structures.* 's-Gravenhage: Mouton, 1957. 116 pp.

Comité International Permanent de Linguistes. *Bibliographie Linguistique de l'Année.* Utrecht: Spectrum, 1949—. 1 vol. per year.

Elson, Benjamin, and Velma B. Pickett. *Beginning Morphology-Syntax.* Santa Ana, Calif.: Summer Institute of Linguistics, 1960. 73 pp.

Firth, John Rupert. *Papers in Linguistics, 1934–1951.* London: Oxford University Press, 1957. 233 pp.

Francis, Winthrop Nelson. *The Structure of American English.* New York: Ronald Press, 1958. 614 pp.

Fries, Charles Carpenter. *American English Grammar.* New York: Appleton-Century-Crofts, 1940. 313 pp.

———. *Teaching and Learning English as a Foreign Language.* Ann Arbor, Mich.: University of Michigan Press, 1945. 153 pp.

———. *The Structure of English: An Introduction to the Construction of English Sentences.* New York: Harcourt, Brace & World, 1952. 304 pp.

Gelb, Ignace J. *A Study of Writing: The Foundations of Grammatology.* Chicago: University of Chicago Press, 1952. 295 pp.

Gray, Louis Herbert. *Foundations of Language.* New York: The Macmillan Co., 1939. 530 pp.

Gudschinsky, Sarah C. *Handbook of Literacy.* Glendale, Calif.: Summer Institute of Linguistics, 1957. 91 pp.

Hall, Robert Anderson, Jr. *Linguistics and Your Language.* Garden City, N.Y.: Doubleday, 1960. 265 pp.

Hamp, Eric P. *A Glossary of American Technical Linguistic Usage.* Utrecht: Spectrum, 1958. 61 pp.

Harris, Zellig Sabbetai. *Methods in Structural Linguistics.* Chicago: University of Chicago Press, 1951. 384 pp. (Also paperback as *Structural Linguistics.*)

Haugen, Einar Ingvald. *Bilingualism in the Americas: A Bibliography and Research Guide.* University, Ala.: University of Alabama Press, 1956. 159 pp.

Heffner, Roe-Merrill Secrist. *General Phonetics.* Madison, Wis.: University of Wisconsin Press, 1949. 253 pp.

Hill, Archibald A. *Introduction to Linguistic Structures: From Sound to Sentence in English.* New York: Harcourt, Brace & World, 1958. 496 pp.

Hjelmslev, Louis, and H. J. Uldall. *Outline of Glossematics.* (Travaux du Cercle Linguistique de Copenhague, vol. 10.) Copenhagen: Nordisk Sprog- og Kulturforlag, 1957—.

Hockett, Charles Francis. *A Manual of Phonology.* Indiana University Pub. in Anthropology and Linguistics, Mem. 11. 1955. 246 pp.

———. *A Course in Modern Linguistics.* New York: The Macmillan Co., 1958. 621 pp.

Hocnigswald, Henry M. *Language Change and Linguistic Reconstruction.* Chicago: University of Chicago Press, 1960. 168 pp.

Hoijer, Harry (ed.). *Language in Culture: Conference on the Interrelations of Language and Other Aspects of Culture.* Chicago: University of Chicago Press, 1954. 286 pp.

Hymes, Dell H. *Lexicostatistics So Far.* Current Anthropology 1:3–44. 1960.

———. *Reader in Linguistic Anthropology.* Evanston, Ill.: Row, Peterson, 1961.

International Institute of African Languages and Cultures. *Practical Orthography of African Languages,* rev. ed. London: Oxford University Press, 1930, 24 pp.

International Phonetic Association. *The Principles of the International Phonetic Association, Being a Description of the International Phonetic Alphabet and the Manner of Using It.* London, 1949. 53 pp.

International Symposium on Anthropology, New York, 1952. *Anthropology Today: An Encyclopedic Inventory.* Chicago: University of Chicago Press, 1953. 966 pp.

Jakobson, Roman, C. Gunnar M. Fant, and Morris Halle. *Preliminaries to*

Speech Analysis, the Distinctive Features and Their Correlates. Cambridge, Mass.: Massachusetts Institute of Technology, 1952. 58 pp.

Jakobson, Roman, and Morris Halle. *Fundamentals of Language.* 's-Gravenhage: Mouton, 1956. 87 pp.

Jespersen, Jens Otto Harry. *Language: Its Nature, Development, and Origin.* London: Allen and Unwin, 1922. 448 pp.

————. *Essentials of English Grammar.* New York: Holt, Rinehart and Winston, 1933. 387 pp.

Jones, Daniel. *An Outline of English Phonetics,* 6th ed. New York: E. P. Dutton, 1940. 326 pp.

————. *The Phoneme: Its Nature and Use.* Cambridge, Eng.: W. Heffer & Sons, 1950. 267 pp.

————. *The Pronunciation of English,* 3d ed. Cambridge, Eng.: Cambridge University Press, 1950. 206 pp.

Joos, Martin. *Acoustic Phonetics.* Language Monographs, no. 23. Baltimore: Linguistic Society of America, 1948. 136 pp.

———— (ed.). *Readings in Linguistics: The Development of Descriptive Linguistics in America since 1925.* Washington, D.C.: American Council of Learned Societies, 1957. 421 pp.

Kenyon, John Samuel. *American Pronunciation: A Textbook of Phonetics for Students of English,* 8th ed. Ann Arbor, Mich.: George Wahr, 1940. 248 pp.

Kroeber, Alfred Louis. *Anthropology: Race, Language, Culture, Psychology, Prehistory.* New York: Harcourt, Brace & World, 1948, pp. 206–251.

Kurath, Hans. *Handbook of the Linguistic Geography of New England.* Vol. 1 of *Linguistic Atlas of New England.* Providence, R.I.: Brown University Press, 1939. 238 pp.

————. *A Word Geography of the Eastern United States.* Ann Arbor, Mich.: University of Michigan Press, 1949. 88 pp. + maps.

————, and Raven I. McDavid, Jr. *The Pronunciation of English in the Atlantic States.* Ann Arbor, Mich.: University of Michigan Press, 1961.

Lado, Robert. *Linguistics across Cultures: Applied Linguistics for Language Teachers.* Ann Arbor, Mich.: University of Michigan Press, 1957. 141 pp.

Lees, Robert B. *The Grammar of English Nominalizations.* Bloomington, Ind.: Research Center in Anthropology, Folklore, and Linguistics, 1960. 205 pp.

McIntosh, Angus. *An Introduction to a Survey of Scottish Dialects.* Edinburgh: Thomas Nelson, 1952. 122 pp.

Marckwardt, Albert H. *American English.* New York: Oxford University Press, 1958. 194 pp.

Marouzeau, Jules. *Lexique de la Terminologie Linguistique, Français, Allemand, Anglais, Italien.* 3e edition. Paris: Geuthner, 1951. 265 pp.

Martinet, André. *Économie des Changements Phonétiques: Traité de Phonologie Diachronique.* Berne: A. Francke, 1955. 395 pp.

————. *La Description Phonologique: Avec Application au Parler Franco-Provençal d'Hauteville (Savoie).* Genève: Librairie Droz, 1956. 108 pp.

Meillet, Antoine. *Introduction à l'Étude Comparative des Langues Indo-Européennes*, 8me ed. Paris: Librairie Hachette, 1937. 516 pp.

———, and Marcel Cohen. *Les Langues du Monde*, rev. ed. Paris: H. Champion, 1952. 1294 pp. + maps.

Merrifield, William R., Constance M. Naish, and Calvin R. Rensch. *Morphology-Syntax: Laboratory Manual.* Glendale, Calif.: Summer Institute of Linguistics, 1960. 140 pp.

Miller, George Armitage. *Language and Communication.* New York: McGraw-Hill, 1951. 298 pp.

Nida, Eugene Albert. *Bible Translating: An Analysis of Principles and Procedures with Special Reference to Aboriginal Languages.* New York: American Bible Society, 1947. 362 pp.

———. *Morphology: The Descriptive Analysis of Words*, 2d ed. Ann Arbor, Mich.: University of Michigan Press, 1949. 342 pp.

———. *Learning a Foreign Language: A Handbook for Missionaries.* New York: Foreign Missions Conference of North America, 1950. 237 pp.

———. *God's Word in Man's Language.* New York: Harper & Brothers, 1952. 191 pp.

———. *A Synopsis of English Syntax.* Norman, Okla.: Summer Institute of Linguistics, 1960. 233 pp.

North, Eric McCoy. *The Book of a Thousand Tongues.* New York: Harper & Brothers, 1938. 386 pp.

Paul, Hermann. *Prinzipien der Sprachgeschichte.* Halle: Niemeyer, 1880. 288 pp. Trans. H. A. Strong, *Principles of the History of Language.* London: S. Sonnenschein, 1890. 511 pp.

Pedersen, Holger. *Linguistic Science in the Nineteenth Century.* Trans. John Webster Spargo. Cambridge, Mass.: Harvard University Press, 1931. 360 pp.

Pike, Kenneth Lee. *Phonetics: A Critical Analysis of Phonetic Theory and a Technic for the Practical Description of Sounds.* Ann Arbor, Mich.: University of Michigan Press, 1943. 182 pp.

———. *Phonemics: A Technique for Reducing Languages to Writing.* Ann Arbor, Mich.: University of Michigan Press, 1947. 254 pp.

———. *Tone Languages.* Ann Arbor, Mich.: University of Michigan Press, 1948. 187 pp.

Pop, Sever. *La Dialectologie: Aperçu Historique et Méthodes d'Enquêtes Linguistiques.* Louvain: l'Auteur, 1950. 2 vols.

Potter, Ralph Kimball. George A. Kopp, and Harriet C. Green. *Visible Speech.* New York: D. Van Nostrand Co., 1947. 441 pp.

Potter, Simeon. *Modern Linguistics.* London: André Deutsch, 1957. 192 pp.

Roberts, Paul. *Patterns of English.* New York: Harcourt, Brace & World, 1956. 314 pp.

Sapir, Edward. *Language: An Introduction to the Study of Speech.* New York: Harcourt, Brace & World, 1921. 258 pp. (Also paperback.)

Sapir, Edward. *Selected Writings in Language, Culture, and Personality.* Berkeley, Calif.: University of California Press, 1949. 617 pp.

Saussure, Ferdinand de. *Cours de Linguistique Générale.* Paris: Payot, 1916. 331 pp. Trans. Wade Basking. *Course in General Linguistics.* New York: Philosophical Library, 1959. 240 pp.

Schlauch, Margaret. *The Gift of Language.* New York: Dover Publications, 1956.

Sledd, James. *A Short Introduction to English Grammar.* Chicago: Scott, Foresman, 1959. 346 pp.

Stetson, Raymond Herbert. *Motor Phonetics: A Study of Speech Movements in Action.* Amsterdam: North Holland, 1951. 212 pp.

Stevick, Earl W. *Helping People Learn English.* Nashville, Tenn.: Abingdon Press, 1957. 138 pp.

Sturtevant, Edgar Howard. *An Introduction to Linguistic Science.* New Haven, Conn.: Yale University Press, 1947. 173 pp. (Also paperback.)

Thomas, Charles Kenneth. *An Introduction to the Phonetics of American English.* New York: Ronald Press, 1947. 181 pp.

Trager, George Leonard, and Henry Lee Smith, Jr. *An Outline of English Structure.* Studies in Linguistics, Occasional Papers 3. 1951. Reprinted, Washington, D.C.: American Council of Learned Societies, 1957. 91 pp.

Trubetskoi, Nikolai Sergieevich. *Grundzüge der Phonologie.* Prague: Cercle Linguistique, 1939. 271 pp. Trans. J. Cantineau. *Principes de Phonologie.* Paris: Klinksieck, 1949. 396 pp.

Twaddell, William Freeman. *The English Verb Auxiliaries.* Providence, R.I.: Brown University Press, 1960. 21 pp.

Ward, Ida Caroline. *Practical Suggestions for the Learning of an African Language in the Field.* London: Oxford University Press, 1937. 39 pp.

———. *The Phonetics of English,* 4th ed. Cambridge, Eng.: W. Heffer & Sons, 1945. 148 pp.

Weinreich, Uriel. *Languages in Contact: Findings and Problems.* New York: Linguistic Circle of New York, 1953. 148 pp.

Welmers, William Everrett. *Spoken English as a Foreign Language.* Washington, D.C.: American Council of Learned Societies. 1953. 27 pp.

Westermann, Diedrich, and Ida C. Ward. *Practical Phonetics for Students of African Languages.* London: Oxford University Press, 1933. 227 pp.

Whorf, Benjamin Lee. *Language, Thought, and Reality: Selected Writings.* Cambridge, Mass.: Technology Press, 1956. 278 pp.

Zandvoort, Reinard Willem. *A Handbook of English Grammar.* London: Longmans, Green, 1957. 351 pp.

Popular and Semi-Popular Introductions: A large number of introductions for general readers have been published. Most of these are either worthless or very bad. Hall's *Linguistics and Your Language,* Potter's *Modern Linguistics,* and Schlauch's *The Gift of Language* are probably the best of recent ones; each is approved by a number of linguists, but none is considered acceptable by all. Sapir's *Language,* in spite of its age, has suffered little obsolescence; its influence within the profession should not obscure the fact that it was written for general readers. Nida's *God's Word in Man's Language* is a good popular account of Bible translation and missionary linguistics.

Textbooks: There have been few recent textbooks in English. Sturtevant's *An Introduction to Linguistic Science* is rather weak on descriptive linguistics but good for historical; it is, therefore, useful as a complement to this book. Nida's *Learning a Foreign Language* gives an introduction to descriptive linguistics as a background for second-language learning, and may be used as a textbook in linguistics, but it is somewhat narrow in scope. Hockett's *A Course in Modern Linguistics* is designed for a comprehensive introductory course and covers historical linguistics and dialect geography in addition to descriptive linguistics. The point of view, while not often basically in conflict, is different enough from that of this book to make them useful supplements to one another.

Manuals: Bloomfield's *Language* has long, and deservedly, been the standard handbook in American descriptive linguistics. It covers most aspects of the field rather well, though it is somewhat contemptuous of phonetics. Certain parts are now obsolete, particularly the treatment of morphology and syntax; others, notably the treatment of comparative method, remain very good. Bloch and Trager's *Outline of Linguistic Analysis* is a good, but overcondensed, statement of the analytic method of descriptive linguistics, now also beginning to show obsolescence. Harris' *Methods in Structural Linguistics* is the most comprehensive treatment of descriptive linguistic method and theory, but idiosyncratic and very difficult reading. Gray's *Foundation of Language*, devoted largely to comparative and historical linguistics and a good summary treatment of older methods, is an excellent reference for many points of detail. Jespersen's *Language* is another older manual, now largely obsolete, although for a few subjects it has not yet been superseded.

History of Linguistics: The roots of modern linguistics are traced out in Pedersen's *Linguistic Science in the Nineteenth Century* and in somewhat less detail in Jespersen's *Language*. Unfortunately, there is no comparable work carrying the history down to the present. Carroll's *Study of Language* gives a sketch, but is concerned mostly with the organization of linguistics as a discipline and its relations with psychology, sociology, anthropology, and philosophy. Something of the development can be traced through Joos' *Readings in Linguistics*, which reprints a number of the decisive papers, but the editorial comments must be used with caution.

There are certain books which, because of their very wide and deep influence, can be considered as classics in the field. Paul's *Prinzipien* states the theory and methods of classical comparative linguistics in the form in which they prevailed when descriptive linguistics started to develop. The cornerstone of synchronic linguistics was laid by De Saussure. His lectures are partially preserved in his *Cours de Linguistique*, certainly the most influential publication in linguistics in this century. Trubetskoi's *Grundzüge der Phonologie* set the course of development for phonology in much of Europe. The French translation is to be preferred because of its lengthy introduction. In American linguistics three landmarks stand out: Boas' Introduction to the *Handbook of American Indian Languages*, Sapir's *Language*, and Bloomfield's *Language*.

Some important current European developments in linguistic theory and method can be seen in Firth's *Papers in Linguistics*, Hjemslev and Uldall's *Outline of Glossematics*, and Martinet's *La Description Phonologique* and *Économie des Changements Phonétiques*.

Terminology: There is no wholly satisfactory dictionary of technical terminology in linguistics. The most comprehensive is Marouzeau's *Lexique de la Terminologie Linguistique* with definitions in French, but covering also terminology in German, English, and Italian. Recent revisions have not brought it up to date. Hamp's *A Glossary of American Technical Linguistic Usage* is more limited in scope and difficult to use without some knowledge of the literature, but it is much more nearly current. It is one of a projected series of dictionaries treating separately each of the important schools of linguistics. *Webster's New International Dictionary, 3d edition*, when it appears, will probably be for some time the best reference work for general use.

Periodical Literature: The greater part of the significant publication in linguistics is in journals, of which there are a growing number. It is impractical to attempt listing important papers here. However, three recent books of readings reprint many of the more significant: Joos' *Readings in Linguistics*, Allen's *Readings in Applied English Linguistics*, and Hymes' *Reader in Linguistic Anthropology*. Very complete bibliographic coverage, including book reviews, may be had in the *Bibliographie Linguistique de l' Année* of the Comité International Permanent de Linguistes, published annually with a delay of two to three years.

Phonetics: The best theoretical treatment of phonetics is Pike's *Phonetics*. This is rather too technical for most purposes. A more useful statement from the same point of view will be found in the introduction to Pike's *Phonemics*. Heffner's *General Phonetics* is probably the most satisfactory general textbook in the field, but still far from what is needed in that the emphasis is too strongly on sounds employed in familiar European languages. Westermann and Ward's *Practical Phonetics* is indispensable for anyone dealing with African languages and useful to many others. Kenyon's *American Pronunciation* is a comprehensive and detailed textbook, based largely on Midwestern American but also making reference to other dialects. Jones' *Outline* does the same for southern British. Kurath's *Handbook* describes the detailed recording used in dialect work. The *Principles* of the International Phonetic Association gives a full statement of the IPA and its use. Joos' *Acoustic Phonetics* is still the best available general statement in this field. As a pioneer effort in a rapidly moving field, it is already somewhat out of date in many details. Potter, Kopp, and Green's *Visible Speech* is a less general work, profusely illustrated, with excellent plates. The latter make it very useful for a beginner, but the phonetic transcriptions in the labels are sometimes difficult to interpret. Stetson's *Motor Phonetics* represents a quite different approach which is sometimes of value as a balance.

Phonology: There are two comprehensive handbooks of phonology. Trubetskoi's *Grundzüge der Phonologie* is the classic and still useful. Hockett's *Manual of Phonology* is the more recent. Jones' *The Phoneme* examines the problems from a strongly phonetic orientation; it is considered by most linguists quite inadequate, but has been widely followed and should not be neglected. A recent statement, strongly influenced by Trubetskoi, is that of Martinet's *La Description Phonologique*. Jakobson and Halle's *Fundamentals of Language* is the best introduction to the approach stressing distinctive features rather than phonemes. This should be followed by Jakobson, Fant, and Halle's *Preliminaries to Speech Analysis*. Pike's *Phonemics* is an elementary textbook, its heavy emphasis on rule-of-thumb procedures and its highly artificial problems limit its usefulness, but there is nothing to replace it. Pike's *Tone Languages* is a very useful treatment of tone, both phonologically and morphologically.

Morphology and Syntax: There are two textbooks: Nida's *Morphology* is the more generally useful. Elson and Pickett's *Beginning Morphology-Syntax* and the accompanying *Laboratory Manual* by Merrifield, Naish, and Rensch are somewhat easier; they are based on the special approach known as 'tagmemics.' For general discussion of morphologic theory the relevant chapters of the more general works must be consulted. One of the few specific recent treatments is in Chomsky's *Syntactic Structures*. This develops the transformational approach and criticizes others rather incisively. It might be well to read with it Lees' *Grammar of English Nominalizations*, the first chapters of which restate Chomsky's theory and may assist the student in understanding it. Much of the pertinent work on syntax has been published in the form of descriptions of English rather than as general theoretical statements. The following are important: Nida's *Synopsis of English Syntax* was one of the first attempts to describe any language by a thoroughgoing IC approach. Fries' *The Structure of English* exemplifies the class and order approach. Hill's *Introduction to Linguistic Structures* exemplifies the analysis of syntax on the basis of phonologic signals.

Writing Systems: Pike's *Phonemics* gives a detailed discussion of some considerations important in setting up an orthography. Nida's *Bible Translating* gives some briefer but also very valuable suggestions. The International Institute's *Practical Orthography* gives detailed recommendations for African languages. North's *Book of a Thousand Tongues* gives facsimile reproductions of Bible translations with historical notes, and is a useful reference on orthographies in use. Gelb's *A Study of Writing* is the best treatment of the history of the alphabet and of other writing systems, but some points of theory are very debatable.

Historical Linguistics: The best introduction to historical linguistics is through the general works, notably Bloomfield's *Language* and Sturtevant's *Introduction to Linguistic Science*. Paul's *Prinzipien* is the classic statement of the methods. Hoenigswald's *Language Change and Linguistic Reconstruction* is one attempt at a modern formulation; it represents, however, a rather specialized development in theory which does not have widespread support. Martinet's *Économie des Changements Phonétiques* represents another direction of development of theory. Hymes' *Lexicostatistics So Far* is a summary of developments centering around glottochronology. A very large part of the work in historical linguistics has been devoted to the Indo-European languages. The best orientation in this field may be had from Meillet's *Introduction à l'Étude Comparative des Langues Indo-Européennes*.

There is no really up-to-date reference work on the classification and enumeration of the languages of the world. Meillet and Cohen's *Les Langues du Monde*, somewhat revised from a 1924 edition, is the best available. The best statement of the methods and problems is that of Greenberg in International Symposium on Anthropology, *Anthropology Today*.

Dialects: McIntosh's *An Introduction to a Survey of Scottish Dialects* gives a lucid popular presentation of dialect work with a good statement of its relevance. Kurath's *Handbook of the Linguistic Geography of New England* sets forth the objectives and mode of operation of the American Survey and suggests some of the connections of dialect distribution with social history. Some of the results of this work are now available in Atwood's *A Survey of Verb Forms*, Kurath's *A Word Geography of the Eastern United States*, and Kurath and McDavid's *The Pronunciation of English in the Atlantic States*. The treatment of dialect geography in Bloomfield's *Language* is good. For details on the progress of dialect work in other countries and general information about the several surveys, see Pop's *La Dialectologie*.

Linguistics and Associated Disciplines: Many anthropology texts contain brief discussions of language from a cultural point of view. Kroeber's *Anthropology* is probably the best of these. Boas and Sapir were both leading anthropologists as well as pioneers in American linguistics; some of their papers, reflecting this dual interest, are reprinted in *Race, Language, and Culture* and *Selected Writings*. Whorf's *Language, Thought, and Reality* reprints writings which have been very suggestive on the question of the interrelationship between language and other aspects of culture. Whorf's hypothesis has been the subject of intense debate among linguists and anthropologists. Some of this debate is gathered in Hoijer's *Language in Culture*. Hymes' *Reader in Linguistic Anthropology* assembles a number of important papers on language from a cultural viewpoint.

Brown's *Words and Things* is probably the best treatment of language from a psychological point of view. Miller's *Language and Communication* treats a few problems that Brown neglects, and is a useful supplement.

Weinreich's *Languages in Contact* gives a comprehensive treatment of competition between languages and the resulting linguistic and social readjustments. Haugen's *Bilingualism in the Americas* gives a useful summary of the problems and a very useful bibliography.

Applied Linguistics: There is a vast literature on practical language problems. Most of it, however, is totally out of touch with linguistic theory, and will not be mentioned here. Useful works oriented toward the linguist's view of language are few, though increasing. Allen's *Readings in Applied English Linguistics* reprints several very useful papers on a variety of problems.

For language learning Nida's *Learning a Foreign Language*, Ward's *Practical Suggestions*, and Bloomfield's *Outline Guide* are all generally useful, in about the order stated. All are inexpensive, and anyone facing language learning in the field will find it worth while to have and study all.

For the teaching of English as a second language the following are to be recommended: Stevick's *Helping People Learn English* is a very useful manual for persons with a minimum of specialized training. Fries' *Teaching and Learning English* gives a thorough treatment of some important procedures, but is based on an analysis of English phonology now superseded. Welmers' *Spoken English* is a very brief teacher's manual to accompany the lesson materials of the English for Foreigners Program. Many of the suggestions in these can be adapted with little other than obvious changes to the teaching of any second language. Lado's *Linguistics across Cultures* attempts to relate linguistic principles to the problems of second language teaching.

Gudschinsky's *Handbook of Literacy* is a general summary of methods of teaching reading, particularly to adults, and applicable to a wide variety of languages.

Few books have been written dealing directly with the linguistic problems that arise in mission work. Nida's *Bible Translating* is intended as a handbook for the technical task of translating the Scriptures, particularly into languages only beginning to develop a literature. It is, however, more widely useful, since the problems discussed are not settled once the Bible has been printed but must be continually faced by those who would use the new translation and those who are attempting to present the same message in other forms. It has also been found useful by non-missionaries engaged in translation work.

English: All general works on linguistics written in English inevitably discuss the language, often very profitably. Recent years have seen the appearance of a few major treatments of English by linguists. The most important of these is Trager and Smith's *Outline of English Structure;* this has formed the base of much of the more recent work. The fullest treatment is Hill's *Introduction to Linguistic Structures.* Twaddell's *The English Verb Auxiliaries* is an important formulation of one of the previously very puzzling problems in English grammar. At the same time there has been a growing interest in linguistic approaches among people working in the field of English. The important bench-mark in this is Fries' *American English Grammar*. This discusses actually observed usages in carefully selected groups of Americans, and so has become indispensable in any work with English. Fries' *Structure of English* is an attempt at formal analysis of syntax based on observed usages.

Based in various proportions on the work of Fries and of Trager and Smith, there have been a number of textbooks presaging some reorientation of English teaching in America. Francis' *The Structure of American English* and Sledd's *A Short Introduction to English Grammar* are probably the best of these written for college English courses. Roberts' *Patterns of English*, written for high school courses, gives a remarkably clear presentation of major sentence patterns, and deserves much wider use. As yet there is no reference grammar which incorporates these newer developments. The older traditional grammars are often very useful for details, though generally unsatisfactory for general framework. Jespersen's *Essentials of English Grammar* and Zandvoort's *A Handbook of English Grammar* are probably the best one-volume works.

A number of treatments of English phonemics were listed and discussed in detail in Chapter 19. The fuller evaluation of that chapter need not be repeated here. Trager and Smith's *Outline of English Structure* presents the system which has most generally been used by linguists in the last few years. This, or slight modifications of it, can be found described in detail in many recent books.

The best introduction to the history of English is Baugh's *A History of the English Language*. This is quite traditional in approach, but nothing of a more modern sort is yet available. For the history of the language in this country it may be supplemented by Marckwardt's *American English*. Most of the treatments of American dialects, listed above, also give important information on the history of American English.

Notes

Examples used in the text are from the following sources, which are hereby acknowledged:

Andrade, M. J. 1933. "Quileute," *HAIL* 3:149–292.
Armstrong, L. E. 1940. *The Phonetic and Tonal Structure of Kikuyu.*
Atwood, E. B. 1953. *A Survey of Verb Forms in the Eastern United States.*
Blake, F. R. 1925. *A Grammar of the Tagálog Language.*
Bloomfield, L. 1946. "Algonquian," *VFPA* 6:85–129.
Chomsky, N. 1957. *Syntactic Structures.*
Collinder, B. 1957. *Survey of the Uralic Languages.*
Crowell, E. E. 1949. "A Preliminary Report of Kiowa Structure," *IJAL* 15:163–167.
de Francis, J. 1950. *Nationalism and Language Reform in China.*
Diringer, D. 1948. *Alphabet: A Key to the History of Mankind.*
Doke, C. M. 1954. *Textbook of Zulu Grammar*, 5th ed.
Forrest, R. A. D. 1948. *The Chinese Language.*
Garvin, P. L. 1948. "Kutenai I: Phonemics," *IJAL* 14:37–42.
Gleason, H. A. 1935. "Melastomaceæ," in Pulle, A. *Flora of Surinam.*
Hall, R. A. 1944. *Hungarian Grammar.*
Hall, R. A. 1948. *Descriptive Italian Grammar.*
Hockett, C. T. 1952. [Class notes for Comparative Algonquian].
Hodge, C. T. 1946. "Serbo-Croatian Phonemes," *Language* 22:112–120.
Liljeblad, S. 1950. "Bannock I: Phonemes," *IJAL* 16:126–131.
Martin, S. A. 1951. "Korean Phonemics," *Language* 27:519–533.
Newman, S. 1947. "Bella Coola I: Phonology," *IJAL* 13:129–134.
Pilhofer, G. 1933. *Grammatik der Kâte-Sprache in Neuguinea.*
Reichard, G. A. 1933. "Cœur d'Alene," *HAIL* 3:519–707.
Rosey, M. [n.d.] *French Irregular Verbs.*
Swanton, J. R. 1911. "Tlingit," *HAIL* 1:159–204.
Tucker, A. N., and Mpaayei, J. T. ole. 1955. *A Maasai Grammar.*
Verdoorn, F. ed. 1932. *Manual of Bryology.*
Voegelin, C. F., and Ellinghausen, M. E. 1943. "Turkish Structure," *JAOS* 63:34–65.
Welmers, W. E. 1952. "Notes on the Structure of Bariba," *Language* 28:82–103.
Westermann, D., and Ward, I. C. 1933. *Practical Phonetics for Students of African Languages.*
Whitney, W. D. 1896. *A Sanskrit Grammar.*

Also the following persons: Gilbert Ansre, Martha Gleason, J. Maurice Hohlfeld, Paul Leser, Obadiah Manjengwe, Samuel Mentee, Paul Nilson, Howard Olson, Dorothy Peck, Wesley Sadler, Henry Lee Smith, Jr.

4.19, p. 50. The analysis of English phonemes used here is basically that of G. L. Trager and H. L. Smith, Jr. I do, however, differ in feeling that the evidence for uniting /h/ and /ʜ/ is insufficient, and so prefer to treat them as two phonemes. The symbol /ʜ/ is used not from any lack of conviction, but merely as a convenience to other instructors who may prefer to treat these as one. I have also changed the symbols for terminals, but intend no difference of analysis. After several years of searching criticism, Trager and Smith's analysis remains without close competition as the most workable available.

6.4, p. 67. The Hebrew examples here and elsewhere represent Massoretic Hebrew, that is, the Old Testament consonantal text as interpreted by the Massoretic tradition embodied in the vowel points and other punctuation. The transcription is one designed for pedagogic purposes. It represents what may be a possible phonemic system underlying the pointing, which will serve as a basis for an exposition of the grammar and provide a pronunciation which can be used in class. It is not intended that this system should fit either Modern Hebrew or the pronunciation at the time the Old Testament was written. Certain inconsistencies in the pointing are resolved by assuming that the features shown are not all contemporaneous and that there are a few instances of arbitrary writing conventions. Eleven vowel nuclei are recognized: i ii e ee a aa o oo u uu ə. Stresses are written ´ `.

6.19, p. 74. The suggested notation, /aw ← (ay)/, is basically that of Nida. However, I have added the parentheses to make it somewhat clearer that the /ay/ does not occur in the form containing /aw ← (ay)/. This has been a source of confusion to students.

10.9, p. 132. The terminology here is not satisfactory. There is much to commend the other usage (**constitute** for what is here called "construction," and **construction** for patterns of combination of constituents into constitutes). The difficulty, however, is that I have found "constitute" and "constituent" confusingly similar and often the cause of misunderstanding. Not desiring to propose a new term (nor, indeed, having any idea of one that would be suitable), I use this older set of terms. Still, "constitute" does need replacement by one with higher redundancy.

Chapter 12, pp. 171–194. This treatment is based on the work of Noam Chomsky. Transformations as developed by Zellig S. Harris are different in many important respects.

13.16, p. 214. Hockett's terms 'Item and Process' and 'Item and Arrangement' have become widely known. Nevertheless, I propose here new terms to replace them. 'Item and Process' is used for both process models and adjustment models, but the distinction is basic, and the confusion must be eliminated. 'Arrangement' is not distinctive. In any case, my experience has been that students more readily understand the distinctions when presented in the terms here used.

14.17, p. 234. This section is based on the work of W. Freeman Twaddell recently published in his *The English Verb Auxiliaries* (1960).

19.8, p. 318. The "centering diphthongs" of Jones and Ward are omitted from consideration since it is not clear to me what the true nature of these may be. It seems evident that there is something more than vowels and semi-vowel glides involved, perhaps /+/, or even terminals.

21.10, p. 349. Sources for these quotations are not cited. There is no intention to condemn individual works, but only to illustrate common failings which may be found even in otherwise excellent books. The works from which these examples were abstracted vary from utterly hopeless to far above the average. At least one of them shows an appreciation of the problems of language learning which is quite unusual. The failing in this instance, as in so many, is insufficient knowledge of English phonology. This underscores the point made in 21.5, p. 345.

21.15, p. 352. It must be distinctly understood that a test such as this is not infallible. Languages do have irregularities, but very often they are caused by inadequate analysis. Unfortunately, sometimes the converse is true; an inadequate understanding of phonemics may conceal some morphophonemic difficulties.

21.17, p. 354. The bell-shaped curves should be interpreted as merely conventional representations of scatter. I have no desire to maintain that the distributions are actually in detail as shown.

23.3, p. 374. I adhere closely to Longfellow's version, however free he may have been with history.

23.4, p. 375. I am not unmindful that information theorists are more accustomed to speaking of the capacity of a channel. But it seems to me that, for linguistic purposes, the concept of the capacity of a code is much more useful and a better place at which to begin an exposition of the elementary notions.

28.19, p. 465. Joseph Greenberg, whom I follow throughout in classification of African Languages, has proposed uniting his Eastern Sudanic and Central Sudanic into a "Macro-Sudanic" phylum. As, however, this name would seem to imply a group comprehending Sudanic, it seems unsatisfactory. I propose the name "Chari-Nile" as a substitute on the analogy of his "Niger-Congo." I also prefer "Nilotic" to his Eastern Sudanic.

The exercises in the *Workbook in Descriptive Linguistics* are keyed to the chapter numbers in the first edition. They should be used with the chapters for which they were designed. The numberings of the two editions are equated below:

Old Edition Chapters 1–9 remain unchanged
         10 is expanded and divided, becoming 10 and 11
         11 becomes 14
         12 becomes 16
         13 becomes 17
         14 becomes 15
         15 becomes 22
         16 becomes 19
         17 becomes 20
         18 becomes 21
         19 becomes 23
         20 becomes 24
         21 becomes 25
         22 becomes 26
         23 becomes 27
         24 becomes 28

Chapters 12, 13, and 18 of this edition are new, as are sections 14.16–14.18.

Index